THE EVOLVING DIMENSIONS OF INTERNATIONAL LAW

This book examines recent developments in sources of public international law, such as treaties and custom operating among nations in their mutual relations, as well as developments in some of the primary rule of law international institutions created by these processes. It finds that public international law has become increasingly dysfunctional in dealing with some of the primary problems facing the world community, such as the maintenance of international peace and security, violations of international human rights and the law of armed conflict, arms control, disarmament and nonproliferation, and international environmental issues, and that international law and international institutions face a problematic future. It concludes, however, that all is not lost. There are possible alternative futures for international law and legal process, but choosing among them will require the world community to make hard choices.

John F. Murphy is Professor of International Law and Business in the Villanova University School of Law, Pennsylvania. He is the author or editor of numerous books and monographs, the most recent of which is *The United States and the Rule of Law in International Affairs* (Cambridge University Press, 2004). He has also written more than 136 articles, comments, and reviews, which have appeared in such publications as the *American Journal of International Law*, the *International and Comparative Law Quarterly*, the *Columbia Journal of Transnational Law*, the *Israel Yearbook of Human Rights*, the *Tulane Law Review*, the *Los Angeles Times*, and the *Baltimore Sun*. His book *The Regulation of International Business and Economic Relations* (coauthored with Alan C. Swan) won a Certificate of Merit from the American Society of International Law in 1992.

The Evolving Dimensions of International Law

HARD CHOICES FOR THE WORLD COMMUNITY

JOHN F. MURPHY
Villanova University School of Law

CAMBRIDGE UNIVERSITY PRESS
Cambridge, New York, Melbourne, Madrid, Cape Town, Singapore,
São Paulo, Delhi, Dubai, Tokyo

Cambridge University Press
32 Avenue of the Americas, New York, NY 10013-2473, USA

www.cambridge.org
Information on this title: www.cambridge.org/9780521709231

First published 2010

Printed in the United States of America

A catalog record for this publication is available from the British Library.

Library of Congress Cataloging in Publication data

Murphy, John Francis, 1937–
The evolving dimensions of international law : hard choices for the world community /
John F. Murphy.
   p.   cm.
Includes bibliographical references and index.
ISBN 978-0-521-88271-2 (hardback)
ISBN 978-0-521-70923-1 (pbk.)
1. International law.   I. Title.
KZ3410.M871   2010
341 – dc22   2009038054

ISBN 978-0-521-88271-2 Hardback
ISBN 978-0-521-70923-1 Paperback

Contents

Acknowledgments

This book has been close to three years in the making. The process of writing it has been slowed down by a few health problems – for example, a hip replacement operation in the summer of 2008 – as well as my undertaking (perhaps foolishly) some other major research and writing responsibilities. I am therefore grateful to John Berger, Senior Editor of Cambridge University Press, for his patience and his guidance throughout this project.

I had the good fortune to have, as the readers of my proposal for this book and some draft chapters, Charlotte Ku, former Executive Director of the American Society of International Law and currently a faculty member of the University of Illinois Law School, and Peter Spiro, Charles Weiner Professor of Law, Temple University James E. Beasley School of Law. I have benefited from their helpful observations and suggestions for improvement. Professor Ku also commented on later draft chapters and made numerous helpful suggestions. Her insights as a political scientist were especially valuable.

Larry D. Johnson, former Legal Adviser to the International Atomic Energy Agency and later Deputy Legal Counsel of the United Nations, and Orde F. Kittrie, Professor of Law, Arizona State University Sandra Day O'Connor College of Law, read Chapter 5, "Arms Control, Disarmament, Nonproliferation, and Safeguards," and gave me extensive and crucially important comments on it.

I am also grateful to former Dean Mark A. Sargent for steadfast support of scholarship and other intellectual activities at the Villanova University School of Law. Similarly, I am grateful to William James, Associate Dean for Information Services at Villanova, and his excellent staff for numerous services. In particular, I benefited from the superb research assistance of Amy Spare, Robert Hegadon, and Matthew McGovern, Faculty Services Librarians and Legal Research Instructors. My former secretary, Terri Laverghetta, helped me in so many ways in my work on this book that I have lost count of them, and my current secretary, Mira Baric, has also been of great assistance. I have benefited greatly, to understate the matter, from the good work of my research assistants – John (Sean) E. Jennings III, Laura Karen Kitell, Emily C. Miletello, Klorkor Okai, and Kristin Scaduto.

Lastly, a special note of gratitude goes to my wife, Laura Sunstein Murphy, who, once again, showed infinite patience with me while I labored to complete this book, and, I should add, a considerable sense of humor.

Introduction

The American Society of International Law held its centennial annual meeting in March 2006, and it was a love fest – a celebration not only of the Society but of international law. Rossalyn Higgins, President Judge of the International Court of Justice, gave the plenary address,[1] and her speech was a panegyric to international law and international institutions. Judge Higgins's remarks reflected the overall tone of the conference; few, if any, of the events at the Society's meeting would lead one to believe that international law and international institutions face any problems of significant consequence.

It is possible, however, to paint a considerably less rosy picture. There are disquieting signs that international law and international institutions face a problematic future. With respect to international institutions, the recently issued Final Paper of the Princeton Project on National Security made the perhaps somewhat hyperbolic claim that: "The system of international institutions that the United States and its allies built after World War II and steadily expanded over the course of the Cold War is broken. Every major institution – the United Nations (U.N.), the International Monetary Fund (IMF), the World Bank, the World Trade Organization (WTO), the North Atlantic Treaty Organization (NATO) – and countless smaller ones face calls for major reform."[2] Similarly, a Geo-Strategic Environment Workshop held at the U.S. Naval War College from August 24–25, 2006, "revealed significant concern about the vitality of international law and institutions" and concluded that "some international organizations are looking long in the tooth and incapable of coping with emerging challenges" and that "bilateral agreements are on the rise as international organizations continue to fall short in their objectives."[3]

International institutions are themselves created by the primary "source" of international law – the international treaty, the quintessential example of which is perhaps the United Nations Charter. As the boundaries between domestic and international rules and institutions have become increasingly blurred, it is important to specify what we mean when we speak of "international law." Traditional public international law meant treaties and custom operating among nations in their mutual relations.[4] Viewing this definition of international law as inadequate, in 1956, Philip Jessup, an eminent international law authority, claimed for international lawyers not only the classic scope of traditional public international law but also "all law which regulates actions or events that transcend national frontiers," which he named "transnational law."[5]

At the risk of appearing flippant, one might characterize Jessup's claim as an exercise in "international law imperialism," an imperialism, moreover, that constantly expands to encompass more and more within its "empire," because, especially with globalization, there are fewer and fewer actions or events that do not, at least to some extent, "transcend national frontiers." Prior to Jessup's renaming, most "transnational law" was classified simply as national law. By way of contrast, it is possible to subdivide international law into various subcategories, such as "private international law," which can refer to conflict of laws at the international level, or to international business transactions or trade. Some other subcategories might include, for example, international organizations law, international human rights law, and international environmental law.

To keep the project manageable, this book will focus its major attention on the primary sources of traditional public international law, that is, treaties and custom operating among nations in their mutual relations, as well as on some of the primary rule of law international institutions created by the processes of public international law. It is in these areas that most of the disquieting developments have taken place. At the same time, the book will consider in some detail other claimed "sources" of international law or alleged components of the international legal process, such as nonbinding resolutions of international institutions, especially resolutions of the United Nations General Assembly, equity, natural law, so-called soft law – for example, nonbinding guidelines and standards – nongovernmental organizations (NGOs), and transnational or multinational corporations.

The increasing dysfunctionality of public international law is based, in no small part, on the nature of modern society. Increasingly, life today is characterized by constant acceleration – indeed the book *Faster*[6] goes into this phenomenon in great detail. Similarly, the many impacts on modern life of the rapidity of change are explored extensively in Alvin and Heidi Toffler's new book, *Revolutionary Wealth*.[7] As Roscoe Pound once noted, "[t]he law must be stable, but it cannot stand still."[8] The rapid pace of life today, however, creates great instability, indeed chaos in some situations. As noted by the Tofflers, this is a significant problem in national legal systems. They suggest that the law is "the slowest of all our slow changing institutions" and describes the body of law as "living – but only barely so."[9] But the Tofflers are referring only to national law. The problem is greatly compounded in the international arena, in part because of the nature of international law itself.

The global treaty or convention, the primary source of international law, takes a long time to negotiate, and is difficult, if not impossible, to amend. The Law of the

Sea Treaty, which took more than ten years to complete, is perhaps the quintessential example, but hardly the only one. The U.N. Charter, perhaps the most important of the global international treaties, has seldom been amended, and most of these amendments have been of a minor nature. The long-standing struggle to amend the Charter to expand the size of the Security Council beyond its current fifteen member states and perhaps the number of its permanent members as well has so far proved to be a fruitless endeavor. Moreover, with the great expansion in the number of countries in this world – Montenegro recently became the 192nd member of the United Nations – and the rise in power of such states as China, India, and Brazil, which are demanding that their interests be recognized, it has become increasingly difficult to conclude global treaties in the first place. The collapse of the World Trade Organization's Doha round of international trade negotiations, the so-called development round, is a salient current example.

In theory, the second primary source of international law, customary international law, is supposed to remedy this problem by supplementing treaties, that is, filling in gaps in them, or by in effect revising them. (It is generally agreed that a general norm of customary international law will prevail over a prior treaty norm under the last-in-time rule that governs a conflict between a treaty and a customary norm at the international level.) But customary international law itself has increasingly been called into question, with some scholars going so far as to call for its elimination.[10] In their book, *The Limits of International Law*,[11] which claims that customary international law has no effect whatsoever on state behavior, Jack Goldsmith and Eric Posner suggest, implicitly if not explicitly, that customary international law does not exist. I believe this claim is patently erroneous and will attempt to demonstrate why throughout this book. Admittedly, however, all is not well with customary international law. As my book, *The United States and the Rule of Law in International Affairs*, demonstrates in some detail,[12] there is no general agreement on how the process of creating a customary norm of international law works, and significant disagreement on precisely what the customary norms of international law are. (There is no definitive source listing these norms.) The result is that claims of the existence of norms of customary international law are often cynically presented as rhetorical maneuvers, with little prospect that the claim will be resolved, either through diplomatic interchange, by the conclusion of a treaty, or by an authoritative third-party decision maker. This is even more the case with claims of *jus cogens*, that is, of a peremptory norm from which no deviation is permitted. Some doubt the very existence of such norms, and there is, in any event, no agreement on the process by which such norms are created, or on what these norms are, and little prospect of an agreement being reached.

One result of this disarray in the primary sources of international law is an increased preference for informal nonbinding guidelines and flexible procedures in place of binding legal instruments. The classic example is the 1975 Helsinki Final Act, which contained human rights provisions that were treated as if they were binding, although the act expressly provided that they were not. Some other examples include the 1985 Plaza Accord on Exchange Rates; the 1988 Basel Accord on Capital Adequacy (a so-called Basel II is currently under negotiation); the 1992 Non-Legally Authoritative Statement on Forest Principles; the 1997 NATO Russian Founding Act; and the 2004 pact of the Paris Club of creditor states to forgive Iraqi sovereign debt. These and similar accords are often referred to as examples of "soft law." For reasons that will be set forth in various places in this book, the term "soft law" is arguably an unfortunate usage that has given rise to some confusion. This is not to claim, however, that nonbinding accords and other examples of "soft law" have no relevance for international law, much less that they have no importance in terms of international governance. On the contrary, nonbinding accords and the informal procedures that accompany them are often turned to because of some of the disadvantages associated with the sources and processes of traditional public international law. Moreover, in many instances, these examples of "soft law" may more effectively fulfill the goals of those who turn to them than traditional international law and legal procedures. Nonbinding accords, for example, may be more faithfully adhered to than binding international treaties, and the flexible procedures adopted for consultation regarding possible changes in the accords to meet unexpected problems may be more effective in resolving these problems than formal meetings of states parties to treaties.

Informal accords are also a central feature of transgovernmental networks, which are an increasingly important mode of cooperation between national regulatory officials. These networks are the central focus of Anne-Marie Slaughter's book, *A New World Order*.[13] Interestingly, there is no reference in the index to Slaughter's book to international law, and the process she describes is informal cooperation, often accompanied by nonbinding memoranda of understanding, between national authorities who are concerned primarily with the effective implementation of their own regulatory law rather than of treaties or customary international law.

Also supporting the thesis that the current pathology of international law is disquieting is the arguable proposition that the primary international institutions designed to support the rule of law in international affairs are performing in an unsatisfactory if not dysfunctional manner. First and foremost among these international institutions is the United Nations. It is no exaggeration to say that the United Nations is currently in a crisis mode. The most important organ of the United Nations, the Security Council, has the primary responsibility under the U.N. Charter to maintain international peace and security, but as Iraq has demonstrated, and as Darfur and perhaps Lebanon are in the process of demonstrating, the Council is, with some exceptions, failing to fulfill this responsibility. The primary problem here, moreover, is not the unrepresentative nature of the Council or its "democratic deficit." It is rather the failure of the permanent members to fulfill their responsibility to play the lead role. Indeed, in many instances, the permanent members have abused their power by imposing peacekeeping or peace enforcement mandates on the United

Nations and then failing to provide the necessary resources to enable the organization to carry out its mandate (the United States has been a primary offender), or by threatening to veto or actually vetoing measures designed to maintain international peace and security.

By and large other efforts to reform the United Nations are also floundering. Although the General Assembly replaced the notorious Commission on Human Rights, with a new Human Rights Council, there is a real risk that the Council will be as dysfunctional as the Commission was.[14] This was a major reason that the United States voted against the establishment of the Council and declined to stand for election to it. Similarly, management reforms proposed by then Secretary-General Kofi Annan and strongly supported by the United States and other developed nations have been strenuously resisted by the developing member states of the United Nations, and the result is a potential major crisis in financing of U.N. activities.[15]

U.N.-related international institutions also are having major difficulties. Elsewhere, I have discussed some of the problems facing the International Court of Justice,[16] but these constitute only part of the picture. Increasingly, the Court is becoming a marginalized institution. The special criminal tribunals established by the U.N. Security Council for the former Yugoslavia and Rwanda have been described by *The New York Times* as "painfully slow, frightfully expensive and sadly inadequate."[17] It remains to be seen whether the new International Criminal Court will perform in a more satisfactory manner. The new Tribunal of the Law of the Sea, whose very establishment was in part due to distrust of the International Court of Justice, reportedly has little to do. In the economic arena, the World Trade Organization (WTO), the International Monetary Fund (IMF), and the World Bank have been sharply criticized. In the wake of the collapse of the Doha trade round, there has been considerable concern expressed that "the WTO is at risk of becoming a 21st-century version of the League of Nations: A well intentioned experiment in global governance that slides into irrelevance."[18]

Even at the regional level the picture is problematical. The European Union, long occupying a pride of place among international lawyers, has its own current crisis with the rejection of its draft constitution by plebiscites in France and the Netherlands and the onset of "expansion fatigue." The European Human Rights regime, generally regarded as the most successful of the human rights institutions in promoting and protecting human rights, faces major challenges posed by new members such as the Russian Federation and some former republics of the Soviet Union, whose human rights records are poor and are resisting complying with judgments of the European Court of Human Rights rendered against them.[19] In the Americas, Mercosur, the trading bloc and customs union formed initially among Argentina, Brazil, Uruguay, and Paraguay, is functioning more as a political than as an economic institution, with the involvement of Venezuela and its volatile president Hugo Chavez. U.S. efforts to create a Free Trade Agreement for the

Americas are a dead letter. Even bilateral efforts toward free trade agreements are facing considerable obstacles.

This book begins, in Chapter 1, with an exploration of the multifaceted nature of "international law." Vastly different from law and legal processes at the national level, there is considerable debate over the precise nature of international law, whether it is accurate to call it "law," in light of its grounding in international politics, and its relevance, if any, to government officials charged with conducting their countries' foreign affairs. Skepticism about international law has a long pedigree, but in recent years, the challenges to it have mounted and have been led, in no small part, by legal scholars and practicing members of the legal profession. As we shall see, many of these challenges, especially those raised by members of the academy, are themselves of questionable merit, but they are having an impact that undermines the effectiveness of international law.

Chapter 2 evaluates the apparent "triumph" of international law and finds that appearances are deceiving. At first blush, international law and institutions appear to be thriving, even triumphing, in their struggle to be "relevant" in international affairs. Hundreds of treaties, the primary source of international law, are concluded each year and are adhered to with little apparent difficulty by most nation-states. The International Court of Justice has a relatively heavy caseload on its docket, and hands down decisions or advisory opinions on a variety of major international law issues. The international criminal law tribunals for former Yugoslavia and Rwanda continue with their proceedings, and the International Criminal Court has been established and has begun its operations. Dispute settlement panels of the World Trade Organization and of the North American Free Trade Agreement hand down decisions on leading issues in international trade and investment. Also in the field of international trade and investment, the International Monetary Fund and the International Bank for Reconstruction and Development are active and have expanded the scope of their responsibilities. But if one looks closer, one finds that quantity is not necessarily the same thing as quality. From a functional perspective, there are numerous problems with the workings of the current international legal processes.

Realists and others skeptical of the relevance of international law have been particularly dubious when it comes to law and legal process designed to put constraints on the use of armed force by states to settle disputes. One scholar has suggested that the record is so unsatisfactory that it has resulted in this law and legal process becoming inoperative. And, to be sure, the recent record in such places as Kosovo, Iraq, and Darfur has been highly unsatisfactory. The United Nations paradigm of the maintenance of international peace and security, especially the role of the Security Council, has been criticized by many as dysfunctional. Alternative approaches have been proposed, such as a coalition of democratic states or reliance on regional agencies for enforcing the peace, but these raise problems of their own. The question remains: who shall enforce the peace? Chapter 3 attempts to answer this question.

The law of armed conflict, or as it is increasingly called by many, international humanitarian law, has traditionally depended on the good faith of nation-states for its implementation. With rare exceptions, this good faith has simply not been present. Recently, the statutes of the international criminal tribunals for the former Yugoslavia and for Rwanda, as well as that for the International Criminal Court, have included certain "war crimes" within their jurisdiction. In large part, all of these tribunals, as well as the so-called hybrid courts, owe their establishment to the failure of national civil or military courts to deal adequately with violations of the law of armed conflict, especially those found in the Geneva Conventions of 1949. There are also problems with the law of armed conflict itself, as demonstrated by the U.S. decision not to ratify either of the two additional protocols to the 1949 Geneva Conventions and by the recent claims by some that the Geneva Conventions of 1949 are so outdated that they have become "quaint" or even dangerous to national security. Chapter 4 evaluates the validity of these charges.

When he was U.S. Undersecretary of State for Arms Control and International Security, John Bolton greatly distrusted arms control and multilateral treaties, and this attitude became part of the Bush administration's approach. The Nuclear Non-Proliferation Treaty (NPT) has been an exception to this negative attitude, but, as demonstrated by the cases of Iran and North Korea, the nonproliferation regime is currently under great strain. Moreover, the Bush administration's proposal to share nuclear information and materials with India, which has declined to become a party to the NPT, arguably further threatens to undermine nonproliferation measures. There also appear to be little in the way of new legal initiatives in the areas of arms control and disarmament. Chapter 5 attempts to answer the question whether, in the areas of arms control, disarmament, nonproliferation, and safeguards, treaties are truly passé.

For much of its history, under the dominance of legal positivism, only states were regarded as the proper subjects of international law.[20] Only states had rights and obligations under international law. For their part, individuals might be, in some cases, the objects of international law, but states owed no duties to them, and there were no international procedures available for individuals to hold states accountable for mistreating them.

To be sure, "[t]he principle that law should protect the rights of individuals against the abuses of government can at least be dated back to John Locke's *Two Treatises of Government*, published in 1690."[21] Similar sentiments were expressed by such other political philosophers as Montesquieu and Jean Jacques Rousseau, and they all had a significant influence on Thomas Jefferson's drafting of the Declaration of Independence and led to democratic revolutions in America and throughout Europe. But the human rights created as a result of these influences, such as those found in the first ten amendments to the U.S. Constitution and in the French Declaration on the Rights of Man and Citizen, were the products of national law, to be protected by national institutions.

The development of international human rights law was a slow and somewhat sporadic process for most of the nineteenth and early twentieth centuries.[22] The cataclysmic event that accelerated and deepened the process was World War II. The gross atrocities committed by the Nazi regime in Europe led to the establishment by the United States, France, the United Kingdom, and the Soviet Union of the International Military Tribunal at Nuremberg, which convicted leading German officials of crimes against the peace, war crimes, and crimes against humanity – all crimes the Tribunal held were established under customary international law. Similar trials were held, and similar convictions were handed down, in Tokyo.

According to Thomas Buergenthal, currently a judge on the International Court of Justice and an eminent authority on international human rights law, "the internationalization of human rights and the humanization of international law" began with the establishment of the United Nations.[23] Following the coming into force of the U.N. Charter, which itself contained several provisions on human rights, the United Nations adopted the landmark Universal Declaration of Human Rights in 1948 and such prominent human rights treaties as the Convention on the Prevention and Punishment of the Crime of Genocide (1948); the International Convention on the Elimination of All Forms of Racial Discrimination (1965); and the International Covenants on Civil and Political Rights and Economic, Social, and Cultural Rights (1966). As of June 29, 2005, the United Nations had adopted twenty-nine human rights conventions.[24] There is little evidence, however, that human rights treaties and conventions have had much of an impact in promoting and protecting human rights, especially because the mechanisms for monitoring compliance with them are weak.[25] Moreover, as noted previously, the Commission on Human Rights, until recently the primary organ of the United Nations responsible for promoting and protecting human rights, became a notorious failure, and at this point it is not clear whether its replacement, the Human Rights Council, will be much better. Chapter 6 examines some of the overall record of the United Nations with respect to human rights, and takes a parenthetical look at the current situation in the European Court of Human Rights.

International environmental issues have received considerable attention in recent days, perhaps highlighted most sharply by former U.S. Vice President Al Gore's documentary movie, *An Inconvenient Truth*.[26] The issue of climate change has received especially intense scrutiny, as "[w]ithout a doubt, the most important development in the twenty-first century is the almost universal consensus that global climate change is well under way and that the international community must undertake heroic measures to attempt to mitigate the most serious adverse impacts. However, debates about the causes and long-term effects continue within the scientific community."[27]

Debate continues, moreover, over the effectiveness of the Kyoto Protocol to the United Nations Framework Convention on Climate Change (Kyoto Protocol).[28] The

United States has been sharply critical of the Kyoto Protocol, which is scheduled to expire in 2012, and even its supporters acknowledge the Protocol needs improvements. Thus efforts are now directed toward reaching at least tentative agreement on what a new Kyoto Protocol might look like and obtaining support for a new Kyoto Protocol from the United States and emerging nations.[29] It remains to be seen whether these efforts will be successful. At present the United States appears to favor national rather than international action, both action the United States is taking and action emerging nations (according to the United States) should take.[30] The United States remains highly skeptical of the usefulness of international treaties on the environment.

In addition to the Kyoto Protocol, the United States remains leery of the Convention on Biological Diversity.[31] The United States views the convention as containing inadequate provisions for the protection of intellectual property rights.[32] Meanwhile, since adoption of the convention in 1992, and as of 2006, the states parties have held eight conferences. The most important development has been the adoption of the Cartagena Protocol on Biosafety to the Convention on Biological Diversity in 2003.[33] The United States signed the Protocol, but has not ratified it. During these conferences the states parties also adopted recommendations on a variety of topics, including agricultural biodiversity, biodiversity in dry and subhumid climates, marine and coastal biodiversity, alien species invasions, and assessment procedures. Despite these steps, however, "[t]he state of the world's ecosystems and biodiversity continues to decline" and "more urgent action is needed."[34] Chapter 7 examines the continuing difficulties surrounding the Kyoto Protocol and the Convention on Biological Diversity and steps taken, or proposed to be taken, to resolve these difficulties.

Chapter 8 first considers some possible causes of the present malaise in international law and the international legal process. Many of the possible causes of the current problems of international law will have been identified in previous chapters. These include, for example, the rapid pace of life and change in today's society; 9/11 and its aftermath; the emergence on the world scene of China, India, and Brazil as world powers; the "clash of civilizations"; and some arguably politicized decisions of international courts. Some of the other possible causes discussed in this chapter include the "democratic deficit"; the "free rider" problem; perceived threats to national sovereignty; increasing provincialism and isolationism in the developed world; and the lack of a rule of law tradition in the developing world.

Chapter 8 then sets forth some concluding observations and a prognosis. The concluding observations are drawn primarily from working through the subjects of the previous seven chapters. The prognosis attempts to develop possible alternative futures for international law and legal process, and to demonstrate why choosing among them will require the making of hard choices by all concerned members of the world community.

Notes

1. *See* Rosalyn Higgins, *A Just World Under Law*, 388 PROC. AM. SOC'Y INT'L L. (2006).
2. *See* Princeton University, Woodrow Wilson School of Public and International Affairs, Project on National Security, G. John Ikenberry and Anne-Marie Slaughter, Co-Directors, *Forging A World of Liberty Under Law* (2006), at 7.
3. As reported in U.S. Naval War College, Final Report on the Legal Experts Workshop on the Future Global Legal Order, Craig H. Allen, *A Stronger And More Prosperous World Through Secure And Accessible Seas* (2006).
4. Article 38 of the Statute of the International Court of Justice provides, in pertinent part:
    1. The Court, whose function is to decide in accordance with international law such disputes as are submitted to it, shall apply:
        (a) international conventions, whether general or particular, establishing rules expressly recognized by the contesting states;
        (b) international custom, as evidence of a general practice accepted as law;
        (c) the general principles of law recognized by civilized nations;
        (d) subject to the provisions of Article 59, judicial decisions and the teachings of the most highly qualified publicists of the various nations, as subsidiary means for the determination of rules of law.
5. PHILIP JESSUP, TRANSNATIONAL LAW 2 (1956).
6. JAMES GLEICK, FASTER (1999).
7. ALVIN and HEIDI TOFFLER, REVOLUTIONARY WEALTH (2006).
8. ROSCOE POUND, INTERPRETATION of LEGAL HISTORY 1 (1923).
9. ALVIN and HEIDI TOFFLER, *supra* note 7, at 38.
10. *See, e.g.*, J. Patrick Kelly, *The Twilight of Customary International Law*, 40 VA. J. INT'L L. 449 (2000).
11. JACK L. GOLDSMITH and ERIC A. POSNER, THE LIMITS of INTERNATIONAL LAW (2005).
12. JOHN F. MURPHY, THE UNITED STATES and the RULE of LAW in INTERNATIONAL AFFAIRS 14–25 (2004).
13. ANNE-MARIE SLAUGHTER, A NEW WORLD ORDER (2004).
14. *See, e.g., Human Rights Council*, N.Y. Times, June 23, 2006, at A26, col. 1. For background to and discussion of the proposal to establish a human rights council, *see* Nazilea Ghanea, *From UN Commission on Human Rights to UN Human Rights Council: One Step Forward or Two Steps Backward?*, 55 INT'L & COMP. L.Q. 695 (2006).
15. *See Crisis Postponed at the UN*, N.Y. Times, July 6, 2006, at A20, col. 1.
16. *See* JOHN F. MURPHY, *supra* note 12, at 250–83.
17. *See The "Killing Fields,"* N.Y. Times, July 6, 2006, at A20, col. 1. For a more wide-ranging criticism of the Yugoslav and Rwanda tribunals, *see* Helena Cobban, *Think Again: International Courts*, FOREIGN POLICY, March/April, 2006, at 22.
18. Greg Hitt, *At a Crossroads: Failed Trade Talks Cloud WTO's Future*, WALL ST. J., July 31, 2006, at A2, col. 3.
19. *See* Chris Stephan, *Human Rights and the War in Chechnya: A Test for Europe*, Crimes of War Project (December 2, 2005), http: www.crimesof war.org/print/onnews/Chechnya2-print.html.
20. *See* Mark W. Janis, *Individuals as Subjects of International Law*, 17 CORNELL INT'L L.J. 61 (1984).
21. MARK W. JANIS & JOHN E. NOYES, INTERNATIONAL LAW 368 (3rd ed. 2006).

22. *See* John H. Humphrey, *The International Law of Human Rights in the Middle Twentieth Century, in* THE PRESENT STATE of INTERNATIONAL LAW and OTHER ESSAYS 75 (Maarten Bos ed., 1973).

23. *See* Thomas Buergenthal, *The Normative and Institutional Evolution of International Human Rights*, 19 HUM. RTS. Q. 703 (1997).

24. *See* RICHARD B. LILLICH, HURST HANNUM, S. JAMES ANAYA, and DINAH L. SHELTON, INTERNATIONAL HUMAN RIGHTS 79–83 (2006).

25. *See* Oona Hathaway, *Do Human Rights Treaties Make a Difference?* 111 YALE L.J. 1935 (2002).

26. It is worth noting that *An Inconvenient Truth* won two Oscars in 2007.

27. EDITH BROWN WEISS, STEPHEN C. McCAFFREY, DANIEL BARSTOW MAGRAW, and A. DAN TARLOCK, INTERNATIONAL ENVIRONMENTAL LAW and POLICY xxi (2d ed. 2007).

28. Conference of the Parties to the Framework Convention on Climate Change: Kyoto Protocol to the United Nations Framework Convention on Climate Change, 37 INT'L LEG. MATERIALS 22 (1998).

29. *See* Bertrand Benoit, Hugh Williamson, and Frederick Studemann, *Germany Seeks to Lead Way on Post-Kyoto Accord*, FIN. TIMES, March 7, 2007, at 1, col. 3.

30. *See* JOHN F. MURPHY, *supra* note 12, at 343–44.

31. Convention on Biological Diversity, 31 INT'L LEG. MATERIALS 818 (1992).

32. For a summary of this view, *see* JOHN F. MURPHY, *supra* note 12, at 342–43.

33. For the text of the Protocol, *see* EDITH BROWN WEISS et al., *supra* 27, at 919.

34. *Id.* at 893.

1

The Multifaceted Nature of International Law

In the chapter on "Law and Legal Process in International Affairs," in my book *The United States and the Rule of Law in International Affairs*,[1] I begin with the lead-in to each program in the *Monty Python* BBC television series: "And now for something completely different."[2] Law and legal process in international affairs are indeed vastly if not completely different from their counterparts in national legal systems. Moreover, it is this vast difference from national law and practice that has given rise to much skepticism about international law and practice and to challenges to claims of its "legal" nature and of its relevance to the conduct of international affairs.

Interestingly, in the early history of international law, there was much less skepticism about international law as "law" and its relevance to international affairs. The end of the Thirty Years War in 1648 and the resultant Peace Treaties of Westphalia[3] are regarded by most historians and international lawyers as the beginning of modern international relations and therefore of modern international law. But prior to the Peace of Westphalia, "an intensification of international trade, improvements in navigation and military techniques, and the discovery of many distant lands . . . stimulated the further development of international practices and the emergence of modern conceptions of a law of nations."[4] In particular, the Hanseatic League, created in the thirteenth century by certain German city-states and by the early fifteenth century comprising more than 150 trading cities and centers, contributed substantially to the growth of international usages and customs. Similarly, in Italy, city-republics, especially Venice, Genoa, and Florence, started sending resident ambassadors to the capitals of other states, thereby contributing to the creation of legal principles governing diplomatic relations and the immunities of ambassadors and their staffs. Expansion of trade resulted in an increasing number of commercial treaties. At the same time, numerous armed conflicts arising in the beginning of the seventeenth century, culminating in the carnage of the Thirty Years War (1618–1648), which inflicted great suffering on both peasants and city dwellers, demonstrated the

12

need for further rules governing the conduct of war. This need stimulated Hugo Grotius, a Dutch jurist generally regarded as the "father of international law," to write his classic treatise, *De Jure Belli Ac Pacis Libri Tres* (De Jure Belli Ac Pacis) (1623–1624), which is generally regarded as the foundation of modern international law.[5]

Grotius was perhaps the best known member of the school of international jurists guided by the philosophy of natural law.[6] Many members of this school closely follow the natural law philosophy of St. Thomas Aquinas (1225–1274), who believed that all human laws derive from, and are subordinate to, the law of God. This law is partly based on the law of nature, a body of permanent principles grounded in the Divine Order and partially revealed in the Scripture. Grotius, however, is a rationalist who derives the principles of the law of nature from universal reason rather than from divine authority. For Grotius, two of the most important principles of the law of nature in the system of the law of nations are first, that restitution must be made for a harm done by one party to another and second, that promises made, through signatures to treaties or otherwise, must be kept (*pacta sunt servanda*). These two principles remain eminent today, even without the doctrinal support of natural law philosophy.

A major problem facing natural law adherents is that they "have been divided, throughout the ages, over the positive meaning of the laws of nature in the world of human institutions and actions."[7] They agreed, however, that the law of nations was based on natural law and did not challenge the legal status of the law of nations. At the same time, it is noteworthy that, in addition to emphasizing the law of nature as a basis of the law of nations, Grotius distinguished between the "*jus naturale* – to which Grotius devotes his main attention – and the *jus gentium*, the customary law of nations (also called *jus voluntarium*, i.e., a body of law formed by the conduct and will of nations)."[8] Grotius's identification of the *jus gentium* as part of the law of nations foreshadowed the later move away from the natural law philosophy and toward the positivist philosophy. Although positivism has a variety of different meanings,[9] "its essential meaning in the theory and development of international law is reliance on the practice of states and the conduct of international relations as evidenced by customs or treaties, as against the derivation of norms from basic metaphysical principles. The rise of positivism in western political and legal theory, especially from the latter part of the 18th century to the early part of the 20th century, corresponds to the steady rise of the national state and its increasingly absolute claims to legal and political supremacy."[10]

The steady rise of the national state gave rise to the concept of sovereignty and its corollary that the national state "recognizes no international obligations other than those to which it has voluntarily agreed through practice hardening into custom, or through specific written consent expressed in treaties or other international agreements."[11] A variety of scholars following the philosophy of positivism attempted to reconcile the validity of international law with the concept of sovereignty, but other positivists rejected their efforts. The most prominent of these was the English jurist John Austin, who dominated jurisprudential thinking in the nineteenth century. According to Austin, a command emanating from a definite superior and punitive sanctions enforcing the command were indispensable elements of law. Because international law has no such superior issuing commands enforceable by punitive sanctions, it does not qualify as law and constitutes merely "positive morality."[12]

Arguably, Austin's definition of law is inaccurate even as applied to law at the national level, and if so, his claim that international law is not law but only positive morality loses much of its cogency. An alternative approach to law is to view it functionally not as a series of commands enforced by punitive sanctions but rather as a process whereby participants in the legal process strive to reach an understanding of how to cooperate to resolve problems that cannot be resolved by individual action alone or, in the case of disputes, as a process that will facilitate the efforts of the participants in the dispute to reach a settlement between their conflicting positions. Even in the field of criminal law, where rules as commands backed by the threat of punitive sanctions have a greater saliency, the rule of law depends primarily on its subjects' acceptance of the legitimacy of its prohibitions rather than on the policeman's gun or nightstick.

Nonetheless, Austin's claim has rung true for many nonlawyers as well as for a number of lawyers outside of the field of international law. A prominent example is John R. Bolton, who, prior to his becoming U.S. Under Secretary of State for Arms Control and International Security and later U.S. Permanent Representative to the United Nations for the Bush administration, made the startling assertion that treaties are "'law' only for US domestic purposes. In their international operation, treaties are simply 'political' obligations."[13] Later, Bolton went so far as to deny the existence of law in international affairs.[14]

More recently, there have been more sophisticated and subtle challenges to the existence of international law. Before turning to these challenges, however, let us look more closely at the nature of international law.

THE "SOURCES" OF INTERNATIONAL LAW[15]

Although it has often been derided as inadequate for purposes of modern international law, the classic statement of the "sources" or kinds of international law is set forth in Article 38 of the Statute of the International Court of Justice (ICJ):

1. The Court, whose function is to decide in accordance with international law such disputes as are submitted to it, shall apply:
   a. international conventions, whether general or particular, establishing rules expressly
   b. recognized by the contesting states;

    c. international custom, as evidence of a general practice accepted as law;

    d. the general principles of law recognized by civilized nations; subject to the provisions of Article 59 [which provides that decisions of the Court have no binding force except between the parties to the dispute], judicial decisions and the teachings of the most qualified publicists of the nations, as subsidiary means for the determination of rules of law.

2. This provision shall not prejudice the power of the Court to decide a case *ex aequo et bono*, if the parties agree thereto.[16]

By way of elaboration Section 102 of the Restatement (Third) of the Foreign Relations Law of the United States provides with respect to the sources of international law:

1. A rule of international law is one that has been accepted as such by the international community of states:

    a. in the form of customary law;

    b. by international agreement;

    c. by derivation from general principles common to the major legal systems of the world;

2. Customary international law results from a general and consistent practice of states followed by them from a sense of legal obligation.

3. International agreements create law for the state parties thereto and may lead to the creation of customary international law when such agreements are intended for adherence by states generally and are in fact widely accepted.

4. General principles common to the major legal systems, even if not incorporated or reflected in customary law or international agreements, may be invoked as supplementary rules of international law where appropriate.

It is worthwhile to pause for a moment to consider just how authoritative these two "authorities" on the sources or kinds of international law are. Article 38 of the Statute of the International Court of Justice is intended simply to guide the Court in its proceedings and does not purport to be a definitive and widely applicable statement on the sources of international law. For its part, the Restatement (Third) of the Foreign Relations Law of the United States is just that: a Restatement produced by the American Law Institute. As such it has no official status and its influence depends on how it is received and utilized by international law practitioners, whether they be lawyers in foreign ministries or other government agencies, international lawyers in private practice, judges on international courts or international arbitral tribunals, or professors of international law in academia. In terms of Article 38 of the Court's statute, the Restatement would appear under section 1(d) as the "teachings of the most qualified publicists of the nations," in light of the prominence of many persons involved in the production of the Restatement. But I am not aware of any study that has examined the extent of the Restatement's influence, and it appears it is not a source relied on by the ICJ or other international courts or by international arbitral tribunals. This is, perhaps, not surprising because none of these courts or tribunals has the authority to create law, unlike common law courts in the United States and Great Britain. U.S. courts, when confronted with an international law question, appear more likely to turn to the Restatement for guidance.

Be that as it may, there are no "official" or "authoritative" other statements of the sources of international law. To be sure, there are numerous writings of scholars on these sources, and to some extent, they fill a vacuum. But Article 38 of the Court's statute and the Restatement still serve as primary guides to the sources of international law. They do so, although neither includes within its listing of the sources of international law other possibilities claimed by some states and commentators to be sources of international law. These include, among others, natural law, equity, and various manifestations of so-called soft law, such as nonbinding declarations and resolutions of international organizations, especially the General Assembly of the United Nations, and nonbinding codes, guidelines, standards, and policy statements. We examine these later in this chapter, as well as in various other parts of the book. But first we turn to a consideration of the most ambiguous and controversial source of international law, customary practices of states accepted as law.

Customary International Law

As a preliminary matter, it is perhaps worth noting that customary law in national legal systems plays at most a minor role. Although custom or usage is routinely listed as a source of law in civil law nations and is a favorite topic for civil law scholars, some eminent comparative law scholars have contended that "[i]n practice the use of custom is limited to the few instances in which statutes expressly refer to custom."[17] Or, it has been suggested, that "[m]ost civil law systems recognize 'customary law' as a subsidiary source of law, i.e., a source that can be used to fill gaps in the written law. In general, the practical importance of this source of law tends to be limited."[18] The role of custom in common law legal systems is even more limited, because the lawmaking authority of judicial decisions has displaced the role that custom played in the early days of the nation.

By contrast, customary international law plays a major, arguably a preeminent, role in international law. As noted earlier, although Grotius based his principle that promises given, through treaties or otherwise, must be kept (*pacta sunt servanda*) on the law of nature (i.e., natural law), he derived this principle also from observing the conduct and the will of nations, which today we view as the basis of customary international law. But dramatic changes in the nature of international relations have made the process of creating customary international law particularly problematic. Examination of the classic description by Manley O. Hudson, a judge on the International Court of Justice and an eminent authority on international law, of the essential elements of the customary international law process in light of current circumstances demonstrates the problem:

1. Concordant practice by a number of States with reference to a type of situation falling within the domain of international relations;
2. continuation or repetition of the practice over a considerable period of time;
3. conception that the practice is required by, or consistent with, prevailing international law; and
4. general acquiescence in the practice by other States.[19]

When this description of the customary international law process was published (1950), the United Nations had sixty member states. The international legal process, including the actions of the United Nations, was dominated by Western states, particularly the United States. Many of the states now constituting the so-called Third World were under colonial rule, and the Soviet Union had relatively little influence in the United Nations and other international institutions. Hence the number of states that had to engage in a concordant practice as part of the customary international law practice was relatively small. Today, by contrast, there are 192 member states of the United Nations and close to 200 states in the world community, and these states have raised a serious challenge to the dominance of the international legal process by the West. As a result, it is by no means clear how many states must participate to constitute the number required by Manley Hudson.

Moreover, there is no agreement on what constitutes state practice.[20] Basically, the divide is between powerful, developed states that would define state practice narrowly to include only the acts of governments and not simply statements made by them, on the one side, and the position of some scholars and less powerful states that would include as state practice normative statements in drafts of the International Law Commission, nonbinding resolutions of the U.N. General Assembly, and recitals in international instruments, on the other. If statements such as those found in General Assembly resolutions adopted by majority vote can alone create international law, the less powerful states can play a strong if not dominant role in the process of creating customary international law. This would also, in effect, endow the General Assembly with legislative power – a result clearly not intended by the drafters of the U.N. Charter.[21]

According to Manley Hudson's approach, state practice – however defined and engaged in by however many states– must continue and be repeated over a considerable period of time. For its part, the International Court of Justice has stated that: "Although the passage of only a short period of time is not necessarily . . . a bar to the formulation of a new rule of customary international law . . . State practice . . . should have been both extensive and virtually uniform."[22] It has also been suggested that the time period necessary may be shorter if there is no conflicting state practice and the proposed rule does not overturn existing rules.[23]

Other commentators have contended that Hudson's formulation reflects a time when international life was slower and communication primitive, and that custom today may be formed rapidly because "every event of international importance is universally and immediately known."[24] Some commentators have gone so far as to suggest that there can be "instant" customary international law,[25] at least if there is close to unanimity among states that a particular rule is necessary and there is no state practice to the contrary.[26] The concept of "instant" customary international law has not been generally accepted by government officials of states, however, and would give a substantial measure of legislative power to such international organizations as the United Nations that have not been adopted in their constitutive charters or to international conferences with nearly universal participation by states.[27]

Hudson's requirements that states engage in a practice with an understanding that it is required by, or consistent with, prevailing international law and that there be general acquiescence in the practice by other states raise the complex issue of *opinio juris*, which is the general acceptance of a norm as a legal obligation by the world community. The concept of *opinio juris* introduces a subjective element in the customary international law process because it requires that when engaging in or refraining from a particular practice states do so under an understanding that they have a legal right to engage in the practice or a legal obligation to refrain from engaging in the practice. For example, it is generally accepted that states have the right, subject to a few exceptions, to exercise jurisdiction over persons and property within their territorial boundaries, but are under an international obligation not to commit acts of genocide.

In many, perhaps most, instances of alleged customary international law norms, however, there may be little clear evidence that the vast majority of states have accepted the norm as a legal obligation.[28] The result is that, in the view of J. Patrick Kelly, "much of international law is announced in books and articles with little input from nations... Much of CIL [customary international law] is a fiction."[29]

One of the many conundrums surrounding customary international law is the role that the consent of nation-states plays in the process of its creation. Although it has long been thought that the explicit or implicit consent of all states is not required for a norm of customary international law to be created, a customary norm, once established, has traditionally been regarded as universally binding. This was the basis for the generally accepted proposition, at least in the West, that new states are bound by customary international law, although they have played no role in its creation. As Professor Kelly has noted, however, after new nations became a majority in the United Nations and the West began to lose control over the customary international law process, especially as it related to the treatment of foreign investment, a persistent objector principle emerged that permits a state that persistently objects during the process of formation to opt out of customary norms.[30] The result, if one accepts the persistent objector principle, and not all states do,[31] is "to make custom consensual for older nations and universally binding on new nations."[32]

In his recent writing, Professor Kelly has been particularly critical of both the current status of customary international law and of the process involved in its creation. He concludes:

> Accordingly, customary international legal theory is incoherent and undefined. There are no defined criteria for determining customary norms. The methodology of customary international law is so malleable that both the left and right in wealthy developed countries manipulate it to advance their own normative agenda, without the participation or consent of most of the nations and peoples of the world. Progressive internationalists, including judges of the International Court of Justice, the World Trade Organization, and the European Court of Human Rights utilize general resolutions and treaties to make environmental and human rights norms universally binding. On the right scholars and unilateralists operating under a theory that only physical acts count as state practice, use custom theory to protect foreign investment and to promote a right of unilateral humanitarian intervention that is said to justify US interventions in Grenada and Panama, and Viet Nam's takeover of Cambodia contrary to the norm against the use of force in the UN Charter. Despite near unanimous condemnation by States, the putative norm of international humanitarian intervention has considerable resonance within the academy.[33]

Elsewhere, Kelly discusses other examples where, in his view, the customary international law process has been misused, especially by judges, academics, NGOs, and a few powerful nations, to find norms of customary international law that have not been accepted by the overwhelming majority of states. Indeed, he contends that "[t]he concept of CIL as empirical law has disappeared . . . If we take the general acceptance requirement seriously, it may be nearly impossible to form legitimate substantive customary norms in an expanded world of many different cultures, values, and perspectives."[34] To Kelly, however, this does not pose a problem because he is of the view that "CIL is not necessary in an era of rapid communications and communications. If there is, in fact, the political will to accept international legal norms, then a binding treaty is possible. CIL is the preferred technique for normative scholars and judges precisely because there is a lack of political will to create binding obligations."[35]

Carrying out Kelly's proposal that customary international law be discarded and replaced by a greater reliance on treaties would be a radical step, and we shall turn to a consideration of its merits later in this study. At this point it suffices to note that if, as Kelly suggests, there is a lack of political will to create binding legal obligations, it would seem to follow that treaties as a source of international law may also be problematic. There is increasing evidence, moreover, that lack of political will to create binding legal obligations has given rise to greater use of so-called soft law, a subject to which we now turn.

Soft Law

In my view use of the term "soft law" in the international legal process is an unfortunate development because it has given rise to considerable controversy and confusion. As an introduction to this problem as I see it, consider the observation of Prosper Weil:

> The term "soft law" is not used solely to express the vague and therefore, in practice, uncompelling character of a legal norm but is also used at time to convey the sublegal value of some non-normative acts, such as certain resolutions of the international organizations . . . It would seem better to reserve the term "soft law" for rules that are imprecise and not really compelling, since sublegal obligations are neither "soft law" nor "hard law"; they are simply not law at all. Two basically different categories are involved here; for while there are, on the one hand, legal norms that are not in practice compelling, because too vague, there are also, on the other hand, provisions that are precise, yet remain at the pre- or sub-normative stage. To discuss both of these categories in terms of "soft law" or "hard law" is to foster confusion.[36]

Weil might have added that to apply the term "soft law" to rules that are imprecise and not really compelling is also to foster confusion. It would be better to refer to such rules as imprecise and ambiguous law, rather than as soft law. This is in part because there is little agreement on what the term "soft law" means.[37] To some, soft law is an oxymoron because, as indicated previously in the quote from Weil, one definition of soft law is that it is not legally binding. Others emphasize the capacity of soft law in the form of resolutions of international organizations or other nonbinding international documents to become hard law. Still others regard this capacity as "beside the point." As Michael Reisman has noted, "[e]ven if soft law does not harden up, soft law performs important functions, and, given the structure of the international system, we could barely operate without it."[38]

Reisman makes an important point, but it is perhaps one that requires further explanation and elaboration. It is generally accepted that often such legally nonbinding international instruments as resolutions of international organizations constitute a first step toward the conclusion of binding international agreements or norms of customary international law. As noted in the introduction to this book, however, perhaps increasingly often legally nonbinding international instruments serve as a substitute for rather than a step toward binding international law. This has especially been the case in the fields of international human rights law and international environmental law, as we shall see in later chapters of this book. In these circumstances, for various reasons to be explored later, the parties seeking to resolve a problem decide that traditional international law will not serve their interests and turn instead to alternative means.

Not entirely facetiously, one might suggest that application of the term "soft law" to nonbinding international instruments is an attempt by international lawyers to remain relevant in international relations. Increased use of nonbinding international instruments, however, in no way threatens the job security of international lawyers because the drafting skills of international lawyers apply to such instruments as well as to the traditional international treaty. As Oscar Schachter has pointed out, "not all nonbinding agreements are general and indefinite. Governments may enter into precise and definite engagements as to future conduct with a clear understanding shared by the parties that the agreements are not legally binding."[39] The key questions then become, according to Schachter, what is the nature of the commitment accepted by the parties in a nonbinding agreement and what, if any, are the legal implications of such an agreement?

The nature of the commitment in a nonbinding agreement is that it is political. Although it is generally agreed that it does not engage the legal responsibility of the parties in the sense that noncompliance by a party would not be the basis for a claim for reparation or for judicial remedies, this point "is quite different from stating that the agreement need not be observed or that the parties are free to act as if there were no such agreement."[40] The 1975 Helsinki Final Act contained human rights provisions that were treated as if they were binding, although the act expressly provided that they were not. Moreover, considerable pressure was bought to bear on the parties to comply with these provisions in the form of follow-up international meetings and the creation of Helsinki watch commissions at the national level. As to the legal implications of nonbinding agreements, Schachter suggests that under certain circumstances parties to a nonbinding international agreement may be barred from deviating from its terms by the doctrine of estoppel.[41]

Even if a party would not be barred from deviating from a nonbinding agreement by some legal principle as estoppel, the agreement may have significant legal effects. For example, a nonbinding agreement may create expectations that national law and practice will be modified to conform with the political commitment set forth in the agreement, and a failure to do so by one party may result in a strong reaction by other parties to the agreement.

It is noteworthy that no one speaks of "soft law" in national legal systems. The term has emerged at the international level in part because of the increasingly dysfunctional nature of international treaties and customary international law – the traditional "sources" of international law. In practice the term "soft law" has been applied to an extraordinarily wide range of instruments and processes in international relations. By way of partial example, Alan Boyle and Christine Chinkin suggest that soft law:

> encompasses *inter alia* inter-state conference declarations such as the 1992 Rio Declaration on Environment and Development; UN General Assembly instruments such as the 1948 Universal Declaration of Human Rights, the 1970 Declaration on the Principles of Friendly Relations Among States, and resolutions dealing with disarmament, outer space, the deep seabed, decolonisation, or natural resources; interpretive guidance adopted by human rights treaty bodies and other autonomous intergovernmental institutions; codes of conduct, guidelines and recommendations

of international organizations, such as UNEP's 1987 Guidelines on Environmental Impact Assessment, FAO's Code of Conduct on Responsible Fisheries or many others adopted by IMO, IAEA, FAO and so on. Also potentially included within the category of soft law are the common international standards adopted by transnational networks of national regulatory bodies, NGOs, and professional and industry associations. Finally, the term "soft law" can also be applied to non-treaty agreements between states or between states and other entities that lack capacity to conclude treaties.[42]

Arguably, to include all of these nonbinding instruments in the category of soft law creates confusion because many of them serve functions that vary considerably from one another. Some documents, such as the Universal Declaration of Human Rights, have played a major role in the creation of "hard," that is, binding law. Others, such as many codes of conduct, guidelines, and recommendations of international organizations, have been adopted in place of binding agreements because of the perception that binding documents would not be appropriate for application to the subject or problem at hand. Still others, such as interpretative guidance adopted by human rights treaties bodies, are designed to facilitate implementation of binding international agreements but, at least in the view of many governments such as that of the United States, carry little authoritative weight.

To the extent that the term "soft law" serves to distinguish these nonlegally binding instruments from instruments containing the "hard law" of legally binding norms, use of the term in this way suffers from a measure of imprecision. In contrast, rather than referring to "soft law" and "hard law," Daniel Bodansky refers to precise norms as rules and less precise rules as standards. In his words, rules "define in advance what conduct is permissible and impermissible," whereas standards "set forth more open-ended tests, whose application depends on the exercise of judgment or discretion."[43]

My quarrel, it is important to note, is not with the proposition that legally nonbinding international instruments and other examples of so-called soft law play an exceedingly important role in the making of international law. On the contrary, the validity of this proposition is strongly and ably demonstrated by Boyle and Chinkin in their treatise.[44] My quarrel, rather, is with the use of the term "soft law" to cover a wide range of phenomena that often are quite distinct from each other. Lumping them all together under the rubric "soft law" creates unnecessary confusion and controversy. Use of this term is especially unfortunate when, as is arguably increasingly the case, legally nonbinding international instruments are utilized not as part of the process of making international law but rather as an alternative to it. To deny the status of "law" to these instruments is not the same as denying that they may play, depending on the circumstances, a crucially important, indeed sometimes indispensable, role in the making of international law. Later in this book we shall see many examples where legally nonbinding international instruments have played such a role. At the same time, we shall see many examples where legally nonbinding international instruments have been utilized as a substitute for international law because of the perception that application of legally binding international norms would not be appropriate under the circumstances.

Jus Cogens

One of the most controversial and problematic doctrines in international law is *jus cogens*, or the concept of a peremptory norm. It is debatable whether *jus cogens* is a form of customary international law or rather a form of natural law,[45] although the weight of authority would seem to favor the proposition that it is a form of customary international law.[46]

In negotiations on the Vienna Convention on the Law of Treaties, the United States opposed incorporating the concept of a peremptory norm in the draft treaty proposed by the International Law Commission.[47] The United States and other states representing the Anglo-Saxon intellectual tradition reportedly "insisted that the concept of *jus cogens* either did not exist or was too vague to be given legal meaning, and that in any case the adoption of such a specific derogation from the free will of the parties to a treaty to conclude whatever agreement they wished would impair the sanctity of the written word and the principle of *pacta sunt servanda.*"[48] In negotiations on the Convention, however, most of the debate did not involve the concept of *jus cogens* but rather how to define the test for recognizing a rule of *jus cogens* and whether the Convention should identify examples of peremptory norms.[49] It proved impossible to agree on examples of peremptory norms, but Article 53 of the Convention provides:

> A treaty is void if, at the time of its conclusion, it conflicts with a peremptory norm of general international law. For the purposes of the present Convention, a peremptory norm of general international law is a norm accepted and recognized by the international community of States as a whole as a norm from which no derogation is permitted and which can be modified only by a subsequent norm of general international law having the same character.

As a corollary to Article 53, Article 64 of the Convention provides:

> If a new peremptory norm of general international law emerges, any existing treaty which is in conflict with that norm becomes void and terminates.

The definition of a peremptory norm in Article 53 of the Convention leaves unclear the process whereby it is determined whether the international community of states as a whole has accepted and recognized a particular norm as being one from which no derogation is permitted. Indeed, the problems of identifying state practice and *opinio juris* as part of the process of creating a "normal" norm of customary international law, discussed previously, would seem to loom especially large if one is attempting to identify a "supernorm" of international law from which no derogation is possible.

The failure of the drafters of the Vienna Convention on the Law of Treaties to agree on a list of *jus cogens* norms has not been followed by any greater success on the part of state representatives in other forums. For its part, the International Court of Justice, in *Nicaragua v. United States*, asserted that the international prohibition on the use of force was "a conspicuous example in a rule of international law having the character of *jus cogens*."[50] But as D'Amato has pointed out, the opinion in the *Nicaragua* case gives no indication as to how the judges reached this conclusion.[51] Indeed, D'Amato has gone so far as to characterize the process whereby the Court reached its decision as a "kitchen-sink approach to the sources of international law." He suggests that "the World Court found it just as easy to promote an ordinary norm into an imperative norm as to create out of thin air an ordinary norm. The only requirement for either of these transformative processes of legal legerdemain to be effected was the garnering of a majority vote of the judges present at the Hague."[52] Decisions by other international courts have determined norms to constitute *jus cogens*, but these too have failed to set forth in convincing fashion the process whereby the courts made their determinations, and it is therefore questionable how authoritative these pronouncements are.[53]

The United States ultimately agreed to the inclusion of Articles 53 and 64 in the Vienna Convention. In doing so, however, it insisted that claims of *jus cogens* be subject to adjudication by the International Court of Justice or arbitration, as provided in Article 66 of the Convention. The United States has not become a party to the Vienna Convention. Accordingly, the procedures of Article 66 cannot be invoked either by or against the United States. Moreover, as pointed out by the Restatement (Third) of the Foreign Relations Law of the United States, although the principles of Articles 53 and 64 arguably are effective as customary international law, "there are no safeguards against their abuse. In such circumstances, the United States is likely to take a particularly restrictive view of these doctrines."[54]

In theory, Article 66 of the Vienna Convention could constitute one safeguard against abuse of the doctrine of *jus cogens* as reflected in the terms of Articles 53 and 64. In practice, however, Article 66 has never been invoked and hence is inoperative. As a result, the doctrine of *jus cogens* has been much abused, by states and writers who seek rhetorical support for their (often outrageous) claims. Perhaps the classic case is the claim by Russian scholar Grigory Tunkin in 1974 that the Brezhnev doctrine was a norm of *jus cogens*.[55] D'Amato has had some fun with this one by suggesting that President Gorbachev attempted to revoke the Brezhnev doctrine by implicitly stating that in the wake of Afghanistan the Soviet Union would no longer necessarily intervene militarily in every socialist nation that had a democratic–capitalist revolution. But this attempt would not succeed because Article 53 of the Vienna Convention provides that a *jus cogens* norm can be modified only by a subsequent norm of general international law having the same character. Hence, D'Amato concludes "international scholars who champion the cause of *jus cogens* might have to assert that the Soviet Union be *compelled*, as a matter of the

Brezhnev Doctrine's peremptory force in international law, to intervene militarily in other states in order to preserve proletarian internationalism."[56]

D'Amato concludes his parody by raising three rhetorical questions intended to demonstrate the weakness of the *jus cogens* doctrine: "(1) What is the utility of a norm of *jus cogens* (apart from its rhetorical value as a sort of exclamation point)? (2) How does a purported norm of *jus cogens* arise? (3) Once one arises, how can international law change it or get rid of it?"[57] Enough said.

General Principles of Law, the Writings of Scholars, and Law Created by International Organizations

As we have seen, Article 38(1) (c) of the Statute of the International Court of Justice directs the Court to apply, as one of the sources of international law, "the general principles of law recognized by civilized nations." In this era of the sovereign equality of states, the adjective "civilized" has in practice been dropped. There is still, however, some question as to the precise meaning of the words "general principles of law."

Because of its positivist orientation the Soviet Union denied that general principles of law were an autonomous source of law, and argued that they could be international law only when drawn from customary international practice. In sharp contrast some scholars have argued that the concept is rooted in natural law and is the basis for the *jus cogens* doctrine. The most widely held view is that general principles of law are to be found in municipal law through the comparative law process. Under this approach, if some proposition of law is to be found in virtually every legal system, it will constitute a general principle of law.

Even under the comparative law approach, there are difficult questions regarding this procedure that still have not been fully resolved.[58] In any event, the use of general principles of law derived from municipal legal systems has been sparing, "nearly always as a supplement to fill in gaps left by the primary sources of treaty and custom."[59]

It has been claimed, however, that "it is also possible for states to adopt general principles not derived from national law, with the intention that courts and states should apply them when relevant."[60] Assuming the correctness of this claim, which is debatable, it is not clear what its significance is. Malcolm Shaw notes that "[i]t is not clear . . . in all cases, whether what is involved is a general principle of law appearing in municipal systems or a general principle of international law. But perhaps this is not a terribly serious problem since because both municipal legal concepts and those derived from existing international practice can be defined as falling within the recognized catchment area."[61] If general principles of law derived from existing international practice and general principles of law appearing in municipal systems of law fall within the same catchment area, presumably this means that both have a limited scope and serve primarily as a gap filler when neither treaty law nor general norms of customary law can resolve an issue. An opinion of the WTO Appellate Body has suggested that a general principle cannot override or amend the express terms of a treaty.[62]

Moreover, it is unclear how precisely a general principle of international law (as distinguished from a general principle of law recognized by civilized nations) is created. Does the process require, like that for customary principles of international law, state practice coupled with *opinio juris*, indicating that the states involved intended to create a general principle of international law rather than a rule of customary international law? Neither court decisions nor the interactions of states, nor the pronouncements of diplomats and statesmen clearly answer this question.

Article 38 (1) (d) of the ICJ's Statute refers to the writings of scholars only as "subsidiary means for the determination of rules of law." Malcolm Shaw, however, notes that "[h]istorically . . . the influence of academic writers on the development of international law has been marked. In the heyday of Natural Law it was analyses and juristic opinions that were crucial, while the role of state practice and court decisions were of less value. . . . With the rise of positivism and the consequent emphasis upon state sovereignty, treaties and custom assumed the dominant position in the exposition of the rules of the international system, and the importance of legalistic writings began to decline."[63]

The *relative* importance of the writings of scholars in the development of international law may have declined since the heyday of natural law in the sixteenth to eighteenth centuries. But because of evidentiary difficulties in determining the state practice and *opinio juris* components of customary international law, it is clear that prominent international law scholars exert a quite extraordinary influence upon decision makers in the customary international law process. The late Louis Sohn, an eminent international law authority, even went so far to suggest, not entirely facetiously, that: "This is the way international law is made, not by states, but by 'silly' professors writing books, and by knowing where there is a good book on the subject."[64]

It is one thing for international and national courts, as well as governmental officials, to rely on scholars for their extensive examinations of state practice and evidence of *opinio juris*. It is quite another to rely on bare statements of scholars whose works do not contain thorough examination of state practice or evidence of *opinio juris*. Unfortunately, it appears that there are very few scholarly works of the latter variety. In Kelly's view, "[t]he concept of CIL as empirical law has disappeared."[65]

As is well known, at the international level, true legislative authority – in the sense of capacity to take action to bind member states without obtaining the consent of them all – is practically nonexistent. In the United Nations, traditionally viewed as the most important of international organizations, with one exception, such legislative authority is limited to the internal governance of the organization, in particular the law applicable to international personnel, the admission and exclusion of member states, and the principles of financial responsibility of member states. The one clear example of U.N. legislative authority that goes beyond the internal governance of the organization is the power of the Security Council to take decisions binding on all members if it determines the existence of a threat to or breach of the peace or act of aggression under Chapter VII of the Charter.[66] As we shall see in Chapter 3, however, the Security Council, and alleged dominance of it by the permanent members, especially the United States, has recently come under severe criticism, and there have been numerous calls for reform of the process.

When one turns from the United Nations itself and to its specialized agencies, as well as to the International Atomic Energy Agency, one finds somewhat more legislative authority being exercised.[67] One must be careful not to overestimate this authority, however. Frederic Kirgis offers the following observations on the "legislative" activities of the specialized agencies and of the International Atomic Energy Agency:

> The examples . . . illustrate both the constructive role that specialized agencies may play as true rule-makers and the reluctance of states to endow the agencies with broad, formal legislative powers. Nonterritorial ocean and airspaces beckon formal international regulation if chaos and severe environmental harm are to be avoided. International drug control does too. Regulation through treaty-making would be far too cumbersome, so a more streamlined method has been found. Of course, there is an intermediate method . . . that could have been chosen: treaty-making with a tacit-consent/opt-out procedure for new standards or amendments to standards, to keep pace with changing conditions. There is also a soft law method that could have been chosen: resolutions formally amounting only to recommendations . . . The streamlined legislative techniques . . . have been adopted because of (a) their limited scope, (b) the need for effective regulation in those limited areas, (c) the assurances provided by procedures that ensure careful preparation of the standards with significant input from governments, and (d) the relatively slight risks that the rules will impose significant disadvantages on governments or their important constituents vis-a-vis their foreign rivals, or will substantially impair other important interests sought to be protected by governments.[68]

Kirgis further suggests that one reason why governments are unlikely to yield significant, formal legislative authority to U.N. agencies in new areas is that to do so would be contrary to democratic principles, because U.N. agencies are not directly accountable to the people in their member states.[69] As we shall see in Chapter 2 of this study, the issue of lack of democratic accountability looms large over many if not most international institutions today. Moreover, if, as has been alleged, the most important of them are truly "broken," member states will not be inclined to expand their legislative authority.

Ex Aequo Et Bono, *Equity, and Unilateral Acts of States*

Paragraph 2 of Article 38 of the Statute of the International Court of Justice provides: "This provision shall not prejudice the power of the Court to decide a case *ex aequo et bono*, if the parties decide thereto." This paragraph would allow the Court to decide a case without reference to the sources of international law enumerated in paragraph 1 of Article 38, or for that matter, "without reference to any principles of law at all."[70] The Court, however, has never decided a case *ex aequo et bono*, and the jurisdiction of the Court to decide a case *ex aequo et bono* has been accepted only once.[71]

It is not surprising that the Court has never decided a case *ex aequo et bono*, because, as Oppenheim suggests, in such a case the decision "will not be based on the application of legal rules but on the basis of such other considerations as the court may in all the circumstances regard as right and proper."[72] This gives the Court extremely broad discretion in its decision making and introduces a substantial measure of uncertainty that most states will not accept. As a result, states have only rarely agreed to this process and then chiefly when the third-party decision maker is an arbitral tribunal.[73]

Equity is to be distinguished from *ex aequo et bono* on the basis that equity is a doctrine of international law, whereas *ex aequo et bono* involves the party to the dispute conferring on the court or arbitral tribunal "the authority to ignore international law in deciding the dispute before it."[74] The International Court of Justice has employed equity as a basis for its decision in several of its opinions. But the Court has not always clearly indicated the source of this equity. Utilizing the classic formulation, Manley O. Hudson, a judge on the Permanent Court of International Justice, the predecessor of the International Court of Justice, in the *Diversion of Water from the Meuse* case,[75] regarded principles of equity as being "general principles of law recognized by civilized nations" under Article 38 (1) (c) of the Court's statute. In contrast, the International Court of Justice made no reference to Article 38 (1) (c) in employing equitable principles as a basis for rejecting the equidistance method to delimit the continental shelf between Denmark, Germany, and the Netherlands in the *North Sea Continental Shelf* cases.[76] Although the Court made a vague reference to equitable principles as "reflecting the *opinio juris* in the matter of delimitation,"[77] which implied that the Court viewed equitable principles as part of customary international law, it nowhere cited state practice evidencing *opinio juris*.

One widely accepted definition of equity is that it is based on generally recognized principles of justice and fair dealing.[78] There are those who believe, however, that such a standard is too vague and imprecise to serve as a rule of international law.[79] One of the sharpest criticisms came from Judge Andre Gross in his dissenting opinion in the *Gulf of Maine* case, challenging the use of equity in maritime delimitation cases:

> [e]quity left, without any objective elements of control, to the wisdom of the judge reminds us that equity was once measured by "the Chancellor's foot." I doubt that international justice can long survive an equity measured by the judge's eye. When equity is simply a reflection of the judge's perception, the courts which judge in this way part company from those which apply the law.[80]

Judge Gross went on to contend that the use of equity as the basis for a court's decision introduces into international law an element of subjectivity, "detached from any established rules."[81]

There is a substantial measure of truth in Judge Gross's challenge. But the *North Sea Continental Shelf* cases are but one of several cases where equity "has been used by the courts as a way of mitigating certain inequities, not as a method of refashioning nature to the detriment of legal rules."[82] Moreover, because international law in the form of "hard" law – that is, treaties and customary international law – can be difficult to change, and doing so usually involves a considerable amount of time under the most favorable circumstances, judges in international courts or arbitrators in international arbitral tribunals may have little choice but to employ equitable principles if they are to serve justice and fair dealing. At the same time, as the ICJ noted in the *Libya/Malta* case,[83] "the justice of which equity is an emanation, is not an abstract justice but justice according to the rule of law; which is to say that its application should display consistency and a degree of predictability; even though it also looks beyond it to principles of more general application." McCaffrey notes that "the ICJ now has considerable experience with the application of equity and has developed a body of jurisprudence that will guide it in future cases" and suggests that "[t]his should be of comfort to those who fear that the explicit application of equity introduces into international law an element of subjectivity . . ."[84] Some comfort, perhaps, but not necessarily enough to ease the minds of those who fear unfettered lawmaking by judges, especially at the international level.

JUDICIAL DECISIONS

Like "the teachings of the most highly qualified publicists of the various nations," under Article 38 (1) (d) of the Statute of the International Court of Justice "judicial decisions" do not constitute a "source" of international law but only "subsidiary means for the determination of rules of law." Moreover, the opening clause of subparagraph (d), "subject to the provisions of Article 59," rules out any *stare decisis* effect or binding precedential effect of decisions of the Court, because Article 59 provides: "The decision of the Court has no binding force except between the parties and in respect of that particular case." Thus the International Court of Justice follows the approach of tribunals in the civil law system rather than that of those in common law states.

Article 38 (1) (d) does not specify the scope of the term "judicial decisions." In practice the Court has referred to its own previous decisions, and the decisions of other international courts and of international arbitral tribunals. Not surprisingly, the Court has regarded its own previous decisions as especially authoritative and, although in no way regarding them as binding, the Court has tended to follow their determinations that a particular rule of law exists, thus furthering the value of consistency. Other international courts and international arbitral tribunals do the same.[85]

Although the decisions of national courts have not been relied on by the International Court of Justice, they are included within the scope of Article 38 (1) (d). They may provide evidence of the existence of a rule of customary international law, and thus be relied on by other national courts or by writers. British and American writers are reportedly especially likely to refer extensively to decisions of national courts.[86]

The role of national court decisions in the international legal process, however, is controversial. Although the Restatement (Third) of the Foreign Relations Law of the United States and some scholars would ascribe considerable importance to the decisions of domestic courts, others have argued that decisions of domestic courts are of minimal value because the judges of such courts generally lack the necessary knowledge of and expertise in international law or reflect a parochial view supporting the political position of the country's executive branch.[87] Moreover, domestic court decisions have been a focus of debate in another sense: whether they can constitute state practice for purposes of the creation of customary international law. Those who are skeptical about the value of domestic court decisions in the international legal process argue that they cannot constitute state practice but only opinions about the existence of customary international law.[88]

The same may be said about international judicial and arbitral decisions, including ICJ decisions. To be sure, all would concede that ICJ decisions carry great weight, but there is nothing in the Court's statute that assigns it law-creating authority. Nonetheless, some commentators have claimed that in practice the ICJ has increasingly assumed a law-creating role.[89]

Unilateral Declarations

Perhaps the most curious of several curious ways in which a state may become subject to a legal obligation under international law is by issuing, in written or oral form, a unilateral declaration. The classic example of this phenomenon is the *Eastern Greenland* case,[90] where M. Ihlen, the Norwegian Minister of Foreign Affairs, first made an oral declaration and then reduced it to writing and initialed it, in which he advised the Danish Minister of Foreign Affairs that "the plans of the Royal Danish Government respecting Danish sovereignty over the whole of Greenland . . . would meet with no difficulty on the part of Norway." The Permanent Court of International Justice held the statement to be binding on Norway with the legal effect of rendering later steps by Norway to occupy parts of Greenland "unlawful and invalid." Dean Rusk, U.S. Secretary of State in the Kennedy and Johnson administrations between 1961 and 1969, related a story that demonstrated his skeptical view of this decision:

> One evening, after a highball or two, I suggested to [the Foreign Minister of Honduras] that we toss a coin for these islands [the Swan Islands in the Caribbean claimed by both Honduras and the U.S.]. Fortunately, he refused because the

International Court of Justice seemed to say in the *Greenland* case that a government has a right to rely upon the statement of a Foreign Minister with respect to a territorial matter. If there is anything clear about our Constitution, it is that the Secretary of State cannot go around the world tossing coins for American territory.[91]

But the holding of the Permanent Court of International Justice may not have been as startling a departure from jurisprudence as Dean Rusk thought it was. The declaration by the Norwegian Foreign Minister was made in the context of a negotiation with the Danish Foreign Minister and in response to a request by the Danish Foreign Minister. Hence it arguably constituted the consummation of a bargain between the two states, with Denmark trading its claims to Spitzbergen, a group of islands in the Arctic Ocean, for assurances from the Norwegian Foreign Minister that Norway would not contest Danish sovereignty over the whole of Greenland.[92]

A more appropriate case for Dean Rusk's concern would be the International Court of Justice's decision in the *Nuclear Test* cases.[93] There, with the support of nine judges, the judgment of the Court stated:

It is well recognized that declarations made by way of unilateral acts, concerning legal or factual situations, may have the effect of creating legal obligations. Declarations of this kind may be, and often are, very specific. When it is the intention of the State making the declaration that it should become bound according to its terms, that intention confers on the declaration the character of a legal undertaking, the State being thenceforth legally required to follow course of conduct consistent with the declaration. An undertaking of this kind, if given publicly, and with an intent to be bound, even though not made within the context of international negotiations, is binding. In these circumstances, nothing in the nature of *quid pro quo* nor any subsequent acceptance of the declaration, nor even any reply or reaction from other States, is required for the declaration to take effect, since such a requirement would be inconsistent with the strictly unilateral nature of the juridical act by which the pronouncement by the State was made.[94]

The Court applied this rationale to a series of unilateral declarations by France concerning the French intention to abstain from future atmospheric nuclear tests in the South Pacific area, holding that the Australian application, asking the Court to adjudge that "the carrying out of further atmospheric tests in the South Pacific Ocean is not consistent with applicable rules of international law," and the New Zealand application asking the Court to rule "[t]hat the conduct by the French Government of nuclear tests in the South Pacific region that give rise to radio-active fallout constitutes a violation of New Zealand's rights under international law: each presented a "claim . . . [that] no longer has any object. . . . "[95]

As noted by Alfred Rubin,[96] the Court gave little indication of the legal basis of its conclusion that unilateral declarations given publicly and with an intent to be bound could give rise to an international legal obligation on the part of the state whose representative made the declarations. The Court appeared to ground its holding on the basic principle of good faith:

> One of the basic principles governing the creation and performance of legal obliga-
> tions, whatever their source, is the principle of good faith. Trust and confidence are
> inherent in international cooperation, in particular in an age when this co-operation
> in many fields is becoming increasingly essential. Just as the very rule of *pacta sunt
> servanda* in the law of treaties is based on good faith, so also is the binding character
> of an international obligation assumed by unilateral declaration. Thus States may
> take cognizance of unilateral declarations and place confidence in them, and are
> entitled to require that the obligation thus created be respected.[97]

But, as Rubin points out,[98] the Court in this paragraph appears to suggest that the principle of good faith becomes relevant only after the unilateral declaration becomes binding through some other, unexplained legal basis, that is, that "good faith merely prevents unilateral revocation of the international obligation, created by the unilateral declaration." After a thorough examination of other cases involving the effects of unilateral declarations, which he distinguishes from the *Nuclear Tests* cases, he emphatically concludes:

> It would appear that the ICJ has found a new rule of international law saddling a
> state with apparently nonrevocable treaty-like commitments *erga omnes*, arising out
> of public unilateral declarations with a presumed intention to be bound and nothing
> more. Whence came the Court's conviction that such unilateral declarations are
> binding? Not from any treaty to which France is a party, thus not from Article 38 (1)
> (a) of the Statute of the Court; not from any known international custom as evidence
> of a practice accepted as law, thus not from Article 38 (1) (b) of the Statute; not
> from any principle accepted by Anglo-American courts or commentators or from
> "any general principles of law," thus not from Article 38 (l) (c) of the Statute; and,
> indeed, not from the unequivocal writings of any publicists or judicial decisions
> that have focused squarely on that question, thus not from Article 38 (1) (d) of the
> Statute. Thus aside from its inherent unpersuasiveness and the language of Article
> 59 of the Statute of the Court which restricts the binding effect of an ICJ decision
> to the particular parties and case before the court, the pronouncement of the Court
> appears to have been ultra vires: The ICJ is not empowered by Article 38 (1) of its
> Statute to decide in accordance with international law any disputes submitted to
> it using other sources of law than the ones enumerated. Thus a serious question is
> raised as to whether the substance of the Judgment relating to the binding force of
> the French unilateral declarations is binding on France at all under Article 94 (1)
> of the UN Charter, even assuming the Judgment is a "decision" and is correct in
> all other aspects, including those aspects relating to jurisdiction.[99]

It is important to note that in the *Nuclear Tests* cases, the ICJ did not rely in any way on the doctrine of estoppel, which is generally accepted as a general principle of law recognized by civilized nations. According to Brownlie: "It is now reasonably clear that the essence of estoppel is the element of conduct which causes the other party, in reliance on such conduct, detrimentally to change its position or to suffer some prejudice."[100] In the *Nuclear Tests* cases neither Australia nor New Zealand relied on the French declarations to its detriment.

Despite Rubin's conclusion that the ICJ acted *ultra vires* in the *Nuclear Tests* cases, the Court has applied the principle it recognized in those cases on at least two other occasions.[101] Moreover, in debates before the International Law Commission, some members have claimed that the existence of unilateral acts producing legal effects and creating specific commitments was now beyond dispute. In contrast, other members have reportedly cautioned that "the diversity of effects and the importance of the setting in which acts occurred made it very difficult to arrive at a 'theory' or 'regime' of unilateral acts."[102] This is a cautionary note well worth heeding.

WITH FRIENDS LIKE THESE . . .

Earlier in our discussion of customary international law, we noted some of the criticisms of this concept by Professor Kelly and his conclusion that it should be abandoned and reliance placed instead on treaties, assuming the political will to enter into a treaty is present. Others have gone so far as to question the very existence of customary international law, describing it as a "myth."[103] But the challenge to customary international law, as well as to international law in general, that has received the greatest notice and response recently has been that of Jack Goldsmith and Eric Posner, first in a law review article[104] and then in a book, *The Limits of International Law.*[105]

In their book, Goldsmith and Posner set forth a rational choice theory of international law that contrasts sharply with the traditional approach of most international law scholars. In particular, they contend that "international law emerges from and is sustained by nations acting rationally to maximize their interests (i.e., their preferences over international relations outcomes), given their perception of the interests of other states, and the distribution of state power."[106] However, they "consistently exclude one preference from the state's interest calculation: a preference for complying with international law."[107] Put another way, "international legal norms, though sometimes useful to states in pursuing their own interests, have no actual constraining effect on states."[108]

In their chapter, "A Theory of Customary International Law,"[109] Goldstein and Posner summarize many of the difficulties other scholars have had with the standard account of customary international law. They point out the disagreements over what type of state action counts as practice; how widespread, long, and uniform state practice must be; what kind of evidence is required to prove the existence of *opinio juris*; and the process by which customary international law changes. These and other issues traditionally subject to debate, however, are not the focus of their analysis. Instead, their focus is "on two sets of issues that are rarely discussed in the international law literature but that are fundamental to understanding customary international law."[110] The first set of issues includes "the unarticulated assumptions that underlie the traditional conception of customary international law . . . that customary international law is *unitary, universal, and exogenous*."[111] Goldsmith's and Posner's theory of customary international law challenges each of these assumptions. By unitary they mean that all the behaviors customary international law describes have an identical logical form. It is universal because it binds all states except those that "persistently object" during the development of the customary international law rule. It is exogenous because it represents an external force that influences state action.

To fully understand Goldsmith and Posner's second set of issues, it is best to quote their own description of them:

> The second set of issues concerns the traditional paradigm's inability to explain international behavior. The traditional paradigm does not explain how customary international law emerges from disorder, or how it changes over time . . . For example, as we discuss in chapter 2, the customary international law rule governing a state's jurisdiction over its coastal seas changed from a cannon-shot rule to a three-mile rule to a twelve-mile rule with many qualifications. On the traditional account, the process of change is illegal, because some states must initiate a departure from the prior regularity that they were bound to follow as a matter of law. More broadly, the traditional account cannot explain why customary international law changes in response to shifts in the relative power of states, advances in technology, and other exogenous forces.
>
> The traditional account also cannot explain the fact that states frequently change their views about the content of customary international law, often during very short periods of time. Nor, relatedly, can it explain why domestic courts and politicians almost always apply a conception of customary international law that is in the state's best interest. In addition, it does not explain why states sometimes say that they will abide by particular customary laws and then violate their promise.
>
> Finally, the traditional account does not explain why states comply with customary international law. Some believe that *opinio juris* is the reason for compliance, but the "sense of legal obligation" is what requires explaining and cannot itself be the explanation. Others say that consent is the reason, but as many have noted, this position begs the question of why states abide by the international rules to which they have consented . . . A prominent theory in the natural law tradition contends that states abide by customary international law because "they perceive the rule and its institutional penumbra to have a high degree of legitimacy," where legitimacy is understood as "a property of a rule or rule-making institution which itself exerts a pull toward compliance on those addressed normatively because those addressed believe that the rule or institution has come into being and operates in accordance with generally accepted principles of right process." . . . Another theory argues that "repeated compliance" [with international law] gradually becomes habitual obedience" as international law "penetrates into a domestic legal system, thus becoming

part of that nation's internal value set.". . . Yet another theory, while nodding to the idea of self-interested state behavior, explains international law compliance mainly on the basis of morality and the "habit and inertia of continued compliance.". . . In our view, "right process," "value set," "habit," and "morality" are stand-ins for the concept of *opinio juris* and do not explain why states are pulled toward compliance by customary international law. There are many other theories of international law compliance . . . but they suffer from similar difficulties.[112]

In place of the traditional view of customary international law, Goldsmith and Posner would substitute their "rational choice" or game theory approach. As already noted, according to Goldsmith and Posner, a state never acts out of a motive to comply with an international law norm, but only out of the desire of the state's political leadership to serve the self-interest of the state as determined by the leaders on an ad hoc basis depending on the circumstances faced at the time the decision is made. To support this thesis, they identify four basic strategic positions to be employed as part of a theoretic game for interstate interaction: coincidence of interest, coordination, cooperation, and coercion. As an example of how these positions might be employed in a strategic game, they pose a situation where states A and B have a common border. They note, correctly, that territorial borders are generally thought to be governed by international law. On the assumption that A and B respect the border, they suggest that their theory of international law "posits that one of four things might explain this behavioral regularity."[113] The first would be a situation where neither A nor B has an interest in projecting power across the border. Here, where a pattern of behavior – not violating the border – results from each state acting in its self-interest "without any regard to the action of the other state," they call this a coincidence of interest.[114]

The second situation would be when each of the two states might be interested in encroaching on the other's territory but has decided not to do so because the costs of such action would outweigh the benefits. Here, "[t]he main concern for the states is to clarify the point at which State A's control ends and State B's begins."[115] To this end they engage in identical or symmetrical actions – which amounts to coordination.

Cooperation characterizes the third situation.[116] Paul Schiff Berman has noted the closeness of "cooperation" to "coordination" but suggests that Goldsmith and Posner "identify cooperation as a kind of mutually assured destruction. States refrain from encroaching based on mutual threats of retaliation."[117]

The fourth and last situation involves coercion – either in the form of an invasion by the more powerful state into the territory of the weaker, or more likely, pressure applied by the stronger state to induce the weaker state to accede to its wishes. In any case, "[c]oercion results when a powerful state . . . forces weaker states to engage in acts that are contrary to their interests."[118]

In chapter 2 of their book,[119] Goldsmith and Posner "examine in detail four areas of customary international law chosen on the basis of their prominence and on the availability of a detained historical record."[120] These four case studies include the "free ships, free goods" rule of wartime maritime commerce, that is, all property on a neutral's ship, including enemy property but excluding contraband, is immune from seizure; the breadth of the territorial sea; ambassadorial immunity; and the wartime exemption from prize for coastal fishing vessels – here they examine the famous U.S. Supreme Court decision in *The Paquete Habana*,[121] which found that a norm of customary international law prohibited condemning two Spanish fishing vessels and their cargoes as prize of war, and find that the available evidence did not support the Supreme Court's decision. In all four case studies they purport to show that "these areas of supposedly robust customary international law never reflected universal behavioral regularities and that the actual state behaviors associated with these laws are most easily and parsimoniously explained using our four models."[122]

In commenting on these case studies, Peter Spiro suggests that "at least three of the four (the territorial sea excluded) are musty old rules of little contemporary relevance or interest... Insofar as international relations, in those contexts and many others, was mostly about relations between states, perhaps Goldsmith and Posner's applications have something to tell us about the evolution of traditional customary norms. But query whether they have much to teach about what is going on today."[123] In response, Goldsmith and Posner state that they "looked for well-settled contemporary rules of CIL against which to test our theory, but frankly could not find a single example. The CIL of human rights is much talked about, of course. But as we explained in a different part of *Limits*, the gap between what this CIL requires and the actual behavior of states is vast. We thus did not think that human rights was a plausible candidate for a case study of a CIL – it would have been *too easy* a case to discredit...."[124]

Although Goldsmith and Posner state at the conclusion of their book that "international law is a real phenomenon,"[125] and elsewhere that they do not think international law is irrelevant or unimportant,[126] it is difficult to conclude that their theory of customary international law supports in any way the existence of customary international law. In an earlier article they stated that "[t]he rational choice account seeks to explain accurately the behaviors associated with CIL. Whether CIL is or is not law is beyond its concern."[127] But, whether customary international law qualifies as law is a key issue with respect to the validity of their thesis that customary international law, as an independent normative force, has little if any effect on national behavior. If they are correct in suggesting that customary international law is "mostly aspirational," and amounts at most, at least in some circumstances, to a political or perhaps a moral obligation, then indeed customary international law would seem to have no independent normative force affecting national behavior. On the other hand, if it does qualify as law, and Goldsmith and Posner admit that government officials, courts, and scholars do "continue to talk as if CIL had independent normative force,"[128] then it is considerably more likely that CIL in fact has independent normative force that affects normative behavior.

Under the Goldsmith/Posner theory of customary international law, the political leaders of states apparently make up customary international law as they go along utilizing one or more of the four possible game theoretic scenarios as circumstances demand. Interestingly, however, nowhere do they indicate that they have spoken with the political leaders of states to ask whether their theory comports with the reality of how they operate. Were they to do so they would find that the political leaders of states, or at least the political leaders of states with any respect for the rule of law, take into account and most seek to act in accordance with norms of customary international law, with the assistance of their legal advisers. They do not, as the authors suggest, engage in theoretic international relations games and thereby decide what the "law" is on an ad hoc basis. On the contrary, as Richard Bilder has recently pointed out,[129] "[s]ome 200 nations and people, coexisting under conditions of interdependence, simply cannot effectively conduct their increasingly complex and interdependent affairs without some measure of predictability and reliable expectations – conditions that only normative arrangements and institutions can provide." The ad hoc approach recommended by Goldsmith and Posner hardly contributes to predictability and reliable expectations.

Goldsmith and Posner state that "international law emerges from and is sustained by nations acting rationally to maximize their interests (i.e., their preferences over international relations outcomes), given their perceptions of the interests of other states, and the distribution of state power."[130] This is correct, but the authors seem to fail to realize that norms of customary international law have traditionally been created through this process.[131] This process, moreover, has resulted in norms of customary international law that reflect the interests of the states involved in their creation. That is why, as Louis Henkin has so famously written: "almost all nations observe almost all principles of international law and almost all of their obligations almost all of the time."[132] That also is why Goldsmith and Posner's claim that the political leaders of states are in no way motivated to adhere to norms of customary international law is simply incorrect. In most instances they are motivated to comply with them because they serve the interests of the states they represent.

Most of the commentary on Goldsmith and Posner's book has focused on their treatment of customary international law.[133] In chapter 3 of their book, however, Goldsmith and Posner turn to a "Theory of International Agreements."[134] They begin by identifying "many interesting issues" that treaties raise:

> The most fundamental issue is: Why ever have a treaty? Why doesn't customary international law suffice? Other important issues include: When and why do states enter into multilateral rather than bilateral treaties? How do multilateral treaties (and the international organizations they often create) work? What role do domestic courts and bureaucracies play in treaty enforcement?

> Another important set of issues concerns the distinction between treaties (legalized agreements) and agreements that are not binding under international law . . . The

literature usually labels nonlegal international agreements "soft law." We avoid this label because nonlegal agreements are not binding under international (or any other) law, so it is confusing to call them law, soft or otherwise . . .

The dominant positivistic approach to international law views nonlegal agreements as aberrational or of secondary importance . . . And yet nonlegal agreements are prevalent and clearly play an important role in international politics. Why do states use nonlegal agreements? How do nonlegal agreements facilitate cooperation among states? If states can cooperate using nonlegal instruments, why do they ever enter into treaties governed by international law? What does legalization add?. . . . [135]

In their analysis of treaties, Goldsmith and Posner seek to explain "the logic of treaties without reference to notions of 'legality' or *pacta sunt servanda* or related concepts. As was the case with customary international law, the cooperation and coordination models explain the behaviors associated with treaties without reliance on these factors, or on what international lawyers sometimes call 'normative pull.' States refrain from violating treaties (when they do) for the same basic reason they refrain from violating nonlegal agreements: because they fear retaliation from the other state or some kind of reputational loss, or because they fear a failure of coordination."[136]

Goldsmith and Posner spend most of their time discussing multilateral rather than bilateral treaties. With respect to multilateral treaties, they have some "sympathy" for the view expressed in the international relations institutional literature that multilateral treaties, "especially ones that create free-standing multilateral organizations," can help to promote multilateral cooperation. But they would limit their approval to multilateral treaties that help resolve technical problems or to multilateral treaties that have a relatively small number of state parties that cooperate for the sake of achieving "relatively narrow goals such as defense against a common enemy by a military alliance (NATO), or the control of world prices of a single commodity that dominates the economies of the state parties (OPEC). . . . "[137] With respect to "true international public goods such as the protection of fisheries, the reduction of atmospheric pollution, and peace," they are "skeptical that genuine multinational collective action problems can be solved by treaty, especially when a large number of states are involved."[138]

There are many other provocative statements about international law and international institutions in Goldsmith and Posner's book, and we will turn to some of them later in this study. For now it suffices to say that at best they are highly skeptical about international law and institutions. Others suggest their attitude amounts to a hostility toward international law. Oona Hathaway and Ariel Lavinbuk, for example, suggest that "[f]or Professors Goldsmith and Posner, as for most revisionist scholars, international law poses a threat to the separation of powers, federalism, and democracy. The only way to secure the sanctity of liberal democracy against over-reaching activist judges who seek to usurp legislative power and undemocratic international institutions that threaten the state's authority to govern itself is to reject international law as a binding force, either legally or morally. Professors Goldsmith and Posner thus argue that when self-interest and morality conflict, states will (as a descriptive matter) choose self-interest, and that is precisely what they *should* do."[139]

Another of the many critics of Goldsmith and Posner's book, Kal Raustialia, asks: "Why [do] NATO, the WTO, the U.N., and the many other international organizations that populate New York, Geneva and elsewhere [exist]," and "why, if international law is so limited, do states keep creating and elaborating it?"[140] The authors answer with a question and a challenge of their own that are a focal point of the present study: "'Why, if international law is *not* so limited, do states keep failing to create effective international law?' There are pressing international problems – war, refugee crises, global warming, the proliferation of nuclear weapons, international terrorism, the depletion of fisheries, intrastate conflict, lingering protectionism – that states are unable to solve."[141] In later chapters the present study seeks to identify some of the primary reasons why international law and international institutions have failed to solve, at least fully and satisfactorily, these problems. For their part, the authors suggest that: "A good theory would explain both why international law exists and why it remains highly imperfect" and note that their book tries to do this.[142] In my view, the search for an overarching theory that would explain both why international law exists and why it remains highly imperfect is like the search for the Holy Grail – such a theory doesn't exist. Rather, the international law developed to apply to these problems, as well as the international institutions developed to apply it, should be approached in pragmatic fashion to ascertain why they have failed and how they might be improved. The present study tries to do this.

At the same time, although the search for an overarching theory that would explain both why international law exists and why it remains highly imperfect is unlikely to be successful, this does not mean there is no higher order value that serves, at least in part, to provide a measure of coherence to the multifaceted nature of international law. One possible candidate for such a higher order value would be the need for the rule of law in international affairs.[143]

To be sure, as I have noted elsewhere, the precise meaning of the term "rule of law" has been a topic of sharp debate; its meaning may be less clear today than ever before, and, especially from commentators from the left end of the political spectrum, has been sharply criticized as a tool that enables the shrewd, the calculating, and the wealthy to manipulate its forms to their own advantage.[144] Moreover, there is little doubt that international law and international institutions deviate in significant respects from the rule of law paradigm.[145]

On the other hand, Brian Z. Tamanaha has pointed out that "politicians, government officials, political and legal theorists, business leaders, development experts, the World Bank and the IMF, and many others around the globe, from liberal and non-liberal societies, from developed countries and developing countries, promote the rule of law as offering a worldwide benefit."[146] This is especially the case, he suggests, "[w]hen the rule of law is understood to mean that the government is limited by the law."[147]

One may interpret Goldsmith and Posner's views of international law as supporting the concept that at the international level, governments are not limited in any meaningful way by law. If so, they might reject the very concept of the rule of law on the global or international level. This raises the important issue of the relationship between law and power at the international level. No one with any sense of reality in the international arena would deny that the interests of powerful states play an important, perhaps even a disproportionate, role in the international legal process, but power is not the only driving force in international law. In their strategic game in which Goldsmith and Posner pose a situation where states A and B have a common border and respect the border, they propose that four basic strategic positions – coincidence of interest, coordination, cooperation, and coercion – have determined their decision to respect the border and that the well-established rule of international law requiring such respect has played no role whatsoever in their decision. But in the real world states usually restrain from violating each others' borders because the international rule is so well established and supported by states. A major, although not the only, reason the member states of the United Nations were willing to support a Security Council resolution authorizing the use of armed force against Iraq in the Gulf War conflict was its blatant violation of its border with Kuwait. Also, there is substantial evidence that the United States and Great Britain strongly believed that their 2003 invasion of Iraq was compatible with international law; other states strongly held a contrary view, but none of these states, pro or con, believed the legality of the invasion was an irrelevant consideration. It is noteworthy as well that attempts by the Bush administration to define torture so narrowly as to permit coercive interrogation techniques that most states, even close allies, and commentators believed constituted torture greatly undermined U.S. relations with other states to the detriment of U.S. foreign policy. Many prominent commentators support the proposition that one of the most important goals of international law is to constrain power and not to serve mainly as a tool for the powerful.

No one would accuse Anne-Marie Slaughter, former Dean of the Woodrow Wilson School of Public and International Affairs at Princeton University, a former president of the American Society of International Law, and currently the Director of Policy Planning for the U.S. Department of State, of being hostile to international law. But Slaughter has proposed "A New World Order" that, if fully implemented, would dramatically transform international law and international institutions as they are constituted today.[148]

In substantial part, Slaughter's proposal is a response to problems created by globalization. Because of globalization, she suggests, "[p]eople and their governments around the world need global institutions to solve collective problems that can only be addressed on a global scale."[149] Yet the international institutions created after

World War II are "outdated and inadequate to meet contemporary challenges. They must be reformed or even reinvented; new ones must be created."[150]

There are some who believe world government is the answer. But Slaughter will have none of it. In her view, "world government is both infeasible and undesirable. The size and scope of such a government presents an unavoidable and dangerous threat to individual liberty. Further, the diversity of the peoples to be governed makes it almost impossible to conceive of a global demos."[151]

The result is the "globalization paradox. We need more government on a global and a regional scale, but we don't want the centralization of decision-making power and coercive authority so far from the people actually to be governed." Slaughter's "new world order" seeks to resolve this paradox.

Slaughter's new world order would resolve this paradox primarily through a series of "government networks." To a considerable extent these government networks already exist. They consist of national regulatory agents and agencies, judiciaries, and legislators who reach out ("network") to their counterparts in other nation-states in an effort to solve problems that transcend national boundaries and have an impact in more than one state. She gives many examples from a variety of fields. Since the terrorist attacks of September 11, 2001, for example, networks of financial regulators have worked to identify and freeze terrorist assets, national law enforcement officials have shared vital information on terrorist suspects, and intelligence operatives have worked together to preempt terrorist attacks. Less spectacularly but equally importantly, central bankers work through the Bank for International Settlements to produce guidelines on capital adequacy known as the Basel Accords; national securities commissioners and insurance supervisors similarly network to discuss common problems and to produce nonbinding guidelines that are usually carried out faithfully. They create their own international organizations, but these are "not 'inter-state' organizations; they are not formed by treaty or even executive agreements; they have no place on the landscape of the international legal system."[152]

A key part of Slaughter's analysis is the concept of the "disaggregated state," which she describes as "simply the rising need for and capacity of different domestic government institutions to engage in activities beyond their borders, often with their foreign counterparts. It is regulators pursuing the subject of their regulations beyond borders; judges negotiating minitreaties with their foreign brethren to resolve complex transnational cases; and legislators consulting on the best ways to frame and pass legislation affecting human rights or the environment.."[153]

The concept of the "disaggregated state" stands in sharp contrast to the "unitary state, a concept that has long dominated international legal and political analysis."[154] The unitary state is presumed to speak with one voice and, in order to enhance cooperation with other states, typically will negotiate with other states in various forums to produce a multilateral international treaty through the use of formal procedures and subsequent ratification of the treaty by state legislatures. The national regulators of the disaggregated state, by contrast, engage in consultations with their counterparts in other states and reach nonbinding "understandings" as to the form their cooperation will take. Most characteristic of the disaggregated state are horizontal networks. "Far less frequent, but potentially very important, are vertical government networks, those between national government officials and their supranational counterparts. The prerequisite for a vertical government network is the relatively rare decision by states to delegate their sovereignty to an institution above them with real power – a court or a regulatory commission."[155] The European Union is the paradigmatic example of vertical government networks. But Slaughter also suggests that there are embryonic vertical networks present between national officials and such international institutions as the World Trade Organization, the International Monetary Fund, the North American Free Trade Agreement, and the United Nations. She further posits that these international organizations are themselves becoming disaggregated. Her core vision of a disaggregated world order is "a concept of an international order in which the principal actors are not states, but parts of states; not international organizations, but parts of international organizations. Those parts, either national or supranational, that perform the same governance function – legislation, execution, adjudication – link up with one another around the world."[156]

Not surprisingly, the governmental networks or even networks of networks envisaged by Slaughter often take the place of the binding treaty characteristic of traditional international law. For example, networks of national antitrust authorities operate under informal memoranda of understandings (MOUs) rather than pursuant to a multilateral treaty regulating competition policy as advocated by some countries.[157] These international governmental networks, in Slaughter's view, thus have the potential to create "order without international law."[158] She suggests that it will be necessary to develop global norms regulating government networks, but these norms would be informal, "like that of the government networks they regulate." In place of proposals for global constitutions, she seeks to develop "an informal alternative – a set of principles and norms that can operate independently of formal codification, even as the actors and activities they would regulate form and reform in shifting patterns of governance."[159] To this end, near the conclusion of her book, she suggests five such norms.[160]

As one would expect, the publication of *A New World Order* has not been met with the kind of hostility that many international lawyers and others have shown toward *The Limits of International Law*. On the contrary, most of the reviews have been highly favorable.[161] Even some of the most highly favorable reviews, however, have raised some serious caveats. For example, in the conclusion to his lengthy review, Kenneth Anderson praises Slaughter for having "deliberately formulated a proposal for global governance that generally removes the NGOs, corporate actors, and private actors from governance." But he goes on to state that "in the end, I cannot see that the system of A New World Order will preserve democracy and democratic accountability. It fails to balance the three horns of the trilemma: global governance, democracy, and democratic accountability . . . A New World Order offers a system in which, for all its good intentions, democracy gradually gives way because the system finally erodes sovereignty to the point at which it serves as no shelter for democracy at all."[162]

Interestingly, in contrast to Anderson, who approves Slaughter's general exclusion of NGOs and the private sector from global governance, Robert Howse suggests that "her identification of 'government networks' as central to the understanding of global governance seems itself to reflect a certain kind of formalism." This is because her "network conception seems to depend on the continuing viability of a clear boundary between public and private . . . When one considers the real-world operation of networks, however, the boundaries of private and public are pervasively interpenetrated and destabilized . . . If actual, real world networks of global governance include both governmental and non-governmental actors as 'insiders,' then the problem of who, on a normatively ideal model of global governance, should be a member of the network becomes more complex, and so also, the issues of accountability."[163]

For his part, Peter Berkowitz warns that "[o]ne should not underestimate the radicalism of Slaughter's proposal." Quoting her, he concedes that "it is perfectly appropriate to suggest that 'U.S. government representatives in every branch, must take account of international events, trends and interests to represent their constituencies adequately.' However, it is quite another thing to argue that U.S. representatives in every branch of government 'should also see themselves as representing a larger transnational or even global constituency.'"[164]

At first blush it appears that Goldsmith and Posner's views are diametrically opposite to those of Slaughter. Goldsmith and Posner basically, although they do not do so explicitly, deny the very existence of customary international law. As to treaties, they acknowledge them as "international law," but then suggest that they have no independent or "exogenous" effect on state behavior and that states feel free to violate them if in any particular instance they are of the view that their state interests are contrary to the treaties' requirements. In contrast, Slaughter does not share their "hostility" or skepticism toward international law. But *A New World Order* is not really a book about international law. Nowhere in the book is there a discussion of customary international law – a primary focus of Goldsmith and Posner's book – and her "radical" proposal for global governance is advanced in large part because of a perceived dysfunctionality of the current international legal order, including, of course, international institutions and multilateral treaties.[165] In many instances she finds that so-called soft law, in the form of nonbinding guidelines or agreements, is preferable to traditional customary international law or treaties.

In an article published after her book, Slaughter, along with William Burke-White, suggests that *The Future of International Law is Domestic (or, The European Way of Law)*.[166] Here, Slaughter and Burke-White note a fundamental shift in the focus of international law away from interstate relations that has resulted in international law penetrating "the once exclusive zone of domestic affairs to regulate the relationships between governments and their own citizens, particularly through the growing bodies of human rights law and international criminal law."[167] Although the cases of human rights law and international criminal law are well known, the authors suggest that the domestic roots of international problems go way beyond these two fields of international law: "From cross-border pollution to terrorist training camps, from refugee flows to weapons proliferation, international problems have domestic roots that an interstate legal system is often powerless to address. To offer an effective response to these new challenges, the international legal system must be able to influence the domestic policies of states and harness national institutions in pursuit of global objectives."[168]

To achieve this influence on the domestic policies of states, the authors argue that international law and international institutions must shift "from independent regulation above the national state to direct engagement with domestic institutions."[169] The three principal forms or methods of such engagement are strengthening domestic institutions, backstopping them, and compelling them to act.

By the "European Way of Law" the authors have in mind the law and practice of the European Union. They recognize the argument that their proposed new functions of international law and international institutions are inapplicable outside of the European context,[170] but seek to refute this point of view, moving "beyond description and prediction to prescription, suggesting ways that the European way of law should become the future of international law writ large."[171]

They begin by noting that "a new generation of worldwide problems . . . arise from within states rather than from state actors themselves."[172] As examples, they point to the terrorist attacks of September 11, 2001; the massive ethnic atrocities committed in Rwanda, Congo, and Sudan; nonstate criminal networks such as those of A.Q. Kahn in the area of nonproliferation; and acute domestic poverty, and suggest that usually, "the origins of these threats can be addressed directly only by domestic governments that have the jurisdictional entitlements, police power, and institutional capability to act directly against them."[173]

If states are strong enough to combat these internal threats directly, then the role of international law is to ensure that these states cooperate sufficiently to address threats before they cross borders. In the far more common situation where national governments lack the will or the capability to deal with the origins of these threats themselves, international law and international institutions must step in and help these states to strengthen their capacity or gain the will to act.[174]

Slaughter and Burke-White acknowledge that this role for international law would be "far more invasive" than its traditional role and that, perhaps quite significantly, "[f]or many countries, ranging from the United States to Russia, from the countries of the Middle East to those of Africa, this new use of international law is also far more frightening."[175]

Turning to the European Union, the authors note that, "[a]s the EU's legal system has evolved, the prime purpose of the European Court of Justice and even of the Commission has been less to create and impose EU law as international law than to spur national courts and regulatory agencies to embrace and enforce EU law as national law."[176] They further point out that much of EU law consists of directives, which specify the goal to be reached but permit national legislatures and courts to decide precisely how the member state in question will fulfill a particular directive. After member states take the necessary steps to carry out the directive under national law, the Court and the Commission perform a monitoring function to ensure that they have fulfilled their obligations. The authors state that "[t]his European way of law is precisely the role that we postulate for international law generally around the world."[177]

The authors then turn to an examination of the three principal forms that they propose international law should take to engage with domestic institutions: strengthening domestic institutions, backstopping them, and compelling them to act. With respect to strengthening domestic institutions, they not surprisingly argue that "[a] critically important tool in strengthening the institutions of national governments is the formalization and inclusion of 'government networks' as mechanisms of global governance."[178] Citing and quoting Stephen Krasner,[179] they note that he "suggests that international law and institutions can strengthen state capacity by engaging in processes of shared sovereignty with national governments. Such shared sovereignty 'involves the creation of institutions for governing specific issue areas within a state – areas over which external and internal actors voluntarily share authority.' Examples of these arrangements include the creation of special hybrid courts in Sierra Leone, East Timor, and, possibly, Cambodia, involving a mix of international and domestic law and judges."[180]

As to backstopping domestic government, the authors point to the complementarity provision of the Rome Statute of the International Criminal Court as "[t]he most obvious example of international law as a backstop." This is because the "ICC is designed to operate only where national courts fail to act as a first line means of prosecution."[181] They also suggest that the dispute resolution mechanisms of the North American Free Trade Agreements function as an international backdrop for domestic resolution of antidumping cases.

Lastly, with respect to compelling action by national governments, the authors note that despite the proliferation of international courts and tribunals, "national governments have retained the nearly exclusive use of their instruments of coercive authority."[182] Nonetheless, they contend that the "use of international law to combat terrorism immediately after September 11, 2001, is a prime example of how specific obligations can be imposed on U.N. member states that they can fulfill only by directing domestic institutions to act in specific ways at the national level."[183] They note in particular U.N. Security Council Resolution 1373, which, among other things, requires member states of the United Nations to "prevent the commission of terrorist acts" and "deny safe haven to those who finance [or] plan . . . terrorist acts."[184] Most important, Resolution 1373 establishes a Counter-Terrorism Committee that has the responsibility to monitor member states' compliance with the resolution and to this end to receive reports from member states on the steps they have taken to comply. In the area of nonproliferation, the authors note Security Council Resolution 1540,[185] which in its second operative paragraph requires member states to adopt national legislation prohibiting the manufacture or possession of weapons of mass destruction by nonstate actors and to establish export control regulations and physical protection regimes for weapons and related technologies. Similarly, the authors point out that "functional international organizations such as the International Atomic Energy Agency (IAEA) have compelled states to act through their own institutions. IAEA Safeguards with nuclear states, for example, require a national system of materials controls and the use of particular accounting mechanisms."[186]

Commendably, in Part III of their article the authors identify some of "The Dangers of Using International Law to Shape and Influence Domestic Politics."[187] Backstopping national institutions, for example, can be "counterproductive" if national governments rely on international institutions to fulfill obligations that they should carry out, if the process of strengthening domestic institutions is carried out ineptly and results in weakening domestic capacity, or if compelling national action undermines local democratic processes and prevents domestic experimentation with alternate approaches.

According to the authors, the "most significant danger inherent in these new functions of international law . . . lies in the potential of national governments to co-opt the force of international law to serve their own objectives . . . by strengthening states capacity, international law may actually make states more effective at the very repression and abuse the interference challenge seeks to overcome."[188] National actions undertaken in the name of the "war on terror" serve as a salient example.

Lastly, and most significantly, the authors concede that their "overall conception of international law and the specific functions described here will meet with fierce resistance from states with very strong domestic legal systems, such as the United States, and from many states with very weak legal systems but strong political rulers . . . many European powers may find it more difficult than they expect to promote an EU-inspired model of pooled sovereignty among wary former colonies."[189]

In Part IV, the concluding section of their article, the authors argue that "the very concept of sovereignty will have to adapt to embrace, rather than reject, the influence of international rules and institutions on domestic political processes."[190] As a "harbinger of this shift," they point to the new doctrine of the responsibility to protect, which, they note, was first set forth in a report of the International Commission on Intervention and State Sovereignty (ICISS), issued in December 2001, which proposed updating the U.N. Charter to incorporate a new understanding of sovereignty.[191] As noted by the authors,[192] the ICISS report contends that "[t]here is no transfer or dilution of state sovereignty. But there is a necessary recharacterization involved: *from sovereignty as control* to *sovereignty as responsibility* in both internal functions and external duties."[193] The ICISS further contends that the primary responsibility to protect the individuals in it lies with the individual state. But "where a population is suffering serious harm, as a result of internal war, insurgency, repression or state failure, and the state in question is unwilling or unable to halt or avert it, the principle of non-intervention yields to the international responsibility to protect."[194]

As is well known, there has long been a debate, especially among international law scholars, over whether there is a doctrine of humanitarian intervention that constitutes an exception to the U.N. Charter's limitations on the use of armed force. The ICISS report avoids this debate by suggesting that if an individual state fails in its responsibility to protect individuals within its territory, then there is a secondary responsibility that "falls on the international community acting through the United Nations."[195] In other words, rather than an individual state or individual states deciding on its or their own to intervene militarily to stop atrocities, the intervention would occur only after the United Nations, presumably through a Security Council resolution, had authorized such an intervention. As we shall see in Chapter 3, the United Nations General Assembly has adopted a nonbinding resolution that claims states have a "responsibility to protect" along the lines suggested by the ICISS. This has resulted in considerable controversy when the doctrine has been applied to specific cases.

What, then, is one to make of all this? In my view, Slaughter and Burke-White have done us a service by focusing in their article on the reality that many of the world's most severe international problems have their origin in nation-states and that such states are in the best position to take the actions necessary to resolve them. Whether, as they suggest, international law and institutions are in a position to strengthen domestic institutions, backstop them, and, if necessary, compel them to act is a much more debatable proposition. If, as claimed by the Princeton Project on National Security, a project codirected by Slaughter, the system of international institutions that the United States and its allies built after World War II is "broken," and every major international institution is in need of "major reform," there is room for serious doubt whether existing international institutions are up to the task. Moreover, Slaughter and Burke-White stress the legal system of the European Union as their model. Increasingly, however, there are those who argue that the European Union itself is "broken"[196] and in need of major reform. Similarly, as this chapter has demonstrated, there is currently considerable controversy over the effectiveness of international law or even over its very existence – customary international law in particular.

The remaining chapters of this study examine these and related issues in some detail. In doing so, there will be numerous occasions to refer to the provocative points made by Slaughter and Burke-White in their article and by Slaughter in her book.

Notes

1. JOHN F. MURPHY, THE UNITED STATES and the RULE OF LAW in INTERNATIONAL AFFAIRS (2004).
2. *Id*. at 11.
3. The Peace Treaties of Westphalia included the Treaty of Osnabruck between Sweden and the Holy Roman Empire and the Treaty of Munster, between France and the Empire. See MARK W. JANIS and JOHN E. NOYES, INTERNATIONAL LAW 34 n.1 (3d ed. 2006).
4. LORI F. DAMROSCH et al., INTERNATIONAL LAW xxix (2001).
5. Another major treatise of the same period was *De Jure Belli Libri Tres* (De Jure Belli) (1598) by Alberico Gentili, the Italian-born professor of civil law at Oxford.
6. Important predecessors of Grotius in this approach include the Spanish theologians Francisco de Vitoria (probably 1486–1546) and Francisco Suarez (1548–1617). The most important of the later natural law philosophers in international law is the German, Samuel Pufendorf (1632–1694), who occupied a chair for the law of nature and nations at the University of Heidelberg. *See* LORI F. DAMROSCH et al., *supra* note 4, at xxx.
7. *Id.* For example, Grotius argued that another basic principle of natural law is the freedom of the seas. But this argument was rejected by the Englishman John Selden (1584–1645), who supported the concept of the closed sea. Grotius's position served to support the interests of the Netherlands as a rising maritime and colonial power. In contrast, Selden's position served the interests of England, whose navy at the time was inferior to that of the Netherlands. Later, "when England became dominant at sea, it also became an ardent champion of the freedom of the seas – at least in times of peace." *Id*. at xxxi.
8. *Id.* at xxxi.
9. *See* WOLFGANG FRIEDMANN, LEGAL THEORY, CH. 21 (5th ed. 1967), cited in *id.*, at xxxi, n. 2.
10. LORI F. DAMROSCH et al., *supra* note 4, at xxxi. Emerich de Vattel (1714–1767), a Swiss lawyer whose treatise, *Le Droit des Gens, ou Principles de la Loi Naturelle, appliques a la Conduite et aux Affaires des Nations et des Souverains* (1758), dominated the philosophy of international law from the eighteenth century to the end of World War I, while acknowledging the existence of natural law, makes clear that he considers "all effective international law to have been derived from the will of nations, a presumed consent expressing itself in treaties or customs." *Id*.
11. *Id.* at xxxii.
12. Denying the validity of international law from a different perspective was the German scholar Wilhelm Friederich Hegel (1770–1831), who, in his *Philosophy of Law and State*, constructed a complex dialectic system that glorified the national state.
13. *See* John R. Bolton, *US Isn't Obligated to Pay the UN*, Wall St. J., Nov. 17, 1997, at A27. For a compelling reply to Bolton, *see* Robert F. Turner, Letter to the Editor, *US and UN: The Ties That Bind*, WALL ST. J., Dec. 1, 1997, at A23, col. 1.
14. *See* John R. Bolton, *Is There Really "Law" in International Affairs?* 10 TRANSNAT'L L. & CONTEMP. PROBS. 1 (2000).
15. This section draws heavily from JOHN F. MURPHY, *supra* note 1, at 13–37.
16. Under this provision, state parties to a dispute may authorize the International Court of Justice to disregard the otherwise applicable law on grounds that it is unreasonable

or unfair under the circumstances and decide the case on the basis of nonlegal criteria. Although some international arbitral tribunals have been authorized by the parties to act *ex aequo et bono*, the International Court of Justice has yet to receive such authorization.

17. *See* JOHN HENRY MERRYMAN et al., THE CIVIL LAW TRADITION: EUROPE, LATIN AMERICA, and EAST ASIA 944 (1994).

18. *See* RUDOLF B. SCHLESINGER et al., COMPARATIVE LAW 669 (6th ed. 1998).

19. M.O. Hudson, [1950] 2 Y. B. INT'L L. COMM'N. 26 UN Doc. A.CN.4Ser.A/1950/Add.1.

20. *See* J. Patrick Kelly, *The Twilight of Customary International Law*, 40 VA. J. INT'L L. 449, 500–507 (2000).

21. For a more extensive discussion of this point, *see* JOHN F. MURPHY, *supra* note 1, at 15–16.

22. North Sea Continental Shelf (F.R.G. v. Den/F.R.G. v. Neth), 1969 ICJ 3, 43.

23. Michael Akehurst, *Custom as a Source of International Law*, 47 BRIT. Y. B. INT'L L. 1, 18–19, 53 (1977).

24. KAROL WOLFKE, CUSTOM in PRESENT INTERNATIONAL LAW 67–68 (1964).

25. Bin Cheng, *United Nations Resolutions on Outer Space: "Instant" International Customary Law ?*, 5 INDIAN J. INT'L L. 23 (1965).

26. *See* Akehurst, *supra* note 23.

27. For further discussion of the "instant" customary international law issue, *see* JOHN F. MURPHY, *supra* note 1, at 16–17.

28. Kelly, *supra* note 20, at 469–75.

29. *See* J. Patrick Kelly, *International Law and the Shrinking Space for Domestic Politics in Developing Countries*, in LAW and RIGHTS: GLOBAL PERSPECTIVES on CONSTITUTIONALISM and GOVERNANCE 259, 261 (Penelope E. Andrews and Susan Bazilli eds., 2008).

30. Kelly, *supra* note 20, at 508–19. In this article, Professor Kelly describes the history of the struggle between the consent and universal paradigms of customary international law and the recent rise of the persistent objector principle.

31. Although the U.S. government and the Third Restatement of the Foreign Relations Law of the United States support the persistent objector principle, there is little evidence that non-western states do so, and there is substantial scholarly debate on this subject. As a result, the status of the persistent objector principle in international law is uncertain. *See* JOHN F. MURPHY, *supra* note 1, at 18.

32. Kelly, *supra* note 29 at 262.

33. *Id.*

34. *Id.* at 263.

35. *Id.*

36. Prosper Weil, *Towards Relative Normativity in International Law*, 77 AM. J. INT'L L. 413, 414, n.7 (1983).

37. *See* JORDAN J. PAUST et al., INTERNATIONAL LAW and LITIGATION in the US 44 (2nd ed. 2005).

38. Remarks by W. Michael Reisman, *A Hard Look at Soft Law*, 82 PROC. AM. SOC. INT'L L. 371, 376 (1988).

39. Oscar Schachter, *The Twilight Existence of Nonbinding International Agreements*, 71 AM. J. INT'L L. 296, 299 (1977).

40. *Id.* at 300.

41. In Schachter's words:

> The conclusion that nonbinding agreements are not governed by international law does not, however remove them entirely from having legal implications. Consider the following situations. Let us suppose governments in conformity with a nonbinding agreement follow a course of conduct which results in

a new situation. Would a government party to the agreement be precluded from challenging the legality of the course of conduct or the validity of the situation created by it? A concrete case could arise if a government which was a party to a gentleman's agreement on the distribution of seats in any international body sought to challenge the validity of the election. In a case of this kind, the competent organ might reasonably conclude that the challenging government was subject to estoppel in view of the gentlemen's agreement and the reliance of the parties on that agreement. *Id.* at 301.

42. ALAN BOYLE and CHRISTINE CHINKIN, THE MAKING of INTERNATIONAL LAW 212–13 (2007).

43. *See* Daniel Bodansky, *Rules v. Standards in International Environmental Law*, 98 AM. SOC'Y INT'L L. PROC. 275 (2004).

44. ALAN BOYLE and CHRISTINE CHINKIN, *supra* note 42, at 210–29.

45. *See* Anthony D'Amato, *Jus Cogens: Definition, in* INTERNATIONAL LAW ANTHOLOGY 115 (Anthony D'Amato ed., 1994).

46. *See* OPPENHEIM'S INTERNATIONAL LAW 7–8 (9th ed. R.Y. Jennings and A. Watts eds., 1992).

47. E. MCWHINNEY, UNITED NATIONS LAW MAKING 73–75 (1984).

48. *Id.*

49. Richard D. Kearney and Robert E. Dalton, *The Treaty on Treaties*, 64 AM. J. INT'L L. 495, 536 (1970).

50. Military and Paramilitary Activities in and Against Nicaragua (Nicaragua v. United States), 1986 ICJ 14 (Judgment on Merits of June 27).

51. *See* Anthony D'Amato, *It's a Bird, It's a Plane, It's Jus Cogens!*, 6 CONN. J. INT'L L. 1, 2–3 (1990).

52. *Id.* at 3.

53. *See, e.g., Prosecutor v. Furundzija* (IT-95–17/1)(judgment 10 December 1998), paras 153–54 (prohibition of torture as *jus cogens*); Inter-American Court of Human Rights, *Juridical Condition and Rights of the Undocumented Migrants* (Adv Op 17 September 2003) (nondiscrimination on the basis of race and sex as *jus cogens*). The International Court of Justice has also pronounced again on *jus cogens. See Armed Activities on the Territory of the Congo* (2006) ICJ Reports, para 64 (prohibition of genocide).

54. Restatement of the Law (Third) of the Foreign Relations Law of the United States 331, Reporters' Note 4 (1987).

55. G. TUNKIN, THEORY of INTERNATIONAL LAW 444 (1974).

56. Anthony D'Amato, *supra* note 51, at 4.

57. *Id.* at 6.

58. For some examples of these questions, *see* JOHN F. MURPHY, *supra* note 1, at 36–37.

59. OSCAR SHACHTER, INTERNATIONAL LAW in THEORY and PRACTICE 52 (1991).

60. ALAN BOYLE and CHRISTINE CHINKIN, *supra* note 42, at 223.

61. MALCOLM N. SHAW, INTERNATIONAL LAW 94 (5th ed. 2003).

62. *Beef Hormones Case* (1998), WTO Appellate Body, paras 124–25.

63. MALCOLM SHAW, *supra* note 61, at 106.

64. Louis Sohn, *Sources of International Law*, 25 GA. J. INT'L & COMP. L. 399, 401 (1996).

65. Kelly, *supra* note 29, at 263.

66. *See*, in particular, Article 39 of the U.N. Charter.

67. For a magisterial examination of the lawmaking capacity of the specialized agencies and the IAEA, *see* Frederic L. Kirgis Jr., *Specialized Law-Making Processes, in* 1 UNITED NATIONS LEGAL ORDER 109 (Oscar Schachter & Christopher C. Joyner eds., 1995).

68. *Id.* at 142–43.

69. *Id.* at 143.
70. *See* STEPHEN C. McCAFFREY, UNDERSTANDING INTERNATIONAL LAW 67 (2006), citing 1 OPPENHEIM'S INTERNATIONAL LAW 44 (R. Jennings and A. Watts eds., 9th ed., 1992) and Michel Virally, *The Sources of International Law, in* MANUAL of PUBLIC INTERNATIONAL LAW 152 (Sorensen ed., 1968).
71. In a dispute with the United Kingdom over British Honduras, Guatemala gave the court such authority but the British government did not.
72. 1 OPPENHEIM'S INTERNATIONAL LAW 44 (R. Jennings and A. Watts eds., 9th ed. 1992), quoted in STEPHEN C. McCAFFREY, *supra* note 70, at 67, n. 223.
73. For some examples, *see* 1 OPPENHEIM'S *supra* note 70, at 44, n. 7.
74. STEPHEN C. McCAFFREY, *supra* note 70, at 68.
75. 1937 P.C.I.J. (Ser.A/B) No. 70, at 76–77.
76. 1969 I.C. J. 3.
77. *Id.* at para 85.
78. *See, e.g.,* the *Cayuga Indians Case,* American and British Claims Arbitration *Nielsen Reports* 203, 307 (1926).
79. *See, e.g.,* Paul Reuter, *Quelques reflexions sur l'equite en droit international,* REVUE BELGE DE DROIT INTERNATIONAL 165 (1980); and Jan Schneider, *The Gulf of Maine Case: The Nature of an Equitable Result,* 79 AM. J. INT'L L. 539 (1985), cited in STEPHEN C. McCAFFREY, *supra* note 70, at 70.
80. *The Gulf of Maine Case,* 1984 I.C. J. 246, 386.
81. *Id.* at 388.
82. MALCOLM SHAW, *supra* note 61, at 101. In footnote 146, Shaw cites several other cases as examples where the ICJ has used equitable principles to avoid rendering an inequitable decision.
83. 1985 I.C.J. 13, 39.
84. STEPHEN C. McCAFFREY, *supra* note 70, at 70.
85. *Id.* at 62. McCaffrey mentions the European Court of Justice and the European Court of Human Rights as examples.
86. *See* MALCOLM SHAW, *supra* note 61, at 105.
87. *See* J. Patrick Kelly, *supra* note 20, at 506.
88. For a contrary view, see the Report of the Committee on the Formation of Customary International Law, *National Court Decisions as State Practice, in* PROCEEDINGS of the AMERICAN BRANCH of the INTERNATIONAL LAW ASSOCIATION 102 (1999–2000).
89. J. Patrick Kelly, *supra* note 20, at 506.
90. Legal Status of Eastern Greenland, [1933] PCIJ Rep. 128.
91. Dean Rusk, *The Role and Problems of Arbitration with Respect to Political Disputes, in* RESOLVING TRANSNATIONAL DISPUTES THROUGH INTERNATIONAL ARBITRATION 15, 18 (Thomas E. Carbonneau ed., 1984), quoted and cited in MARK W. JANIS & JOHN E. NOYES, *supra* note 3, at 89.
92. In support of this analysis, see Alfred P. Rubin, *The International Legal Effects of Unilateral Declarations,* 71 AM. J. INT'L L. 1, 4–5 (1977).
93. Nuclear Tests (Australia v. France), [1974] ICJ Rep. 253 and Nuclear Tests (New Zealand v. France), *id.* at 457.
94. The six dissenting judges opposed the decision on a variety of grounds. They declined to take a position on this rationale for the court's judgment on the ground that the point was not argued before the court. Alfred P. Rubin, *supra* note 92, at 1, n. 3.
95. For the court's recital of the Australian and French applications and its disposition of them, see Nuclear Tests, *supra* note 93, paras. 11 and 62 (Australia v. France) and 11 and 65 (New Zealand v. France).

96. Alfred P. Rubin, *supra* note 92, at 2.
97. Nuclear Tests, *supra* note 93, at paras. 43 and 46 (Australia v. France), paras. 46 and 49 (New Zealand v. France).
98. Alfred P. Rubin, *supra* note 92, at 2.
99. *Id.* at 28–29.
100. IAN BROWNLIE, PRINCIPLES OF PUBLIC INTERNATIONAL LAW 646 (5th ed. 1998).
101. In Nicaragua v. United States and by chamber of the Court in the Case Concerning the Frontier Dispute (Burkina Faso v. Mali). Id. at 644.
102. Report of the International Law Commission, 57th Sess., 2 May–3 June and 11 July–5 August 2005, General Assembly Off. Rec. 60th Sess. Supplement No. 10 (A/60/10), at 133–34.
103. *See, e.g.,* NCH Dunbar, *The Myth of Customary International Law*, 1983 AUSTL. Y.B. INT'L. 1.
104. Jack L. Goldsmith & Eric A Posner, *A Theory of Customary International Law*, 66 U. CHI. L.R. 1113 (1999).
105. JACK L. GOLDSMITH and ERIC A. POSNER, THE LIMITS OF INTERNATIONAL LAW 23–78 (2005).
106. *See* Jack Goldsmith and Eric A. Posner, **RESPONSE** *The New International Law Scholarship*, 34 GA. J. INT'L and COMP. L. 463 (2006).
107. JACK L. GOLDSMITH & ERIC A. POSNER, *supra* note 105, at 9.
108. Paul Schiff Berman, *Book Review Essay – Seeing Beyond the Limits of International Law*, 84 TEX. L. REV. 1265, 1270 (2006).
109. JACK L. GOLDSMITH & ERIC A. POSNER, *supra* note 105, at 23–43.
110. *Id.* at 25.
111. *Id.*
112. *Id.* at 25–26.
113. *Id.* at 11.
114. *Id.* at 12.
115. *Id.*
116. *Id.*
117. Paul Schiff Berman, *supra* note 108, at 1275.
118. JACK L. GOLDSMITH and ERIC A. POSNER, *supra* note 105, at 12.
119. *Id.* at 45–78.
120. *Id.* at 45.
121. The Paquete Habana, 175 U.S. 677 (1900).
122. JACK L. GOLDSMITH and ERIC A. POSNER, *supra* note 105, at 45.
123. Peter J. Spiro, *A Negative Proof of International Law*, 34 GA. J. INT'L & COMP. L. 445, 455 (2006).
124. Jack Goldsmith and Eric A. Posner, *supra* note 106, at 476.
125. JACK GOLDSMITH and ERIC A. POSNER, *supra* note 105, at 225.
126. Jack Goldsmith and Eric A. Posner, *supra* note 106, at 467.
127. Jack L. Goldsmith and Eric A. Posner, *Understanding the Resemblance Between Modern and Traditional Customary International Law*, 40 VA. J. INT'L L. 639 (2000).
128. *Id.* at 663.
129. *See* Richard Bilder, *On Being an International Lawyer*, 3 LOY. U. CHI. INT'L L. REV. 135, 137 (2006).
130. Jack Goldsmith and Eric A. Posner, *supra* note 106, at 463.
131. For the classic description of this process, *see* Myres S. McDougal et al., *The World Constitutive Process of Authoritative Decision*, 19 J. LEGAL EDUC. 253, 254–55 (1967).
132. LOUIS HENKIN, HOW NATIONS BEHAVE: LAW and FOREIGN POLICY 47 (2d ed. 1979).

133. The amount of commentary on their book has been substantial. Particularly noteworthy are the series of essays in *Symposium: The Limits of International Law*, 34 GA. J. INT'L & COMP. L. 253–462 (2006) and the authors' response, *supra* note 106; Paul Schiff Berman, *supra* note 108; and Oona A. Hathaway and Ariel N. Lavinbuk, *Book Review: Rationalism and Revisionism in International Law*, 119 HARV.L. REV. 1404 (2006). Citations to other leading commentaries may be found in Peter J. Spiro, *supra* note 123, at 446, n. 2.
134. JACK L. GOLDSMITH and ERIC A. POSNER, *supra* note 105, at 83–106.
135. *Id.* at 81–82.
136. *Id.* at 90.
137. *Id.* at 87.
138. *Id.*
139. Hathaway & Lavinbuk, *supra* note 133, at 1419–20.
140. Kal Raustialia, *Refining the Limits of International Law*, 34 GA. J. INT'L & COMP. L. 423, 429 (2006).
141. Jack Goldsmith and Eric Posner, *supra* note 106, at 472.
142. *Id.*
143. I am obliged to Charlotte Ku, formerly Executive Director of the American Society of International Law and now a faculty member of the University of Illinois Law School, for this suggestion. In an e-mail message to me, Ku reports that "[a]t a recent conference presentation, I likened the current situation to having pieces of a puzzle and trying to put them together without having the picture on the box to guide placement of the pieces."
144. *See* JOHN F. MURPHY, *supra* note 1, at 1.
145. For a thoughtful discussion of this reality, *see* BRIAN Z. TAMANAHA, on the RULE of LAW: HISTORY, POLITICS, THEORY 127–136 (2004).
146. *Id.* at 137.
147. *Id.*
148. ANNE-MARIE SLAUGHTER, A NEW WORLD ORDER (2004).
149. *Id.* at 8.
150. *Id.*
151. *Id.*
152. *Id.* at 38.
153. *Id.* at 12.
154. *Id.*
155. *Id.* at 13.
156. *Id.* at 162.
157. *Id.* at 174.
158. *Id.* at 199.
159. *Id.* at 245.
160. *Id.* at 259. The five norms or principles she suggests are first, a norm of global deliberative equality. Second, a norm of "legitimate difference – the requirement that in their various deliberations, members of government networks understand and act on the principle that 'different' does not equal 'wrong.'" Third, "positive comity," the substitution of a norm of affirmative cooperation between nations in place of the traditional deference by one state to another state's action. Fourth, the principle of "subsidiarity, or the location of government power at the lowest level practicable among local, regional, national, and supranational authorities."
161. For examples of reviews of A New World Order, see G. John Ikenberry, *Book Review*, 83 FOREIGN AFFAIRS 136 (May/June 2004); *Book Review*, PUBLISHER'S WEEKLY (Feb. 2, 2004); Tony Judt, *Dreams of Empire*, 51 N.Y. REV. of BOOKS 38 (2004); Kenneth

Anderson, *Squaring the Circle? Reconciling Sovereignty and Global Governance Through Global Government Networks*, 118 HARV. L. REV. 1255 (2005); Peter Berkowitz, *Laws of Nations*, Hoover Institution, Policy Review (April & May 2005); Andras Sajo, *Transnational Governance and Constitutionalism: International Studies in the Theory of Private Law*, 3 INT'L J. CONST. L. 697 (2005); and Robert Howse, *Book Review*, 101 AM. J. INT'L L. 231 (2007).

162. Kenneth Anderson, *supra* note 161, at 1311–12.

163. Robert Howse, *supra* note 161, at 232–33.

164. Peter Berkowitz, *supra* note 161.

165. For example, Slaughter suggests that "the advantages of transgovernmentalism have become more prominent while the disadvantages of many more formal international institutions have become clearer." ANNE-MARIE SLAUGHTER, *supra* note 148, at 44.

166. *See* Anne-Marie Slaughter and William Burke-White, *The Future of International Law is Domestic (or, The European Way of Law)*, 47 HARV. INT'L L. J. 327 (2006).

167. *Id.*

168. *Id.* at 328.

169. *Id.*

170. *Id.* at 329, n. 8. As an example, they quote Eric Posner and John Yoo, *Reply to Helfer and Slaughter*, 93 CAL. L. REV. 957, 966 (2005) ("There is no reason to think that a court that works for Europe, where political and legal institutions in most countries are of high quality, would work for a world community that lacks the same level of cohesion and integration. Whatever one thinks about the EU, it is nothing like the international community.").

171. *Id.* at 329.

172. *Id.* at 330.

173. *Id.*

174. Slaughter and Burke-White's point about weak or failing states is well taken. Sadly, recent data indicate that the problem may be getting worse rather than better and that "[f]ew encouraging signs emerged in 2006 to suggest the world is on a path to greater peace and stability." *See The Failed State Index 2007*, FOREIGN POL'Y, July/August 2007, at 54.

175. Slaughter and Burke-White, *supra* note 166, at 331.

176. *Id.* at 332.

177. *Id.*

178. *Id.* at 334.

179. Stephen D. Krasner, *Building Democracy After Conflict: The Case for Shared Sovereignty*, 16 J. DEMOCRACY, Jan. 2005, at 69, 76.

180. Slaughter and Burke-White, *supra* note 166, at 337.

181. *Id.* at 340.

182. *Id.* at 343.

183. *Id.* at 344.

184. S.C. Res. 1373, para 2 (c)–(d), U.N. Doc. S/RES/1373 (Sept. 28, 2001).

185. S.C. Res. 1540, U.N. Doc. S/RES 1540 (Apr. 28, 2004).

186. Slaughter and Burke-White, *supra* note 166, at 345–46.

187. *Id.* at 346–49.

188. *Id.* at 347.

189. *Id.* at 349.

190. *Id.* at 350.

191. Int'l Comm'n on Intervention and State Sovereignty, THE RESPONSIBILITY TO PROTECT: REPORT OF THE ICISS (2001).
192. Slaughter and Burke-White, *supra* note 166, at 351.
193. Int'l Comm'n on Intervention and State Sovereignty, *supra* note 191, at para 2.14.
194. *Id.* at XI.
195. Slaughter and Burke-White, *supra* note 166, at 351.
196. For some recent arguments to this effect, *see* Clive Crook, *Think Again: Europe*, FOREIGN POL'Y, July/August, at 22.

2

International Institutions

As we have seen in the Introduction to this study, there are numerous claims that the elaborate system of international institutions that was developed after World War II is "broken" and that every major international institution, as well as countless smaller ones, faces calls for major reform. To attempt to cover all or only the major international institutions would require a multivolume treatise and is way beyond the scope of this chapter and of this study.[1] For present purposes, this chapter examines some of the most salient aspects of criticisms and calls for reform of the United Nations, the International Court of Justice, and the international criminal tribunals, including the International Criminal Tribunal for the Former Yugoslavia, the International Criminal Tribunal for Rwanda, and the International Criminal Court, as well as the so-called hybrid tribunals.

In order to evaluate the performance of these international institutions, it is necessary first to consider the criteria to be applied in judging their successes and failures. Has the performance of the institution concerned established its credibility and its relevance in fulfilling the goals of its founders? How effective has the institution been in helping states settle their disputes, for example, and has it avoided taking on issues where it cannot make an effective contribution? Has the institution at least avoided making a bad situation worse?

In evaluating the performance of these international institutions, it is also important to realize the enormity of many of the problems they were created to resolve. The terrible carnage of World War II, for example, finally shocked humankind into making a major effort to create an international institution that would induce states to settle their disputes peacefully and have enough military assets at its disposal to prevent would-be aggressors from resorting to armed force against their neighbors. As we shall see in some detail in Chapter 3 of this study, the record of the United Nations has been mixed at best in fulfilling this goal when viewed from an ideal perspective, but when considered in light of the multitude of obstacles that the organization has faced in attempting to fulfill its primary obligation under the U.N. Charter, the picture is somewhat brighter. The same may be said of efforts by the

United Nations and other international institutions to promote and protect human rights. Similarly, international environmental problems have greatly increased in intensity, especially the problem of climate change, but the obstacles facing international institutions seeking to resolve them have grown stronger as well and efforts to remove them face daunting challenges.

UNITED NATIONS

Throughout its history, there have been numerous proposals to "reform" the United Nations, most of which have never been implemented.[2] In a speech to the United Nations General Assembly in September 2003, however, Kofi A. Annan, then Secretary-General of the United Nations, suggested that "a decisive moment" had arrived for the United Nations and "in particular for the aspiration set out in the [U.N.] Charter to provide collective security for all."[3] He noted the "deep divisions among the Member States on the nature of the threats that we faced and the appropriateness of the use of force to address those threats." He concluded by announcing his intention "to convene a high level panel of eminent persons to provide me with a shared, comprehensive view about the way forward on the critical issues."[4] The High-level Panel on Threats, Challenges and Change was convened,[5] and on December 1, 2004, transmitted its report, *A more secure world: our shared responsibility*,[6] to the Secretary-General. The High-level Panel's report sets forth a number of wide-ranging recommendations for possible reform of the United Nations, including a number of structural reforms.

On March 21, 2005, Secretary-General Kofi Annan produced his own report that, among other things, sets forth his reactions to the High-level Panel's report.[7] Both the High-level Panel's report and the Secretary-General's report were made available to member states of the United Nations for purpose of their consideration in preparation for the summit meeting of heads of government in September 2005.

On September 16, 2005, the U.N. General Assembly adopted a resolution by which the assembled Heads of State and Government set forth the 2005 World Summit Outcome.[8] The document sets forth a wide range of proposals, many of which relate directly to the maintenance of international peace and security. Some of these proposals are discussed in Chapter 3 of this study. Discussion of other proposals set forth in the document appears in other later chapters of this study.[9] For purposes of this chapter, the focus is on the creation of the Human Rights Council to replace the discredited Commission on Human Rights and the subsequent performance of the Council up to the time of writing.

The Human Rights Council

Article 1 (3) of the U.N. Charter provides that one of the principal purposes of the United Nations is to "achieve international cooperation in solving international problems of an economic, social, cultural, or humanitarian character, and in promoting and encouraging respect for human rights and for fundamental freedoms for all without distinction as to race, sex, language, or religion." Under Article 7 of the Charter, the Economic and Social Council (ECOSOC) is established as one of the principal organs of the United Nations, and Article 68 of the Charter directs it to set up a commission "for the promotion of human rights." In 1946, ECOSOC carried out this mandate and established the Commission on Human Rights.[10]

The Commission was intended to be and for a number of years was the keystone of an elaborate system of U.N. activities designed to promote and protect human rights.[11] In the early years of its existence the Commission developed a framework of international human rights law, consisting of the Universal Declaration of Human Rights, the International Covenant on Civil and Political Rights, and the International Covenant on Economic, Social, and Cultural Rights, as well as other core human rights treaties. During its annual meeting the Commission served as a forum for discussion of and debates on human rights issues and developed a system of independent and expert special procedures to help promote compliance with human rights norms.

In its report of December 1, 2004, however, the High-level Panel on Threats, Challenges and Change noted that "[i]n recent years the Commission's capacity to perform these tasks has been undermined by eroding credibility and professionalism . . . in recent years States have sought membership of the Commission not to strengthen human rights but to protect themselves against criticism or to criticize others."[12] To rectify this situation, the panel proposed that the membership of the Commission be expanded to universal membership. In the view of the panel this would "underscore that all members are committed by the Charter to the promotion of human rights, and might help to focus attention back on to substantive issues rather than who is debating and voting on them."[13]

In his report of March 21, 2005, the Secretary-General rejected the proposal of the High-level Panel and set forth a much more radical recommendation. In sharp contrast to the panel's view that the Commission on Human Rights should be expanded to universal membership, the Secretary-General recommended that member states of the United Nations "should agree to replace the Commission on Human Rights with a smaller standing Human Rights Council."[14] Its members would be elected by the General Assembly by a two-thirds majority of members present and voting. "The creation of the Council would accord human rights a more authoritative position, corresponding to the primacy of human rights in the Charter of the United Nations . . . Those elected to the Council should undertake to abide by the highest human rights standards."[15]

The relatively restrained criticism of the Commission on Human Rights by the High-level Panel and the Secretary-General was supplemented by more strident voices that accused the Commission of rampant corruption, politicization, and partisanship.[16] Other critics complained that the Commission met too infrequently, because it only convened for six weeks a year.[17] Especially strident were the criticisms of several states, including the United States, that the Commission's membership included such notorious human rights violators as Libya, Sudan, and Zimbabwe.[18]

The U.N. General Assembly formally established the Human Rights Council in March 2006 by adoption of a resolution.[19] As a subsidiary organ of the General Assembly, the forty-seven-member Council is directly accountable to the full membership of the United Nations, unlike the Commission on Human Rights, which reported to the fifty-four-member ECOSOC. Elections to membership in the Council are decided by a simple majority vote of the General Assembly, rather than by the two-thirds vote recommended by the Secretary-General. The Council is to hold no fewer than three meetings per year, with each meeting lasting longer than the Commission meetings. The Council also has the authority to call emergency meetings for fast developing human rights crises.

The General Assembly is directed to scrutinize closely the human rights records of state candidates for membership on the Council.[20] The Council held elections for state membership in May 2006, and officially replaced the Commission in June when it convened in Geneva for its first meeting.[21] It is debatable, however, whether the General Assembly adequately examined the human rights records of the candidates to exclude states with unsatisfactory human rights records.

Critics of the results of the elections note that China, Cuba, Pakistan, Russia, Saudi Arabia, and Azerbaijan, all states identified by human rights groups as states with poor human rights records, were elected to the Council.[22] On the other hand, Iran and Venezuela failed to get the necessary votes, and states with notorious human rights records that had been on the Commission, such as Sudan, Zimbabwe, Libya, Democratic Republic of Congo, Syria, Vietnam, Nepal, Sri Lanka, Eritrea, and Ethiopia, declined to run for the Council.

Under the rules of the new Council, all members of the United Nations must submit to reviews of their human rights records, and members of the Council are to be scrutinized first. It was unclear at the beginning how soon the procedures for this review would be in place.[23]

The United States was especially critical of the establishment of the Council, being only one of four states voting against passage of the resolution doing so.[24] The United States also declined to offer itself as a candidate for membership on the Council. John Bolton, then U.S. Permanent Representative to the United Nations, explained that the United States was not running for a position on the Council in order to pressure the Council to adopt more stringent membership criteria to exclude egregious human rights violators from the Council. Some commentators, however, have claimed that the United States decided not to run because of concern that its own human rights record might result in its failing to win election to the Council.[25]

It is fair to say that the Council got off to a rocky start. Writing at a time when the Council had met five times since its establishment, twice in regular session and three times in special sessions,[26] Patrizia Scannella and Peter Splinter, Amnesty International's Deputy Representative and Representative to the United Nations in Geneva, respectively, first noting the accomplishments of the Council, pointed out that the Council had adopted by consensus the International Convention for the Protection of All Persons from Enforced Disappearances as well as, by majority vote, the U.N. Declaration on the Rights of Indigenous Peoples. The Council also continued special procedures developed by the Commission that created working groups and special reporters to examine the human rights situation in particular countries or to consider particular human rights problems like extrajudicial killings.[27] Unfortunately, the Council also continued another practice of the Commission on Human Rights: the "unprincipled" handling of situations involving Israel, which had been discussed every time the Council had met and had been the subject of one adopted decision, three adopted resolutions, and three draft decisions and resolutions.[28] At the same time, "many of the main proponents of the Council's action in respect of situations involving Israel have also argued against, if not actively sought to block, the Council's consideration of the human rights situations in other acute situations such as Sudan (Darfur and Eastern Chad) and Sri Lanka," thus demonstrating "the dangerous double standards that are being imposed on the new Council by many of the same States that were so vocal in decrying the evident application of double standards in the Commission."[29]

The willingness of the Council constantly to condemn Israel while trying to block consideration of the situation in other states with egregious human rights records is in part the result of the way seats in the Council are distributed among regional groups. Of the forty-seven seats in the Council, thirteen go to the African Group, thirteen seats to the Asian Group, six to the Eastern European Group, eight to the Latin American and Caribbean Group, and seven to the Western European and Others Group. This means that if the African and Asian Groups vote together, they are ensured a majority. The practice of working through regional and other groups was common in the Commission and carried over to the Council. As noted by Scannella and Splinter, "[t]his often makes for relatively inflexible positions as the most conservative members are able to impose a lowest common denominator on positions adopted by the group. This phenomenon has been most noticeable, although by no means limited to, the inflexible positions taken by proponents and opponents of the draft resolutions during the special sessions on the situation in the Palestinian and other Occupied Territories and on Lebanon."[30]

Antipathy toward Israel is engendered in no small part by the seventeen members of the Organization of Islamic Conference on the Council. Their presence also led to the adoption of a resolution, by a twenty-four to fourteen vote, with nine abstentions, on "combating defamation of religions" that calls upon states to limit speech in such a way to further "respect for religions and beliefs" and to require that freedom of speech be exercised "with responsibility."[31] The problem with this language, which appears anodyne at first glance, is that "[t]he right to free speech is not a right if it cannot be exercised irresponsibly and, so long as it does not promote violence, jinx trials, libel individuals without cause or, in rare circumstances, threaten national security, freely is how many feel it should be exercised."[32] Of the seventeen members of the Organization of Islamic Conference on the Council, all but one voted for the resolution, along with China, Russia, and South Africa. Fourteen Western countries voted against, including all eight EU states, plus Japan, Ukraine, and South Korea. Nine developing countries abstained.[33]

Other sessions of the Council have devoted an arguably disproportionate time to Israel's alleged sins in the Occupied Palestinian Territories and Lebanon, but the Council's focus has widened to take in a variety of other human rights issues. One notable accomplishment of the Council was the adoption, without a vote on June 18, 2007, of a Draft Code of Conduct for Special Procedures Mandate-Holders of the Human Rights Council at its Fifth Session.[34] Earlier, there were concerns that the code might be drafted in such a way to restrict the independence of the special procedures system, that is, the reporters and working groups on human rights themes and on country situations.[35] This has not happened.

The Bush administration announced that it again would not seek election to the Human Rights Council in elections later in 2007 because of its concerns about the Council's lack of credibility and its bias against Israel.[36] Some members of the U.S. Congress sharply criticized the administration's decision not to seek election.[37]

Arguably, the most salient challenge initially facing the Council was how it would conduct its universal periodic review of the human rights records of U.N. member states, especially those on the Council. This was a new venture for the United Nations, and there were not very many models to follow.[38] According to Scannella and Splinter, "[a] principal issue that is emerging in the discussion of the universal periodic review mechanism is its relationship to other means by which the Council can address the human rights situations in particular countries . . . Some other emerging issues concern the nature of the information that should be used as the basis for the universal periodic review; the periodicity of the review; whether Council observers, including NGOs, should be able to participate in the review process and the interactive dialogue at its centre; whether the review should be carried out in the Council meeting in plenary or in subsidiary bodies; and the character of the outcome of the review and how that outcome is to be adopted."[39]

On June 18, 2007, one year after its first meeting, and in compliance with General Assembly Resolution 60/251,[40] the Council agreed on the procedures, mechanisms, and structures that would govern its Universal Periodic Review (UPR).[41] Under this new mechanism, all U.N. member states would be reviewed within a period of four years in the first cycle, with forty-eight states to be reviewed every year. All members of the Council would be reviewed during their term of membership. The review would be carried out by a working group composed of members of the Council that would meet three times a year for two weeks and would be aided by groups of three members of the Council that would act as Rapporteurs (or "troikas") appointed by the Council. Recommendations from the so-called special procedures, that is, involving working groups or reporters who address either specific country situations or thematic issues in all parts of the world, and "human rights treaty bodies, as well as information from other sources, such as nongovernmental organizations and national human rights institutions," would be considered as elements of the review in addition to the report of the state concerned.[42]

As of May 2009, eighty countries have been subject to UPR. This leaves 112 countries still to be reviewed. The process has involved a threefold assessment of the reviewed state's compliance with its human rights obligations: the assessment of a self-evaluation by the country under review, a report by the Office of the High Commissioner for Human Rights on any applicable treaties and domestic laws, and a compilation of observations from nongovernmental organizations and concerned states. How effective this review has been remains to be determined, but Paula Schriefer, director of advocacy at Freedom House, a U.S.-based research institute, reportedly is of the view that countries with poor human rights records can easily ignore the recommendations that come out of the UPR.[43]

Ms. Schriefer's opinion is in some measure confirmed by the recent UPR of China. On February 11, 2009, the Working Group on the Universal Periodic Review adopted its report on China.[44]

The first step in the proceedings of the review process involved a presentation by China. Not surprisingly, this presentation was largely laudatory of China's human rights record and heavily emphasized economic, social, and cultural rights, high-lighting China's impressive record of poverty reduction while directing relatively little attention to civil and political rights. The next step consisted of an interactive dialogue and responses by China. The nature of this dialogue and China's responses varied considerably depending on whether the questions were largely critical in tone or friendly. Two examples are worthy of notice. First, Australia:

> welcomed the considerable improvements made by China over the past 30 years but expressed concern that Chinese officials continue to repress religious activities considered to be outside the State-controlled religious system. Noting grave concerns about reports of harassment, arbitrary arrest, punishment and detention of religious and ethnic minorities, including Tibetans, it recommended that China (a) strengthen the protection of ethnic minorities' religious, civil, socio-economic and political rights. While encouraged by positive developments in the handling of death-penalty cases, it remained concerned about the reportedly high number of executions and lack of transparency in such cases and recommended that China (b) abolish the death penalty and, as interim steps, reduce the number of crimes for

which the death penalty can be imposed and publish figures on executions. Welcoming the softening of media regulations for foreign journalists and encouraging China to ensure restrictions are not imposed on journalists' access to the Tibetan Autonomous Region and to rural areas, it recommended (c) that new regulations be extended to Chinese journalists. Australia further recommended that China (d) respond positively to outstanding visit requests by special procedures and issue a standing invitation to (e) ratify the International Covenant on Civil and Political Rights (ICCPR) as quickly as possible and with minimal reservations (f) establish a national human rights institution . . . ; and (g) investigate reports of harassment and detention of human rights defenders, including alleged mistreatment while in police custody, with a view to ending impunity.[45]

China's response to Australia's questions and comments was brief and dismissive: It "noted with regret that there were a few countries like Australia, which made some ill-founded comments on Tibet. China categorically rejects this attempt to politicise (sic) the issue."[46]

There was no need for China to respond to the comments and recommendations of the Russian Federation:

The Russian Federation commended China's role in the work of the Human Rights Council and its efforts to strengthen international interaction in the area of human rights. It noted that the emphasis placed in China's national report on ensuring the realization of a basket of socio-economic rights, including questions of increasing the level of social protection, education and health, was fair. This policy on the part of the Government of the most heavily populated country of the world is particularly important in light of the global financial crisis. China is investing enormous resources aiming to develop Tibet province and in this regard the Russian Federation recommended it continue to invest financial and material resources with a view to supporting economic and social developments in the country as a whole and in the Tibet Autonomous Region in particular. It welcomed the fact that China has managed to develop a mutually acceptable formula for interaction between the authorities and civil society and noted the progress made in the work of the judiciary, law enforcement and penitentiary systems, and on questions related to conditions of certain groups of society.[47]

The conclusions and recommendations section of the Report first lists the recommendations formulated during the interactive dialogue that enjoy the support of China.[48] These recommendations are set forth in forty-two paragraphs, and many relate to economic, social, and cultural rights that China emphasizes in its report. The very first recommendation approved by China, however, is that it "[c]reate conditions for an early ratification of the International Covenant on Civil and Political Rights."[49] The Chinese response next notes recommendations that it claims it is already implementing, such as guaranteeing "that all detainees, regardless of their crimes, are held in facilities with decent standard and treatment,"[50] and then lists recommendations that it intends to examine and respond to in due time, such as a recommendation that it reduce the number of crimes carrying the death penalty.[51]

Last, and most significantly, the Chinese response rejects seventy recommendations by U.N. member states related to alleged human rights abuses in China,[52] such as "all recommendations related to freedom of expression and freedom of association, independence of the judiciary, guarantees for the legal profession, protection of human rights defenders, rights of ethnic minorities, reduction of the death penalty, abolition of reeducation-through-labor, prohibition of torture, media freedom, and effective remedies for discrimination."[53]

The reaction of the international human rights NGOs to the Chinese response has been highly critical.[54] Human Rights Watch, for example, alleged that the Chinese government's "defense of its human rights record during the review process was characterized by statements such as, 'There is no censorship in the country,' and responses that the Chinese government would 'never allow torture to be allowed on ethnic groups,' despite ample documentation by civil society groups and international organizations of such abuses."[55] For its part, Amnesty International contended that:

> China's rejection in its UPR session in February of a large number of recommendations covering a broad range of human rights has undermined the meaningfulness of its Universal Periodic Review. . . .
>
> The UPR process was meant to be an opportunity for states to provide frank assessments on how they are promoting and achieving international human rights standards, as well as an opportunity for other states to make recommendations on how best to work towards fulfilment of these standards.
>
> By rejecting so many recommendations China threatens the effectiveness and credibility of the process. Rejected recommendations were not politically motivated as alleged but based on international human rights obligations that China has accepted.[56]

China's appalling human rights record has been extensively documented in too many reports to mention. It is thus perhaps naive to expect the UPR to have any significant impact in improving China's human rights record. But the process may at a minimum serve to expose the extreme hypocrisy of China's position on human rights.

More generally, the UPR may be of limited use with respect to other U.N. member states with extremely poor human rights records. The same may not be true, however, with respect to states that approach the process in good faith and have a real desire to improve their human rights records. In their case the comments and recommendations of other U.N. member states presented during the UPR process, as well as the comments of international human rights NGOs, may prove to be of real benefit.

Lastly, it is noteworthy that the Obama administration repudiated the policy of the Bush administration and decided to run for election to the Human Rights Council. U.S. participation in the Council can only help the effort to induce the Council to overcome the discredited legacy of its predecessor, the Commission on Human Rights.

INTERNATIONAL COURT OF JUSTICE

There has long been a hope that nation-states would be willing to employ international adjudication in place of armed force as a method for settling disputes. The first movement toward the establishment of an international adjudicatory body came at the Hague Peace Conferences of 1899 and 1908.[57] Despite enjoying considerable support at the conferences, however, proposals for a permanent international court failed to be accepted by the majority of participants. The only institution to emerge from these conferences was the Permanent Court of Arbitration (PCA, created in 1899). But the so-called permanent court is not a true judicial institution. Rather, the PCA merely provides facilities for international arbitration, including lists of available arbitrators.

In the wake of the extensive carnage caused by World War I, the Permanent Court of International Justice (PCIJ) came into being as the judicial organ of the League of Nations. The years 1922 to 1939 were the most active for the PCIJ. During that time it heard sixty-five cases, issued twenty-seven advisory opinions, and rendered thirty-two judgments.[58] It enjoyed some success in resolving several boundary disputes and a dispute between Denmark and Norway over the sovereignty of Eastern Greenland. In 1946 it ceased operations, shortly after the formation of the International Court of Justice (ICJ). The International Court of Justice is in every sense the direct successor of the Permanent Court of International Justice, because the Statute of the ICJ is essentially the same as that of the PCIJ. Also, the jurisprudence of the PCIJ is often cited by the ICJ and remains highly relevant to its decisions.

By way of background and context to a discussion of the issue whether the International Court of Justice is "broken," there follows a brief summary of how the Court is chosen, its structure, and its jurisdiction in contentious cases and advisory opinion situations.[59]

All members of the United Nations are parties to the ICJ Statute and therefore eligible to submit disputes to it. There are fifteen judges on the Court elected by the Security Council and the General Assembly in separate elections by majority vote. Although not required by the Court's Statute, in practice each of the permanent members of the Security Council has a national on the Court. All questions are decided by a majority vote of the judges present. In the event of a tie, the president has a casting vote that has been used in several of the Court's most controversial cases.[60]

The jurisdiction of the Court in contentious cases is based on the principles of consent and reciprocity. Article 36 of the Court's statute provides:

1. The jurisdiction of the Court comprises all cases which the parties refer to it and all matters specially provided for in the Charter of the United Nations or in treaties and conventions in force.

2. The states parties to the present Statute may at any time declare that they recognize as compulsory *ipso facto* and without any special agreement, in relation to any other state accepting the same obligation, the jurisdiction of the Court in all legal disputes concerning:
   (a) the interpretation of a treaty;
   (b) any question of international law;
   (c) the existence of any fact which, if established, would constitute a breach of an obligation;
   (d) the nature or extent of the reparation to be made for the breach of an international obligation.

3. The declarations referred to previously may be made unconditionally or on condition of reciprocity on the part of several or certain states, or for a certain time.

4. Such declarations shall be deposited with the Secretary-General of the United Nations, who shall transmit copies thereof to the parties to the Statute and to the registrar of the Court.

5. Declarations made under Article 36 of the Statute of the Permanent Court of International Justice and which are still in force shall be deemed, as between the parties to the present Statute, to be acceptance of the compulsory jurisdiction of the International Court of Justice for the period which they still have to run and in accordance with their terms.

6. In the event of a dispute as to whether the Court has jurisdiction, the matter shall be settled by the decision of the Court.

Under Article 36 there are basically three ways in which a state can give its consent to the Court's jurisdiction. First, the parties to a dispute may decide on an ad hoc basis to refer it to the Court. The parties usually do so by way of a special agreement called a *compromis*. Second, the parties to a bilateral or multilateral treaty may agree in advance to submit disputes regarding interpretation or application of the treaty to the Court, through the inclusion of a compromissory clause in the treaty. In cases involving compromissory clauses, the primary jurisdictional question facing the Court is whether the dispute falls within the relevant treaty containing the clause. Third, under Article 36 (2), which covers the so-called compulsory jurisdiction of the Court, states may agree in advance that the Court shall have jurisdiction over *all* legal disputes concerning the four topics listed in subparagraphs (a)–(d). This is done through a state's filing a declaration with the Court that, under Article 36 (3), "may be made unconditionally or on condition of reciprocity on the part of several or certain states, or for a certain time."

It is useful to compare the consent to the Court's jurisdiction that a state gives under a compromissory clause in a treaty with the consent it gives when it files a declaration under Article 36 (2). Under a compromissory clause, states consent only to the Court's jurisdiction over disputes arising over the interpretation and application of a particular treaty. By contrast, a state filing a declaration under Article 36 (2) consents to the Court's jurisdiction over a broad range of future disputes that may be beyond its contemplation at the time the declaration is filed or even beyond its imagination. Clearly, for example, it was never contemplated by the United States that it would be subject to the Court's jurisdiction in a suit involving the facts of *Nicaragua v. United States*. Such a broad consent in advance of a dispute may be especially problematic in an age when the subjects covered by international law are growing at an exponential pace. In any event, of the 192 states that are parties to the Court's statute, only about 67 currently have made declarations under Article 36 (2). Most significantly, the United Kingdom is the only one of the five permanent members of the U.N. Security Council that accepts the so-called compulsory jurisdiction of the Court.

Although one might assume that a state, in agreeing to a compromissory clause in a treaty referring a dispute over the interpretation or application of the treaty to the ICJ, is consenting to a much narrower jurisdiction than would be the case if the state filed a declaration under Article 36 (2), in several cases the Court has interpreted a treaty with a compromissory clause as having a greater scope of coverage than anticipated. In *Nicaragua v. United States*, for example, the Court held that a compromissory clause in a Treaty of Friendship, Commerce and Navigation between the United States and Nicaragua provided a basis for the Court's jurisdiction, despite a strong dissent by Judge Schwebel that the bilateral treaty "is a purely commercial agreement whose terms do not relate to the use or misuse of force in international relations." In addition, he noted that the treaty expressly precluded its application to "traffic in arms" and to measures "necessary to protect [the] essential security interests" of a party.[61] Similarly, in the *Oil Platforms* case[62] where Iran challenged the lawfulness of the destruction by U.S. military forces of several Iran oil production platforms in the Persian Gulf during the last stages of the 1980–1988 war between Iran and Iraq, the Court upheld its jurisdiction based on a compromissory clause in a 1955 U.S.-Iran Treaty of Amity, Economic Relations, and Consular Rights over U.S. objections that the destruction of the platforms was governed by the law regulating the use of force and self-defense, and did not fall within the scope of the treaty. As a result, although it is currently a party to more than seventy bilateral treaties with compromissory clauses, the United States has become less inclined to include such clauses in future bilateral treaties and regularly makes a reservation to multilateral treaties with compromissory clauses in them that refer disputes arising under the treaty to the ICJ for resolution.[63]

Oscar Schachter has nicely summarized the reasons states are reluctant to submit their disputes to an international judicial body for resolution:

> It is no great mystery why they are reluctant to have their disputes adjudicated. Litigation is uncertain, time consuming, troublesome. Political officials do not want to lose control of a case that they might resolve by negotiation or political pressures. Diplomats naturally prefer diplomacy; political leaders value persuasion, manoeuvre and flexibility. They often prefer to "play it by ear," making their rules fit the circumstances rather than submit to pre-existing rules. Political forums, such as the United Nations, are often more attractive, especially to those likely to get wide support for political reasons. We need only compare the large number of disputes brought to the United Nations with the few submitted to adjudication. One could go on with other reasons. States do not want to risk losing a case when the stakes are high or be troubled with litigation in minor matters. An international tribunal may not inspire confidence, especially when some judges are seen as "political" or as hostile. There is apprehension that the law is too malleable or fragmented to sustain "true" judicial decisions. In some situations, the legal issues are viewed as but one element in a complex political situation and consequently it is considered unwise or futile to deal with them separately. Finally, we note the underlying perception of many governments that law essentially supports the *status quo* and that courts are not responsive to demands for justice or change.[64]

States are especially reluctant to submit disputes to international adjudication when the issues involve – at least in the perception of the state concerned – matters affecting their national security or other vital interests. Increasingly, however, the International Court of Justice has accepted cases involving such interests – to its great detriment in my view.

The quintessential case is *Nicaragua v. United States*.[65] Rightly or wrongly, the United States regarded the military actions it undertook against Nicaragua as vital to its national security.[66] Hence, a ruling by the Court on the legality of these actions was simply unacceptable to the United States, and this opposition explains its enormous expenditure of time and effort during the jurisdiction phase of the proceedings. It also explains the sharp reaction of the United States to the Court's decision on jurisdiction and its decision to walk out of the proceedings in protest and to terminate its acceptance of the Court's compulsory jurisdiction under Article 36 (2) of the Court's statute.

This is not the time and place to go into a discussion of the merits of the Court's decision in either the jurisdictional or the merits phase of the proceedings.[67] In my view the Court was wrong on both jurisdiction and the merits. But even assuming *arguendo* the correctness of the Court's decisions, the Court did a disservice to the cause of international adjudication by issuing decisions that caused as significant a state as the United States to walk out of the proceedings and terminate its acceptance of the Court's compulsory jurisdiction. Both of these steps, moreover, were predictable in the light of the sensitivity of the issues to the United States.

Equally sensitive, in this case to the government of Iran, were the issues before the Court in *United States v. Iran*.[68] Although, unlike the case of Nicaragua versus the United States, there was no question that the Court rendered a correct decision in both the jurisdictional and merits phases of the proceedings, there is a serious question whether the Court served the cause of international adjudication in a situation where Iran refused to appear in the case, there was no question of Iran abiding by the decision, and the United States pursued this litigation, not because there were any close legal issues that needed to be resolved, but rather because of a desire to use the Court's judgment for political purposes in debates before the Security Council, in negotiations with allies seeking to impose tougher economic sanctions against Iran, or in efforts to persuade the U.S. public that it "was doing something" to resolve the crisis.

More recently, in *Legal Consequences of the Construction of a Wall in the Occupied Palestinian Territory*,[69] the Court issued a highly controversial advisory opinion that arguably undermined the cause of international adjudication in numerous ways. As might be expected, the *American Journal of International Law* has published an extensive Agora containing articles supporting and opposing the Court's advisory opinion.[70] The articles address a large number of issues arising out of the Court's opinion. No effort will be made here to cover all or even most of these. Rather, the effort will be to highlight aspects of the Court's opinion that support the proposition that it undermines the cause of international adjudication.

To begin with, it is clear that the proceedings in the U.N. General Assembly that led to the Assembly forwarding a request to the Court for its advisory opinion were part of the same syndrome that has so far marred the record of the Human Rights Council: the pervasive bias against Israel and the consequent obsessive effort to attack it on every possible occasion. As Michla Pomerance notes,[71] Article 65 (1) of the Court's Statute, which provides that the Court "may give an advisory opinion on any legal question at the request of whatever body may be authorized by or in accordance with the Charter of the United Nations to make such a request," grants the Court the discretion to decline to accept a request to issue an advisory opinion. But the International Court of Justice has never exercised its discretion to do so. To be sure, its predecessor, the Permanent Court of International Justice, declined to accept a request from the Council of the League of Nations to issue an advisory opinion in only one case, a dispute between Russia and Finland over the status of Eastern Carelia.[72] And the reason it declined to do so, by a seven to four vote, was primarily because Russia, as a nonmember of the League, had not agreed to have the Council handle its dispute, thus rendering that body incompetent to refer the matter to the Court, even in its advisory capacity.[73]

For the PCIJ, however, there normally was little reason for it to decline to issue an advisory opinion because the Council adopted the practice of proceeding to request an advisory opinion from the Court only if the Council agreed to do so by unanimous vote, including the votes of the states principally concerned. This practice provided, in effect, an alternative consent-based avenue to the Court and minimized the problem of compliance with the Court's advisory pronouncements. It also "averted, overall, what would become one of the negative UN phenomena: the embroilment of the Court in politically volatile issues where the probability of compliance by the losing side was small, and the chances that the advisory opinions would remain ineffective, correspondingly great."[74]

There is no question but that, by agreeing to issue its advisory opinion in the *Wall* case, the Court embroiled itself in politically volatile issues. Because of this and other reasons, all the permanent members of the Security Council except China, the members of the European Union, Australia, and Canada urged the General Assembly not to request the opinion, and the vote in the Assembly on the requesting resolution (90–8–74) included "an unusual number of nays and abstentions for an anti-Israel resolution."[75] Michla Pomerance summarized the many "compelling reasons" the Court should have resisted the Assembly's request for an advisory opinion: "These included the formulation of the request; the transparent motives of its sponsors; the unprecedented number of states urging judicial restraint; the absence of an agreed factual basis for adjudication; the legitimacy and consequences of judicial intervention in an acute and ongoing conflict in which, additionally, the Security Council was actively engaged; and, above all, the objection of Israel, the targeted state, to back-door nonconsensual adjudication of matters impinging so crucially on its existence, its territorial rights, and the defense of citizens from a continuing terrorist onslaught."[76]

Having decided to issue an advisory opinion, the Court reaches some startling conclusions of law in it. Most startling, perhaps, is the Court's statement that: "Article 51 of the Charter thus recognizes the existence of an inherent right of self-defence in the case of armed attack by one State against another State. However, Israel does not claim that the attacks against it are imputable to a foreign State."[77]

This statement is simply incredible. To begin with, by its very language, Article 51 of the Charter does *not* recognize the existence of an inherent right of self-defense in the case of armed attack by one *state* against another state. On the contrary, it recognizes the existence of an inherent right of self-defense "if an armed attack occurs against a Member of the United Nations . . . " There is no mention of any requirement that the armed attack be by a state. In his masterful contribution to the Agora, Sean Murphy suggests that "[a]t best the position represents imprecise drafting, and thus calls into question whether the advisory opinion process necessarily helps the Court 'to develop its jurisprudence and contributes to the progress of international law.' At worst, the position conflicts with the language of the UN Charter, its *travaux preparatoires*, the practice of states and international organizations, and common sense."[78]

Murphy goes on in his essay to demonstrate quite convincingly that the worst assumption about the Court's position is the more convincing. I will only emphasize that not only does the Court's position conflict with common sense. More important, it is a position no rational decision maker who has to decide how to respond to an armed attack by a terrorist group will take seriously. One is reminded of the comments of John Lawrence Hargrove, former Legal Adviser to the U.S. Mission to the United Nations and, at the time of this writing, Executive Director of the American Society of International Law, on the Court's highly controversial definition of an "armed attack" in *Nicaragua v. United States*. There, Hargrove suggested that the Court's definition "degrades the concept of international law, diminishes the inducement for a responsible political leader to take its constraints seriously into account in conflict situations in the actual planning and conduct of that state's affairs." He suggested, as an alternative procedure, that "[t]he way to develop a law of force or self-defense that will be taken seriously by real-world states is not to appoint the Court or any other body to such a futile function. It is to what the Charter already does: permit real force to be resisted by force, but scrupulously require that the defense fit the conduct defended against."[79] Arguably, Hargrove's comments apply *a fortiori* to the *Wall* case, because there Israeli was building a wall as an alternative to the use of armed force as an exercise of individual self-defense.

The Court's opinion also sets forth the highly questionable thesis that an occupying power may not take measures in the occupied territory whose object is to defend the territory of the occupying power from attacks originating in the occupied territory.[80] David Kretzmer, however, convincingly notes that "[s]uch a thesis ignores the fact that the law of occupation is part of the law of armed conflict. Becoming an occupying power in the course of an armed conflict cannot prevent a state from taking measures in the occupied territory necessary to protect the population in its own territory against attacks originating in the occupied territory," subject only to the well-accepted principle of the law of armed conflict that such measures be proportionate to the magnitude of the attack in question.[81]

On June 30, 2004, just nine days prior to the ICJ's advisory opinion, the Supreme Court of Israel, sitting as the High Court of Justice,[82] issued its opinion in *Beit Sourik Village Council v. Israel*,[83] which invalidated orders for the construction of several parts of the fence and instructed the Israeli Defense Force to reroute the wall so as to minimize the negative impact on daily Palestinian life. More recently, on September 4, 2007, a three-judge panel of the High Court ruled unanimously that a mile-long section of the wall should be redrawn and rebuilt in a way that would not split a West Bank village from much of its farmland.[84] Geoffrey R. Watson, in his contribution to the *American Journal of International Law's* Agora, has usefully compared the High Court of Justice's 2004 decision's holding and methodology with that of the ICJ in its *Wall* advisory opinion.[85] In doing so, he identifies both "commonalities" and "differences" between the High Court's decision and the ICJ's opinion. Perhaps the most noteworthy similarity was that both tribunals found that the wall, or perhaps more accurately, "security fence," violated to some extent the law of armed conflict in that it disrupted the daily life and livelihood of the civilian Palestinian population, although the ICJ's finding was, of course, by far the more sweeping in that it declared the entire wall illegal. Watson suggests, however, that the High Court's methodology was "more meticulous, both in enunciating the law and in applying it to the facts in a particularized fashion."[86]

Not surprisingly, Watson finds that the differences between the decision and the opinion outweigh the similarities. His discussion of these is worth quoting at some length:

> .... The International Court of Justice adopted a broad, sweeping holding that every inch of the fence violates international law. The Israeli Court found that many, but not all, segments of a portion of the wall violate international law. The ICJ applied a wide range of legal sources, including humanitarian law, the two Human Rights Covenants, the Convention on the Rights of the Child, and the right of self-determination. The Supreme Court focused narrowly on humanitarian law and Israeli administrative law....
>
> The Israeli Court employed a meticulous and particularized methodology that seems more satisfying than the generalized approach of the International Court, even allowing for the fact that the latter court was ruling in an advisory capacity. In ascertaining and applying the law, the International Court spoke in conclusory terms, whereas the Israeli Court engaged in a much fuller (though sometimes also conclusory) analysis. The International Court asserted without explanation that the "military necessity" exceptions in humanitarian law were inapplicable. It curtly announced that Article 51 of the Charter had "no relevance" to the case. It characterized the case as different from those described in the 2001 Security Council terrorism resolutions because the terror attacks originated within occupied territory, but it did not explain why that difference matters. It found that the fence violated the right of self-determination without fully explaining how. By contrast, the Israeli Court spent several paragraphs developing, in painstaking detail, a three-part test of "proportionality" that rivals the most intricate constructions of American constitutional law. Intricacy is not always a good thing, but at least the analysis was full-bodied enough to give the reader a thorough understanding of the Israeli Court's reasoning.
>
> Likewise, the Israeli Court was much more careful about finding facts and applying law to those facts. It engaged in a careful, detailed, case-by-case analysis of a number of segments of the wall involving lengths of about five to ten kilometers each. It frankly weighed security concerns against humanitarian ones, and more often than not found that insufficient attention had been paid to the humanitarian concerns. By contrast, the International Court had little to say about facts relating to security and terrorism ...
>
> .... The Israeli Supreme Court's jurisprudence is not just restrained – too restrained at times, as when it avoids questions relating to the applicability of the Fourth Geneva Convention – but also eminently pragmatic ... The decision is a reasonable mix of the retrospective (finding past and present violations of law) and prospective (fashioning practical relief to cure those violations).

By contrast, the decision of the International Court is not simply expansive and sweeping: it is primarily retrospective and relatively unconcerned with practical implementation. ... Those sections devoted to prospective implementation have the virtue of simplicity – they merely instruct Israel to tear down the entire wall – but they are not likely to influence Israeli (or American) decision making.[87]

An especially useful feature of the AJIL's Agora is the Editors' Introduction.[88] In it, the editors point out that even the authors who are generally supportive of the Court's opinion "question the quality of judicial reasoning in aspects of the advisory opinion and offer alternative explanations (of the law of self-defense and humanitarian law respectively) that are more precisely reasoned than those stated by the Court."[89] This is a disquieting observation because well-founded claims of low-quality legal crafts-manship can severely undermine a court's reputation.

Richard A. Falk, an eminent international law scholar, is the one contributor to the Agora who appears to have no reservations about the Court's advisory opinion.[90] Stressing the 14–1 vote of the Court, and the acknowledgment even by dissenting judge Thomas Buergenthal that "there is much in the Opinion with which I agree," Falk emphatically supports the Court's decision to reject Israel's challenge to jurisdiction and the finding of the Court that there was no reason for the Court to exercise its discretion to decline the General Assembly's request for an advisory opinion. He further is of the view that the advisory opinion will have the effect of enhancing the chances of reaching a peaceful settlement of the dispute between Israel and the Palestinians over the occupied territories. In sharp contrast, in the words of the editors, Michla Pomerance believes that "a Court bent on aggrandizing its own role beyond consensual jurisdiction jeopardizes its own authority, which poses a threat to the search for a peaceful settlement."[91] For my part, I suspect that the opinion will simply be ignored in the negotiations on this dispute and therefore will play no role whatsoever in any final settlement – hardly a happy prospect for those who believe in the importance of the rule of law in international affairs.

Most recently, on February 26, 2007, the Court handed down its decision in a contentious case, *Bosnia and Herzegovina v. Serbia and Montenegro*.[92] In that case, Bosnia and Herzegovina brought an action before the Court accusing Serbia and Montenegro of committing genocide in Bosnia during the time when Slobodan Milosevic was president of Serbia. After fourteen years of litigation the Court held that Serbia had violated its obligation to prevent the Srebrenica genocide and to cooperate with the International Criminal Tribunal for Yugoslavia (ICTY) in the prosecution of those responsible. But, to the surprise and disappointment of many, the Court did not find that genocide had been committed in the many other instances of mass killings and rapes across Bosnia, that the Serbian government had been directly complicit in any acts of genocide, or that Serbia was financially responsible for its failure to prevent the Srebrenica atrocities. A primary reason for the Court's declining to issue such findings, in the view of many, was its failure to engage in adequate fact finding. The result, according to Jose E. Alvarez, then president of the American Society of International Law, was that "[e]ven those who might be inclined to accept the central conclusions on the merits reached by the Court . . . are not likely to be persuaded by an opinion whose factual underpinnings are so weakly supported."[93]

Alvarez also sharply criticizes the Court's determination that Bosnia's burden of proof would be "beyond the reasonable doubt standard of criminal law" rather than the balance of probabilities approach normally followed in a civil case, as well as the Court's adherence to its "effective control" test for attribution from the *Nicaragua v. United States* case, rather than the "overall control" test adopted by the ICTY in its proceedings. In his view, "one is entitled to expect a practicable, and not an impossible, standard and burden of proof. Instead, the majority fails to explain why it is fair or just to require Bosnia to prove (1) that Serbia exercised effective control over the non-state actors engaged in the killings at Srebrenica and (2) that on the day those killings occurred Serbian officials shared the same genocidal intent as the killers – when such evidence would appear to be in the control of Serbia and the Court extracts only redacted government documents from that state."[94]

Ruth Wedgwood has suggested that the Court's judgment has broad and disturbing implications. Most significantly, she contends that the Court's judgment "amounts to a posthumous acquittal of Mr. Milosevic for genocide in Bosnia."[95] "Worse yet," she states, "by saying that only the Srebrenica massacre amounted to genocide, the International Court of Justice limits the charges that can be brought against the Bosnian Serb leaders Radovan Karadzic and Ratko Mladic, if Belgrade at last allows them to be arrested."[96] It should be noted that Radovan Karadzic has since been arrested and transferred to the ICTY for trial.

There have been other highly critical comments on the Court's decision.[97] Alvarez has predicted that it will be "seen as one of the Court's greatest self-inflicted wounds, especially by those who expected, after 14 years of litigation, a definitive statement on what occurred in Bosnia during Milosevic's rule."[98] The wounds may be especially deep when coupled with the Court's similar failure to engage in rigorous fact finding in the *Wall* advisory opinion.

To be sure, any fair-minded overall evaluation of the record of the International Court of Justice will determine that the Court has, in both its contentious cases and in its advisory opinions, made major contributions to the development of international law and the peaceful resolution of disputes between states. It is widely acknowledged, for example, that the Court has enjoyed considerable success in helping to settle traditional border and maritime jurisdiction disputes. Yet in the 1982 Law of the Sea Convention, the drafters of the convention decided to adopt highly complex provisions for the settlement of various disputes under the convention that, in effect, serve to minimize the role of the ICJ.[99] If recourse to such informal methods of dispute settlement as negotiation and consultation fails, parties may choose among several third-party tribunals. Under Article 287, their choices include the International Tribunal for the Law of the Sea (ITLOS), established by the convention; the International Court of Justice; an arbitral tribunal; or a special tribunal for specified categories of disputes. If the parties to a dispute have not accepted the same procedure for the settlement of the dispute, it shall be referred to arbitration, unless the parties otherwise agree. Similarly, if a state party to a dispute has not made a declaration as to its preferred type of tribunal, its default position is arbitration. Most state parties to the Law of the Sea Convention have chosen ITLOS or arbitration in preference to the ICJ.[100]

The dispute settlement provisions of the Law of the Sea Convention reflect the reality that states involved in international disputes today have an increasingly wide range of third-party dispute settlement choices. The divergent approaches to state responsibility for acts of genocide of the ICJ in the *Bosnia and Herzegovina v. Serbia and Montenegro* case and of the ICTY in its jurisprudence illustrate the concern of some that divergent interpretations of international law will threaten the coherence of international law. Most commentators on this issue, however, are of the view that "the variety of international tribunals functioning today do not appear to pose a threat to the coherence of an international legal system . . . "[101]

Nor is it likely that the ICJ is in danger of not having enough to do in light of the current fullness of its caseload. Nonetheless, the questionable legal craftsmanship and possible political bias demonstrated by the Court in such politically charged cases as *Nicaragua v. United States, Bosnia and Herzegovina v. Serbia and Montenegro*, and the *Wall* lend a measure of support to the proposition that the Court has become dysfunctional or, in the words of the Princeton national security project report, "broken."

INTERNATIONAL CRIMINAL TRIBUNALS AND HYBRID COURTS

International criminal tribunals and so-called hybrid courts, or mixed national–international tribunals, are a topic that forms a subset of the relatively recently created but fast developing field of international criminal law. Parenthetically, it should be noted that the very term "international criminal law" is one of considerable definitional ambiguity.[102] The eminent British international law scholar, Georg Schwarzenberger, writing in 1950, concluded that "international criminal law in any true sense does not exist."[103] Defining "international" narrowly to cover only rights and obligations of states and not those of individuals, Schwarzenberger was of the opinion that "an international criminal law that is meant to be applied to the world powers is a contradiction in terms. It presupposes an international authority which is superior to these states."[104]

Turning to piracy and war crimes, the examples most often "adduced as evidence *par excellence* of the existence of international criminal law,"[105] Schwarzenberger denied that these actions constitute crimes under international law. Rather, in his view:

> The rules of international law both on piracy *jure gentium* and war crimes constitute prescription to States to suppress piracy within their own jurisdiction and to exercise proper control over their own armed forces, and an authorization to other States to assume an extraordinary criminal jurisdiction under their own municipal law in the case of piracy *jure gentium* and of war crimes committed prior to capture by the enemy.[106]

Most other commentators have come to a different conclusion.[107] With respect to piracy the International Law Commission (ILC), a subsidiary organ of the United Nations General Assembly, in drafting the articles on piracy that ultimately helped constitute the 1958 Geneva Convention on the High Seas, adopted what Alfred Rubin has termed the "naturalist" model, that is, the view of "'piracy' as a crime against international law seeking only a tribunal with jurisdiction to apply that law and punish the criminal," as opposed to the "positivist" view of piracy "as solely a municipal law crime, the only question of international law being the extent of a state's jurisdiction to apply its criminal law to an accused foreigner acting outside the territorial jurisdiction of the prescribing state."[108] As to war crimes, the decision of the International Military Tribunal at Nuremberg and subsequent action by the U.N. General Assembly have arguably supported the "naturalist" view.

Volumes have been written about the Nuremberg Trials. One issue arising from the trials is the contribution, if any, they made to the development of international criminal law. For his part, Georg Schwarzenberger has contended that they made no contribution. In his view, although the Nuremberg Tribunal explicitly applied customary and treaty international law in the trial of the defendants, it was sitting as a *municipal* war crimes court rather than as an *international* tribunal, because "the signatories to the Charter of the Tribunal only did jointly what each of them, if in sole control of Germany, could have done alone. In the exercise of their *condominium* over Germany, the occupying powers were not limited to the application to Germany of the customary laws of warfare. In their capacity as co-sovereigns of Germany they were free to agree on any additional legal principles which they cared to apply."[109]

It is debatable whether the Nuremberg Tribunal is viewed accurately as a municipal or an international tribunal. Certainly, the Tribunal's judgment stated that the making of the Charter was the "exercise of the sovereign legislative power by the countries to which the German Reich unconditionally surrendered," and concluded that these countries had the "undoubted right" to legislate for occupied Germany.[110] On the other hand, the London Charter, which established the Tribunal, was an international agreement, and the Tribunal applied international law as the basis for its decision. Assuming *arguendo*, however, that the Tribunal is properly viewed as a municipal court, it does not follow that its decision made no contribution to the development of international criminal law, as Schwarzenberger posits.

On the contrary, the Tribunal's judgment may be viewed as a truly landmark step in the progressive development of international law. Albeit controversially, the Tribunal proclaimed the existence of two "new" crimes under international law – crimes against peace and crimes against humanity. With respect to the more traditional concept of war crimes, the Tribunal declared that it had evolved from its initial status as treaty law, binding only on state parties, to the status of customary international law binding on all nations. In 1947, moreover, the U.N. General Assembly adopted a resolution affirming "the principles of international law recognized by the Charter of the Nuremberg principles and the judgment of the Tribunal,"[111] thereby further supporting the proposition that proscription of the Nuremberg crimes has been recognized broadly as international customary law. The Nuremberg principles also endorsed the controversial propositions that individuals as well as states have obligations under international law and that the proscriptions of international law prevail over national laws that authorize or at least allow such acts.

The concept of crimes against humanity was affirmed further when the General Assembly adopted, on December 9, 1948, the Convention on the Prevention and Punishment of the Crime of Genocide.[112] The convention declares genocide, as defined therein, to be a crime under international law, and directs that persons charged with genocide shall be tried "by a competent tribunal of the State in the territory of which the act was committed, or by such international tribunal as may have jurisdiction."[113] Although the convention did not succeed in establishing an operative framework for the prosecution and punishment of those who have committed genocide, it is nevertheless widely regarded as a critical step in establishing genocide as a crime under international law and, as we shall see, its definition of genocide has been incorporated into the jurisdictional provisions of the statutes for the International Criminal Tribunal for the Former Yugoslavia, the International Criminal Tribunal for Rwanda, and the International Criminal Court.

Following the General Assembly's affirmation of the Nuremberg principles, the International Law Commission began work on a Draft Code of Offences Against the Peace and Security of Mankind as well as on a Draft Statute for an International Criminal Court. A Draft Statute for the latter was prepared in 1951, and a revised text in 1953. By 1954 a Draft Code of Offenses Against the Peace and Security of Mankind had been developed by the ILC. Both the Code and the Statute, however, were tabled pending definition of the crime of "aggression." In 1974 the General Assembly adopted a resolution defining the term "aggression," and in 1978 work began again on the Draft Code, despite the opposition of the United States, which opposed reconsideration of the Draft Code as a useless exercise, arguing that the likelihood of achieving consensus was small, a consolidated code would add nothing to existing conventions and declarations, and the General Assembly's 1974 definition of aggression was too imprecise to serve as the basis for a criminal indictment.[114] For a variety of reasons, however, work on the Draft Statute for an International Criminal Court was not resumed, and for many years the idea of an international criminal court was regarded as of academic interest only. After much controversy and delay, the International Law Commission, on July 5, 1996, adopted the final text of twenty draft articles constituting the Draft Code of Crimes Against the Peace and Security of Mankind. Although there initially was some support for the idea that the Draft Code might constitute the basis for the statute of an international criminal court, this idea was abandoned, and the Draft Code remained a nonbinding document and a substitute for a binding international convention on crimes against the peace and security of mankind – an example of so-called soft law.

The International Criminal Tribunal for the Former Yugoslavia

Early in the 1990s, various reports of atrocities in the former Yugoslavia gained the attention of the U.N. Security Council, which was seeking ways to respond to the violence there.[115]

Especially influential was a report by an independent commission of experts established by the Council that concluded that "ethnic cleansing" had been carried out in the former Yugoslavia "by means of murder, torture, arbitrary arrest and detention, extra-judicial executions, rape and sexual assault, confinement of civilian population in ghetto areas, forcible removal, displacement and deportation of civilian population, deliberate military attacks or threats of attacks on civilians and civilian areas, and wanton destruction of property."[116] As a result, on February 22, 1993, the Security Council adopted Resolution 808, whereby it decided that the widespread violation of the law of armed conflict and of international human rights in the former Yugoslavia constituted a threat to international peace and security and decided to establish an international tribunal for the former Yugoslavia.[117] Resolution 808 also requested the Secretary-General to submit to the Council a report "on all aspects of this matter, including specific proposals [regarding the creation of such a court]." The Secretary-General's report, submitted on May 3, 1993, discussed the legal basis for the establishment of the ICTY and included a draft statute for the ICTY with commentary.[118]

On May 25, 1993, the Security Council unanimously adopted Resolution 827, which established the ICTY and authorized it to prosecute "persons responsible for serious violations of international humanitarian law committed in the territory of the former Yugoslavia between 1 January 1991 and a date to be determined by the Security Council upon the restoration of peace." Utilizing its extraordinary powers under Chapter VII of the Charter, the Council commanded that "all States shall cooperate fully with the International Tribunal and its organs in accordance with the present resolution and the Statute of the International Tribunal." The seat of the ICTY is in The Hague, Netherlands.

Initially, the Tribunal had two trial chambers of three judges each and a single five-judge appellate chamber. But the limited number of trial chambers created significant delays in trying cases, and the number of judges was increased. The ICTY currently has a total of twenty-eight judges, including sixteen permanent judges supplemented by twelve "ad litem" judges designated to sit on a particular case.[119]

The ICTY got off to a rocky start. Despite having, at least in theory, the full enforcement powers of the Security Council behind it, the Tribunal found that some of the states of the former Yugoslavia refused to cooperate and surrender key suspects to it. According to Gabrielle Kirk McDonald, a former president of the Tribunal, as of spring 1998, "the Tribunal had issued some 205 arrest warrants and only six had been executed by the states."[120] This sorry record raised concerns that the Tribunal would not be able to function with any degree of effectiveness.

Fortunately, the record soon improved dramatically. In the words of the authors of a major U.S. international law coursebook:

> Beginning in late 1997, though, the tide began to turn. The Tribunal started to use sealed indictments, which diminished the chances that persons would go into hiding after being indicted, and the NATO-led military Stabilization Force (SFOR) in Bosnia began to arrest ICTY fugitives. The United States and other countries brought economic and diplomatic pressure to bear on the countries of the former Yugoslavia, and governments in those states that had been sympathetic to the regimes responsible for the atrocities began to give way to regimes interested in improving relations with Europe and the U.S. By the time of the ICTY's Fifth Annual Report to the General Assembly and Security Council in August 1998, the increase in activity at the Tribunal led it to declare that the year had been "characterized by the unprecedented growth and development of the institution, which has now, without any doubt, become a fully-fledged international criminal institution.". . . .[121]

In what appeared to be a major breakthrough, in 2001 Serbia turned over its former president, Slobodan Milosevic, to the ICTY, which had indicted him for a wide range of war crimes. His trial began in February 2002, but it did not turn out to be the Tribunal's finest hour. To the contrary, from the outset of the trial, it became clear that Milosevic's primary purpose was not to defend himself against the charges contained in the indictment, but rather to turn the proceedings into a diatribe against the Tribunal and into a political free-for-all that would play well in Serbia. As Mark A. Drumbl has noted, "[p]opular trials create a platform that places the defendant onto the world's center stage. If the defendant can make the trial all about himself, and selfishly control the stage through grandstanding, histrionics, and manipulation, then the proceedings drift away from the victims and their terrible losses."[122]

Indeed, Patricia M. Wald, who served as a judge on the ICTY from 1999–2001, has stated that "one of their [the ICTY and ICTR] greatest failures has been, despite a few attempts at outreach through judicial visits and TV coverage, an inability to reach the 'hearts and minds' of the populace who suffered as victims of the leaders and their subordinates who committed the war crimes. . . . Ironically, the most vivid impressions the Serbs have was gleaned from the notorious Milosevic trial which, until his recent death before the trial ended [in 2006], was beamed into most parts of Serbia and enjoyed high viewer ratings, which unfortunately ended up boosting Milosevic's standing to the point that he won a seat in Parliament."[123]

Because of the success of Milosovic's efforts in swaying Serbian public opinion to his side, some have doubted whether the final result in his trial, had it proceeded to a conclusion, would have been a conviction. If that would be the case, we may be grateful that fate interrupted the proceedings. At a minimum, Drumbl has suggested, "Milosevic's premature death is an obstacle to the ICTY's narration of an overarching story of death and destruction in the Balkans. The ICTY has mitigated the impact of this obstacle by indicting 161 individuals in total; and, quickly following Milosevic's death, by moving ahead with other high-profile trials, including regarding atrocity at Srebrenica and in Kosovo."[124] As of early 2009, the Tribunal had completed proceedings with regard to 116 of the indicted persons. Ten had been acquitted, 57 sentenced, and 13 had their cases transferred to local courts. Another 36 cases had been terminated. Proceedings remained ongoing with regard to 45 accused: 10 were at the appeals stage, 6 were awaiting the Trial Chamber's judgment, 21 were currently on trial, and 6 were at the pretrial stage.[125] Only two arrest warrants were pending against persons at large.[126] The most prominent of these two was Ratko Mladic, the general in charge of Bosnian Serb forces during the killings at Srebrenica in 1995. Radovan Karadzic, the former president of the self-proclaimed Bosnian Serb Republic, had been arrested in Belgrade in July 2008 and extradited to the Netherlands for trial before the ICTY.

Because many of the primary criticisms of the ICTY apply as well to the ICTR, we will wait until after there has been some discussion of the Rwanda Tribunal to address these.

The International Criminal Tribunal for Rwanda

Rwanda has an unhappy history of recurrent outbreaks of ethnic conflict between the Hutus, who have constituted approximately 85 percent of the population, and the Tutsis, less than 15 percent.[127] In April 1994, in response to the assassination of President Juvenal Habyarimana of Rwanda, Hutu extremist troops, militia, and mobs engaged in genocidal attacks against the Tutsi minority and Hutu moderates. Between April and July 1994, at least half a million and perhaps 800,000 or more Tutsis and moderate Hutus were killed. Unhappily, largely because of the unwillingness of the military powers, including the United States, to get involved, the United Nations took no action to prevent the slaughter. President Bill Clinton later apologized for U.S. inaction. After the fighting stopped, and because of charges of "Eurocentrism" from less developed countries, especially in Africa, there was increased pressure on the Security Council to set up an international criminal tribunal along the lines of the Yugoslav model. Accordingly, on November 8, 1994, the Security Council decided to set up an ad hoc tribunal similar to the ICTY to prosecute persons responsible for genocide and other serious violations of international humanitarian law in the territory of Rwanda during 1994.[128] Ironically, although the government of Rwanda had initially requested that an international criminal tribunal for Rwanda be created, it ultimately voted against the Security Council resolution establishing the Tribunal, in part because the statute annexed to the resolution did not authorize the death penalty to be imposed on those convicted of genocide by the Tribunal. As a result of this sentiment, Rwanda has instituted its own program of wholesale arrest and detention of genocide suspects.

The International Criminal Tribunal for Rwanda is closely modeled after the ICTY. There are, however, some salient differences. The conflict in Rwanda was essentially internal, whereas the conflict in the former Yugoslavia was in part international. As a result, the competence of the ICTR covers crimes commonly committed within a single territory, namely, genocide, crimes against humanity, and serious violations of common Article 3 of the Geneva Conventions of 1949 and Additional Protocol II of 1977, but not grave breaches of the Geneva Conventions or war crimes under the 1907 Hague Convention, because the latter apply only to international conflicts. Like the ICTY the ICTR has a presidency, a Registrar, and several trial chambers of three judges. But the ICTY and the ICTR share the same appeals chamber, where the ICTR has two judges, and initially both tribunals were served by a single prosecutor, though currently each has its own.

Like the ICTY, the ICTR had a rocky start. After the Security Council selected Arusha, Tanzania, as the site for the Tribunal in February 1995, the severe financial crisis of the United Nations delayed construction of the ICTR's facilities and the hiring of staff, including investigators and prosecutors. The Tribunal nonetheless did manage to hold its first sessions in Arusha and indicted eight persons on December 12, 1995. Charges of mismanagement and neglect of the Tribunal's operations then surfaced, and the Prosecutor and the Registrar resigned under pressure on February 25, 1997. Since the change of administration, the operations of the Tribunal have improved, and it has succeeded in bringing to trial major figures in the past Rwanda government. As of early 2009, the ICTY had arrested more than seventy individuals accused of involvement in the 1994 genocide in Rwanda. These persons included the former prime minister and several other members of the interim government of Rwanda during the genocide, as well as senior military leaders and high-ranking government officials. The Tribunal had completed trials of several of those arrested, including that of the former Prime Minister Jean Kambanda. Kambanda's trial was the first time that a Head of Government had been convicted for genocide.[129]

A common criticism leveled at both the ICTY and the ICTR is that their pro-ceedings have been exceedingly slow and laborious and that their cost has been excessively high. From their inception to early 2007, the total cost of operating the two tribunals has reportedly exceeded $ 2 billion, and the cumulative budgets of the ICTY alone have totaled more than $1.2 billion.[130] Both of the tribunals have responded to these criticisms by formulating plans according to which they will pros-ecute only "the highest-ranking political, military, paramilitary and civilian leaders" and will refer the cases of some indicted persons to national courts.[131] For its part, the Security Council has adopted a resolution that "calls on the ICTY and the ICTR to take all possible measures to complete investigations by the end of 2004, to complete all trial activities at first instance by the end of 2008, and to complete all work in 2010."[132] To this end, the ICTY has reportedly, as of March 2007, transferred twelve indictees to Bosnia, Croatia, and Serbia for trials before domestic courts. The ICTR has indicated it intends to transfer five of those currently in custody to national courts for trial, "although neither the defendants nor the states to which they will be transferred has been decided yet."[133] On July 7, 2009, however, the Security Council extended the mandate of the judges of the ICTY until December 2010 or until "the completion of the ongoing cases."[134] Similarly, on July 7, 2009, the Security Council gave the ICTR until the end of 2010 to finish the trials of suspects.[135]

Patricia M. Wald has suggested that we "will not see again any court modeled after the ICTY or the ICTR. They have proven too expensive, slow and bureaucratic; the U.N. will not take on such a burden again."[136] Instead, she believes that "the hybrid court is the likely wave of the future."[137]

Helena Cobban has recently made a frontal attack on the whole concept of inter-national courts.[138] Besides noting the usual problems of delay and expense, Cobban denies that the ICTY and ICTR have contributed to peace and reconciliation in the former Yugoslavia or Rwanda, citing surveys that report that few Serbs, Croats, Bosnians, or Rwandans believe that the tribunals have helped to achieve reconcili-ation in their countries; contends that war crimes tribunals and truth commissions do not always advance human rights, citing the case of Uganda, where the newly established International Criminal Court in October 2005 issued arrest warrants against five top leaders of the Lord's Resistance Army (LRA), a rebel group launch-ing an insurgency against the Ugandan government in the north of the country, with the result that the LRA stepped up attacks against civilians and aid workers; argues that victims of war crimes do not always demand prosecutions, often prefer-ring instead simply to bring the fighting to an end and to reintegrate wrongdoers into society; and claims that there is little proof or evidence that "giving amnesty to war criminals encourages impunity" or that "war crimes prosecutions deter future atrocities."[139]

Not surprisingly, Cobban's allegations stimulated a quick response from support-ers of international tribunals in the form of letters to the editor. David Scheffer, for example, formerly U.S. Ambassador at Large for War Issues during the Clinton administration and now Mayer, Brown, Rowe, & Maw/Robert A. Helman Professor of Law and Director, Center for International Human Rights, Northwestern University, suggested that Cobban had misstated the goals of international criminal tribunals. In his view, these tribunals are "convened to pursue justice and, over the long term, influence the attitudes of perpetrators and victims. No one ever assumed that they would have a significant short-term impact on warring parties."[140] As evidence to support this proposition, Scheffer pointed to the highly negative view of most German and Japanese citizens of the Nuremberg and Tokyo trials after 1945 but the great support for international criminal tribunals and human rights from subsequent generations in both countries.

For his part, Michael P. Scharf, Professor of Law at Case Western Reserve University and coauthor of leading treatises on the Yugoslav and Rwanda Tribunals, concedes that these tribunals are expensive but argues that they are "worth every penny." As evidence to support this argument, Scharf notes that the indictment of Slobodan Milosevic "led to his removal from power and surrender to the Hague, where he no longer posed a threat to the region. During the war crimes trials, the NATO peacekeeping force in Bosnia has been reduced from 60,000 to just 7,000, as peace has taken hold. And though Milosevic's popularity may have climbed in the early days of his trial, it ultimately plummeted."[141] Scharf further argues that the "former Serb leader's nationalist policies were thoroughly discredited when the prosecution presented a graphic video of the genocidal acts committed at Srebrenica – evidence that was subsequently broadcast countless times throughout Serbia and Bosnia." Although acknowledging that "[i]t is impossible to prove that war crimes prosecutions deter future atrocities," he contends that "evidence presented at the recent tribunals strongly suggests that the failure to prosecute perpetrators such as Pol Pot, Idi Amin, Saddam Hussein, Augusto Pinochet, and Papa Doc Duvalier convinced the Serbs and Hutus that they could commit genocide with impunity."[142]

Regardless of who has the better argument regarding the Yugoslav and Rwanda tribunals, it is clear that they will soon be history and that it is highly likely, as suggested by Patricia Wald, that "we will not see again any court modeled after the ICTY or the ICTR." Certainly, the recently established International Criminal Court follows a very different model.

The International Criminal Court

As we saw earlier, the United Nations produced a Draft Statute for an International Criminal Court in the early 1950s. However, it did not resume work on the Draft Statute when the International Law Commission again took up the Draft Code of Offences Against the Peace and Security of Mankind in 1982.

Instead, in 1992, the U.N. General Assembly requested the Commission to draft a statute for a permanent international criminal court. After much debate the Commission's efforts led to a conference held in Rome in 1998, which adopted the so-called Rome Statute of the International Criminal Court.[143] In sharp contrast to the tribunals for the former Yugoslavia and Rwanda, therefore, the International Criminal Court (ICC) was created not by the U.N. Security Council, but by an international treaty. Moreover, unlike the Yugoslav and Rwanda tribunals, the jurisdiction of the ICC is not geographically limited in scope but is global in its reach. The Rome Statute was adopted by a vote of 120 states in favor, 7 against (China, Iraq, Israel, Libya, Syria, Sudan, and the United States), and 21 abstentions. The treaty came into force in 2002, and the Court held its opening session in The Hague on March 11, 2003. As of July 23, 2009, 110 states have ratified the Rome Statute.[144]

Under Article 5 of the Rome Statute, the jurisdiction of the ICC is "limited to the most serious crimes of concern to the international community as a whole." These crimes include (1) the crime of genocide; (2) crimes against humanity; and (3) war crimes. In addition, the crime of aggression is within the Court's jurisdiction, but this jurisdiction will be exercised only if the state parties are able to agree on a definition of the crime and on the conditions that would have to be fulfilled before the ICC could exercise jurisdiction over it. Should such agreement be reached, it would then be necessary to adopt a provision on aggression under the articles on amendment of the Statute. The United States strongly opposed the inclusion of aggression as one of the crimes within the Court's jurisdiction.

As is well known, although the United States participated actively and constructively in the deliberations on the International Criminal Court, in the end, it voted against and strongly opposed adoption of the Rome Statute. It also has taken a number of extraordinary steps in an effort to ensure that no U.S. national, especially military personnel, will be subject to the Court's jurisdiction. These steps include, among others, threatening to veto U.N. peacekeeping operations unless the Security Council adopts a resolution granting Americans involved in peacekeeping operations immunity from the Court's jurisdiction, and pressuring countries to conclude bilateral so-called Article 98 agreements in which both parties agree not to surrender the other's nationals to the Court.

A discussion of the reasons advanced by the United States to support its opposition to the Court is beyond the scope of this chapter.[145] It is clear, however, that a major reason for the U.S. opposition is its concern that its military personnel and government officials will be subject to politically motivated prosecutions. Other commentators have argued that the protections against such prosecutions in the Rome Statute are adequate to ensure that it operates responsibly.[146] Another view that I share is that the substantial limitations on the Court's operations create a risk that it will be unable to perform its task of prosecuting and punishing the perpetrators of the atrocities within its jurisdiction.[147]

Besides the limited scope of its subject matter jurisdiction, the ICC has other significant limitations on its jurisdiction. It only has jurisdiction over crimes committed after the Rome Statute entered into force on July 1, 2002. Any crimes committed before that date are excluded from the scope of its jurisdiction. States that ratify or accede to the Rome Statute after July 1, 2002, are only exposed to the Court's jurisdiction after the date they became parties, unless they grant the Court jurisdiction retroactively to July 1, 2002 (Rome Statute, Article 11).

Under Articles 12–14 of the Rome Statute, "the I.C.C. may only investigate and prosecute acts when one of several situations arises: (1) the state where the alleged crime was committed is a party to the Rome Statute (including where the crime was committed on an aircraft or vessel of the state); (2) the person suspected of committing the crime is a national of a party to the Rome Statute; (3) the state where the alleged crime was committed, or whose national is suspected of committing the crime, consents *ad hoc* to the jurisdiction of the I.C.C.; or (4) the crime is referred to the I.C.C. by the Security Council under Chapter VII of the U.N. Charter."[148]

A major limitation on the Court's exercise of jurisdiction is the principle of "complementarity." Under this principle (Rome Statute, Articles 1 and 17) the Court is to rule a case inadmissible if there is a state with jurisdiction that is willing and genuinely able to carry out an investigation or prosecution. If a state has investigated a matter and decided that prosecution is not warranted, this does not provide the Court with a basis to exercise jurisdiction unless the national proceedings were clearly not carried out in good faith.

The prosecutor has the authority to initiate an investigation on the basis of a referral from any state party or from the Security Council, unless he determines that there is no reasonable basis to proceed under the Rome Statute (Article 53). He also can initiate investigations *proprio motu*, on his own authority, on the basis of information on crimes within the jurisdiction of the Court received from individuals or organizations, but he must first conclude that there is a reasonable basis to proceed (Article 15). During an investigation, each situation is assigned to a pretrial chamber. If the prosecutor requests, the pretrial chamber may issue a warrant of arrest or a summons to appear if there are reasonable grounds to believe a person has committed a crime within the jurisdiction of the Court. Once a wanted person has been surrendered to or voluntarily appears before the Court, the pretrial chamber holds a hearing to confirm the charges that will be the basis for the trial.

Once the charges are confirmed, the case is assigned to a trial chamber of three judges, which conducts the trial. Under the Rome Statute, the accused enjoys a number of rights, including the right to be present at trial and to be presumed innocent until proven guilty beyond a reasonable doubt. Upon conclusion of the trial, the trial chamber issues its decision, acquitting or convicting the accused by at least a majority vote (Article 74). If the accused is convicted, the trial chamber issues a sentence for a specified term of up to thirty years, or, in extreme cases, life in prison (Article 77). The trial chamber may also order reparations to victims (Article 75). Under Articles 81–83 of the Rome Statute, throughout the proceedings, either the accused or the prosecutor may appeal decisions of the chambers. All appeals are decided by the appeals chambers of five judges.

As of July 16, 2009, the ICC has indicted fourteen persons and has four persons in custody.[149] All of the situations leading to these indictments have been referred to the Court by state parties, with one major exception: the situation in Darfur. This situation was referred to the Court by the Security Council and has resulted in a major challenge to the Court.

On March 31, 2005, the Security Council adopted a resolution[150] whereby the Council referred the situation in Darfur, Sudan, to the Prosecutor of the International Criminal Court. The resolution was adopted by a vote of eleven in favor and four abstentions (Algeria, Brazil, China, and the United States). Although, as we have seen, the Bush administration was a strong opponent of the Court, it decided not to veto the resolution, perhaps in part because, as we shall see in greater detail in Chapter 3, other efforts to stop the slaughter in Darfur had proven fruitless.

After a lengthy investigation by the Prosecutor, on March 4, 2009, Pre-trial Chamber I of the ICC issued an arrest warrant for Omar Hassan Ahmad Al Bashir, the president of the Sudan.[151] The prosecutor had requested the issuance of an arrest warrant against Bashir for the commission of genocide, crimes against humanity, and war crimes. Pre-Trial Chamber I, however, decided to limit the arrest warrant to crimes against humanity and war crimes. Article 59 of the Rome Statute provides that all parties to the Statute "shall immediately take steps to arrest the person in question in accordance with [their] laws. . . . " Article 16 of the Rome Statute authorizes the Security Council to request by a resolution that an investigation or prosecution be delayed for a period of one year, in which case no investigation or prosecution may be commenced or proceeded for twelve months after the Council's request, and that request may be renewed by the Council under the same conditions. A number of states wished the Council to issue such a request, but the Obama administration, as well as the British and French representatives to the Council, made it clear that it would veto any such resolution.

The reaction of the Arab and African states to the arrest warrant, however, has been extremely hostile. When Arab leaders gathered for their annual summit in Doha, Qatar, on March 30, 2009, they greeted Mr. Bashir warmly, and the Secretary-General of the Arab League said that member states would "continue our efforts to halt the implementation of the warrant."[152] In their view, the Court's action revealed the West's double standard by indicting Mr. Bashir while taking no action against what they saw as war crimes committed by Israel during its offensive in Gaza. They also argued that the indictment and arrest warrant undermined efforts to bring about a negotiated settlement in Darfur by inflaming the situation. For their part, African leaders and the African Union have characterized the case against Bashir as "hypocritical."[153] They note that the Security Council, which referred the situation in Darfur to the Court, has three permanent members that never signed the Rome Statute: the United States, Russia, and China. Also, they point out that all of the situations taken up by the ICC have involved Africa, and they accuse the Court of bias.[154]

The unified opposition of African and Arab states to implementation of the arrest warrant against President Bashir constitutes a major crisis for the ICC, especially because so few African or Arab states are parties to the Rome Statute.[155] The Court's chief prosecutor, Luis Moreno-Ocampo, has said that the ICC would have far more power to arrest criminals and stop genocide if it had U.S. backing.[156] As indicated earlier, the Obama administration is more favorably disposed to the ICC than the Bush administration was, and President Obama was reportedly greatly disturbed by Mr. Bashir's decision to expel aid groups from the Sudan in response to the ICC's arrest warrant.[157] The effect of this expulsion is to eliminate a lifeline that was keeping more than a million people alive in Darfur.

The Obama administration reportedly is considering the possibility of the United States becoming a party to the Rome Statute. This would be a dramatic change indeed from the policy of the Bush administration and would take a step beyond the change in policy recommended by the Independent Task Force convened by the American Society of International Law.[158] Although the Task Force recommended that "the United States should announce a policy of positive engagement with the Court, and that this policy should be reflected in concrete support for the Court's efforts and the elimination of legal and other obstacles to such support," it did not "recommend U.S. ratification of the Rome Statute at this time."[159] But it urged "engagement with the ICC and the Assembly of States Parties in a manner that enables the United States to help further shape the Court into an effective accountability mechanism. The Task Force believes that such engagement will also facilitate further consideration of whether the United States should join the Court."[160]

It is highly likely that the Obama administration will decide to follow the policy recommendations of the Task Force. Even if in the unlikely event it decided that U.S. ratification of the Rome Statute would be desirable at this time, it would be a mission impossible. The Republican members of the Senate would be adamantly opposed, as would a large number of the Democratic members, and therefore the Senate would not give its advice and consent to ratification. Moreover, although space and time limitations preclude discussing these in this chapter, there are, as suggested by the Task Force, a number of legal and other obstacles to U.S. ratification that will need to be resolved before movement toward ratification may commence.

Might "concrete support for the Court's efforts" include helping to implement the arrest warrant against Bashir? Ideally it would, but in light of the strong opposition to the arrest warrant of the Arab and African states, U.S. involvement in apprehending Bashir could create major complications in U.S. relations with these states and undermine other important U.S. interests. In short, the obstacles to bringing Bashir to justice before the court are formidable.

The creation of an international criminal tribunal for the prosecution of war crimes, crimes against humanity, and genocide is justified only if national courts either have failed to do so or are deemed incapable of doing so. This has certainly been the case in most situations where these crimes have been committed. Under the doctrine of "complementarity," however, set forth in Article 17 (a) and (b) of the Rome Statute, the ICC is to determine that a case is inadmissible where "[t]he case is being investigated or prosecuted by a State which has jurisdiction over it, unless the State is unwilling or unable genuinely to carry out the investigation or prosecution" or "[t]he case has been investigated by a State which has jurisdiction over it and the State has decided not to prosecute the person concerned, unless the decision resulted from the unwillingness or inability of the State genuinely to prosecute." It is hoped that this doctrine might induce more states to undertake themselves the prosecution and punishment of these atrocities.

There already is some evidence that states may be more willing to pursue these atrocities through proceedings in national courts. Such proceedings may increasingly take place in hybird courts.

Hybrid Courts

Hybrid courts are a recent addition to the kinds of tribunals that may be available for the trial of alleged perpetrators of war crimes, crimes against humanity, and genocide. These courts are "hybrid" in the sense that they are composed of both national and international or foreign personnel. The archetype for hybrid courts is the tribunal set up, with U.N. backing, in Sierra Leone.[161] The backdrop to the hybrid court in Sierra Leone is a political situation rife with corruption and mismanagement that degenerated into an extraordinarily brutal civil war involving the cutting of limbs and other mutilations of women and children and the intervention of outside forces, especially from Liberia. After years of fighting, peace was finally imposed in Sierra Leone when, in May 2000, rebel forces took 500 U.N. peacekeepers hostage, prompting intervention by British soldiers. For its part, the U.N. Security Council adopted a resolution authorizing the Secretary-General to begin negotiations with the government of Sierra Leone toward the creation of a special court that would have subject matter jurisdiction over crimes against humanity, war crimes, and other serious violations of the law of armed conflict. A bilateral agreement between the United Nations and the government of Sierra Leone, as well as a statute for the special court, was signed in Freetown, the capital of Sierra Leone, on January 16, 2002.

Under the Court's statute, there is a three-judge trial chamber and a five-judge appellate chamber. The government of Sierra Leone appoints one judge to the trial chamber and the U.N. Secretary-General appoints two. The appellate chamber has two judges picked by the government of Sierra Leone and three selected by the Secretary-General. Further, after consultation with the government of Sierra Leone, the Secretary-General appoints the prosecutor. During the start-up period of the court, most of the key posts in the Office of the Prosecutor, including the

Prosecutor, were filled by Americans, which generated some criticism, but now many of these posts have been turned over to non-Americans.

Writing around 2004, Patricia M. Wald gave the Sierra Leone Court's performance up to that time a tentative positive evaluation:

> It is still too early to call the Sierra Leone court an unqualified success, but its record thus far is promising. It demonstrates that some lessons have been learned from earlier international courts, but it too has not been able to overcome entirely the persistent problems of volatile out-of-country financing or political controversy from indicting powerful people in high places. It also may suffer disappointments in leaving a legacy for national courts due to an almost complete absence of infrastructure – working organs of civil society – to take up the cause and continue the struggle for justice when the hybrid closes down. But an evaluation of its first years by the U.S. based International Center for Transitional Justice gives it high marks for efficiency and staff competency.[162]

Not too long after Wald gave her optimistic evaluation, however, the Sierra Leone Court faced a major new challenge.

Ironically, the troubles of the tribunal began with an event heralded as a milestone for justice in Africa: the arrest of Charles Taylor, the former president of Liberia, in March 2006 and the authorization by the U.N. Security Council, acting under Chapter VII of the U.N. Charter, of his transfer to The Hague for trial by a "special chamber" of the Sierra Leone hybrid court. His trial, the first war crimes trial of an African former president, was scheduled to start in April 2007.

After being postponed for four times in 2007, however, the trial was rescheduled to begin in 2008.[163] The latest postponement was the result of Taylor's dismissal of his court-appointed lawyer, Karim Khan. His new lawyer, Courtenay Griffiths, told the court that his team needed at least four months to study the 40,000 pages of evidence already before the court.. He also claimed that Taylor's personal archives, about 50,000 pages, had only just surfaced and needed to be examined.[164]

It appears that the delay was caused by a variety of factors. Those most often cited include undue haste on the part of the judges in trying to schedule the complex case, an inept and short-of-funds court administration, the move from the relatively inexpensive city of Freetown in Sierra Leone to the much costlier city of The Hague, in The Netherlands, and stalling tactics on the part of Taylor. Alleged stalling tactics on the part of Taylor included staying in his cell on the opening day of the trial, and firing Mr. Khan.

As previously noted, the hybrid court in Sierra Leone was touted as being cheaper, faster, and leaner than the ICTY or the ICTR. It also was praised for being closer to the location of the wars' victims. But in practice the Sierra Leone hybrid court has had considerable difficulties in fulfilling its mandate. Clearly, operating on two continents – in Europe for Taylor and Africa for its other cases – has greatly increased the expenses of the tribunal and contributed to the delay in its proceedings, but contrary to the reports cited by Patricia Wald, critics have claimed the court has been slow and inept from the start. According to *The New York Times*, "[i]ts orginal three-year mandate is expected to turn into eight years. The original budgeted cost of $54 million, based on voluntary contributions, has tripled and is growing." The budget crunch was reportedly so substantial that court officials had to divide their time between court proceedings and traveling to raise voluntary contributions from such states as the United States.[165] Antonio Cassese, an eminent international lawyer, has reportedly said that: "Because of numerous mistakes and cost-cutting, it [the Sierra Leone hybrid court] has become comparatively more expensive and slower than the other tribunals."[166]

The Sierra Leone Court did manage to resume proceedings in 2008, and the Prosecution formally rested its case against Charles Taylor on February 27, 2009, almost four months after it began.[167] Lawyers for Taylor began presenting their defense against war crimes and crimes against humanity on July 13, 2009. The indictment holds Taylor accountable for the barbaric methods employed by the rebels in Sierra Leone, which include pillaging, killing, raping, using drug-crazed children as soldiers, and hacking off limbs, ears, or noses to subdue civilians.[168]

Taylor's defense lawyers argue, however, that he did not exercise sufficient control over the rebel group to be held criminally liable for their actions. To prove that he did, the Prosecutor presented ninety-one witnesses, many making a 7,000-mile round trip to The Netherlands. Because the Prosecution does not have documents or orders signed by Taylor, it has had to rely on circumstantial evidence. Taylor is expected to take the stand, and his lawyers have said his testimony is expected to go on for weeks.[169]

Besides Sierra Leone, hybrid courts also have been established in East Timor, Kosovo, Cambodia, and Lebanon. Because of space and time limitations, we shall briefly consider only the situations in Cambodia and Lebanon.

After long and torturous negotiations that at one point broke down entirely, the United Nations and Cambodia concluded a framework agreement on June 6, 2003, to establish a hybrid court to prosecute members of the Khmer Rouge, the Marxist insurrectionists who ruled Cambodia from 1975 until 1978, for crimes committed while they were in power.[170] These crimes included massive killings, estimated to be between 1.5 and 2 million people out of a population of perhaps 7 million.

Under the framework agreement,[171] the hybrid court, or "Extraordinary Chambers," as they are referred to in the agreement, consists of Cambodian and "international" judges, the latter being nominated by the U.N. Secretary-General. Cambodian judges constitute a majority of both the trial and appellate chambers, but at least one of the international judges must join in any decision. There are coinvestigating judges and coprosecutors, one Cambodian and one international. The tribunal has jurisdiction over genocide (as defined in the Genocide Convention), crimes against humanity (as defined in the ICC Statute), grave breaches of the 1949

Geneva Conventions, and other crimes as defined in the 2001 Cambodian law that created the Chambers. The tribunal is directed to prosecute only Khmer Rouge "senior leaders" and "those most responsible" for atrocities committed during Pol Pot's reign.

It took until May 2005 for the United Nations to raise sufficient financial pledges from states for the tribunal to begin its work. Even then, however, a sharp disagreement between Cambodian and foreign judges over the rules of evidence and procedure prevented trials from going forward.[172] As a result, there were serious doubts that the tribunal would ever hold trials of even the few leaders of the Khmer Rouge still alive.[173] Finally, the tribunal began its first proceedings against five former leaders of the Khmer Rouge in late 2007.[174] The first person to stand trial is Kaing Geuk, 65, also known as Dutch, a former high school math teacher who was director of the notorious 5–21 prison where more than 14,000 of the Khmer Rouge's victims died. The youngest of the detainees, Dutch has admitted his guilt but says he was only following orders. It is worth noting that some of the victims of Khmer Rouge brutality feel that the trials have come too late and that Cambodia and the United Nations should instead spend their energy and time in efforts to improve the lives of young Cambodians. In their view, "placing elderly Khmer Rouge leaders on trial will not bring back those who lost their lives in the Killing Fields, or bring peace to the survivors. It will only stir more anger and misery and hate. Pol Pot, the chief criminal, is long dead. So are many of the others who killed and tortured at his command."[175]

The backdrop to the efforts to establish a hybrid court for Lebanon is the 2005 assassination of former Prime Minister Rafik Hariri. Mr. Hariri's death set off nationwide protests that forced Syrian President Bashar Assad to withdraw all Syrian troops from Lebanon after nearly thirty years of a substantial presence there. U.N. investigators have implicated elements of Syria's intelligence community services in the car bombing that killed Mr. Hariri and twenty-two others. Syria has subsequently been charged with involvement in a string of other political assassinations and bombings in Lebanon.

On November 25, 2006, Lebanon's Cabinet, despite opposition from Hezbollah, approved a U.N. plan to establish an international tribunal to try suspects in the assassination of Hariri. On November 13, 2006, the Lebanese Cabinet had unanimously approved an earlier U.N. plan to create an international tribunal.[176]

In the wake of the November 13 vote, members of Hezbollah and their allies quit the government, calling for demonstrations and civil unrest as acts of protest. Prior to the vote, President Emile Lahoud protested and a sixth Cabinet member quit. The eighteen ministers approving the tribunal did not include any members of the Shiite Muslim sect, in all probability the majority group in Lebanon. Hezbollah and its Christian allies called the vote unconstitutional, and General Michel Aoun, head of a powerful Christian party and a political ally of Hezbollah, said the government had lost its legitimacy.

Parliamentary speaker Nabih Berri, a close ally of Hezbollah, subsequently refused to convene the Parliament to hold a vote on the U.N. plan for an international tribunal, citing the lack of Shiite ministers in the Cabinet.[177] In response, Prime Minister Fuad Siniora requested the U.N. Security Council to circumvent Lebanon's Parliament by passing a resolution under Chapter VII of the U.N. Charter, which would permit the hybrid tribunal to be established independently.

On May 30, 2007, acting under Chapter VII of the Charter, a sharply divided Security Council adopted a resolution[178] that calls for the establishment of a "Special Tribunal" to prosecute suspects in the assassination of former Lebanese Prime Minister Rafik Hariri. The vote on the resolution was ten in favor and five abstentions (Russia, China, South Africa, Indonesia, and Qatar).

Attached to the resolution as an annex is the November 25, 2006, Agreement Between the United Nations and the Lebanese Republic on the Establishment of a Special Tribunal for Lebanon (the Agreement), along with the attached Statute of the Special Tribunal for Lebanon. Pursuant to the terms of the resolution, the Agreement and the Statute entered into force on June 10, 2007.

The Special Tribunal has its seat in The Netherlands. The Special Tribunal has jurisdiction over persons alleged to be responsible for the February 14, 2005, attack resulting in the murder of former Prime Minister Hariri, as well as over persons alleged to have engaged in other attacks that occurred in Lebanon between October 1, 2004, and December 12, 2005, and were found by the judges to be connected with Mr. Hariri's assassination. Any political killings taking place after December 2005 could also fall within the Special Tribunal's jurisdiction, but only with the consent of the Security Council. The Special Tribunal shall apply, among others, the provisions of the Lebanese Criminal Code relating to the prosecution and punishment of acts of terrorism and crimes and offenses against life and personal integrity. In other words, the Special Tribunal will apply the criminal law of Lebanon rather than international law.

The Special Tribunal consists of four organs: the Chamber, the Prosecutor, the Registry, and the Defense Office. The Chambers will include an international Pre-Trial Judge, a three-judge Trial Chamber (one Lebanese judge and two international judges), and a five-judge Appeals Chamber (two Lebanese and three international judges). A second Trial Chamber may be created if after at least six months from the commencement of the functioning of the Special Tribunal, the Secretary-General or the President of the Special Tribunal so requests. The Pre-Trial Judge will review and confirm indictments and may also issue warrants, transfer requests, and any other orders required for the conduct of the investigation and for the preparation of the trials. The Defense Office will be responsible for protecting the rights of the defense, drawing up the list of possible defense counsel, and providing support and assistance to defense counsel and persons entitled to legal assistance.

The four Lebanese judges will be appointed by the Secretary-General, from a list of twelve nominees presented by the Lebanese government. The seven international judges will be appointed by the Secretary-General from nominations received by member states of the United Nations, or other competent persons. All judges will serve three years. An international Prosecutor will be appointed by the Secretary-General in consultation with the Lebanese government. The Prosecutor will serve for three years. A Lebanese Deputy Prosecutor, who will assist the Prosecutor, will be appointed by the Lebanese government in consultation with the Secretary-General and the Prosecutor. The Secretary-General will appoint the judges and the Prosecutor upon the recommendation of a selection panel, made up of two judges currently sitting on or retired from an international tribunal, and a representative of the Secretary-General.

As to funding, 51 percent of the costs of the Special Tribunal will be borne by voluntary contributions from states, and the Lebanese government will finance 49 percent of the costs. The Special Tribunal will be established once sufficient contributions to finance its establishment and activities for one year, as well as pledges equivalent to anticipated expenses for the following two years, have been received.

The Special Tribunal has the authority to impose penalties leading up to and including life. There is no death penalty. Sentences will be served in a state designated by the President of the Tribunal from a list of states that have expressed their willingness to receive convicted persons.

The Special Tribunal opened for business on March 1, 2009. It is the first international criminal tribunal with a subject matter jurisdiction based exclusively on national rather than international law. It is also the first international criminal tribunal that has jurisdiction to try a crime described as "terrorist" by the United Nations.

It remains to be seen whether the Special Tribunal will be successful in bringing the killers of Rafiq Hariri and other political figures in Lebanon to justice. The Special Tribunal is estimated to cost $35 million to run in its first twelve months, $45 million in its second year, and $40 million in its third year. If the experiences of Yugoslavia and Rwanda and of Sierra Leone are any guide, these estimates are likely to be too low, and the 51 percent funding from the international community, much less the 49 percent from the Lebanon government, may not be forthcoming. The use of Chapter VII powers by the Security Council to establish a hybrid court in the unstable Middle East is a bold but risky endeavor. Its success or failure, as well as that of the Cambodian hybrid court, may well determine whether, as suggested by Patricia Wald, hybrid courts are indeed to be the "wave of the future."

It well may be that the "wave of the future" will be trial of these atrocities in national courts or perhaps in what Michael Scharf has termed "internationalized domestic tribunals."[79] According to Scharf, the Iraqi High Tribunal (IHT) that tried and convicted Saddam Hussein "merits characterization as an internationalized domestic tribunal because its statute and rules of procedure are modeled on the U.N. war crimes tribunals for the former Yugoslavia, Rwanda, and Sierra Leone, and its statute provided that the IHT is to be guided by the precedent of the U.N. Tribunals and that its judges and prosecutors are to be assisted by international experts." At the same time, he points out that the IHT is not an international tribunal "or even international enough to be dubbed a hybrid court, because it is seated in Baghdad, its prosecutor is Iraqi, it uses the Iraqi Criminal Code to supplement the provisions of its statute and rules, and its bench is composed exclusively of Iraqi judges."[180]

To be sure, the IHT has not been a "model" internationalized domestic tribunal. On the contrary, it was "snake-bitten from its conception."[181] But operating under extremely difficult conditions, it has had its successes as well as its failures, and because there are still defendants to be tried by the IHT, it may be that lessons learned from the Saddam trial may help to improve the future proceedings of the IHT.[182] Moreover, as Scharf suggests, internationalized domestic tribunals may serve as "a potentially vital supplement to the International Criminal Court, which lacks the resources and personnel to prosecute all but a tiny portion of cases in situations where the domestic system is unable or unwilling to do so. As one of the first internationalized domestic tribunals, the perceived success or failure of the IHT is likely to have an affect (sic) on the future use of that model of international justice."[183]

It also may be that trials of these atrocities in purely domestic courts will be the wave of the future. If the "complementarity" procedures of the International Criminal Court work effectively, national judiciaries may decide in numerous cases to undertake the trial themselves rather than surrender an accused to the ICC.

Aside from the International Criminal Court there are indications that states are increasingly seeking, through extradition requests or other methods of rendition, to gain custody for trial of individuals accused of committing atrocities within their territory. For example, Chile has extradited Alberto Fujimori, the former president of Peru, to Peru to face human rights and corruption charges, and two Argentine judges reportedly want Spain to send Isabel Peron, the country's former president, to Argentina to face war crimes charges. And Hissene Habre, the former president of Chad, after living in exile in Senegal for seventeen years, is now facing trial before a war crimes court set up by the Senegalese government on the orders of the African Union. Reportedly, it was "only after Belgium had threatened to try Mr. Habre under its 'universal jurisdiction' law that African leaders decided to abandon their tradition of mutual protection and vote for his prosecution by one of their own."[184]

Notes

1. For an evaluation of the many criticisms of the major economic international institutions, see JOHN W. HEAD, the FUTURE of the GLOBAL ECONOMIC ORGANIZATIONS: AN EVALUATION of CRITICISMS LEVELED at the IMF, THE MULTILATERAL DEVELOPMENT BANKS, and the WTO (2005).

2. See, e.g., United States General Accounting Office, UNITED NATIONS: *Reforms Progressing, but Comprehensive Assessments Needed to Measure Impact* (Feb. 2004).

3. *Note by the Secretary-General*, U.N. General Assembly, 59th Sess., Agenda Item 55, at 1, U.N. Doc. A/59/565 (2004).

4. *Id.*

5. The High-level Panel consisted of Anand Panyarachun, former Prime Minister of Thailand, chair, Robert Badinter (France), Joao Baena Soares (Brazil), Gro Harlem Brundtland (Norway), Mary Chinery Hesse (Ghana), Gareth Evans (Australia), David Hannay (United Kingdom of Great Britian and Northern Ireland), Enrique Iglesias (Uruguay), Amre Moussa (Egypt), Satish Nambiar (India), Sadako Ogata (Japan), Yevgeny Primakov (Russian Federation), Qian Qiqian (China), Salim Salim (United Republic of Tanzania), Nafis Sadik (Pakistan), and Brent Scowcroft (United States).

6. See *A more secure world: our shared responsibility*, Report of the High-level Panel on Threats, Challenges and Change, to the Secretary-General (Dec. 1, 2004), in *Note by the Secretary-General*, *supra* note 3, at 6.

7. *In larger freedom: towards development, security and human rights for all*: Report of the Secretary-General, U.N. GAOR, 59th Sess. Agenda Items 45 and 55, U.N. Doc.A/59/2005 (2005).

8. G.A. Res. 60/1 U.N. GAOR, 60th Sess., U.N. Doc. A/RES/60/1 (2005).

9. For a helpful oversight of many of these proposals, see Frederic L. Kirgis, *International Law Aspects of the 2005 World Summit Outcome*, ASIL INSIGHT, Oct. 4, 2005, http://www.asil.org/insights/2005/10/insights051004.html. For a recent, and thoughtful, review of the U.N. record in its primary endeavors, see PAUL KENNEDY, THE PARLIAMENT of MAN: THE PAST, PRESENT, and FUTURE of the UNITED NATIONS (2006).

10. Economic and Social Council Res. 5 (Feb. 16, 1946).

11. For a diagram of this elaborate system (as of 2006) *see* RICHARD B. LILLICH et al., INTERNATIONAL HUMAN RIGHTS 565 (4th ed. 2006).

12. See *A more secure world: our shared responsibility*, *supra* note 6, para. 283, at 74.

13. *Id.* at para 285.

14. See *In larger freedom: towards development, security and human rights for all*, *supra* note 7, para 183, at 45.

15. *Id.* at 45–46.

16. *See, e.g.*, Human Rights Watch, *Human Rights Council: New Approaches to Addressing Human Rights Situations*, Sept. 15, 2006, http//hrw.org/english/docs/2006/09/15/global14209/htm.

17. *See* Lawrence G. Albrecht et al., *The U.N. Human Rights Council*, 41 INT'L LAW. 643, 644 (2007).

18. *See* Warren Hoge, *New U.N. Rights Group Includes Six Nations with Poor Records*, N.Y. TIMES, May 10, 2006, at A12, col. 5.

19. G.A. Res. A/RES.60/251 (Apr. 3, 2006), at pmbl.

20. *Id.* at para. 8.

21. *See* Human Rights Council, *First Sess. of the Human Rights Council, 19–30 June 2006: Human Rights Council Concludes First Sess.*, June 30, 2006, http:www.ohchr.org/english/bodies/hrcouncil/1 session.

22. *See* Warren Hoge, *supra* note 18.

23. As of the end of its fourth regular session on March 30, 2007, the Council reportedly had taken no steps to this end and was criticized by Louise Arbour, the U.N. High Commissioner for Human Rights, for this failure. The Council then gave itself a year to establish procedures for such a review. *See* THE ECONOMIST, April 7, 2007, at 58, 59.

24. The vote on G.A. Resolution 60./251 was 170 to 4 (United States, Israel, Palau, and Marshall Islands). At the time, John Bolton, then the U.S. Permanent Representative to

the United Nations, reportedly stated, by way of explanation of the vote, that "We want a butterfly. We don't intend to put lipstick on a caterpillar and call it a success." *Id.* at 58.

25. *See* Lawrence G. Albrecht et al., *supra* note 17, at 645.

26. The first regular session of the Council was held from June 19–30, 2006, and the second from September 18 to October 6, 2006. The first special session met from July 5–6, 2006, at the request of Tunisia, on behalf of the Group of Arab States "to consider the latest escalation of the situation in the Palestinian and other occupied Arab territories." The second was on August 11, 2006, again at the request of Tunisia, on behalf of the Group of Arab States and the Organization of the Islamic Conference, "to consider and take action on the gross human rights violations by Israel in Lebanon, including the Qana massacre, country-wide targeting of innocent civilians, and destruction of vital civilian infrastructure." The third special session took place on November 15, 2006, at the request of Bahrain on behalf of the Group of Arab States and of Pakistan on behalf of the Organization of the Islamic Conference to consider the "gross human rights violations emanating from Israeli military incursions in the Occupied Palestinian Territory including the recent one in Northern Gaza and the assault on Beit Hanoun." *See* Patrizia Scannella and Peter Splinter, *The Human Rights Council: A Promise to be Fulfilled*, 7 HUM. RTS. L. REV. 41, 51 (2007).

27. *Id.* at 55–61.

28. *Id.* at 61.

29. *Id.* at 61–62.

30. *Id.* at 70.

31. Human Rights Council Res. 4/9 Para 10, in Report to the General Assembly on the Fourth Session of the Human Rights Council, A/HRC/4/123, June 12, 2007, at 19,21.

32. THE ECONOMIST, *supra* note 23, at 59.

33. *Id.*

34. *See* Report to the General Assembly on the Fifth Session of the Council, A/HRC/5/21, Aug. 7, 2007, at 40.

35. *See* Patrizia Scannella and Peter Splinter, *supra* note 26, at 59.

36. U.S. Dep't of State Daily Press Briefing (Mar. 6, 2007), at http://www.state.gov/t/pa/prs/dph/2007/mr.81471.htm. For highlighting of these remarks, *see* John R. Crook, *Contemporary Practice of the United States*, 101 AM. J. INT'L L. 484, 485 (2007).

37. *See* House Committee on Foreign Affairs Press Release, Lantos Blasts Administration Decision Not to Take Part in United Nations Human Rights Council (Mar. 6, 2007), at http://www.internationalrelations. House.gov/press__display.asp?id=313. John R. Crook, *supra* note 36, at 485.

38. The primary example would be the annual extensive country reports produced by the U.S. Department of State pursuant to congressional mandate. Some NGOs also produce reports on the human rights situations in various countries. For discussion, *see, e.g.,* LILLICH et al., *supra* note 11, at 1115–22.

39. Patrizia Scannella and Peter Splinter, *supra* note 26, at 64.

40. GA Res. 60/251 (March 15, 2006). Operative paragraph 5 (e) of the resolution provides that the Council shall "Undertake a universal periodic review, based on objective and reliable information, of the fulfillment by each State of its human rights obligations and commitments in a manner which ensures universality of coverage and equal treatment with respect to all States; the review shall be a cooperative mechanism, based on an interactive dialogue, with the full involvement of the country concerned and with consideration given to its capacity-building needs; such a mechanism shall complement and not duplicate the work of treaty bodies; the Council shall develop the modalities and

necessary time allocation for the universal periodic review mechanism within one year after the holding of its first session."

41. *See* Human Rights Council, 5/1 Institution-building of the United Nations Human Rights Council, 9th meeting, 18 June 2007.
42. *See* Factsheet: Work and Structure of the Human Rights Council, July 2007.
43. *See* Lauren Vriens, *Troubles Plague UN Human Rights Council,* Council on Foreign Relations, July 16, 2009.
44. *See* Human Rights Council, Universal Periodic Review, Report of the Working Group on the Universal Periodic Review China, A/HRC/11/25, 3 March 2009.
45. *Id.*, para 27, at 6–7.
46. *Id.*, para 113, at 27.
47. *Id.*, para 34, at 9.
48. *Id.*, para 114, at 27–31.
49. *Id.* at 27.
50. *Id.*, para 115, at 31.
51. *Id.*, para 116, at 31.
52. *Id.*, para 117, at 31.
53. *See* Human Rights Watch, *China: Government Rebuffs UN Human Rights Council,* June 11, 2009, at http://www.hrw.org.
54. *See, e.g., id.*; Human Rights Watch, *Human Rights Watch Statement on UPR Report of China,* June 11, 2009, at http://www.hrw.org; and Amnesty International Public Statement, *China Undermines Universal Periodic Review,* June 11, 2009, at www.amnesty.org.
55. *See* Human Rights Watch, *supra* note 53.
56. Amnesty International Public Statement, *supra* note 54.
57. *See* DAVID J. BEDERMAN, INTERNATIONAL LAW FRAMEWORKS 239 (2001).
58. *See* BARRY E. CARTER, PHILLIP R. TRIMBLE, and ALLEN S. WEINER, INTERNATIONAL LAW 298 (5th ed. 2007).
59. This summary is taken in part from JOHN F. MURPHY, THE UNITED STATES and the RULE of LAW in INTERNATIONAL AFFAIRS 250–52 (2004).
60. *See id.*, at 251.
61. Schwebel, Dissenting Opinion, paras 117–29, [1984] ICJ Rep. at 628–37. For further discussion, see JOHN F. MURPHY, *supra* note 59, at 258.
62. Oil Platforms (Islamic Republic of Iran v. United States of America) 1996 ICJ 803 (Preliminary Objections Judgment of Dec. 12, 1996).
63. According to an e-mail communication from Duncan Hollis, an Associate Professor of Law at Temple University and previously an attorney/adviser in the treaty section of the Office of the Legal Adviser, U.S. Department of State.
64. OSCAR SCHACHTER, INTERNATIONAL LAW in THEORY and PRACTICE 218 (1991).
65. Case Concerning Military and Paramilitary Activities in and against Nicaragua (Nicaragua v. United States) (Jurisdiction), [1984] ICJ Rep. 392.
66. For an extensive defense of these actions and the need for them, *see* J.N. MOORE, the SECRET WAR in CENTRAL AMERICA (1987).
67. For an extensive discussion of the Court's decisions, and their aftermath, *see* JOHN F. MURPHY, *supra* note 59, at 255–66 and authorities cited therein.
68. Case Concerning United States Diplomatic and Consular Staff in Tehran (United States of America v. Iran), Judgment of May 24, 1980, [1980] ICJ Rep. 3.
69. Legal Consequences of the Construction of a Wall in the Occupied Palestinian Territory, Advisory Opinion, 2004 ICJ 136 (July 9).

70. *See Agora: ICJ Advisory Opinion on Construction of a Wall in the Occupied Palestinian Territory*, 99 Am. J. Int'l L. 1–141 (2005).

71. Michla Pomerance, *The ICJ's Advisory Jurisdiction and the Crumbling Wall Between the Political and the Judicial*, 99 Am. J. Int'l L. 26, 29 (2005).

72. Status of Eastern Carelia, 1923 PCIJ (ser. B) No. 5 (July 23).

73. *See* Michla Pomerance, *supra* note 71, at 27–28.

74. *Id.* at 28.

75. *Id.* at 31, n. 31.

76. *Id.* at 31.

77. Legal Consequences of the Construction of a Wall in the Occupied Palestinian Territories, Advisory Opinion, para 139 (Int'l Ct. Justice July 9, 2004).

78. Sean Murphy, *Self-Defense and the Israeli Wall Advisory Opinion: An Ipse Dixit From the ICJ?*, 99 Am J. Int'l L. 63 (2005).

79. John Lawrence Hargrove, *The Nicaragua Judgment and the Future of the Law of Force and Self-Defense*, 81 Am. J. Int'l L. 135, 139 (1987).

80. *See* Legal Consequences of the Construction of a Wall in the Occupied Palestinian Territories, *supra* note 77, at para 139.

81. David Kretzmer, *The Advisory Opinion: The Light Treatment of International Humanitarian Law*, 99 Am. J. Int'l L. 88, 100–101, n. 101 (2005).

82. Israeli Law authorizes the Supreme Court to sit as a High Court of Justice in the first instance on certain questions of administrative and constitutional law. BASIC LAW: Judiciary section 15 (c), (d) (Isr).

83. HCJ 2056/04, Beit Sourik Village Council v. Israel (June 30, 2004), 43 Int'l Leg. Mat. 1099 (2004)

84. HCJ 8414/05, Ahmed Issa Abdallah Yassin, Head of Bill'in Village Council v. Government of Israel et al. (September 4, 2007).

85. Geoffrey R. Watson, *The "Wall" Decisions in Legal and Political Context*, 99 Am. J. Int'l L. 6, 21–25 (2005).

86. *Id.* at 22.

87. *Id.* at 24–25.

88. *See* Lori Fisler Damrosch and Bernard H. Oxman, *Editors' Introduction*, 99 Am J. Int'l L. 1 (2005).

89. *Id.* at 6.

90. Richard A. Falk, *Towards Authoritativeness: The ICJ Ruling on Israel's Security Wall*, 99 Am. J. Int'l L. 42 (2005).

91. Lori Fisler Damrosch and Bernard H. Oxman, *supra* note 88, at 6.

92. Application of the Convention on the Prevention and Punishment of the Crime of Genocide (Bosnia and Herzegovina v. Serbia and Montenegro), Judgment, 2007 I.C.J. General List No. 91 (Feb. 26).

93. *See* Jose E. Alvarez, *Burdens of Proof*, ASIL Newsletter, vol. 23, issue 2, Spring 2007, at 1.

94. *Id.* at 7. Alvarez cites the dissenting opinion of Judge Al-Khasawneh, who notes that, in comparable circumstances, other adjudicators have shifted the burden of proof or drawn adverse inferences against the party in control of relevant evidence who refuses to supply it, *e.g.*, the ICJ itself in the Corfu Channel case. *See* Dissenting Opinion, Vice-President Al-Khasawneh, para 35.

95. Ruth Wedgwood, *Slobodan Milosevic's Last Waltz*, N.Y. Times, Mar. 12, 2007, at A23, col.1.

96. *Id.*
97. *See, e.g.,* the various views reported in Marlise Simons, *Genocide Court Ruled for Serbia Without Seeing Full War Archive,* N.Y. TIMES, Apr. 19, 2007, at Al, col. 1; and in *Council Comment: The International Court of Justice's Decision in Bosnia and Herzegovina v. Serbia and Montenegro,* ASIL NEWSLETTER, vol. 23, Issue 2, Spring 2007, at 8–9.
98. Jose E. Alvarez, *supra* note 93, at 1.
99. For a brief summary of these provisions, *see* JOHN F. MURPHY, *supra* note 59, at 230–40.
100. *See* Helmut Tuerk, *The Contribution of the International Tribunal for the Law of the Sea to International Law,* 26 PENN ST. INT'L L. REV. 289 (2007).
101. *See* Jonathan I. Charney, *The Impact on the International Legal System of the Growth of International Courts and Tribunals,* 31 N.Y.U. J. INT'L L. & POL. 697, 704 (1999).
102. Much of the following discussion of the backdrop to the Nuremberg Trials is taken from John F. Murphy, *International Crimes, in* 2 UNITED NATIONS LEGAL ORDER 993 (Oscar Schachter & Christopher C. Joyner eds., 1995).
103. Georg Schwarzenberger, *The Problem of an International Criminal Law,* 3 CURRENT LEGAL PROB. 263, 295 (1950).
104. *Id.*
105. *Id.* at 268.
106. *Id.* at 270.
107. *See, e.g.,* Gerhard Mueller and Douglas J. Besharov, *Evolution and Enforcement of International Criminal Law, in* 1 INTERNATIONAL CRIMINAL LAW 59 (M.C. Bassiouni ed., 1986).
108. ALFRED P. RUBIN, THE LAW OF PIRACY 328 (1988).
109. Schwarzenberger, *supra* note 103, at 290–91.
110. The text of the judgment of the International Military Tribunal may be conveniently found in 6 FRD 69, 107 (1946).
111. GA RES. 95 (I), UN Doc. A/64/Add. 1, at 188 (1947).
112. Convention on the Prevention and Punishment of the Crime of Genocide, GA Res. 260A (III), UN GAOR 3d Sess. (L), at 174, U.N. Doc. A/810(1948).
113. *Id.,* art. VI.
114. *See* LORI F. DAMROSCH et al., INTERNATIONAL LAW 410 (2001), citing Reply of the United States, U.N. Doc. A35.210/Add. 1 at 11 (1980), and U.N. Doc. A/C.6/35/ SR. 12 at 9 (1980).
115. Much of this section on the ICTY and the next on the ICTR is taken from JOHN F. MURPHY, *supra* note 59, at 312–16.
116. U.N. Doc.S/252704 at 16, para 56 (1993).
117. SC Res. 808 (Feb. 22, 1993).
118. Report of Secretary-General Pursuant to Paragraph 2 of Security Council Resolution 808 (1993), U.N. Doc. S/25704, Corr. 1 and Add. 1 (1993).
119. *See* BARRY CARTER, PHILLIP R. TRIMBLE, and ALLEN S. WEINER, INTERNATIONAL LAW 1186 (5th ed. 2007).
120. Gabrielle Kirk McDonald, *Problems, Obstacles, and Achievements of the ICTY,* 2 J. INT'L CRIM. JUST. 558, 563 (2004).
121. BARRY CARTER et al., *supra* note 119, at 1186.
122. MARK A. DRUMBL, ATROCITY, PUNISHMENT, and INTERNATIONAL LAW 178 (2007).
123. Patricia M. Wald, *International Criminal Courts–A Stormy Adolescence,* 46 VA. J. INT'L L. 319, 336 (2006).

124. MARK A. DRUMBL, *supra* note 122, at 177.
125. *See* LORI F. DAMROSCH et al., INTERNATIONAL LAW CASES and MATERIALS 1330 (5th ed. 2009).
126. *See* Update: International Criminal Tribunal for the Former Yugoslavia, at http://www.icty.org.
127. Much of the introduction to this section is taken from JOHN F. MURPHY, *supra* note 59, at 315.
128. SC Res. 955 (Nov. 8, 1994), 33 Int'l Leg. Materials 1598 (1994).
129. *See* LORI F. DAMROSCH et al., *supra* note 125, at 1355.
130. BARRY CARTER et al., *supra* note 119, at 1187.
131. Daryl A. Mundis, *The Judicial Effects of the "Completion Strategies" on the Ad Hoc International Tribunals*, 99 AM J. INT'L L. 142, 143 (2005), cited in id. at 1188.
132. SC Res. 1503 (2003).
133. BARRY CARTER et al., *supra* note 119, at 1188.
134. SC Res 1877 (July 7, 2009).
135. SC Res 1878 (July 7, 2009).
136. *See* Patricia M. Wald, *supra* note 123, at 335.
137. *Id.* at 339.
138. Helena Cobban, *Think Again: International Courts*, FOREIGN POL'Y, March/April, 2006, at 22.
139. *Id.* at 26.
140. David Sheffer, *Jostling Over Justice*, FOREIGN POL'Y, May/June, at 4.
141. Michael P. Scharf, *Jostling Over Justice*, FOREIGN POL'Y, May/June, at 6.
142. *Id.* at 7.
143. Rome Statute of the International Criminal Court, U.N. Doc. 32/A/CONF. 183/9, 37 Int'l Leg. Mat. 999 (1998).
144. *See* the Web site of the ICC at http:www.icc-cpi.int/menusASP/states +parties/.
145. For a recent summary of these reasons and other arguments against the International Criminal Court, *see* DAVID DAVENPORT, THE NEW INTERNATIONAL CRIMINAL COURT: RUSH to JUSTICE? (2002).
146. *See especially* LEILA NADYA SADAT, THE INTERNATIONAL CRIMINAL COURT and the TRANSFORMATION of INTERNATIONAL LAW (2002).
147. For my views, see John F. Murphy, *The Quivering Gulliver: US Views on a Permanent International Criminal Court*, 34 INT'L LAW. 45 (2000).
148. *See* LORI F. DAMROSCH et al., *supra* note 125, at 1352.
149. *See* the ICC Web site: http:www.icc-cpi.int/menus/icc situations +and +cses/
150. S.C. Res. 1593 (Mar. 31, 2005).
151. Warrant of Arrest for Omar Hassan Ahmad Al-Bashir, No. ICC-02/05–01/109 (Mar. 4, 2009), http://www.icc-cpi.int.
152. *See* Michael Slackman and Robert F. Worth, *Often Split, Arab Leaders Unite for Sudan's Chief*, N.Y. TIMES, Mar. 31, 2009, at http://www.nytimes.com/2009/03/31/world/africa/31 arab.html?page wanted.
153. *See* Colum Lynch, *International Court Under Unusual Fire: Africans Defend Sudan's Indicted Leader*, WASH. POST, June 30, 2009, at http://www.washingtonpost.com/wd-dvn/content/article/2009/06/29/AR20009062904322.
154. For a defense of the Court's initial focus on Africa, *see* Marlise Simons, *Gambian Defends the International Criminal Court's Initial Focus on Africans*, N.Y. TIMES, Feb. 26, 2007, at A13, col. 1. According to this article, Fatou Bensouda, the deputy to the chief prosecutor and a native of Gambia, has stated that "This court does not intend to focus

only on Africans; it will prove that in the future . . . But at the moment, Africa presents the gravest situations."

155. Uganda is a party to the Rome Statute, which, according to reports, did result in some inconvenience to Mr. Bashir. He had been invited to a development summit to be held in Uganda, but Uganda's Minister for International Affairs told the press that Mr. Bashir faced arrest in Uganda. Two days later, Uganda's president telephoned Mr. Bashir to apologize for the Minister's statement. Nonetheless, Bashir decided to cancel his plans for travel to Uganda. BBC News, July 16, 2009, http:/news.bbc.co.uk/go/pr/fr/-2/hi/africa/8154730.stm.

156. *See* Indira A.R. Lakshmanan, *Obama War-Crime Verdict May Echo Bush Objection to Global Court,* May 4, 2009, http://www.Bloomberg.com/apps/news?pid=20670001&sid=axBVOVbOJIbM.

157. *See* Nicolas D. Kristof, *Watching Darfuris Die,* N.Y. Times, Mar. 8, 2009, http://nytimes.com/2009/03/08/opinion/08kristof.html?Sq=rwanda&st=nv&scd=48&page wanted=print.

158. Report of an Independent Task Force Convened by the American Society of International Law, *U.S. Policy Toward the International Criminal Court: Furthering Positive Engagement,* at http://www.asil.org/files/ASIL-08-DiscPaper2pdf (March 2009).

159. *Id.,* Executive Summary, at iii.

160. *Id.*

161. For discussion and analysis of the Sierra Leone tribunals, *see, e.g.,* Celina Schocken, *The Special Court for Sierra Leone: Overview and Recommendation,* 20 Berkeley J. Int'l L. 436 (2002); International Center for Transitional Justice, *The Special Court for Sierra Leone: The First Eighteen Months,* March 2004, http://www.ictj.org/downloads/SC_SL_Case_Study_designed.pdf.

162. *See* Patricia M. Wald, *supra* note 123, at 339, citing Thierry Cruvellier, *The Special Court for Sierra Leone: The First Eighteen Months,* Int'l Center for Transitional Just. Mar. 2004, http://ictj.org/images/content/1/0/104.pdf.

163. *See* Jason McClurg, *Taylor Trial Delayed Until January 7, 2008,* 23 Int'l Enforcement L. Rep. 435 (Nov. 2007).

164. *See* Marlise Simons, *Trial of Liberia's Ex-Leader Languishes Amid Delays, Bureaucracy and Costs,* N.Y. Times, Aug. 27, 2007, at A6, col. 1.

165. *Id.*

166. *Id.*

167. *See* Jason McClurg, *Taylor Defense Team to Begin Presenting Case on July 13, 2009,* 25 Int'l Enforcement L. Rep., Aug. 2009, at 333.

168. *See* Marlise Simons, *War Crimes Trial to Hear from Ex-Liberia President,* N.Y. Times, July 13, 2009, at A9, col. 1.

169. *Id.*

170. *See* Bruce Zagaris, *UN and Cambodia Finally Reach Agreement on Prosecuting Khmer Rouge,* 19 Int'l Enforcement L. Rep. 194 (May 2003).

171. The framework agreement is annexed to G.A. Res. 57/228B (May 22, 2003).

172. *See* Bruce Zagaris, *Cambodian Special Tribunal Controversy Continues,* 23 Int'l Enforcement Law Rep. 58 (February 2007).

173. Most recently, "[a] United Nations Development program report sharply criticized Cambodia for what it said was widespread malpractice in hiring local staff members for the United Nations-backed tribunal that is to try Khmer Rouge figures, saying that lucrative salaries had been out to unqualified people. In their report, the auditors also suggested that the agency, which administers donors' funds for the Cambodian side

of the tribunal, seriously consider withdrawing from participation if the Cambodian administrators fail to make needed changes." *Cambodia: U.N. Finds Flaws in Tribunal*, N.Y. Times, Oct. 3, 2007, at A6, col. 3.

174. For a list of the indictments issued by the tribunal, *see* http://www.cambodia.gov.kh/krt/english/indictments.htm.
175. Marshall Kim, *Too Late for Revenge*, N.Y. Times, July 16, at A23, col. 2.
176. *See* Bruce Zagaris, *Lebanon Approves U.N. Plan for International Criminal Court for Hariri Assassination*, 23 Int'l Enforcement Law Rep. 29 (Jan. 2007).
177. *See* Jay Solomon, *U.S. Backs Plan on Trying Suspects in Hariri Killing*, Wall St. J., Apr. 20, 2007, at A17, col. 1.
178. S.C. Res. 1757 (May 30, 2007).
179. *See* Michael P. Scharf, *Foreward: Lessons From the Saddam Trial*, 39 Case W. Res. J. Int'l L. 1 (2006–2007).
180. *Id.*
181. *Id.* at 2.
182. For an extensive examination of these lessons, *see* the various articles and the appendices in *Lessons From the Saddam Trials*, 39 Case W. Res. J. Int'l L. 1–291 (2006–2007).
183. Michael P. Scharf, *supra* note 143, at 1–2.
184. *See How the Mighty Are Falling*, The Economist, July 7, 2007, at 59.

3

Who Shall Enforce the Peace?

As is well known, the primary motivation of the founders of the United Nations was to create an international institution that would be more effective than the League of Nations was in maintaining international peace and security. Under the U.N. Charter the Security Council is given the "primary responsibility for the maintenance of international peace and security,"[1] and it was the vision of the founders of the United Nations that the permanent members of the Security Council, especially the United States and the Soviet Union, would continue the cooperation that characterized their actions during World War II and be the backbone for the efforts of the new institution to prevent and, if necessary, to suppress by armed force aggression and other threats to and breaches of the peace.

With rare exceptions the vision of the founders has not been realized. To be sure, the record is not one of consistent failure. From time to time various permanent members have played key roles in efforts to meet aggression or threats to the peace. But the record on the whole is scandalously bad. Surprisingly, with the exception of the Gulf War in 1991, the record has been especially poor since the end of the Cold War.

In a speech to the United Nations General Assembly in September 2003, Kofi Annan, then Secretary-General of the United Nations, suggested that "a decisive moment" had arrived for the United Nations and "in particular for the aspiration set out in the [U.N.] Charter to provide collective security for all."[2] He noted the "deep divisions among the Member States on the nature of the threats that we faced and the appropriateness of the use of force to address those threats."[3] He concluded by announcing his intention "to convene a high level panel of eminent persons to provide me with a shared, comprehensive view about the way forward on the critical issues."[4] The High-level Panel on Threats, Challenges and Change, which we considered briefly in Chapter 2, was convened, and on December 1, 2004, transmitted its report, *A more secure world: our shared responsibility*, to the Secretary-General.[5]

The High-level Panel's report sets forth a large number of wide-ranging recommendations for possible reform of the United Nations, including structural reforms. Of the recommendations for structural reforms, the one that has received the most attention is that the Security Council be expanded along the lines of two possible models. One would add additional permanent members without a veto, along with further term-limited members; the other would add only additional term-limited members. Both would expand the total size of the Security Council to twenty-four members.[6]

The High-level Panel's report makes no recommendations for change in the composition of the current five permanent members of the Security Council and recognizes that there is "no practical way of changing the existing members' veto powers."[7] It does state, however, its view that "as a whole the institution of the veto has an anachronistic character that is unsuitable for the institution in an increasingly democratic age and we would urge that its use be limited to matters where vital interests are genuinely at stake."[8] It also requests "the permanent members, in their individual capacities, to pledge themselves to refrain from the use of the veto in cases of genocide and large-scale human rights abuses."[9]

Somewhat gingerly, the report criticizes the record of the permanent members in maintaining international peace and security. It suggests that "[t]he financial and military contributions to the United Nations of some of the five permanent members are modest compared to their special status . . . Even outside the use of a formal veto, the ability of the permanent members to keep critical issues of peace and security off the Security Council's agenda has further undermined confidence in the body's work."[10]

The record of the permanent members is not, however, the focus of the report's comments and recommendations for reform of the Security Council. Rather, the focus is on enlargement of the Security Council, whether this enlargement should include the creation of new permanent members (without the veto), as well as the addition of more nonpermanent members, how the new seats should be distributed among major regional areas, and what criteria should govern the selection of the new members.

On March 21, 2005, Secretary-General Kofi Annan produced his own report that, among other things, sets forth his reactions to the High-level Panel's report.[11] In this report he endorses the recommendations of the High-level Panel's report regarding reform of the Security Council and urges member states to consider the two options, Models A and B, "or any other viable proposals in terms of size and balance that have emerged on the basis of either model."[12] Although the Secretary-General suggested that member states should make a decision on Security Council enlargement before the summit meeting of Heads of State and Government in September 2005, he later acknowledged that this would not be possible by then and moved his target date from September to December.[13]

On September 16, 2005, the General Assembly adopted a resolution by which the assembled Heads of State and Government set forth the 2005 World Summit Outcome.[14] The Outcome document sets forth a number of proposals, some of which are referred to later in this chapter. As to the Security Council the Heads of State and Government support its "early reform" "in order to make it more broadly representative, efficient, and transparent and thus to further enhance its effectiveness and the legitimacy and implementation of its decisions," and "commit" themselves to "continuing [their] efforts to achieve a decision to this end and request the General Assembly to review progress on the reform set out above by the end of 2005."[15]

I am of the view that the current problems of the Security Council do not stem from a lack of enough permanent members or from the "unrepresentative" nature of the current membership. Indeed, the current focus on the alleged unrepresentative nature of the membership of the Security Council is a red herring. The focus should be on the actions and inactions of the current permanent members of the Security Council that have so often resulted in the failure of the Council to fulfill its primary responsibility under the Charter to maintain international peace and security. The remarks of Edward Luck, a longtime observer of and commentator on the United Nations, are apposite: "The United Nations, sadly, has drifted far from its founding vision. Its Charter neither calls for a democratic council nor relegates the collective use of force to a last resort. It was a wartime document of a military alliance, not a universal peace platform."[16]

A key question arising out of these developments is where do we go from here? If the permanent members of the Security Council will not fulfill their responsibilities, or at best do so only sporadically, who or what shall enforce the peace? Various possibilities have been suggested. These include, among others, a renewed commitment on the part of the permanent members to fulfill their responsibilities; a greater role for more "robust" U.N. peacekeeping; greater involvement in peace enforcement by regional agencies, including especially the African Union; an alliance of democratic states, including one with its own institutional military capability; and some combination of these possibilities. As we shall see, none of these possibilities is a panacea. All, however, are deserving of serious consideration because the alternative is to continue with the highly unsatisfactory status quo.

THE PERMANENT MEMBERS' FAILURE TO FULFILL THEIR RESPONSIBILITIES

At the San Francisco conference, held from April to June, 1945, it was generally accepted that the Security Council would have the primary responsibility for the maintenance of international peace and security and that the Great Powers were entitled to a special position on the Council by virtue of their exceptional responsibility for world security.[17] The expectation was that it would seldom be necessary for the Council to order military measures; the mere threat of military action by the Great Powers should serve to "deter states from aggressive acts and would be an added incentive to settle disputes by peaceful means."[18] At the same time, "the drafters of the Charter recognized that it was unrealistic to attempt to establish a system of United Nations enforcement action which would be effective in the event a major power violated the peace. Indeed, most felt that the United Nations should not even attempt to take action if those powers were not in agreement."[19]

Thus, the founders of the United Nations recognized the possibility that a permanent member might itself create a threat to or breach of the peace. One may speculate, however, that they did not envisage in 1945 that the Soviet Union would seek to promote the spread of communism on a worldwide basis through the use of armed force, that communists would take control of China, or, for that matter, that France, Great Britain, and Israel would engage in blatant aggression against Egypt during the Suez crisis.

Although France lobbied hard for one, the San Francisco Conference refused to authorize the creation of an international police force.[20] Instead, the conference agreed to accept a clause (Article 43 of the Charter) requiring member states to make available troops and bases to the Security Council through "special agreements." There was no serious opposition to these provisions because "every state wanted to guarantee that the United Nations would protect them against future wars."[21] It was to prove a vain hope.

The Charter Paradigm: A Brief Excursus

Although there are a few dissenting voices, the generally accepted view is that the U.N. Charter places severe constraints on the use of armed force by member states.[22] Under the generally accepted view, the prohibition on the use of armed force contained in Article 2 (4) of the Charter[23] is subject to only two exceptions: the right of individual or collective self-defense under Article 51 of the Charter[24] and "military action taken or authorized by the Security Council in a binding decision, following determination of the existence of a threat to the peace, a breach of the peace, or an act of aggression."[25]

Perhaps the alleged exception to the Charter's prohibition of the use of armed force that has had the most support among the commentators is the so-called doctrine of humanitarian intervention, which would permit the use of armed force on the basis of humanitarian concerns, especially in the case where it is used to stop another country's government from engaging in a massive violation of the human rights of its own citizens.[26] Other eminent scholars have categorically rejected the arguments in support of the doctrine.[27] Most important, the doctrine has not been accepted by the overwhelming majority of states, including the United States.[28]

To be sure, there has been a good deal of debate over the precise scope of the self-defense authorized under the Charter, especially whether Article 51 requires an actual "armed attack" or instead permits anticipatory self-defense.[29] Moreover, the

Bush administration has stimulated considerable controversy by adopting a strategy of "preemptive" attack according to this strategy: "[t]he greater the threat, the greater is the risk of inaction – and the more compelling the case for taking anticipatory action to defend ourselves, even if uncertainty remains as to the time and place of the enemy's attack. To forestall or prevent such hostile acts by our adversaries, the United States will, if necessary, act preemptively."[30]

There has also been considerable debate over whether particular Security Council resolutions have authorized member states to use armed force.[31] Debate has been especially sharp over whether Security Council Resolution 1441[32] authorized the invasion of Iraq.[33] As I have suggested elsewhere, although Resolution 1441 was unanimously adopted by the Security Council, it was a "masterpiece of diplomatic ambiguity that masked real differences of opinion between the United States and the United Kingdom, on the one hand, and France, Germany and Russia, on the other, in how Iraq's failure to fulfill its obligations under Resolution 687 should be handled."[34] Nonetheless, as pointed out by Sean Murphy, "the debate at the Security Council reflects a belief by all the members (with the exception of the United States) that they had, after intensive weeks of negotiation, reached a consensus on a 'two-stage process' whereby, if Iraq failed to disarm, the Security Council would decide at a future, second stage whether to authorize the use of force."[35] Moreover, it is doubtful whether an authorization of the use of force may ever be implicit rather than explicit in a Security Council resolution, and Resolution 1441 contains no explicit authorization.

For present purposes, however, the issue is not whether particular resolutions do or do not authorize the use of force. Rather, the debate over these resolutions reflects the reality that the Security Council, despite various obstacles, continues to play a, indeed the, key role in the maintenance of international peace and security. But, as the rest of this chapter demonstrates, the permanent members have often blocked the Council from performing this role through their abuse of the privilege of the veto and their failure to support Council action when it has been clearly needed.

Abdication from the Outset: The Failure to Conclude Article 43 Agreements

As noted previously, the San Francisco Conference refused to authorize the creation of a U.N. international police force or a standing army. Instead, under Article 43 of the Charter, member states are obligated to make available to the Security Council the armed forces necessary to maintain international peace and security, but only "in accordance with a special agreement or agreements," which would cover, among other matters, the number and types of forces, their degree of readiness and general location.[36] Article 43 further requires that the special agreements "shall be negotiated as soon as possible on the initiative of the Security Council."[37] Pending the coming into force of the special agreements referred to in Article 43, Article 106 provides that the five permanent members shall consult with a view to taking "such joint action on behalf of the Organization as may be necessary for the purpose of maintaining international peace and security."[38]

It is clear from the language of Article 43 that the Security Council is not required to conclude special agreements with all U.N. members or even all permanent members,[39] although it would clearly be dysfunctional for the Council to conclude such agreements with some permanent members and not others. Nonetheless, Article 43 surely requires that the Council seek to conclude at least a sufficient number of agreements with member states capable of enforcing the peace to enable the Council to fulfill its primary responsibility for maintaining international peace and security. The permanent members, moreover, could reasonably be expected to take the lead in inducing the Council to begin negotiations toward the conclusion of such agreements. But the two leading powers in the Council, the United States and the Soviet Union, were unable to agree on the terms of agreements making available the armed forces necessary to permit the Council to discharge its responsibility to enforce the peace. The disagreement between the United States and the Soviet Union reportedly related to such matters as the size and the composition of the armed forces to be contributed by the permanent members, the provisions of bases, the location of forces when not in action, and the time of their withdrawal.[40] This impasse continued throughout the period of the Cold War, and although some hoped that the collapse of the Soviet Union in the early 1990s might result in the conclusion of some Article 43 agreements, such was not to be the case.[41]

The failure of the permanent members to take the lead in inducing the Security Council to conclude Article 43 agreements has greatly undermined the Council's capacity to maintain international peace and security. As noted by Yoram Dinstein:

> The rationale underlying the scheme of the special agreements is plain. The Council cannot accomplish the mission assigned to it by the Charter unless it acts swiftly once a crisis breaks out. Since no permanent international force exists, advance preparations have to be made for the rapid deployment of forces belonging to Member States. In particular, Member States must identify combat-ready units that can be drawn upon by the Council at a moment's notice.[42]

To be sure, as Dinstein also notes,[43] and as we shall see, the failure to conclude Article 43 agreements has not prevented the Security Council from taking action to enforce the peace if the political will is present. All too often, however, it has not been.

It was not present, for example, to deal with the conflict in Palestine.

The Conflict in Palestine

The implications of the failure on the part of the permanent members to conclude Article 43 agreements with the Security Council became clear early in the history of the United Nations as the conflict in Palestine between Jews and Arabs became more violent.[44] Secretary-General Trygve Lie attempted to salvage the talks on permanent military forces by suggesting informally to Great Britain and the United States that an armed force be established in Palestine out of the "minimum units which the Big Five were committed to place at the Security Council's disposal," which he believed would be "more than adequate" to keep the peace.[45] Both Great Britain and the United States rejected the proposal because of fear of Russian troops in Palestine, and the Secretary-General never introduced it to the Council. Accordingly, it proved impossible for the Security Council to implement the General Assembly's plan for a partition of Palestine into a Jewish and an Arab state. Indeed, the United States reversed its position on partition in the Security Council and called instead for a temporary trusteeship over Palestine.[46] This proposal was not adopted. The mandate was terminated on May 14, 1948.[47] The Jewish community in Palestine immediately proclaimed the State of Israel within the territorial boundaries of the partition plan, and the new state was quickly recognized by a number of states, including the United States and the Soviet Union. Almost simultaneously, however, Egypt, Syria, Transjordan, Lebanon, and other Arab states intervened, as stated in a cablegram of May 16 from the Secretary-General of the League of Arab States to the United Nations Secretary-General, "to restore law and order and to prevent disturbances prevailing in Palestine from spreading into their territories and to check further bloodshed."[48]

The Security Council was initially slow to react to the crisis, and when it did react on May 22 it limited itself to a call for a cease-fire.[49] This resolution was ignored by the Arab states, and there then ensued a series of Security Council Resolutions, several cease-fires and violations of the cease-fires; ultimately negotiations between Israel and Egypt, under the chairmanship of Ralph Bunche, began at Rhodes in January 1949.[50] Largely through Bunche's efforts, for which he was awarded a Nobel Peace Prize, these negotiations resulted in the signing of an armistice agreement on February 24. This was followed by similar agreements between Israel and Lebanon, Jordan, and Syria. These armistice agreements specified that they were concluded without prejudice to territorial rights and that the armistice demarcation lines were not to be construed as political boundaries. The agreements also established demilitarized zones and set up Mixed Armistice Commissions (MACs) to supervise implementation of the truce. The chairman of each MAC was the chief of staff of the U.N. Truce Supervision Organization (UNTSO).[51]

Conclusion of these armistice agreements was an outstanding accomplishment of the United Nations. The same may not be said, however, of the other U.N. actions regarding the situation in Palestine. In particular, the Security Council failed to take the steps necessary to implement the General Assembly's partition plan, although it was crystal clear that the Arab states were going to resort to force against the projected Jewish state. But neither Great Britain nor the United States was willing to provide the Security Council with the forces necessary to prevent the outbreak of violence in Palestine and the invasion of the territory by Arab states.

The reasons for this unwillingness are worth a brief examination – although one has to speculate somewhat to do so – because neither Great Britain nor the United States spelled out their positions publicly in great detail. We have already noted the reluctance of Great Britain and the United States to have Soviet troops introduced into the Middle East. Under the plan proposed by Secretary-General Lie, however, the Soviet component would have been only a small part of the overall force and would have been under the command of the United Nations. Moreover, even if the Cold War had progressed to the stage where the introduction of any Soviet armed force into Palestine was simply unacceptable, it was incumbent upon the United States and Great Britain to suggest other alternatives. But the British announced categorically and self-righteously that they would have no part in implementing a partition plan that was opposed by the Arab states.[52] For his part, the Permanent Representative of the United States to the United Nations, Warren Austin, argued that the Security Council had no authority under the Charter to use force to implement the partition plan.[53] Secretary-General Lie's observation on this contention is compelling:

> Ambassador Austin's doctrine that the United Nations did not have the power to enforce any type of political settlement is sound as a general proposition ... The United Nations does not have the power to impose a political settlement, whether it be unification or partition, except in special circumstances. Such circumstances exist when all the parties in control of a territory hand it over to the United Nations for disposition. Clearly, I felt, the Organization in these circumstances had full constitutional power, not only to maintain order inside the territory but, even more, to resist any attempt from outside to overthrow its decision.[54]

One might add to Secretary-General Lie's observation that, in any event, the Security Council had the authority and the primary responsibility under the Charter to maintain peace, through the use of force if necessary. Great Britain's abandonment of the mandate, the Jewish community's proclamation of the State of Israel, and the Arab states' threats to intervene with force precipitated an imminent threat to peace that, had its permanent members been willing, the Council had ample authority to handle.

As a result of the Council's failure to deal with the crisis in Palestine, the United Nations has had the Arab-Israeli conflict on its agenda for the length of its existence.

Korea

As noted earlier in this chapter, the drafters of the U.N. Charter were well aware that the collective security system they were devising would not function effectively in the event a major power violated the peace, and a majority of the drafters were of the opinion that the United Nations should not even attempt to take action if there was no agreement among the major powers. In the case of North Korea's invasion of South Korea on June 25, 1950, however, both the Security Council and the General Assembly took action, although North Korea's clear aggression[55] had the support of the Soviet Union, and the People's Republic of China intervened militarily on the side of North Korea when U.S. and other armed forces crossed the 38th parallel dividing the two Koreas in an effort to occupy North Korea and win a decisive military victory.

For its part, the Security Council was able to act only because of the fortuitous circumstance that the Soviet delegate had previously walked out in protest of the Council's decision to seat the Nationalist Chinese as the lawful representative of China. The Council first passed a resolution calling for a cessation of North Korea's actions.[56] When this resolution was ignored, it recommended that member states "furnish such assistance to the Republic of Korea as may be necessary to repel the armed attack and to restore international peace and security in the area."[57] Passage of the second resolution allowed the United States to bring its defense of Korea – an action it would have taken in any event – under the auspices of the United Nations.[58]

The Soviet delegate returned to the Security Council on August 1, 1950, and blocked any further action by the Council. On October 7, 1950, the General Assembly, noting that the objectives of the Security Council had not been attained, established the United Nations Commission for the Unification and Rehabilitation of Korea.[59]

In the meantime, the Inchon landing of September 15 had radically turned the tide of battle in Korea, and the North Korean army was in full retreat. This sudden change of circumstances raised a crucial question: Should United Nations forces cross the 38th parallel dividing the two Koreas or be content with having driven the North Korea forces out of South Korea? The view of the United States, which was shared by the Secretary-General and many other member states, was that U.N. forces should proceed into North Korea in order to defeat decisively the North Korean forces, preclude any further aggression on their part, set up conditions for free elections throughout Korea, and thereby unify the country.[60]

In response to the stalemate in the Council and at the initiative of the United States, the General Assembly adopted on November 3, 1950, the famous "Uniting for Peace" Resolution.[61] The resolution provided that the General Assembly would meet to recommend collective measures in situations where the Security Council was unable to deal with a breach of the peace or act of aggression. Under the resolution, whenever a veto prevented the Council from acting, a special emergency Assembly session could be convened within twenty-four hours by a procedural vote of any seven members. By way of institutional provisions, the resolution recommended that all member states earmark units of their armed forces to be maintained in readiness for future use under either Council or Assembly resolutions and authorized the Secretary-General to appoint a panel of military experts to advise governments, on their request, about setting up the earmarked national units. It also established a fourteen-member Collective Measures Committee to study further methods to improve the ability of the United Nations to meet future cases of aggression.

It wasn't long before the United Nations had occasion to use the new procedures. The fundamental premise underlying the decision to cross the 38th parallel – that the People's Republic of China would not intervene in the fighting with its own forces – proved false. On November 29, as the U.N. forces were driving to the Yalu River, North Korea's boundary with Manchuria, Chinese troops intervened in massive numbers. Imminent victory threatened to become a rout as U.N. forces retreated rapidly. Initially, the Secretary-General attempted to work out a cease-fire through negotiations with the communist Chinese. These proved to be of no avail, and on February 1, 1951, with the Security Council unable to act, the General Assembly, acting under the Uniting for Peace procedures, passed a resolution condemning the Chinese action as aggression, calling upon them to withdraw their forces from Korea, and recommending that all states lend every assistance to the U.N. action in Korea.[62]

During the winter of 1951 the initiative passed again to the U.N. forces, and the North Korean forces were driven back to the 38th parallel. This time there was no sentiment in favor of crossing the line. Nonetheless, the negotiations were long and difficult, and the conflict continued until an armistice agreement was finally concluded at Panmunjom on July 28, 1953. Accordingly, as a result of Soviet opposition, and armed intervention by the People's Republic of China, the United Nations was unable to fulfill even its limited goal of ensuring that North Korea would not resume its aggression against the South. On the contrary, with the Chinese intervention and the difficulty of the U.N. forces in returning to the 38th parallel, the North Koreans were in a position to drive a hard bargain in negotiations over an armistice and prolonged the process for two years. The observation of the drafters of the Charter on the difficulties facing the collective security system of the United Nations in the event of the opposition of a major power proved apt.

Suez

The Suez crisis – one of the most spectacular and dangerous examples of interstate violence arising out of the Arab-Israeli conflict – involved an extraordinary situation where the Security Council was prevented from fulfilling its primary responsibility for maintaining international peace and security by two permanent members, France and Great Britain, which had generally been regarded as dedicated to upholding the United Nations in its peacekeeping functions.

As noted previously, the first Arab-Israeli conflict ended in the armistice agreements of 1949. However, the armistice between Israel and Egypt deteriorated rapidly.[63] Fedayeen raids occurred frequently from the Sinai and the Gaza Strip and led to increasingly severe Israeli retaliation. On the ground that it was exercising legitimate belligerent rights, Egypt closed the Suez Canal to Israeli shipping and kept it closed in disregard of a 1951 Security Council resolution[64] that denied the compatibility of the exercise of belligerent rights with the armistice. Egypt also controlled the entrance to the Gulf of Aqaba at Sharm el Sheikh, which overlooks the Strait of Tiran. In justification of this action, Egypt again relied on belligerent rights and on the location of the navigable passage of the straits within its territorial waters. In response, Israel contended that the Gulf could not legally be closed to blockade one riparian and that the straits constituted an international waterway, zone which, under customary international law, could not be unilaterally closed to Israeli shipping.[65]

Tensions between Israel and Egypt continued to mount, and despite strenuous efforts on the part of the Security Council to induce the parties to resolve their problems peacefully,[66] conditions along the demarcation lines continued to deteriorate. At the same time, relations between Egypt, on the one hand, and Great Britain, France, and the United States on the other, came under increased strain, culminating in the U.S. decision not to finance the construction of the Aswan Dam and Egypt's on July 26, 1956, regarding the nationalization of the Suez Canal and its intention to use funds from the collection of tolls to defray the costs of building the dam. Although the decree of expropriation provided for compensation to the shareholders in the company established to operate the canal on the basis of the market value of their shares as of July 25, and President Nasser of Egypt indicated that he remained bound by the obligation in the Constantinople Convention of 1888 to keep the canal open at all times, the hostility of the British, French, and United States reaction was pronounced. Attempts at compromise were unsuccessful, and on September 12 the United Kingdom and France placed the issue before the Security Council for the first time. Due in large part to the good offices of Secretary-General Dag Hammarskjold, private negotiations among the French, British, and Egyptian foreign ministers resulted in substantial agreement among the three countries on steps to be taken to resolve the dispute peacefully.[67] These steps were then incorporated into a draft resolution,[68] which was unanimously adopted by the Security Council on October 13.

From all appearances then, prospects for a peaceful settlement of the dispute were favorable. But appearances were deceiving, because in London, Paris, and Tel Aviv, government officials were deciding in secret to use force in the form of an Anglo-French "police" action, following an Israeli attack upon Egypt. The United States was not informed of these plans.

The Israeli attack upon Egypt came on October 29, whereupon the United States promptly asked the Security Council to determine that a breach of the peace had occurred and to order Israel to withdraw behind the armistice lines.[69] The chief of staff of UNTSO confirmed that Israeli troops had violated the armistice and crossed the international frontier. Israel defended its action as security measures to eliminate Egyptian fedayeen bases in the Sinai Peninsula and claimed that this action was self-defense under Article 51 of the U.N. Charter. On October 30, Britain and France, through their veto power, prevented the Security Council from taking action and sent a joint ultimatum to Egypt and Israel, calling upon both sides to stop all warlike action and withdraw ten miles away from the canal. The ultimatum also demanded that Egypt permit the "temporary occupation by Anglo-French forces of key positions at Port Said, Ismailia, and Suez," and threatened force if compliance was not forthcoming.

With the Security Council unable to act, the matter was then transferred to the General Assembly under the Uniting for Peace procedure. The result was the United Nations' first peacekeeping operation. The U.N. Emergency Force (UNEF) was established by the General Assembly[70] to position itself between the hostile forces and to supervise the withdrawal of British and French forces from the Suez Canal and Israeli forces from the Sinai Peninsula. It was then deployed along the armistice line until May 1967, when the so-called Six Day War broke out.

One is left with two strong impressions with respect to the Suez crisis. First, the Security Council performed extremely well in attempting to resolve the disputes peacefully. Second, ironically, during the grim days of the Cold War, the Council functioned as envisaged by the founders of the United Nations, that is, the United States and the Soviet Union acted in concert in dealing with blatant acts of aggression. Only the extraordinary fact of British and French aggression and their consequent vetoes prevented the Council from fulfilling its responsibilities.

To be sure, the Suez Crisis was an aberration. Most often, it was the Cold War and the threat of a Soviet veto that prevented the Security Council from taking measures to enforce the peace. Faced with this inability, the United Nations in practice employed other methods to maintain international peace and security. The most important of these methods has come to be known as *peacekeeping*. We explore the role of the permanent members of the Security Council in peacekeeping in the next section of this chapter.

THE COLLAPSE OF COLLECTIVE SECURITY AND ENFORCED INNOVATION: THE RISE OF PEACEKEEPING

Interestingly, the word "peacekeeping" does not appear in the U.N. Charter. Moreover, the constitutional basis for it has been hotly debated.[71]

As defined by a former Legal Counsel of the United Nations, peacekeeping operations are "actions involving the use of military personnel on the basis of the consent of all parties concerned and without resorting to the use of armed force except in self-defense."[72] As noted in the previous section, the first U.N. peacekeeping operation was the U.N. Emergency Force (UNEF) established by the General Assembly during the 1956 Suez crisis. Robert Riggs and Jack Plano have aptly contrasted "peacekeeping" with "enforcement action" and described its functions:

> Instead of acting to deter or defeat an aggressor, the U.N. peacekeeping mission is deployed against no identified enemy. Its purpose is to help maintain peace when tension is high but no party is determined to pursue armed conquest. It may perform this function by observing border violations, policing a cease-fire or truce line, serving as a buffer between hostile forces, and even helping to maintain domestic order during a transition period. A peacekeeping force is deployed only with the consent of the sovereign of the territory where it operates, and usually with the consent or acquiescence of all the governments concerned. While U.N. forces or military observers are normally armed, weapons are to be used only in self-defense and not to enforce the will on any of the contending parties. Except for the Congo operations, 1960–64, U.N. peacekeeping operations have never been large enough to enforce order against serious military opposition.[73]

To these observations one might add that traditionally U.N. peacekeeping forces have been introduced after the fighting has stopped in an effort to avoid a new outbreak of violence. As indicated by Riggs and Plano, the contrast between peace-keeping and collective security is sharp. Peacekeeping operations have been made up largely of units from smaller states rather than the forces of permanent members, and they have operated with the consent of the member states concerned. Their function initially and to this day has been to discourage hostilities, not to restore or enforce peace.

This neat division between peacekeeping and peace enforcement, however, has not always worked well in practice. The most salient early example was the U.N. operation in the Congo in the early 1960s. There, amid great controversy, U.N. forces went way beyond the use of force in self-defense and, ultimately with the express sanction of the Security Council, brought to the end the armed resistance of the Katanga forces and put to an end the attempted secession of Katanga province.[74] The situation in the Congo involved internal rather than international armed conflict, although there were threatened and actual (in the case of Belgium) interventions on the part of outside states. As we shall see later in this chapter, since the 1990s, internal armed conflicts have posed major challenges to the whole concept of peacekeeping and have raised in sharp relief the issue of the extent to which, if at all, U.N. forces should be authorized to use force for purposes other than self-defense.

One should also note the rise in recent years of what is sometimes referred to as "second-generation" peacekeeping.[75] The paradigmatic case of such peace-keeping is Cambodia. In 1975, the Khmer Rouge gained control of Cambodia, and attempted a total restructuring of Cambodian society, committing mass state-sponsored killing and other gross violations of human rights.[76] This came to an end in 1979, when Vietnam invaded Cambodia and installed a regime known as the People's Republic of Kampuchea, which controlled most of Cambodia during the 1980s but faced four factions that conducted a guerrilla war in an attempt to gain control of Cambodia.

In 1991, the four Cambodian warring factions endorsed a United Nations plan designed to help rebuild Cambodia and signed a number of agreements aimed at a comprehensive settlement.[77] Under these agreements, the four warring factions agreed to create a Supreme National Council (SNC), composed of representatives of the factions, to act as the "unique ... source of authority" and embody Cambodian sovereignty. The SNC delegated to the United Nations all authority necessary to ensure the implementation of the comprehensive settlement. In 1992, the United Nations set up the U.N. Transitional Authority (UNTAC) to monitor the disarmament of the four Cambodian factions and supervise free elections. In order to create a neutral environment for elections, the factions delegated to UNTAC control of five ministries and supervision of others, access to all government documents, and power to issue binding directives and replace personnel.[78]

Perhaps in part because of the rise in "second-generation" peacekeeping, on September 16, 2005, the Heads of State and Government agreed, as part of the 2005 World Summit Outcome, to establish a Peacebuilding Commission as an intergovernmental body "to bring together all relevant actors to marshal resources and to advise on and propose integrated strategies for post-conflict peacebuilding and recovery."[79]

There now appears to be general agreement that traditional U.N. peacekeeping involving the consent of all the parties to the dispute and the use of force only in self-defense has played a highly constructive role in maintaining international peace and security, evidenced most dramatically by the award in 1988 of the Nobel Peace Prize to U.N. peacekeeping forces. The creation and operation of these forces, however, have raised some crucial and controversial legal issues.

The fundamental disagreement has been over the allocation of authority under the Charter for peacekeeping among the Security Council, the General Assembly, and the Secretariat, represented by the Secretary-General. In the words of Erik Suy:

> The main problem areas are, on the one hand, the competence to establish peace-keeping operations and, on the other hand, the continuing authority over established operations, i.e., the competence with regard to the day-to-day running of the operations. The latter involves mainly the question of the division of authority between the Security Council and the Secretary-General, while the former primarily relates to the issue of sharing of power between the Security Council and the General Assembly.[80]

The International Court of Justice in the Certain Expenses case[81] has advised on both of these issues. In Certain Expenses a majority of the court was of the opinion that, contrary to the arguments of the Soviet Union and France, the General Assembly has residual authority, under Articles 11 and 14 of the Charter,[82] to establish peacekeeping operations except when enforcement action is required. As to the division of authority between the Council and the Secretary-General, the majority of the Court confirmed the Council's prerogatives but advised that, in the case of the Congo, the Council had either authorized or ratified the Secretary-General's actions.

The Court's opinion, however, did not end the debate. France and the Soviet Union rejected the validity of the Court's opinion, which as an advisory opinion had no binding effect on them, and refused to pay any expenses associated with UNEF or the Congo operation, and the General Assembly took no action to deprive either country of its vote as arguably it was required to do under Article 19 of the Charter.[83] In 1965, the General Assembly established the Special Committee on Peacekeeping Operations to examine the problem of peacekeeping in all its aspects. From the deliberations of this committee there evolved a tacit understanding that the Security Council should assume its role as the organ with primary responsibility in the field of peacekeeping to the fullest extent possible.[84] As a result, there gradually arose a tacit understanding between the United States and the Soviet Union that peacekeeping operations should be authorized by the Security Council rather than by the General Assembly under the Uniting for Peace procedure.[85]

END OF THE COLD WAR: COLLECTIVE SECURITY REDUX?

According to Louis Henkin, during the first decades of the United Nations, "the United States was, and was generally recognized to be, a principal champion of the law of the Charter, insisting on its validity and its interpretation to limit strictly the permissible uses of force."[86] Henkin then goes on to suggest, however, that there were compelling grounds to question the commitment of the United States to the law forbidding the use of force during the 1980s, especially during the Reagan administration. In particular, Henkin pointed to the U.S. invasion of Grenada in 1983, the U.S. bombing of Libya in 1986 for its support of international terrorism, and the U.S. mining of Nicaraguan harbors and its support of rebellion by the contras.[87] It should be noted that all of the U.S. actions criticized by Henkin have their defenders and that there has been considerable debate over both the law and the facts in each of these cases. The debate over the U.S. mining of the Nicaraguan harbors and its support of the contras has been especially fierce, as the decisions by the International Court of Justice in the *Nicaragua v. United States* case, first, that it had jurisdiction[88] and then on the merits[89] were highly controversial.[90]

For its part, during the first decades of the United Nations, the Soviet Union engaged in various actions incompatible with its status as a permanent member of the Security Council. We have already seen how the Soviet Union supported North Korea's invasion of South Korea. In addition, it engaged in "indirect aggression" in Czechoslovakia in 1948, in Hungary in 1956, and again in Czechoslovakia in 1968. The Soviet Union attempted to justify these interventions under the so-called Brezhnev Doctrine, named after Premier Leonid Brezhnev, which asserted the right of the Soviet Union and other socialist states to intervene in support of any socialist government threatened by antisocialist forces. The United States and most other states outside of the Soviet bloc flatly rejected the Brezhnev Doctrine as a violation of the U.N. Charter. In 1979 the Soviet Union invaded Afghanistan, a step that, at least in part, may have contributed to the ultimate dissolution of the Soviet Union.

There was one instance of major cross-border violence during the 1980s when both the Soviet Union and the United States, as well as the other permanent members of the Security Council, utterly failed to fulfill their responsibilities: Iraq's invasion of Iran on September 22, 1980. Iraq's invasion of Iran illustrates *realpolitik* at its most pernicious.

Iraq-Iran

In northern Iraq the Kurds had long sought autonomy from Iraqi rule, and Iraq had long resisted their demands. In 1970, Iraq offered the Kurds significant self-rule in a Kurdistan Autonomous Region, but it covered only half of the territory Kurds considered theirs and excluded Kurdish-populated oil rich provinces.[91] Although the Kurds rejected the offer, Saddam Hussein imposed the plan unilaterally in 1974. Believing they would receive support from Iran, Israel, and the United States (because of U.S. unease over Iraq's recent friendship treaty with the Soviet Union), the Kurds revolted. In 1975, however, with U.S. backing, Iran and Iraq concluded the Algiers agreement, which presumably settled a historic border dispute. Iraq agreed to recognize the Iranian position on the border, and the Shah of Iran and the United States withdrew their support of the Kurds.

With the invasion of Iran in 1980, Iraq disregarded the 1975 Algiers agreement. Viewing the weakness of Iran following the overthrow of the Shah and the confrontation with the United States over the taking of hostages as an opportunity to settle old grievances, Iraq invaded Iran and occupied the Shatt al Arab waterway, which Iraq had claimed in the territorial dispute with Iran.

The response of the Security Council was to issue a resolution[92] merely calling for a cease-fire and for the Secretary-General to lend his good offices to resolving the conflict. Not surprisingly, Iran rejected any cease-fire while Iraq was illegally occupying its territory.

The reasons for the Council's limited response were several. Most of the Arab states, with the exception of Libya and Syria, which backed Iran, approved of Iraq's invasion because of their opposition to the efforts of Ayatollah Khomenei's regime to stir up religious strife in the Muslim world. Great Britain and France reportedly stood aloof from efforts to draft a strong resolution because of their heavy investments in both Iraq and Iran and their desire to tread warily between the two countries.[93] For its part, the United States at first took no major initiative, but finally – more than a month after the invasion began – the American representative spoke out in the

Council warning of the possible dismemberment of Iran because of the Iraq invasion. He reportedly discussed in private with other members of the Council the elements of a possible resolution that would include a call for an Iraqi withdrawal from Iran, with evacuated territory converted to a cease-fire zone patrolled by U.N. observers. The resolution also proposed the mutual control of the Shatt al Arab waterway under the chairmanship of a neutral third nation, a mechanism or negotiating forum to settle Iraq's claims for land in Iran, and a pledge by both sides against interference in each other's internal affairs.[94] No resolution, however, was forthcoming from these efforts, and war dragged on for eight years until Iran finally accepted a cease-fire in 1988 after Iranian offenses in 1986 and 1987 failed to capture Basra and Iraqi forces pushed the exhausted Iranians back across the border into Iran.

One can only speculate as to the precise reasons for the United States' failure to support forceful action in the Security Council against Iraq, but there appear to be several primary reasons for the U.S. position. First, the United States wished to ensure that the Soviet Union would not use an action by the United States as a pretext for itself becoming involved in the conflict. Similarly, the United States apparently did not wish to appear to be favoring Iran when Jordan and Saudi Arabia, friendly states, were supporting Iraq, and the unfriendly states of Libya and Syria were supporting Iran.

Another, perhaps the most compelling, reason was that Iran was still holding fifty-two American diplomats hostage, despite a call by the Security Council and a unanimous decision by the International Court of Justice that they should be released. But Iraq's invasion of Iran, a pure territorial grab, was in no way intended to secure the release of the hostages. Moreover, the Iraqi invasion rallied the people of Iran around the previously shaky regime of the Ayatollah Khomenei, caused even the moderates in Iran to believe that the United States was behind it, and made the release of the hostages more rather than less problematic.

Finally, 1980 was an election year, and the administration wished to appear to be taking a hard line against Iran. Nonetheless, any administration has a responsibility to educate the public (and the world community) about the importance of fundamental United Nations Charter norms against aggression.

Sadly, not only did the United States fail to support meaningful action by the Security Council in response to Iraq's invasion of Iran, the Reagan administration, unwilling to see an Iranian victory, began in December 1982 to intervene to offset Iranian gains.[95] Specifically, the United States granted Iraq an initial $210 million in agricultural credits to buy U.S. grain, wheat, and rice, a figure that soon climbed to $500 million per year. Because Iraq's poor credit rating and high rate of default made banks reluctant to loan it money, these credits were highly valuable to the Saddam Hussein regime. The United States also gave Iraq access to export–import credits for the purchase of goods manufactured in the United States, and removed Iraq from its list of countries sponsoring terrorism after Iraq expelled the Abu Nidal Black June terrorist group.[96] In November 1984 the United States and Iraq resumed diplomatic relations, which had been severed during the 1967 Arab-Israeli conflict.

This rapprochement between the United States and Iraq continued even when Saddam Hussein acquired between 2,000 and 4,000 tons of deadly chemical agents and began experimenting with the gases against the Iranians.[97] According to Samantha Power, "Iraq used chemical weapons approximately 195 times between 1983 and 1988, killing or wounding, according to Iran, some 50,000 people, many of them civilians."[98]

Nor did the United States protest when, in May 1987, Iraq became the first country ever to attack its own citizens with chemical weapons.[99] According to reports from Iraqi Kurds who fled to Iran, Saddam Hussein's planes had dropped mustard gas on some two dozen Kurdish villages along the Iranian-Iraqi border. The headquarters of the two main Kurdish political parties reportedly also had been bombed with poison gas, and similar reports continued to be made for the rest of 1987 and into 1988.[100]

Perhaps the most notorious of Iraq's gas attacks was the March 1988 gassing of the Kurdish town of Halabja. According to Samantha Power, "[i]n three days of attacks, victims were exposed to mustard gas, which burns, mutates DNA, and causes malformations and cancer; and the nerve gases sarin and tabum, which can kill, paralyze, or cause immediate and lasting neuropsychiatric damage. Doctors suspect that the dreaded VX gas and the biological agent aflatoxin were also employed. Some 5,000 Kurds were killed immediately. Thousands more were injured."[101] Again, however, there were no U.S. condemnation of the attacks or efforts to refer the issue to the Security Council. On the contrary, in the Security Council the United States reportedly blocked an Iranian effort to raise the question of responsibility for the Halabja attack.[102]

The United States was not, of course, the only permanent member of the Security Council unwilling to take forceful action against the Saddam Hussein regime for its chemical weapons attacks against the Kurds. The Soviet Union had long had cozy relations with Iraq, as evidenced by the friendship treaty between the two nations. France had a thriving arms business with Iraq. Germany sold insecticide and other chemicals to them, and Britain had considerable commercial interests in Iraq.[103]

It would not be long, however, before all of the permanent members would have to decide how to react to Iraq's invasion of Kuwait.

Iraq-Kuwait

The 1990s were, by any measure, an extraordinary decade. The breakup of the Soviet Union, and the emergence of the countries in central and eastern Europe from under the Soviet yoke, the demise of apartheid in South Africa, and the emergence of a less confrontational atmosphere in the U.N. General Assembly all contributed to a lessening of support for wars of national liberation (with the important exception of Arab attitudes toward Israel) and promised to usher in a new era of international cooperation, inside and outside the United Nations, in maintaining international peace and security. The first major test of this promise came on August 2, 1990, when Iraq invaded Kuwait.

The newly revitalized Security Council immediately responded to the challenge by unanimously adopting a resolution that condemned the invasion and demanded that Iraq "withdraw immediately and unconditionally all its armed forces."[104] When Iraq failed to do so, on August 6, 1990, the Council, acting under Chapter VII of the Charter, imposed mandatory economic sanctions against Iraq.[105] On August 9, in response to Iraq's declaration of a "comprehensive and internal merger" with Kuwait, the Council adopted a resolution[106] by which it decided that annexation of Kuwait by Iraq had no legal validity and was considered null and void, called on states and international organizations not to recognize the annexation, and demanded that Iraq rescind its annexation.

The Security Council continued to adopt resolutions on various aspects of the Gulf crisis.[107] At the same time there was a major military build-up in the Persian Gulf of U.S. and other states' military troops.[108] Neither this military build-up nor the adoption of further resolutions by the Security Council, however, succeeded in inducing Iraq to withdraw from Kuwait, and on November 29, the Security Council adopted Resolution 678 that authorized the use of military force to drive Iraq out of Kuwait.[109]

Resolution 678 was adopted by a vote of twelve in favor (Yemen), two against (Cuba) and one abstention (China). In it the Security Council demanded that Iraq comply fully with all of the Council's previous resolutions and allowed Iraq "one final opportunity, as a pause of goodwill, to do so." Unless Iraq did so, "on or before January 15, 1991," member states were authorized, in cooperation with Kuwait, "to use all necessary means to uphold and implement [the previous Council resolutions] and to restore international peace and security in the area." Iraq did not withdraw from Kuwait by the January 15 deadline, and the military coalition supporting Kuwait began air strikes at that time. After the air strikes, which lasted several weeks, a ground war began that lasted until February 27, 1991, when President Bush went on television to announce his intention to suspend offensive combat operations and stated that the United States was willing to abide by all U.N. resolutions.

Parenthetically, it should be noted that President Bush's decision to stop the fighting when he did and not continue on to Baghdad to eliminate the military capability of Iraq and replace its leadership raised both policy and legal issues. The primary legal issue is whether Resolution 678 and previous Security Council resolutions would have authorized anything more than the liberation of Kuwait.[110]

In any event, the political decision was to stop the attack in Iraq well short of occupying Baghdad. Although, as always when the use of force is involved, not all would agree,[111] most commentators and states would support the proposition that the U.S. and the coalition's use of force in Kuwait and Iraq was in full compliance with international law, either as an act of collective self-defense or as a U.N.-authorized collective security action.[112] Some, moreover, including President Bush, envisaged a "new world order" in which the U.N. Security Council would finally be able to perform its collective security function along the lines of the Charter paradigm.

Note, however, that in the voting on Resolution 678, one permanent member of the Security Council (China) abstained on the vote,[113] rather than casting a veto, allegedly because the United States, during a then current Chinese crackdown on political dissidents, consented to lift trade sanctions in place since the Tiannamen Square massacre of prodemocracy protesters, to support a $114.3 million loan to China from the World Bank, and to grant a long-sought Washington visit by the Chinese Foreign Minister.[114] Similarly, allegedly, the Russian affirmative vote came about largely because the United States agreed to help Russia keep Estonia, Latvia, and Lithuania out of the November 1990 Paris Summit Conference and pledged to persuade Kuwait and Saudi Arabia to provide Moscow with the hard currency it needed to catch up on overdue payments to commercial creditors.[115] Most important, perhaps, neither Russia nor China provided troops or materials to the coalition in the Gulf or otherwise contributed to the success of the military effort there – hardly in keeping with the role of permanent members under the Charter paradigm for collective security.

A harsher reality soon intruded itself. In a sense this harsher reality began on April 3, 1991, when the Security Council unanimously adopted Resolution 687, which, among many other things, decided that Iraq must unconditionally accept the destruction, under international supervision, of all its chemical and biological weapons and all its ballistic missiles with a range greater than 150 kilometers and must unconditionally agree not to acquire or develop nuclear weapons or nuclear-weapons-usable material and to place all such materials under the exclusive control, for custody and removal, of the International Atomic Energy Agency (IAEA). It also constituted a formal cease-fire to the Gulf conflict.[116]

Shortly after the cease-fire, however, in March 1991 there were reports of widespread attacks by Iraqi forces against Iraq's Kurdish and Shiite populations, causing nearly two million refugees to flee toward the Turkish and Iranian borders. On April 5, 1991, "Recalling Article 2, paragraph 7, of the Charter of the United Nations," the Security Council adopted Resolution 688,[117] which condemned Iraq's repression of its civilian population and noted that this repression led to a "massive flow of refugees towards and across international frontiers and to cross-border incursions, which threaten international peace and security in the region." Resolution 688 further demanded that Iraq, "as a contribution to removing the threat to international peace and security in the region," immediately cease this repression, insisted that Iraq allow immediate access by international humanitarian organizations to all those in need of assistance in all parts of Iraq, requested the Secretary-General to pursue his humanitarian efforts in Iraq and to use all the resources at his disposal to address the critical needs of the refugees, and appealed to all member states and to all humanitarian organizations to contribute to these humanitarian relief efforts.

The United States, the United Kingdom, and France cited this resolution as support for the establishment by force of refugee camps in northern Iraq, and later of no-fly zones in northern Iraq (to protect the Kurds) and in southern Iraq (to protect the Shiites), but the Secretary-General disagreed and suggested the need for Iraq's consent or further Security Council action.

The Secretary-General's position is not easily dismissed. As a preliminary matter one should note that Resolution 688 does *not* invoke Chapter VII of the Charter; rather, it recalls Article 2 (7), which precludes the United Nations from intervening in matters that are "essentially within the domestic jurisdiction of any state," unless the application of enforcement measures under Chapter VII is involved. By adopting Resolution 688, the Council thus decided that Iraq's repression of its civilian population was not a matter essentially within its domestic jurisdiction. But it does not follow that the resolution thereby authorized the use of armed force to prevent that repression by setting up enclaves in northern and southern Iraq. On the contrary, nothing in the language or negotiating history of Resolution 688 suggests the right of any member state to deploy troops to that end. Unlike the Council's earlier resolutions authorizing the trade embargo or the armed attack against Iraq, nothing in Resolution 688 even hints at the use of armed force to protect the civilian population of Iraq. Moreover, as pointed out by Jane Stromseth,[118] who does not agree with these arguments, in the vote on Resolution 688:

> China and India abstained, expressing their concern for the humanitarian needs of the refugees, but also their desire to protect the principle of nonintervention in internal affairs. China's representative, for example, indicated that the situation in Iraq involved both "internal affairs" and "international aspects." While supporting the Secretary-General in "rendering humanitarian assistance to the refugees through the relevant organizations," China also reiterated its position that the Security Council "should not consider or take action on questions concerning the internal affairs of any State."

To be sure, the U.N. General Assembly never adopted a resolution condemning the interventions in either northern or southern Iraq. This inaction, plus various statements made by governments and nongovernmental entities over an extended period of time, as suggested by Sean Murphy, arguably "leads to a conclusion that, while many governments and others expressed serious reservations, ultimately the interventions in Iraq were regarded by the world community as somehow emanating from authority granted by the Security Council."[119] One is reminded by this argument of the practice of "jury nullification" that one finds in domestic legal orders, especially that of the United States.

With or without authority granted by the Security Council, throughout the rest of 1990s and into the 2000s, the United States and other states employed the use of armed force in and over Iraqi territory. The no-fly zones were enforced by coalition aircraft from a base in Turkey or from aircraft carriers in the Persian Gulf. The

United States and other states mounted air strikes or other military actions when Iraq violated the terms of the cease-fire resolution, trespassed into Kuwait, renewed attacks on its Kurdish or Shiite populations, or otherwise acted in a hostile manner. In January 1993, U.S., British, and French forces carried out air strikes in response to cease-fire violations, including unauthorized incursions into Kuwaiti territory and the refusal to guarantee the safety and free movement of the Special Commission (of weapons inspectors) established under Resolution 686 (UNSCOM).[120]

Iraq's interference with the free movement of UNSCOM intensified over the 1990s and resulted in the departure of the UNSCOM inspectors in 1998 and Iraq's refusal to permit them or a successor team to resume their functions. The response of the United States and the United Kingdom (France was no longer involved) was fierce. Operation Desert Fox, as the military action was called, was a major operation lasting four days and nights and involving more missiles than used in the entire 1991 conflict.[121] As the legal basis for their use of force, the United States and the United Kingdom cited Security Council resolutions[122] and claimed that the use of force was a lawful response to a breach by Iraq of the cease-fire.[123] But these arguments are problematic because neither of the two cited Security Council resolutions explicitly authorizes the use of force, and arguably the Security Council rather than individual U.N. member states should decide what response is appropriate in the event of a violation of a cease-fire imposed by the Security Council.[124]

Assuming arguendo that the U.S. and U.K. legal case for Operation Desert Fox is weak, it is noteworthy that the other permanent members of the Security Council were unwilling to authorize the use of force in the face of such a blatant violation by Iraq of its responsibilities under the cease-fire resolution. Indeed, China and Russia sharply criticized the action as an unprovoked use of force that violated the U.N. Charter,[125] and the debates on the Security Council resolutions cited by the United States and the United Kingdom indicate quite clearly that most members of the Security Council did not view the resolutions as in any way authorizing the use of force.[126] As we shall see later in this chapter, this unwillingness to use force on the part of France, Russia, and China continued up to the point where the United States and the United Kingdom decided to effect a regime change in Iraq in March 2003. Before we explore this situation, however, we turn next to the dissolution of the former Yugoslavia and the trials and tribulations facing the Security Council in dealing with that crisis.

Yugoslavia

In the previous section we have taken a look at the difficulties surrounding the U.S., British, and (initially) French use of force in Iraq to protect Kurdish and Shiite populations. These difficulties pale in comparison, however, with those associated with the dissolution of the former Yugoslavia in 1991. In the wake of "the shock waves of a collapsed Soviet Union that reverberated throughout Central and Eastern

Europe,"[127] on June 25, 1991, Slovenia and Croatia declared their independence. On June 27, armed forces controlled by Serbia attacked the provisional Slovenia militia, and by July had initiated hostilities in Croatia. The response of the Security Council, on September 25, was the unanimous adoption of a resolution that expressed support for the collective efforts of the European Community and the Conference on Security and Cooperation in Europe to resolve the conflict.[128] By the same resolution the Council decided under Chapter VII of the Charter to impose an embargo on all deliveries of weapons and military equipment. There was no suggestion in the resolution that an international act of aggression had taken place. By early 1992, however, most of the former Yugoslavian republics had attained international recognition, thus turning what had begun as an internal conflict into an international conflict.

In January 1992, special U.N. envoys had managed to secure a cease-fire in Croatia.[129] The result, however, was to shift the locus of the fighting to the republic of Bosnia-Herzegovina, which contained a majority of Muslims in its population but with substantial Serbian and Croatian minorities. In 1992 those minorities were supplied with extensive military assistance for use against the Bosnian army. Serbia in particular was actively involved in providing the Bosnain Serbs with significant firepower. Perversely, the arms embargo imposed against the former Yugoslavia as a whole greatly undermined Bosnia's ability to obtain arms to defend itself.[130] In April 1992, Serb forces launched an attack against Bosnia-Herzegovina from Serbia and commenced the "ethnic cleansing" and other atrocities that ultimately caused the Security Council to create the International Tribunal for the former Yugoslavia to prosecute the persons responsible.

In February 1992, the Security Council had authorized the creation of a U.N. Protection Force (UNPROFOR).[131] Initially, it was envisioned that this force would be interposed, in classic peacekeeping fashion, between the Serbian and Croatian forces that had been fighting in Croatia, as one step toward an overall settlement. UNPROFOR's mandate was later extended to Bosnia-Herzegovina. On December 11, 1992, the Security Council approved a deployment of 700 U.N. personnel to Macedonia, another former Yugoslavian republic – the first time U.N. peacekeepers had been deployed as an exercise of "preventive diplomacy."[132]

In March 1993, the United States, in coordination with the United Nations, began supplying food and medicine by air to Muslim enclaves in Bosnia-Herzegovina that could not be reached by land.[133] In April and May 1993, the Security Council established six of these enclaves as "safe areas" for Bosnian civilians. UNPROFOR was given a mandate to use force "to enable it to deter attacks against those areas, to occupy certain key points on the ground to this end, and to reply to bombardments against the safe areas."[134] This mandate envisaged a use of force that went beyond that traditionally utilized by U.N. peacekeeping force. To carry out this mandate, the Secretary-General estimated that UNPROFOR would need an additional 34,000 troops at a cost of $250 million for the first six months and $26 million per month thereafter.[135] But no such additional troops were forthcoming. As a result, UNPRO-FOR was simply incapable of protecting the so-called safe areas in Bosnia. This was most tragically demonstrated on July 11, 1995, when Bosnian Serb forces overran the U.N.-designated safe area of Srebrenica, captured 430 Dutch members of UNPRO-FOR, and massacred Muslim civilians in such numbers that it was "said to be the worst atrocity in Europe since World War II."[136]

In short, the so-called U.N. peacekeeping operation in Bosnia-Herzegovina was a disastrous failure. In Bosnia, there was no peace to keep, and UNPROFOR was never given the numerical strength or military firepower to impose itself on all or even any of the warring parties. Nor did the Security Council have the political will to induce NATO to introduce sufficient troops to enforce a truce. It was only after NATO finally decided to bomb heavily Bosnian Serb positions, coupled with the use of Croatian ground troops, that it became possible to enforce a peaceful settlement.[137] The peacekeeping force established to implement the peace agreement for Bosnia and Herzegovina negotiated in Dayton, Ohio, and signed on December 14, 1995, in Paris operates under NATO auspices. By resolution the Security Council authorized the NATO peacekeeping force to replace U.N. peacekeepers in Bosnia and to take "such enforcement action . . . as may be necessary to ensure implementation" of the peace agreements.[138] This new implementation force or IFOR, unlike the hapless UNPROFOR, had the wherewithal (in the form, e.g., of 60,000 troops) to serve as an enforcement force.

This pattern of a Security-Council-approved ambitious mandate, coupled with a failure to carry out their mandate, was also present in Somalia, with tragic results. And this pattern has continued. The United States, in particular, has often urged the Council to adopt ambitious peacekeeping mandates without the military clout to ensure a peaceful resolution of the dispute.[139]

We shall return to the issue of the appropriate role of permanent members of the Security Council in U.N. peacekeeping forces later in this chapter. For now, however, it is time to resume consideration of some of the developments that led to regime change in Iraq.

The Downfall of Saddam Hussein

Despite the ferocity of its attacks, Operation Desert Fox did not result in Iraq readmitting the UNSCOM and IAEA inspectors. Because of a belief by several members of the Security Council that UNSCOM needed to be reconstituted so as to reflect a more balanced body, there ensued a year of discussions that resulted in Resolution 1284,[140] which established a new inspection agency, the U.N. Monitoring, Verification and Inspection Commission (UNMOVIC), to verify Iraq's compliance with Resolution 687. UNMOVIC took steps toward resuming its inspections, but Iraq continued to block the return of inspectors unless there was an immediate lifting of U.N. sanctions against Iraq.[141]

Elsewhere, U.S. and British efforts to gain support from other states and at the United Nations for armed intervention in Iraq have been described in detail.[142] Elsewhere, the arguments for and against the proposition that Resolution 1441 authorized the use of force to remove Saddam Hussein from power have been set forth in detail. For my part I find the arguments against this proposition to be the more persuasive,[143] and am of the view that Resolution 1441 required that the Security Council meet and decide by the adoption of a further resolution what actions, if any, member states should take against Iraq for violations of Resolution 1441.[144] But there is now compelling evidence that there was no possibility that France, Russia, or China would ever have agreed to a Security Council resolution that authorized the removal by force of the Saddam Hussein regime. This is because all three permanent members had for years been involved in deals with the regime and had no interest in bringing this cozy relationship to an end.

Such Good Friends

Various recent investigations and reports have demonstrated convincingly that France and Russia had long-standing friendly relations with Saddam Hussein's government and used their status as permanent members of the Security Council to undermine the effectiveness of U.N. sanctions against the Hussein regime.[145] Indeed, as noted previously in this chapter, at the time of Iraq's invasion of Iran, the United States also was supportive in various ways of Saddam's aggression. Moreover, it should be remembered, although the evidence of Saddam's use of chemical weapons against the Iranians and against the Kurds was overwhelming, the United States failed to take any action, inside or outside of the Security Council, in response to these atrocities.[146]

Oil-for-Food

After six years of being subject to international economic sanctions, Iraq was permitted by the United Nations Security Council to resume its export of crude oil in December 1996 under the Oil-for-Food Program. Under the rules of the program, Iraq was allowed to sell its oil so long as it was sold at what the United Nations decided was a fair market price and the proceeds of each sale were deposited to a U.N.-controlled escrow account to be used only for humanitarian and other purposes permitted by the Security Council.[147]

The program permitted Iraq, not the United Nations, to choose its oil buyers. This "empowered Iraq with economic and political leverage to advance its broader interest in overturning the sanctions regime. Iraq selected oil recipients in order to influence foreign policy and international public opinion in its favor."[148] Specifically, "[at]the outset of the Programme, Iraq preferred to sell its oil to companies and individuals from countries that were perceived as 'friendly' to Iraq, and, in particular, if they were permanent members of the Security Council in a position to ease the restrictions of sanctions. Russian companies received almost one-third of oil sales under the Programme. Through its Ministry of Fuel and Energy, Russia coordinated with Iraq on the allocation of crude oil to Russian companies. French companies were the second largest purchaser of oil under the Programme."[149]

In contrast, Iraq disfavored companies from countries viewed as unfriendly to Iraq. Interestingly, at the beginning of the program, Iraqi Vice President Taha Yassin Ramadan and Oil Minister Amer Rashid convinced Saddam Hussein to give allocations to U.S. companies in the hope of persuading the United States to soften its attitude toward Iraq. When there was no change in the U.S. position, the oil allocated to U.S. companies was given to Russian companies.[150] This Iraqi disfavor, however, did not prevent companies from disfavored countries from obtaining Iraqi crude oil, because companies based in the United States and other countries entered into contracts with Russian companies for the purchase and for the financing of purchases of substantial amounts of oil.[151]

Several years after the program began, Iraq decided it could generate illicit income outside of the United Nations' oversight by requiring its oil buyers to pay surcharges of generally between ten to thirty cents per barrel of oil. Russian companies contracted for approximately $19.3 billion worth of oil from Iraq under the program. This amounted to approximately 30 percent of all oil sales, which was by far the largest portion among all participating countries.[152] Although most of the oil provided to Russia was allocated to major oil companies, some of it was allocated in the names of political figures and parties in Russia, including the Communist Party of the Russian Federation and the Russian Liberal Democratic Party.[153]

Surcharges on oil contracts sometimes were paid in cash at Iraqi embassies abroad, including in Russia, Greece, Egypt, Switzerland, Italy, Malaysia, Turkey, Austria, Vietnam, Yemen, and Syria.[154] But by far the largest portion of total surcharge payments went through the Iraqi Embassy in Moscow. Between March 2001 and December 2002, more than $52 million in surcharges was paid through the Iraqi Embassy in Moscow.[155] Cash payments were stored by the commercial counselor in the safe in his office at the Embassy. The cash, along with copies of relevant receipts, was transported periodically in red canvas diplomatic bags from Moscow to Baghdad by the diplomatic staff of the Iraqi Embassy. Diplomatic bags, which could hold up to $1.5 million in $100 bills, were used to transport the money when a sufficient amount accumulated at the Embassy.[156]

As indicated previously, French companies were the second-largest purchaser of Iraqi oil under the Oil-for-Food Program.[157] Besides preferring companies based in France, Iraq also allocated oil to individuals based in France who espoused pro-Iraq views. Several of the individuals receiving the most generous allocations had previously held positions of influence, either with the French government or with international organizations like the United Nations.[158]

Under the Oil-for-Food Program, Iraq was expected to use revenues derived from the sale of its oil to purchase "humanitarian goods," such as food and medicines, to relieve the suffering of its people from the economic sanctions. Like its selection of oil purchasers, political considerations governed its selection of humanitarian vendors. As a consequence, Russian and French companies together accounted for nearly one-fifth of Iraq's imports (about $6.8 billion).[159] For its part China added an additional 5 percent to Iraq's imports (more than $1.7 billion).[160]

Iraq's largest source of illicit income with respect to the program came from "kickbacks" paid by companies that it selected to receive contracts for humanitarian goods. Iraq reportedly derived more than $1.5 billion in income from these kickbacks.[161]

Interestingly, for the first several years of the program's operation, Iraq had no kickback policy. The kickback policy developed in mid-1999 because Iraq wanted to recoup costs it incurred to transport goods to inland destinations after their arrival by sea at the Persian Gulf port of Umm Qasr. Eschewing approval from the United Nations for compensation for such costs from the program's escrow account, Iraq instead required humanitarian contractors to make such payments directly to Iraqi-controlled bank accounts or to front companies outside Iraq that would forward the payments to the government of Iraq. Iraq imposed "inland transportation" fees that far exceeded its actual transportation costs.[162]

In mid-2000, Iraq decided to impose generally a 10 percent kickback requirement on all humanitarian contractors – including contractors shipping goods by land as well as contractors shipping to Umm Qasr. Iraq called its broader kickback requirement an "after-sales-service" fee. This fee was in addition to the requirement that contractors pay inland transportation fees. After-sales-service provisions often were incorporated into contracts as a way to inflate prices and permit contractors to recover from the United Nations escrow account amounts they had paid secretly to Iraq in the form of kickbacks.[163] The Volcker Committee calculated that more than 2,200 companies worldwide paid kickbacks to Iraq in the form of inland transportation fees, after-sales-service fees, or both.[164]

To be sure, Russian officials have claimed that the documents cited as evidence by the Volcker Committee that Russian companies and politicians paid hefty kickbacks to Iraq in the Oil-for-Food Program are forgeries.[165] But they have presented no evidence to support their claims, and the findings of the Volcker Committee have been confirmed by the results of other investigations, especially those of the U.S. Senate Permanent Subcommittee on Investigations – Committee on Homeland Security and Governmental Affairs, the so-called Coleman Committee, named after its chairman, Senator Norm Coleman.[166] Parenthetically, it may be noted that the Coleman Committee reports also support some of the findings of the Volcker Committee regarding France and former French officials.[167]

The Duelfer Report

Many of the findings of the Volcker Committee regarding actions taken by French, Russian, and Chinese companies, as well as by their governments themselves, that undermined the effectiveness of the Oil-for-Food Program have also been confirmed by the so-called Duelfer Report, named after Charles Duelfer, Senior Advisor to the U.S. Director of Central Intelligence, and issued on September 30, 2004.[168] The Duelfer Report, however, goes beyond the Volcker Committee's report and discusses actions by these countries and their companies that supplied Iraq with conventional weapons and, in some instances, materials that would be helpful in producing chemical or biological weapons.

The Duelfer Report is the product of the Iraq Survey Group (ISG), which was created in June 2003 and consisted of numerous Australian, British, and American soldiers, analysts, and support personnel.[169] Its purpose was to provide as comprehensive an investigation as possible into Iraq's weapons of mass destruction (WMD) program. The Director of Central Intelligence initially named David Kay as the senior Special Adviser for Iraqi WMD, who served in Iraq from June until December 2003, to provide direction to the overall effort. Under his leadership, ISG began a systematic survey and examination of the existence and location of WMD capabilities, through interviewing many key participants in the WMD programs, site visits, and the review of captured documents.[170] Kay provided an initial report to the Director of Central Intelligence in September 2003 on the early findings of the investigation. Charles Duelfer succeeded Kay as the Special Adviser for Iraqi WMD at the end of December 2003.

According to the Duelfer Report, by 2000, sanctions against Iraq had been so weakened that "[p]rohibited goods and weapons were being shipped into Iraq with virtually no problem. The only notable items stopped in this flow were some aluminum tubes, which became the center of debate over the existence of a nuclear enrichment effort in Iraq. Major items had no trouble getting across the border, including 380 liquid-fuel rocket engines. Indeed, Iraq was designing missile systems with the assumption that sanctioned material would be readily available."[171] Procurements supporting Iraq's weapons delivery systems expanded after the 1998 departure of U.N. inspectors, because revenue was flowing in under the Oil-for-Food Program and Iraqi front companies took advantage of the freedom to operate without U.N. oversight.[172]

Iraq hired technicians and engineers from Russian companies to review the designs and assist development of the Al Samud II rocket, thereby contributing to its rapid evolution. It also entered into negotiations with North Korean and Russian entities for more capable missile systems, and in 2002, Iraq approached Russian entities about acquiring the Iskander-E-short-range ballistic missile (SRBM). Iraq further imported missile guidance and control systems from entities in Belarus, Russia, and the Federal Republic of Yugoslavia.[173]

In early July 2001, the United States and the United Kingdom withdrew their joint proposal to substantially modify the existing economic sanctions against Iraq and institute in their place a regime of so-called smart sanctions. These smart sanctions were designed to further relieve the impact of sanctions on the Iraqi people while tightening the effectiveness of sanctions against the Saddam regime. Specifically, the smart sanctions were directed toward preventing the illicit procurement of weapons and dual-use goods and the illicit generation of revenue from Iraqi oil sales outside the Oil-for-Food Program. The United States and Great Britain withdrew their proposal because of Russian, Chinese, and French opposition.[174]

The Duelfer Report is full of reports regarding illicit transactions between Iraq and Russian companies and officials involving the supply of conventional weapons.[175] It also reports that, in 2002, Iraq made improvements to a nitric acid plant with equipment, material, and expertise obtained in part from Russia.[176] In the field of biological weapons, in 1995, Iraq reportedly attempted to purchase two turnkey 50-cubic-meter fermentor plants from a Russian company with expertise in botulinum toxin production. Iraq negotiated a deal for equipment and assistance, and Iraqi scientists and technicians traveled to Russia to discuss the deal. But it fell through because the Russian company could not obtain an export license.[177]

The Duelfer Report also had much to say about Iraq's dealings with France, although it described the Iraqi-French relationship as being "more tumultuous" than Iraq's "relatively predictable relationships with China and Russia."[178] It noted that, before 1991 when the sanctions against Iraq began, France used to be a "major conventional arms supplier for the Iraq Regime."[179] In 2001, Tariq Aziz, Deputy Prime Minister of Iraq, "characterized the French approach to U.N. sanctions as adhering to the letter of sanctions but not the spirit. This was demonstrated by the presence of French CAs [commercial attaches] in Bagdad, working to promote the interest of French companies while assisting them in avoiding U.N. sanctions."[180]

An example of how France provided Iraq with military goods was the tank carrier supplied to the Iraqi Ministry of Defense by the French company Lura. A French expert arrived in Iraq in September 1999 to provide training and offer technical expertise regarding the carrier.[181] Similarly, recovered documents dated November 1999 revealed that a French company was "willing to collaborate and supply spare parts for the French Mirage aircraft," and in the same year, Mr. William Libras, head of the Iraqi-French Friendship Society, offered to supply Iraq with Western-manufactured helicopters and told Iraq that French suppliers would be able to update the aircraft and add any system Iraq requested.[182]

Between 2000 and 2002, the Iraqi government purchased thousands of supply and personnel transport vehicles for Iraq's Republican Guard and Special Republican Guard. According to a former senior Iraqi cabinet minister, Turkey, Russia, France, Germany, and South Korea were the primary suppliers of these vehicles.[183]

Lastly, in 1999, a French company reportedly supplied raw materials to be used in the production of solid propellants for missiles to an Iraqi company. These raw materials included six tons of ammonium perchlorate and five tons of aluminum powder. The Duelfer Report noted, however, that it had "no evidence that the French Government either sanctioned or approved this transaction."[184]

According to the Duelfer Report, Iraq successfully targeted scientists from China (along with scientists from Russia, Belarus, Poland, Bulgaria, Yugoslavia, and several other countries) to acquire new military and defense-related technologies for Iraq. Payments were made in U.S. dollars. Iraq also recruited foreign scientists to work in Iraq as free-lance consultants. The result, in the Duelfer Report's view, was that "[p]resumably these scientists, plus their Iraqi colleagues, provided the resident 'know how' to reconstitute WMD within two years once sanctions were over, as one former high-ranking Iraqi official said was possible."[185]

As to military assets, Chinese firms supplied Iraq with limited but critical items, including gyroscopes, accelerometers, graphite, and telecommunications. Interestingly, the Duelfer Report indicated that there was "no evidence to suggest the [sic] Chinese Government complicity in supplying prohibited goods to Iraq. It is likely that newly privatized state-owned companies were willing to circumvent export controls and official U.N. monitoring to supply prohibited goods."[186] On the contrary, the Report stated, "we suspect that some contracts that were abruptly stopped may have been a result of Beijing's direct intervention . . . Most transactions, however, were orchestrated through newly privatized state-owned companies competing in a bloated and highly competitive, newly founded commercial system where they were able to participate in illegal trade with little oversight."[187]

The Bottom Line: No Security Council Resolution Authorizing Saddam's Removal

As the Volcker Committee Report and the Duelfer Report, as well as other sources, demonstrate, for most of the 1990s and into the 2000s, France, Russia, and China worked assiduously to undermine the effectiveness of U.N. sanctions against the Saddam regime and to continue and enhance the many commercially beneficial relationships they had with the regime. The reports also demonstrate that these efforts were successful and that, by the early 2000s at the latest, the sanctions had become largely ineffective. Their motives appear to be largely commercial, although both France and Russia had long-standing political ties to Iraq as well. In short, the Saddam regime was one favored by the three permanent members of the Security Council, and it is reasonable to conclude that they had no interest in its removal and would exercise their veto power to block any Security Council resolution that sought to authorize such removal.

To be sure, there has been considerable debate over whether it was necessary or desirable to remove the Saddam regime to maintain international peace and security. The arguments for and against this proposition are beyond the scope of this chapter. But one may reasonably conclude that permanent members of the Security Council should never allow commercial interests to trump their responsibility to maintain international peace and security. This, however, is what happened with respect to Iraq, and as we shall see, this pattern has continued.

Darfur

Perhaps the most striking recent example of permanent members' commercial interests trumping considerations of war and peace, as well as humanitarian values, has been the situation in Darfur and the Sudan. For more than two and a half years, the government of the Sudan combined with a band of thugs known as the *janjaweed* to "butcher, rape, and expel non-Arabs living in the western region of Darfur."[188] The estimated dead included, as of May 2005, 70,000 killed and another 130,000 dead from disease and malnutrition created by the conflict.[189] During this period, the U.N. Security Council, especially the permanent members, did little to stop the slaughter. China is the main customer for Sudan's oil exports, Russia is the Sudan's main provider of weapons and aircraft, and French oil companies have interests in extracting Sudanese oil.[190]

A United Nations Commission of Inquiry created by the Security Council to investigate violence in the Darfur region found a pattern of mass killings and forced displacement of civilians that, although they did not constitute genocide (contrary to an allegation by Colin Powell, U.S. Secretary of State), did in many instances constitute such international offenses as crimes against humanity and war crimes that were as serious as genocide and should be referred to the International Criminal Court (ICC).[191]

Because of its opposition to the ICC, the United States initially opposed any referral of the situation to the ICC and instead proposed the establishment of a new tribunal to be run jointly by the African Union and the United Nations and to be based in Arusha, Tanzania, which is the location of the International Criminal Tribunal for Rwanda, which is trying suspects in the 1994 genocide in Rwanda.[192] The U.S. proposal received little support, however, and the United States ultimately reluctantly agreed not to block a referral to the ICC once the Council agreed to language in the resolution that would exempt Americans from prosecution in the court. Accordingly, on March 31, 2005, the Security Council adopted, with the United States abstaining, a resolution referring the situation in Darfur since July 1, 2002, to the Prosecutor of the International Criminal Court.[193] On April 5, 2005, U.N. Secretary-General Kofi Annan presented a list of fifty-one suspects in the ethnic killing campaign in Darfur compiled by the U.N. Commission of Inquiry in January to Luis Moreno-Ocampo, the Chief Prosecutor of the International Criminal Court.[194] The Sudan, however, stated that it would refuse to hand over any of its citizens to face trial abroad and would instead prosecute war crimes suspects itself.[195] Sudan has been true to its promise to refuse to hand over any indicted person to the ICC, but it has failed to carry out its promise to prosecute war crimes suspects itself.[196]

A week before it decided to refer the situation in Darfur to the International Criminal Court, the Security Council adopted a resolution whereby it established the United Nations Mission in Sudan (UNMIS) and decided that UNMIS would consist of up to 10,000 military personnel and a civilian component of up to 715 civilian police personnel.[197] UNMIS, however, had as its primary mission the monitoring of the peace agreement in the south of Sudan between the Sudanese government and black African Christians, and its ability to help stop the slaughter in Darfur was questionable. The Council also adopted a resolution imposing modest economic sanctions, including an asset freeze and a travel ban on those who impeded the peace process in Darfur.[198]

African Union efforts to effect a solution to the crisis in Darfur culminated in the signing of the Darfur Peace Agreement on May 5, 2006.[199] The Agreement consisted of four substantive chapters – on power sharing, wealth gathering, a comprehensive cease-fire and security arrangements, and the Darfur-Darfur Dialogue and Consultation. Not all participants in the conflict in Darfur, however, signed on to the Agreement and those who did failed to implement it. As a result, violence continued throughout Darfur, and "it was feared that any attempt to implement the Agreement through force, including the forced return of internally displaced persons, could push Darfur into an even bloodier round of conflict."[200]

In response, on August 31, 2006, the Security Council, by its Resolution 1706,[201] decided to expand the UNMIS mandate to include Darfur without prejudice to the mission's existing mandate and operations. The mandate of UNMIS was to support implementation of the Darfur Peace Agreement (DPA) and the N'djamena Agreement on Humanitarian Ceasefire of the Conflict in Darfur. Acting under Chapter VII of the U.N. Charter, the Council authorized UNMIS to use all necessary means, as it deemed within its capabilities, to prevent disruption of the implementation of the DPA by armed groups, without prejudice to the responsibility of the government of the Sudan, and to protect civilians under threat of physical violence.

UNMIS was unsuccessful in accomplishing its mission, and on July 31, 2007, again acting under Chapter VII of the U.N. Charter, the Security Council adopted Resolution 1769,[202] which authorized a joint African Union/United Nations operation, called UNAMID, to augment UNMIS for an initial period of twelve months. UNAMID has as its core mandate the protection of civilians, providing security for humanitarian assistance, monitoring and verifying implementation of agreements, contributing to the promotion of human rights and the rule of law, and monitoring and reporting on the situation along the borders with Chad and the Central African Republic. The Council decided that UNAMID should consist of up to 19,555 military personnel and a civilian component including up to 3,772 police personnel and 19 formed police units comprising up to 140 personnel each.

As of February 5, 2008, however, UNAMID had barely a third of its planned 26,000 personnel deployed.[203] Resistance on the part of the government of Sudan to accept the deployment of nonAfrican military personnel contributed to this problem. Also, despite appeals by U.N. Secretary-General Ban Ki-Moon to every U.N. member state capable of providing the transport and attack helicopters necessary to operate in the vast territory of the Sudan, none had come forward with offers. When the U.N. forces were attacked by Sudanese forces, they withdrew without returning fire.[204] Sadly, at this time, despite pious statements that "never again" should atrocities along the lines of those committed in Rwanda be allowed to occur, the Rwanda precedent was being followed in Darfur,[205] and both Rwanda and Darfur demonstrated that "nations are not prepared to intervene beyond their spheres of perceived influence."[206]

Since early 2008, there have been both negative and positive developments with respect to Darfur. Perhaps the major negative development has been the March 4, 2009, expulsion of thirteen international nongovernmental aid organizations and the dissolution of three national nongovernmental aid organizations operating in Northern Sudan by President Bashir in response to the arrest warrant issued by the International Criminal Court.[207] "The loss of the nongovernmental organizations initially affected some 1.1 million beneficiaries receiving food assistance, 1.5 million accessing health services, 1.6 million receiving water and sanitation support, and 670,000 receiving non-food items...As of 30 June 2009, the number of national and international aid workers in the region had dropped from a pre-expulsion level of 17,700 to 12,658."[208]

On the positive side, as of June 30, 2009, the total strength of UNAMID military personnel was 13,430 out of a total authorized strength of 19,555, including 12,806 troops, 365 staff officers, 178 military observers, and 84 liaison officers.[209] But "delays by the Government of Sudan in granting both customs clearances and permission for United Nations-contacted vessels to disembark in Port Sudan have slowed the movement of critical equipment into Darfur and resulted in more than $1 million in demurrage charges to the United Nations."[210] Nonetheless, it is expected that "all pledged units will be in place and fully operational by 31 December 2009, constituting 92 percent of the mission's total authorized strength."[211]

At the moment "[l]arge-scale violence stretching over a wide territory and for lengthy periods is now infrequent... Nevertheless, the situation for the civilians of Darfur continues to be deeply troubling, with 2.6 million internally displaced persons unable to return to their homes and some 4.7 million Darfurians in need of assistance. Meanwhile, banditry and sexual violence continue to plague civilians throughout Darfur."[212]

The failure of the United Nations to prevent the atrocities in Darfur would seem to mock the affirmation by the U.N. General Assembly and the Security Council of the so-called responsibility to protect. The U.N. Summit Declaration of 2005, adopted by the General Assembly, affirmed that the United Nations has the responsibility to protect populations from genocide, war crimes, ethnic cleansing, and crimes against humanity, stating: "We are prepared to take collective action, in a timely and decisive manner, through the Security Council, in accordance with the Charter, including Chapter VII, on a case-by-case basis and in cooperation with relevant regional organizations as appropriate, should peaceful means be inadequate and national authorities are manifestly failing to protect their populations."[213] For its part, the Security Council, on April 28, 2006, adopted Resolution 1674, which affirmed this statement.[214] But the Council has yet to fulfill this responsibility by taking the necessary action in concrete cases.

WHO SHALL ENFORCE THE PEACE?

As the foregoing discussion demonstrates, since the founding of the United Nations, the permanent members of the Security Council have all too often failed to fulfill their primary obligation to enforce the peace and have on occasion, to the contrary, actively sought to prevent action being taken against those states who threaten or breach the peace. It is noteworthy, however, as reported by a recent study,[215] that despite this uninspiring record by the permanent members of the Security Council, over the past dozen years, civil wars, genocides, and international crises have all declined sharply. International wars currently constitute only a small minority of all conflicts, and have been in a steady decline for a much longer period. The same is true for military coups and the average number of people killed per conflict per year.[216]

The only form of political violence that appears to be getting worse is international terrorism, but even here the data are subject to debate. Some data have shown an overall decline in international terrorism incidents since the early 1980s, but the most recent data suggest a dramatic increase in the number of high casualty attacks since the September 11 attacks on the United States in 2001.[217]

The authors of *the* Human Security Report 2005 (Report) ascribe much of this drop in conflict numbers to the end of the Cold War.[218] Between 1946 and 1991 there was a twelvefold rise in the number of civil wars, and the data suggest that anticolonialism and the geopolitics of the Cold War were the major causes of this dramatic increase.[219] The wars of liberation from colonial rule accounted for 60 percent to 100 percent of all international wars fought since the early 1950s, but by the early 1980s they had virtually ended with the demise of colonialism. By the late 1980s, the Cold War, which had been a contributing factor for approximately one-third of all wars – civil and international – in the post – World War II period, also came to an end. According to the authors of the Report, "[t]his not only removed the only risk of violent conflict between the major powers and their allies, it also meant that Washington and Moscow stopped supporting their erstwhile allies in many so-called proxy wars in the developing world. Denied external support, many of these conflicts quietly ground to a halt."[220]

Interestingly, the authors of the Report argue that the single most significant contributing factor to the sharp decline in political violence around the world that started in the 1990s and has continued ever since has been a "veritable explosion" of conflict prevention, peacemaking, and postconflict peace-building activities in the early 1990s, spearheaded by the United Nations but involving as well U.N. specialized agencies like the World Bank, a number of regional organizations, and thousands of NGOs working closely with U.N. agencies and often playing independent roles of their own.[221]

Michael Glennon has famously contended that because the use of armed force contrary to the norms of the U.N. Charter has been so widespread, "international 'rules' concerning the use of force are no longer considered obligatory by states."[222] To the contrary, the authors of the Report suggest that a major reason for the decline in wars is that there has been "a gradual normative shift against the use of violence in human relationships."[223] The authors of the Report go on to say:

> Nowhere is this normative shift more evident than in changing public attitudes toward war. Prior to the 20th century, warfare was a normal part of human existence. For governments, war was simply an instrument of statecraft.

> Today the forcible acquisition of territory is universally perceived as a blatant transgression of international law, and resort to force against another country is only permissible in self-defence, or with the sanction of the U.N. Security Council....

> Ideologies that glorify violence and see war as a noble and virtuous endeavor are today notable mostly by their absence. Insofar as similar ideologies still exist they are mainly found not in governments but in small, fanatical, terrorist organizations, such as those associated with al-Qaeda. In addition, the sort of hyper-nationalism that drove Nazi German and Imperial Japanese aggression in the 1930s and 1940s is now extremely rare.

> Some scholars argue that the rise of war-adverse sentiment in the industrialized countries has been the critical factor in the worldwide decline in international war.[224]

There is much to be said in support of these scholars' arguments. Michael Glennon has cited NATO's bombing of Serbian forces in Kosovo and the invasion of Iraq by the United States and other members of the "coalition of the willing" in 2003, both actions arguably in violation of the U.N. Charter, as the final "death knell" for international law norms on the use of force.[225] But both Kosovo and the war in Iraq have been subject to widespread criticism from governments and scholars, and this widespread criticism arguably is a reaffirmation of the Charter norms on the use of force rather than a rejection of them. Also, the United States and other members of NATO largely avoided trying to justify the bombing of Kosovo in legal terms, not because they were rejecting the legal constraints or viewing them as having fallen into desuetude, but because they knew that the legal case was weak under Charter norms and did not want NATO's actions in Kosovo to be viewed as a precedent.[226] In contrast, the United States and its supporters have argued strenuously that the use of force against Iraq to remove the Hussein regime was compatible with U.N. Charter norms, because, among other reasons, it was authorized by Security Council resolutions.[227]

Regardless of the technical legal status of Charter norms on the use of force, and despite the encouraging findings of the Human Security Report that there has been a substantial decline in armed conflict over the last decade, there is still the reality that there continue to be occasions when it is necessary to enforce the peace. Who or what should do this in the future is somewhat unclear at this juncture. It is time to consider some of the possibilities.

Permanent Members of the Security Council

Although much of the discussion in this chapter has revolved around the use of armed force to enforce the peace, it is important to keep in mind that enforcement of the peace also may involve the use of economic sanctions, either as a complement to the use of armed force or as a substitute for it. Indeed, the permanent members of the Security Council, as well as other member states of the United Nations, are often much more willing to impose economic sanctions against a state that threatens or breaches the peace than they are to resort to the use of armed force.[228]

This preference for economic sanctions in place of the use of armed force is likely to continue. The permanent members of the Security Council are likely to assign their own forces to battle only in situations where they perceive that their vital interests are threatened and economic sanctions will be insufficient to protect them. Moreover, as we have seen in the cases of the Oil-for-Food scandal and Darfur, one or more of the permanent members may resist the imposition of economic sanctions against a state threatening the peace, or undermine them once they are in place.[229]

A major barrier to the permanent members acting as a coherent unit through the Security Council to maintain the peace is that, although the Cold War is over, there remains a major disparity of values between the United States, France, and the United Kingdom, on the one hand, and Russia and China, on the other. Despite its taking steps to liberalize its economy, China maintains tyrannical control in the political arena, with an appalling record of human rights abuses. For its part, Russia, under President Vladimir V. Putin, has become increasingly authoritarian and also has a poor human rights record, especially in Chechnya. As a result, Russia and China may have significant sympathetic relations with states that threaten international peace and security.

Moreover, even in the rare instance when Russia and China are willing to vote for, or at least abstain from voting on, a Security Council resolution authorizing the use of force, their contribution to the effort tends to be minimal, both in military and economic terms. The 1990 Gulf War, where neither Russia nor China provided troops or economic support to the coalition forces, is a prime example.

An Alliance of Democratic States

Because of the difficulties the Security Council has had in dealing with threats to the peace, as well as the difficulties the U.N. General Assembly has had in this regard,[230] some commentators have proposed that a coalition or alliance of democratic states assume this responsibility.[231] One form this proposal has taken is to call for a coalition of democratic states to operate within the United Nations itself to counter the autocratic states and their sympathizers. Its more ambitious form would be an international institution whose membership would be limited to countries "where democracy is so rooted that reversion to autocratic rule is unthinkable."[232] This more ambitious form would have member states of the alliance accomplish their objectives in part by working through existing international institutions like the United Nations, but "[t]o achieve its full potential the alliance would also have to develop its own capabilities. On the military front that means emulating NATO. The alliance would develop doctrine, promote joint training and planning and enhance inter-operability among its member militaries. These efforts could cover high-intensity warfare and peacekeeping operations."[233]

There would seem little that would be objectionable in a proposal to form an alliance of democratic states that would serve as a caucus to pursue various objectives within existing international institutions like the United Nations. Creating a new international institution for such an alliance would, however, be much more problematical. The European Union's plan to create a rapid deployment force outside of the NATO framework has met with objections from the United States that it might at best duplicate NATO arrangements and at worst undermine NATO's effectiveness. These problems would be greatly compounded by the creation of a global institution composed of member states from around the world. Moreover, this global institution, unlike NATO, would function not as an exercise of collective self-defense but rather as a collective security agency. As such, its compatibility with the U.N. Charter would be questionable because, although the Charter envisages "regional arrangements or agencies" engaging in "enforcement action" if authorized by the Security Council,[234] the international institution of democracies would be a global rather than a regional agency, and the U.N. Charter does not provide for the possibility of a global institution other than the Security Council performing a collective security function.

Parenthetically, one might question the wisdom of this alliance of democracies emulating NATO in light of the difficulties NATO is currently experiencing in Afghanistan. At this writing, the United States is asking its NATO allies to provide more troops to stabilize the military situation in Afghanistan, but "it is discovering that some allies appear more eager to reduce their forces than to add to them."[235] U.S. Secretary of Defense Robert Gates has credited the Netherlands, Britain, Australia, and Canada with "doing their part in Afghanistan," but indicated that other NATO members have contributed far less.[236] For its part, Canada has threatened to withdraw from the southern province of Kandahar early next year unless other NATO countries agree to send 1,000 addition combat troops there. Tensions within the alliance have also risen because of the unwillingness of some members, including Germany, Italy, and Spain, to send troops to the south of Afghanistan, where the bulk of the fighting is taking place.[237]

Robert Gates has recently emphasized "the direct threat posed to European security by extremists in and around Afghanistan" in a speech reflecting growing

American concerns that weak public support in Europe risked undermining NATO's mission in the country.[238] As evidence of increased danger to Europe from terrorist attacks, Gates cited, among other things, the arrest of fourteen extremists in Barcelona, suspected of planning attacks against public transport systems in Spain, Portugal, France, Germany, and Britain. On the reluctance of European states to commit more troops to Afghanistan, or to allow those already there to move to the south and other areas where the fighting was most intense, Gates warned against the alliance becoming a two-tiered coalition, of those willing to fight and those that were not. He reportedly added that "[s]uch a development, with all its implications for collective security, would effectively destroy the alliance."[239]

Regional Arrangements or Agencies

As noted in the previous section, the U.N. Charter provides for the possibility of regional arrangements or agencies enforcing the peace if authorized to do so by the Security Council, and it should be remembered that Winston Churchill, who proposed separate councils for Asia, Europe, and the Americas, favored a regional approach to enforcing the peace. The U.N. Charter does not define what a regional arrangement or agency is, and there is ambiguity regarding the definition. David Scheffer has suggested an expansive definition that would not limit the composition of regional arrangements to member states of the geographical region in question. Under this definition, "[i]f it had exhibited more explicit organizational trappings, the multinational force that was created in 1990 to confront Iraqi aggression might have qualified for a Chapter VIII 'arrangement' and therefore have been authorized by the Security Council to use military force pursuant to that chapter rather than Chapter VII."[240]

The validity of Scheffer's provocative proposition is debatable in light of the language of Chapter VIII of the Charter. It is, in any event, unlikely to be put to the test, for there appears to be no reason why the Security Council would prefer to operate under Chapter VIII rather than Chapter VII in a situation like the Gulf War crisis where a worldwide coalition of willing states is formed to meet an act of aggression.

The Organization of American States (OAS) is perhaps the quintessential example of a regional arrangement or agency. The OAS, however, has no military force structure, and peace enforcement measures under OAS auspices would therefore be basically by U.S. troops. The United States has relied on OAS recommendations in the past to support the use of armed force, arguing that the actions in question did not constitute "enforcement action" and therefore did not require Security Council approval. Prominent examples include the Cuban quarantine of 1962[241] and the 1965 U.S. intervention in the Dominican Republic.[242]

The 1983 U.S. intervention in Grenada was justified in part on the basis that it was in response to a request for help from a group of Caribbean states called the

Organization of Eastern Caribbean States. There was significant debate over such issues as whether this group of states constituted a regional organization within the meaning of Article 52 of the U.N. Charter and whether the invasion of Grenada in 1983 by the United States and several Caribbean states was a lawful "regional action" under the U.N. Charter.[243]

On October 3, 1991, in response to the overthrow of President Aristide of Haiti by military coup, the OAS unanimously recommended that its member states take "action to bring about the diplomatic isolation of those who hold power illegally in Haiti" and "suspend their economic, financial, and commercial ties."[244] These and other economic sanctions proved to no avail, and in 1994 the Security Council authorized a multinational force led by the United States to "use all necessary means to facilitate the departure from Haiti of the military leadership . . . [and] the prompt return of the legitimately elected President."[245] The OAS never adopted a resolution authorizing the use of force in Haiti and, with the spread of democracy in Latin America, has not been involved in peacekeeping during the last half of the 1990s and the early years of the twenty-first century.

In 1991, Oscar Schachter predicted that: "It is probable that peacekeeping actions and perhaps limited enforcement will be employed by regional organizations more frequently in the future. They are likely to be used to assist in monitoring and border patrol and perhaps to help provide order to a country in internal conflict or near anarchy."[246] As has so often been the case, Schachter's suggestion has proven to be prescient.

The constitutive Act of the African Union gives it the authority to play a peacekeeping and peace enforcement role.[247] As we saw earlier in this chapter, the African Union has attempted to play such a role in Darfur, but it has lacked the resources and expertise to do so, and the United Nations has had considerable difficulty in trying to establish a more robust African Union/U.N. force. Nonetheless, the African Union is likely to be the regional agency most involved in peacekeeping and peace enforcement, if only because the need for such action is likely to be greatest on the African continent. For a variety of reasons, some of which will be explored in the next section of this chapter, other regional agencies are likely to be less active than the African Union.[248]

The United Nations

From the discussion of U.N. peacekeeping earlier in this chapter, one may safely conclude that, should a state with the military capacity of Milosovic's Serbia, or Saddam Hussein's Iraq, commit an act of armed aggression, it is highly unlikely that a U.N. peacekeeping force will be raised to resist it. Rather, at least ideally, the Security Council might authorize a coalition of military powers to undertake this task.

This does not mean, however, that future U.N. peacekeeping will be conducted only among the lines of the traditional model where U.N. peacekeeping units resort to the use of force only in self-defense. To the contrary, it is likely that civil wars, often involving widespread atrocities, especially in Africa, will continue to be the primary kind of armed conflict in the twenty-first century. Because the military powers, including the permanent members of the Security Council, have shown little interest in committing their own troops to such conflicts, U.N. peacekeeping forces will need to fill the gap. U.N. peacekeeping has recently become more robust,[249] and this is a trend that is likely to continue,[250] as illustrated by the continuing efforts to induce Sudan to accept a 27,000-member U.N. peacekeeping force in Darfur.[251]

Moreover, as a recent Rand study has reported,[252] the United Nations has been actively engaged in "nation-building," defined as "the use of armed force in the aftermath of a crisis to promote a transition to democracy."[253] Although the use of armed force characteristic of such nation-building missions has often been along the traditional peacekeeping model, there have been exceptions – the Congo has been the quintessential example.[254] U.N. peacekeeping missions in Liberia, Sierra Leone, Kosovo, Burundi, and Ivory Coast – each with their own rules of engagement – have also moved well beyond the traditional notion of peacekeeping.[255]

To be sure, as noted in the Rand study, when the U.N. peacekeeping missions have moved beyond the traditional model, and thereby encountered more difficult circumstances, certain deficiencies in their modus operandi have become apparent:

- the slow arrival of military units;
- the even slower deployment of police and civil administrators;
- the uneven quality of military components;
- the even greater unevenness of police and civil administrators;
- the United Nations' dependence on voluntary funding to pay for such mission-essential functions as reintegration of combatants and capacity building in local administrations;
- the frequent mismatches between ambitious mandates and modest means; and
- the premature withdrawal of missions, often immediately after the successful conclusion of a first democratic election.[256]

Another recently disclosed deficiency is lack of control over U.N. peacekeeping troops, who have engaged in sexual abuse of woman and girls in the Congo and elsewhere.[257] In general, the quality of U.N. peacekeeping forces has often been a problem. In Sierra Leone, an intervention by Nigerian troops was conducted in brutal fashion and resulted in a near defeat for Nigeria. Also, U.N. peacekeeping forces in Sierra Leone were often stymied by outside support of the Revolutionary United Front by Liberia.[258]

In an effort to improve the quality of U.N. peacekeeping forces, the military powers of the United Nations member states have begun to provide military training and equipment to the forces of countries likely to contribute troops, especially member states of the African Union. The process has been slow, however, with contributors often failing to make good on their pledges.[259] The ultimate success or failure of this effort may depend on the ability of member states of the African Union to move away from dictatorships and toward a democratic form of government, because the Human Security Report found that risk of civil conflict is reduced by equitable economic growth, good governance, and inclusive democracy.[260] In contrast, the Report found that countries with governments that are partly democratic and partly authoritarian – called "anocracies" by political scientists – are *more* likely to engage in civil wars than either democracies or autocracies.[261]

According to the Rand study, U.N. enforcement missions are not suited to missions that require forced entry or employ more than 20,000 men, which to date has been the effective upper limit for U.N. operations.[262] Forced entry or the employment of more than 20,000 troops, the Rand study suggests, demands the involvement of the military powers. If this suggestion is correct, it calls into question the viability of the proposed U.N. force for Darfur. Although at this point the United Nations has made it clear that the presence of the force in the Sudan depends on the willingness of the Sudanese government to accept it, it is envisaged that the number of troops in the force may be as many as 26,000, which would make it the largest of the U.N. peacekeeping forces. And any involvement of the military powers will be limited to providing equipment and training for the U.N. force. In short, assuming the current obstacles to establishing such a force for Darfur can be overcome, it will remain to be seen whether the force's responsibilities can be limited to so-called robust peacekeeping or will require enforcement measures that would seem to demand the participation of the armed forces of the military powers.

It is likely that U.N. exercises in nation-building will require the use of robust peacekeeping forces. As noted previously, in December 2005, the General Assembly and the Security Council adopted resolutions[263] creating a Peacebuilding Commission to help stabilize and rebuild nations emerging from war. This was the first concrete achievement flowing from the proposals adopted in principle by the September 2005 General Assembly meeting of Heads of State and Government. Jan Eliasson of Sweden, president of the General Assembly, reportedly said the commission was critical for keeping war-torn countries from reverting to hostilities, which he said had occurred in half the cases over the past twenty years where conflicts had ended.[264] At the present time, there is considerable risk in several places in Africa of war-torn countries reverting to hostilities.

CONCLUSION

As we have seen throughout this chapter, the permanent members of the Security Council have often failed to fulfill their primary responsibility under the U.N. Charter to maintain international peace and security and have, on occasion, gone so far as to aid and abet aggressor states. They have become especially reluctant to commit their ground troops to the currently most prevalent form of armed conflict, civil wars, or to prevent the commission of such atrocities as genocide, war crimes, or crimes against humanity by a government against its own citizens – what the Human Security Report refers to as "one-sided violence."[265] Surely this reluctance has increased because of the difficulties facing the United States and the "coalition of the willing" in Iraq and NATO in Afghanistan. At the same time, the permanent members, as well as some other militarily powerful states such as some E.U. member states, have recognized, if haltingly, an obligation to provide training and military assets to U.N. or regional peacekeeping forces to enable them to suppress aggression. Moreover, although it is less likely than it was during the Cold War days, there is still a possibility that a military power will engage in cross-border aggression that will require a response that is beyond the military capabilities of U.N. or regional peacekeeping forces. One thinks of Iran or North Korea as possibilities. In such a case the role of the United Nations, at least initially, is likely to be limited to a call on the aggressor state to cease its aggression or to the passage of a Security Council resolution authorizing member states to use force to meet the aggression.

An alliance of democratic states working within the United Nations and other international institutions that had as a primary goal increasing the overall number of democratic states would seem a good idea, because, according to the Home Security Report, "[o]ver the long term, the evidence suggests that the risk of civil conflict is reduced by equitable economic growth, good governance, and inclusive democracy. Development, in other words, appears to be a necessary condition for security, just as security is a necessary condition for development."[266]

None of these possible vehicles for maintaining the peace should be regarded as mutually exclusive. On the contrary, in creating a Peacebuilding Commission, the General Assembly and the Security Council recognized the importance of involving as many participants as possible.[267] Nor should participants be limited to governments or intergovernmental institutions. In recent years, "literally thousands of NGOs, have both complemented U.N. activities and played independent prevention and peacebuilding roles of their own."[268]

In closing, we should note a striking paradox. Although, as this chapter demonstrates, the permanent members of the Security Council have generally failed to fulfill their responsibility to maintain international peace and security, there has been in recent years a substantial decline in both international and internal violence. If, as alleged by the Human Security Report,[269] this is in large part due to U.N. efforts, the permanent members of the Security Council should at a minimum be expected to contribute to the enhancement of such efforts through increased funding, the training of military forces, intelligence and military support, and support in Security Council deliberations. This would be a much more modest role for the permanent members than that envisaged by the founders of the United Nations, but it just might be the most useful role these military powers could play under current circumstances.

Notes

1. U.N. Charter, Article 24 (1).
2. *Note by the Secretary-General,* U.N. General Assembly, 59th Sess., Agenda Item 55, at 1, U.N. Doc. A/59/565 (2004).
3. *Id.*
4. *Id.*
5. *See A more secure world: our shared responsibility,* Report of the High-level Panel on Threats, Challenges and Change, to the Secretary-General (Dec. 1, 2004), in *Note by the Secretary-General, supra* note 2, at 6.
6. The High-level Panel's report sets forth two alternative approaches to Security Council enlargement: Model A and Model B. Both models involve a distribution of seats among four major regional areas, identified by the report as "Africa," "Asia and Pacific," "Europe," and "Americas." Model A provides for six new permanent seats, with no veto power, and three new two-year term nonpermanent seats. The new permanent seats would be divided among the major regional areas as follows: two to Africa, two to Asia and Pacific, one to Europe, and one to Americas. The two-year nonpermanent and nonrenewable seats, including the three new two-year seats, would be divided as follows: two to Africa, two to Asia and Pacific, two to Europe, and four to Americas. There would, in total, then be twenty-four members of the Security Council. Model B provides for no new permanent seats but creates a new category of eight four-year renewable term seats and one new two-year nonpermanent (and nonrenewable) seat, divided among the major regional areas as follows: the eight four-year renewable seats would be divided equally among the four major regions. As for the eleven two-year nonrenewable seats, including the one new one, four would go to Africa, three to Asia and Pacific, one to Europe, and three to Americas. Again, there would, in total, be twenty-four members of the Security Council. *Id.* at 67–68. It is noteworthy that a congressionally created bipartisan task force on U.N. reform, cochaired by Newt Gingrich, a Republican former speaker of the House of Representatives, and George Mitchell, a Democratic former majority Senate leader, has decided to take no position on expansion of the Security Council. *See* AMERICAN INTERESTS and U.N. REFORM: REPORT of the TASK FORCE on the UNITED NATIONS 7 (2005).
7. *A more secure world: our shared responsibility, supra* note 5, at 68.
8. *Id.*
9. *Id.*
10. *Id.* at 66.
11. *In larger freedom: towards development, security and human rights for all:* Report of the Secretary-General, U.N. GAOR, 59th Sess., Agenda Items 45 and 55, U.N. Doc. A/59/2005 (2005).
12. *Id.* at 42–43.
13. *See Annan Acknowledges Delays in Council Reform,* N.Y. TIMES, Aug. 11, 2005, at A 10, col. 1. Momentum for change had been undermined the previous week by the refusal of the African Union to support a joint effort by Japan, Germany, Brazil, and India to be named as new permanent members. *Id.*
14. G.A. Res. 60/1 U.N. GAOR, U.N. Doc. A/RES/60/1 (2005).
15. *Id.,* para 153.
16. Edward C. Luck, *Making the World Safe for Hypocrisy,* N.Y. TIMES, Mar. 22, 2003, at A11, col.1.
17. At Dumbarton Oaks the United States, Great Britain, the Soviet Union, and China were reportedly in complete agreement with this proposition. RUTH B. RUSSELL, A HISTORY

of the UNITED NATIONS CHARTER: THE ROLE of the UNITED STATES 1940–1945 440 (1958). The main sticking point after Dumbarton Oaks was a disagreement between the United States and the Soviet Union over the Soviet proposal for an absolute veto. Eventually, however, the Soviet Union agreed to abandon this proposal and to accept the approach of Leo Pasvolsky, a key advisor to Franklin Roosevelt, which distinguished between "substantive" matters subject to the veto and "procedural" questions not subject to the veto. STEPHEN C. SCHLESINGER, ACT of CREATION: THE FOUNDING of the UNITED NATIONS 219–222 (2003).

18. LELAND M. GOODRICH, EDVARD HAMBRO, and ANNE PATRICIA SIMONS, CHARTER of the UNITED NATIONS: COMMENTARY and DOCUMENTS 291 (3rd ed. 1969).

19. *Id.*

20. STEPHEN C. SCHLESINGER, *supra* note 17, at 240.

21. *Id.*

22. For further discussion and support of this thesis, *see, e.g.*, John F. Murphy, *Force and Arms, in* UNITED NATIONS LEGAL ORDER 247 (Oscar Schachter and Christopher C. Joyner eds., 1995); YORAM DINSTEIN, WAR, AGGRESSION and SELF-DEFENCE (4th ed., 2005); Oscar Schachter, *The Right of States to Use Armed Force*, 82 MICH. L. REV. 1620 (1984).

23. Article 2 (4) of the U.N. Charter provides: "All Members shall refrain in their international relations from the threat or use of force against the territorial integrity or political independence of any state, or in any other manner inconsistent with Purposes of the United Nations."

24. Article 51 of the U.N. Charter provides: "Nothing in the present Charter shall impair the inherent right of individual or collective self-defense if an armed attack occurs against a Member of the United Nations until the Security Council has taken measures necessary to maintain international peace and security. Measures taken by Members in the exercise of this right of self-defense shall be immediately reported to the Security Council and shall not in any way affect the authority and responsibility of the Security Council under the present Charter to take at any time such actions as it deems necessary in order to maintain or restore international peace and security."

25. Yoram Dinstein, *Comments on War*, 27 HARV. J.L. & PUB. POL'Y 877,878 (2003–2004).

26. *See, e.g.*, Richard Lillich, *Humanitarian Intervention. A Reply to Ian Brownlie and a Plea for Constructive Alternatives, in* LAWS and CIVIL WAR in the MODERN WORLD 229 (John Norton Moore ed., 1974); W. Michael Reisman, *Humanitarian Intervention to Protect the Ibos, in* HUMANITARIAN INTERVENTION App. A (Richard Lillich ed., 1973).

27. *See especially* YORAM DINSTEIN, *supra* note 22, at 90, 315.

28. In a scholarly and exhaustive study of humanitarian intervention, Sean Murphy has examined state practice since the enactment of the Charter (up to 1996) and found little or no support for the doctrine. SEAN MURPHY, HUMANITARIAN INTERVENTION: THE UNITED NATIONS in an EVOLVING WORLD ORDER (1996). For its part, the United States has never expressly endorsed a right of humanitarian intervention under the U.N. Charter, although various U.S. officials have from time to time cited humanitarian concerns as a policy justification for the use of force. By contrast, the British government has apparently expressly accepted the doctrine. The then British Secretary of State for Defense, George Robertson, reportedly said, in defending NATO's bombing of Kosovo: "We are in no doubt that NATO is acting within international law and our legal justification rests upon the accepted principle that force may be used in extreme circumstances to avoid a humanitarian catastrophe." An earlier British note of October 1998 had stated that "as matters now stand and if action through the Security Council

is not possible, military intervention by NATO is lawful on grounds of overwhelming military necessity." *See* Lori F. Damrosch et al., International Law 1000 (4th ed. 2001), reporting quotes from Simon Duke, Hans-Georg Ehrhart, and Matthias Karadi, *The Major European Allies: France, Germany and the United Kingdom in,* Kosovo and the Challenge of Humanitarian Intervention 128, 137 (Albrecht Sechnabel and Ramesh Thakur eds., 2000). For further discussion of the British position and other issues, see Adam Roberts, *NATO's "Humanitarian War" Over Kosovo,* 41 Survival 102 (Oct. 1, 1999).

29. *See* Murphy, *supra* note 22, at 257–58,
30. The National Security Strategy of the United States of America 15 (2002). For an argument that applies a "reformulated" test for using force in anticipatory self-defense in support of the legality of the U.S. invasion of Iraq in 2003, *see* John Yoo, *International law and the War in Iraq,* 97 Am J. Int'l L. 557, 574 (2003). For a refutation of this and other arguments in support of the legality of the invasion *see* Sean Murphy, *Assessing the Legality of Invading Iraq,* 92 Geo. L.J. 173 (2004).
31. There have been, for example, extensive debates over whether Security Council resolutions authorized NATO to resort to bombing of Serbian forces in Kosovo or the invasion of Iraq by the United States, Great Britain, and other members of the U.S.-led "coalition of the willing." *See generally,* John F. Murphy, the United States and the Rule of Law in International Affairs (2004), at 157–58 (Kosovo), 169–73 (Iraq).
32. S.C. Res. 1441, U.N. SCOR, 4644th mtg., U.N. Doc. S.Res/1441 (2002).
33. For the U.S. position that it does, *see especially,* William H. Taft and Todd F. Buchwald, *Preemption, Iraq, and International Law,* 79 Am. J. Int'l L. 557 (2003). *Per contra, see* Murphy, *supra* note 30.
34. John Murphy, *supra* note 31, at 169.
35. Sean Murphy, *supra* note 30, at 219.
36. Article 43 provides:
   1. All Members of the United Nations, in order to contribute to the maintenance of international peace and security, undertake to make available to the Security Council, on its call and in accordance with a special agreement or agreements, armed forces, assistance and facilities, including rights of passage, necessary for the purpose of maintaining international peace and security.
   2. Such agreement or agreements shall govern the numbers and types of forces, their degree of readiness and general location, and the nature of the facilities and assistance to be provided.
   3. The agreement or agreements shall be negotiated as soon as possible on the initiative of the Security Council. They shall be concluded between the Security Council and Members or between the Security Council and groups of Members and shall be subject to ratification by the signatory states in accordance with their respective constitutional processes.
37. Article 43, para 3.
38. Article 106 provides:

Pending the coming into force of such special agreements referred to in Article 43 as in the opinion of the Security Council enable it to begin the exercise of its responsibilities under Article 42, the parties to the Four-Nation Declaration, signed at Moscow, October 30, 1943, and France, shall, in accordance with the provisions of paragraph 5 of that Declaration, consult with one another and as occasion requires with other Members of the United Nations with a view to such joint action on behalf of the Organization as may be necessary for the purpose of maintaining international peace and security.

39. For further confirmation of this point, *see* YORAM DINSTEIN, *supra* note 22, at 305.
40. LELAND M. GOODRICH, the UNITED NATIONS in a CHANGING WORLD 113 (1974).
41. For the view that "[t]he time is overdue for the creation of standby U.N. military forces for peace enforcement as well as peacekeeping now that the Cold War no longer blocks the way," *see Recommendation and Report on Peacekeeping, Peacemaking, and Peace Enforcement* (under the auspices of the Working Group on Improving the United Nations) *in* THE UNITED NATIONS at 50: PROPOSALS for IMPROVING its EFFECTIVENESS 45, 47 (John E. Noyes ed., 1997).
42. YORAM DINSTEIN, *supra* note 22, at 305.
43. *Id.* at 306–307.
44. This section of the chapter draws heavily on JOHN F. MURPHY, THE UNITED NATIONS and the CONTROL of INTERNATIONAL VIOLENCE 26–29 (1982).
45. TRYGVE LIE, in the CAUSE of PEACE 166 (1954).
46. *Id.* at 169–70.
47. At least one prominent authority has contended that the mandate over Palestine was never terminated. The late Professor Eugene V. Rostow, former U. S. Undersecretary of State for Political Affairs and Director, U. S. Arms Control and Disarmament Agency, argued that General Assembly Resolution 181 (II), which the Assembly adopted on November 29, 1947, only recommended (and could only recommend) termination of the mandate. Actual termination could be effected only by the Security Council. Since the Council failed to adopt the Assembly's plan, Professor Rostow argued, the mandate remains in effect, at least for the West Bank and the Gaza Strip, the "Unallocated Territories of the Palestine Mandate." As to them, only the fact of British administration has ended. The mandate over the territories now comprised by Israel has ended, but only because of the world community's recognition of the state of Israel, not because of the General Assembly's resolution. *See* Eugene V. Rostow, *Palestinian Self-Determination: Possible Future for the Unallocated Territories of the Palestine Mandate,* 5 YALE STUD. WORLD PUBLIC ORDER 147–72 (1979). Professor Rostow's position is debatable. It is true that the General Assembly did not purport by Resolution 181 (II) itself to terminate the mandate. But neither does that resolution recommend that the Security Council terminate the mandate. Rather, it recommends to the United Kingdom, as mandatory, and to all other members of the United Nations, the adoption and implementation of the partition plan, which includes a statement that the mandate shall terminate not later than August 1, 1948. Then, in a separate paragraph, the resolution requests the Security Council to take the necessary measures as provided in its plan for its implementation. This request is made for the practical reason that only the Security Council has the authority to enforce the partition plan. The aid of the Council, however, was not needed to terminate the mandate. This could be done by the mandatory accepting the recommendation of the General Assembly and declaring the mandate at an end. Hence, the General Assembly and the mandatory, acting together in tacit agreement, could terminate the mandate. The normal method of terminating U.N. trusteeships was for the General Assembly and the administering authority to agree that the trust had ended. There normally was no need for the Security Council to be involved.
48. Reprinted in 3 THE ARAB–ISRAELI CONFLICT 352–57 (John Norton Moore ed., 1974).
49. S.C. Res. 49, U.N. Doc. S/773 (1948).
50. For discussion, *see* MURPHY, *supra* note 44, at 26–27.

51. For a thorough discussion of the background to and the documents of UNTSO, see 1 ROSALYN HIGGINS, UNITED NATIONS PEACEKEEPING 1946–1967, DOCUMENTS AND COMMENTARY 1–217 (1969).

52. To be fair, there is a serious question whether the partition plan, as originally drafted, set forth tenable boundaries for the proposed new Jewish and Arab states. *See* FREDERICK H. HARTMANN, the RELATIONS of NATIONS 244–45 (1978).

53. *See* TRYGVE LIE, *supra* note 45, at 167.

54. *Id.*

55. The reason there was relatively little debate over whether North Korea or South Korea had been the aggressor was that, at the time of the invasion, the General Assembly had previously established a United Nations Temporary Commission on Korea to facilitate elections designed to unify the country, and staff of the Commission in Korea were therefore in a position to report that North Korea's forces had crossed the border into South Korea. For discussion, *see* MURPHY, *supra* note 44, at 29.

56. S.C. Res. 82, UN Doc. S/501 (1950).

57. S.C. Res. 83, UN Doc. S/1511 (1950).

58. At the same time the United States resisted efforts on the part of the Secretary-General to involve the United Nations more deeply in the defense of Korea. The Secretary-General proposed informally to the United States the formation under Security Council auspices of a "Committee on the Coordination of Assistance for Korea" to promote and supervise U.N. participation in the military action. TRYGVE LIE, *supra* note 45, at 333. Although the proposal had the support of the Europeans, the strong resistance of the Pentagon to anything more than a minimal role for the United Nations led the United States to reject it. In view of the United States' monopoly over available armed forces, the Council had no choice but to accept the U.S. decision. As a result, U.N. "supervision" over the forces in Korea was limited to the receipt of periodic reports from the United States. Secretary-General Lie later expressed the opinion that American resistance to letting the United Nations play a more substantial role "no doubt contributed to the tendency of members to let Washington assume most of the responsibility for fighting." *Id.* at 334. Be that as it may, the U.N. role was not insignificant. Fifteen governments ultimately contributed ground, naval, or air forces, and many others made significant contributions of ancillary support, such as shipping, medical facilities, and supplies. *Id.* at 339–40.

59. G.A. Res. 376, 5 U.N. GAOR, Sup. No.20, U.N. Doc. A/1775, at 9 (1950).

60. TRYGVE LIE, *supra* note 45, at 345.

61. G.A. Res. 377A, 5 U.N. GAOR, Supp. No.20A, at 10, U.N. Doc. A/1175/Add 1 (1950).

62. G.A. Res. 498, 5 U.N. GAOR, Supp. No. 20A, at 1, U.N. Doc. A/1175/ADD 1 (1950). It is questionable whether the General Assembly has the authority it claims in the Uniting for Peace resolution to recommend the establishment of an armed force under its auspices to enforce the peace against an aggressor state. For discussion, *see* Murphy, *supra* note 22, at 280. The question is largely academic now, however, because with the loss of their control of voting patterns in the General Assembly, the permanent members, including the United States, have tacitly agreed to the Soviet position – that only the Security Council should authorize the use of armed force.

63. For a concise summary of the background to the Suez crisis, *see* ROSALYN HIGGINS, *supra* note 51, at 222–27.

64. S.C. Res. 95, U.N. Doc. S/2322 (1951).

65. For an examination of many of these issues, *see* Carl F. Salans, *Gulf of Aqaba and Strait of Tiran: Troubled Waters*, 12 U. S. NAVAL INST. PROC. 54 (1968); D.H.N. Johnson, *Some*

Legal Problems of International Waterways, With Particular Reference to the Straits of Tiran and the Suez Canal, 31 Mod. L. Rev. 153 (1968); Majid Khadduri, *Closure of the Suez Canal to Israeli Shipping*, 33 Law & Contemp. Probs. 159 (1968).

66. These efforts included, among others, a request to the Secretary-General to undertake urgently a study of the amount of compliance with the armistice agreements – the report of the Secretary-General was submitted on May 9, 1956; *see* Report of the Secretary-General to the Security Council pursuant to the Council's resolution of 4 April 1956 (May 9, 1956), *reprinted in pertinent part* in Higgins, *supra* note 51, at 179 – and the unanimous adoption, on June 4, 1956, of a resolution, S.C. Res. 114, U.N. Doc. S/3605 (1956), urging the parties to cooperate with the chief of staff and the Secretary-General in order to put into effect the proposals of the report.

67. Specifically, substantial agreement was reached on six points: (1) free and open passage through the canal without discrimination, overt or covert; (2) respect for the sovereignty of Egypt; (3) the insulation of the canal from the politics of any country; (4) the manner of fixing tolls and dues to be settled between Egypt and the users; (5) a fair proportion of the dues to be allotted to development; and (6) in the case of disputes, unresolved affairs between the Suez Canal Company and the Egyptian government to be resolved by arbitration. *See* Murphy, *supra* note 44, at 35–36.

68. S.C. Res. 118, U.N. Doc. No. S/36 75 (1956).

69. *See* Murphy, *supra* note 44, at 36.

70. *See* GA Res. 997,998 and 1000 (ES-1) (1956).

71. This section of the chapter draws heavily from Murphy, *supra* note 22, at 292.

72. Erik Suy, *Peace-Keeping Operations, in* A Handbook on International Organizations and World Politics 379 (R. Dupuy ed., 1988).

73. Robert Riggs and Jack Plano, The United Nations: International Organizations and World Politics 134–35 (1988).

74. For further discussion, *see* Murphy, *supra* note 44, at 148–61; Oscar Schachter, *Authorized Uses of Force by the United Nations and Regional Organizations, in* Law and Force in the New International Order 65, 84–86 (Lori F. Damrosch and David J. Schefer eds., 1991); George Abi-Saab, The United Nations Operation in the Congo (1978).

75. *See, e.g.,* Steven R. Ratner, The New U.N. Peacekeeping: Building Peace in Lands of Conflict After the Cold War (1995).

76. This background to the U.N. involvement in Cambodia is based largely on Lori R. Damrosch et al., International Law 1030–31 (4th ed. 2001).

77. *See* Paris Conference on Cambodian Agreements Elaborating the Framework for a Comprehensive Political Settlement of the Cambodian Conflict, U.N. Doc. A/46/608 and S/ 233177, *reprinted in* 31 Int'l Legal Mat. 174 (1992).

78. *See* Steven R. Ratner, *The Cambodian Settlement Agreements*, 87 Am J. Int'l L. 1 (1993).

79. *See* 2005 World Summit Outcome, GAOR A/60/L. 1, 15 September 2005, at 25.

80. *See* Erik, Suy, *supra* note 72, at 384.

81. Certain Expenses of the United Nations, 1962 ICJ 151 (Advisory Opinion).

82. Articles 11 and 14 of the Charter provide:
Article 11.

1. The General Assembly may consider the general principles of cooperation in the maintenance of international peace and security, including the principles governing disarmament and the regulation of armaments, and may make recommendations with regard to such principles to the members or to the Security Council or to both.

2. The General Assembly may discuss any questions relating to the maintenance of international peace and security brought before it by any Member of the United Nations, or by the Security Council, or by a state which is not a Member of the

> United Nations in accordance with Article 35, paragraph 2, and, except as provided in Article 12, may make recommendations with regard to any such questions to the state or states concerned or to the Security Council or to both. Any such question on which action is necessary shall be referred to the Security Council by the General Assembly either before or after discussion.
>
> 3. The General Assembly may call the attention of the Security Council to situations which are likely to endanger international peace and security.
> 4. The powers of the General Assembly set forth in this Article shall not limit the general scope of Article 10.
>
> Article 14.
>
> Subject to the provisions of Article 12 [which precludes the General Assembly from making recommendations on a dispute or situation while the Security Council is exercising 'the functions assigned to it in the present Charter' with respect to that dispute or situation unless the Council so requests], the General Assembly may recommend measures for the peaceful adjustment of any situation, regardless of origin, which it deems likely to impair the general welfare or friendly relations among nations, including situations resulting from a violation of the provisions of the present Charter setting forth the Purposes and Principles of the United Nations.

83. Article 19 of the U.N. Charter provides:

> A member of the United Nations which is in arrears in the payment of its financial contributions to the Organization shall have no vote in the General Assembly if the amount of its arrears equals or exceeds the amount of the contributions due from it for the preceding two full years. The General Assembly may, nevertheless, permit such a Member to vote if it is established that the failure to pay is due to conditions beyond the control of the Member. For discussion of the quite extraordinary ICJ's opinion in the Certain Expenses case, *see* MURPHY, *supra* note 44, at 121–23.

84. *See* Murphy, *supra* note 22, at 295.
85. Ironically, in light of the U.S. sponsorship of the Uniting for Peace resolution in 1950, it was the Soviet Union that invoked the resolution in the aftermath of the 1967 Arab-Israeli war when the Security Council failed to pass a resolution condemning Israel as the aggressor, and it was the United States that opposed the convocation of the Assembly. In the General Assembly it proved impossible for either side to the controversy to obtain the two-thirds majority required to adopt a resolution on the conflict. *See* MURPHY, *supra* note 44, at 183.
86. Louis Henkin, *Use of Force: Law and US Policy, in* RIGHT V. MIGHT 37,52 (Louis Henkin et al., eds., 1989). To be sure, Henkin claims that the United States "committed violations of the Charter" through such actions as supporting the invasion by Cuban exiles of the Bay of Pigs (1961), sending troops to the Dominican Republic (1965), its believed role in toppling governments in Guatemala (1957) and Chile (1973), and its intervention in Vietnam. He suggests, however, that "the United States did not preach what it may have practiced; it did not seek to reinterpret the law of the Charter so as to weaken its restraints. In sum, there were no compelling grounds for questioning the commitment of the United States to the law forbidding the use of force." *Id.* at 53.
87. *Id.* at 53–54.
88. Case Concerning Military and Paramilitary Activities In and Against Nicaragua (Nicar. v. U.S.) 1984 ICJ 392 (jurisdiction).
89. Case Concerning Military and Paramilitary Activities In and Against Nicaragua (Nicar. v. U.S.) 1986 ICJ 14 (Judgment of June 27).

90. *See, e.g.,* Harold C. Maier, *Appraisals of the ICJ's Decision: Nicaragua v. United States,*
     81 AM. J. INT'L L. 77 (1987).
91. This brief background to the Iraq-Iran war is taken largely from SAMANTHA POWER, A
     PROBLEM FROM HELL: AMERICA and the AGE of GENOCIDE 174–75 (2003).
92. S.C. Res. 479 (Sept. 28, 1980).
93. N.Y. TIMES, Nov. 5, 1980, at A7.
94. N.Y. TIMES, Oct. 24, 1980, at A7.
95. SAMANTHA POWER, *supra,* note 91, at 176.
96. *Id.* at 177.
97. *Id.* at 178.
98. *Id.*
99. *Id.* at 186–87.
100. *Id.* at 187.
101. *Id.* at 189.
102. *Id.* at 195.
103. *Id.* at 222.
104. S.C. Res. 660 (Aug. 2, 1990), *reproduced in* 29 Int'l Leg. Materials 1325 (1990).
105. S.C. Res. 661 (Aug. 6, 1990), *reproduced in id.*
106. S.C. Res. 662 (Aug. 9, 1990), *reproduced in* 29 Int'l Leg. Materials 1327 (1990).
107. For discussion of these resolutions, *see* Murphy, *supra* note 22, at 282–86.
108. Reportedly, "[b]y the end of November 1990 . . . the US had more than 250,000 military
     personnel in the region, part of a planned deployment of 400,000 troops by mid-January.
     Other states, including Egypt, Saudi Arabia, Britain, France, Argentina, and Canada,
     had reportedly deployed between 200,000 and 250,000 troops.": DAMROSCH et al., *supra*
     note 76, at 1014.
109. S.C. Res. 678 (Nov. 29, 1990), *reproduced in* 29 INT'L LEGAL MATERIALS 1327 (1990).
110. For discussion of this issue, *see* Murphy, *supra* note 22, at 287–88.
111. *See, e.g.,* John Quigley, *The United States and the United Nations in the Persian Gulf
     War: New Order or Disorder?,* 25 CORNELL INT'L L.J. 1 (1992); Burns Weston, *Security
     Council Resolution 678 and Persian Gulf Decision Making: Precarious Legitimacy,* 85
     AM. J. INT'L L. 516 (1991).
112. As Oscar Schachter has noted, Resolution 678 could be regarded either as an autho-
     rization of collective self-defense under Article 51 or U.N. action under Article 42. In
     his view, however, it is more accurate to classify the Security Council's action as an
     endorsement of collective self-defense than as a U.N. enforcement action, since the
     Council did not establish a U.N. command or call upon the Military Staff Committee
     for assistance and advice. Oscar Schachter, *United Nations Law in the Gulf Conflict,*
     85 AM. J. INT'L L. 452, 458 (1991).
113. In U.N. practice, despite the "concurring votes" language of Article 27 (3) of the Charter,
     an abstention on a nonprocedural issue does not count as a veto. *See* LELAND M.
     GOODRICH, EDVARD HAMBRO and ANNE PATRICIA SIMONS, CHARTER of the UNITED
     NATIONS 229–31 (3rd ed. 1969).
114. Burns Weston, *supra* note 111, at 523.
115. *Id.*
116. *See* Operative para 1 of S.C. Res. 687 (Apr.3, 1991), *reproduced in* 30 INT'L LEGAL
     MATERIALS 847 (1991).
117. S.C. Res. 688 (April 5, 1991), *reprinted in* 30 INT'L LEGAL MATERIALS 858 (1991).
118. Jane E. Stromseth, *Iraq's Repression of its Civilian Population: Collective Responses
     and Continuing Challenges, in* ENFORCING RESTRAINT: COLLECTIVE INTERVENTIONS
     in INTERNAL CONFLICTS 77, 87 (Lori F. Damrosch ed., 1993).

119. JOHN MURPHY, *supra* note 28, at 194.
120. *Id.*
121. For a concise summary of the response of the United States and the United Kingdom and the legal authority cited for their actions, *see* Christine Grey, *From Unity to Polarization: International Law and the Use of Force Against Iraq*, 13 EUR. J. INT'L L. 1, 11–12 (2002).
122. S.C. Res. 1154, U.N. SCOR, U.N. Doc. S/RES/1154 (1998), and S.C. Res. 1205, U.N. SCOR, U.N. Doc. S/RES/ 1205 (1998).
123. *See* Christine Grey, *supra* note 121, at 11–12.
124. For further development of these arguments, *see* Christine Grey, *supra* note 121, at 12–13, JOHN MURPHY, *supra* note 31, at 153–54.
125. *See* Sean Murphy, *supra* note 30, at 214.
126. *See id.* at 212–15.
127. *Id.* at 198.
128. S.C. Res. 713, U.N. SCOR, U.N. Doc. S/RES/713 (1991).
129. JOHN MURPHY, *supra* note 28, at 199.
130. As noted in *id.*, at 200, Bosnia's inability to obtain these arms was later part of the suit it brought against Serbia and Montenegro before the International Court of Justice charging it with genocide. On April 8, 1993, the Court issued a provisional order demanding that Serbia and Montenegro take measures to prevent the crime of genocide in Bosnia-Herzegovina, but did not rule on Bosnia's request to be exempted from the Security Council's arms embargo. Application of the Convention on the Prevention and Punishment of the Crime of Genocide (Bosn. & Herz. v. Yugoslavia (Serb. and Mont.)), 1993 ICJ 3 (Apr. 3).
131. S.C. Res 743, U.N. SCOR, U.N. Doc S/RES/713 (1992).
132. Secretary-General Boutros-Ghali had called for such an approach in his Agenda for Peace. U.N. Doc. A/47/277, S/24111 (1992).
133. *See* SEAN MURPHY, *supra* note 28, at 206.
134. *Id.*
135. *Id.* at 207.
136. *See* LORI DAMROSCH et al., *supra* note 28, at 1040. For a detailed description of the massacres in Srebrenica, *see* SAMANTHA POWER, *supra* note 91, at 411–421. In 2005, the Special Bosnian Serb Government Working Group, which had been compiling a report since 2003, stated that it had identified more than 17,000 people who had taken part directly and indirectly in the Srebrenica massacre. *Bosnian Serb Panel Links 17,000 to Roles in Srebrencia Massacre*, N.Y. TIMES, Oct.5, 2005, at A5, col. 1.
137. For the sad history of failure in Bosnia, *see* Paul C. Szasz, *Peacekeeping in Operation: A Conflict Study of Bosnia*, 28 CORNELL INT'L L.J. 685 (1995); Tibor Varady, *The Predicament of Peacekeeping in Bosnia*, 28 CORNELL INT'L L.J. 701 (1995); Valerie Bunce, *The Elusive Peace in the Former Yugoslavia*, CORNELL INT'L L.J. 709 (1995).
138. S.C. Res. 1284, U.N. SCOR, 54th Sess., 4084th mtg., U.N. Doc. S/RES/1284 (1999).
139. For a detailed description of this process, see *Hearing on United Nations Peacekeeping Missions and Their Proliferation*, Before the Subcommittee on International Operations of the Senate Committee on Foreign Relations, 106th Cong. 13, 115–17 (2000) (Statement of Dr. John Hillen).
140. S.C. Res. 1284, U.N. SCOR, 54th Sess., 4084th mtg., U.N. Doc. S/RES/1284 (1999).
141. *See* Sean Murphy, *supra* note 30, at 216.
142. *See, e.g., id.* at 217–24.
143. *See* JOHN MURPHY, *supra* note 31, at 169–72.

144. In my view, the most compelling exegesis of Resolution 1441 is that of Professor Sean Murphy. *See* Sean Murphy, *supra* note 30, at 218–27.
145. *See, e.g.,* the series of reports issued by the Independent Inquiry Committee into the United Nations Oil For-Food Programme, chaired by Paul Volcker, the so-called Volcker Committee. These include: Briefing Paper, Internatl Audit Reports on the United Nations Oil-For-Food Programme (Jan. 9, 2005); First Interim Report (Feb. 3, 2005); Second Interim Report (Mar. 29, 2005); Third Interim Report (Aug. 8, 2005); The Management of the United Nations Oil-For-Food Programme, Vol. I – The Report of the Committee (Sept. 7, 2005); and Report on the Manipulations of the Oil-For Food Programme (Oct. 27, 2005). *See also* the three-volume Comprehensive Report of the Special Adviser to the DCI on Iraq's WMD (Charles Duelfer, Sept. 30, 2004) (hereinafter "The Duelfer Report"). The series of reports issued by the Senate Security and Governmental Affairs Committee, chaired by Senator Norm Coleman (the so-called Coleman Reports), include Report on Oil Allocations Granted to Charles Pasqua & George Galloway (May 12, 2005); Report on Oil Allocations Granted to Vladimir Zhirinovsky (May 16, 2005); Report on Oil Allocations Granted to the Russian Presidential Council (May 16, 2005); Report on Illegal Surcharges on Oil-for-food Contracts and Illegal Oil Shipments from Khor Al-Amaya (May 17, 2005). Hearing on United Nations Operations: Integrity and Accountability before the Subcom. On Oversight and Investigations of the House Com. On International Relations, 109th Cong. (March 2, 2005). RICHARD Z. CHESNOFF, THE ARROGANCE of the FRENCH (2005).
146. *See* SAMANTHA POWER, *supra* note 91, at 171–245.
147. This summary is taken from the Fifth Report of the Independent Inquiry Committee Into the United Nations Oil-For-Food Programme on "Manipulations of the Oil-For-Food Programme by the Iraqi Regime" (Oct. 27, 2005), www.iic-offp.org.
148. *Id.* at 2.
149. *Id.*
150. *Id.* at 2–3.
151. *Id.* at 3.
152. *Id.* at 22.
153. *Id.* at 23.
154. *Id.* at 38.
155. *Id.*
156. *Id.* at 41.
157. According to the Fifth Report of the Volcker Committee, "[i]f the purchase of a London-based subsidiary of a Chinese state-owned company are [sic] factored into China's total oil purchases, then Chinese companies would surpass French companies as the second largest purchaser of oil under the Programme." *Id.* at 47, n.70.
158. For example, Jean-Bernard Merrimee began receiving oil allocations that would ultimately total approximately 6 million barrels from the government of Iraq. From 1991–1995 Merimee served as France's Permanent Representative to the United Nations. *Id.* at 49–50. Similarly, Charles Pasqua, who in 1986 and again in 1993 was the Minister of Interior in France, had allocations designated in his name for a total of 11 million barrels of oil from the government of Iraq. Id., at 53. Lastly, Serge Boidevaix, a French consultant and former diplomat, was hired to obtain Iraqi crude contracts for Vitro S.A., a Swiss company based in Geneva. He received allocations of 32 million barrels of oil from Iraq. *Id.* at 67.
159. *Id.* at 261.
160. *Id.*

161. *Id.* at 249.
162. *Id.*
163. *Id.*
164. *Id.* at 250.
165. *See* Andrew Kramer, *Evidence Cited in Oil Report Was Forged, Russia Says*, N.Y. TIMES, Oct. 29, 2005, at A8, col. 7.
166. *See, e.g., Report on Oil Allocations Granted to Vladimir Zhirinovsky.* Prepared by the Majority and Minority Staffs of the Permanent Subcommittee on Investigations, released in conjunction with the Permanent Subcommittee on Investigations May 17, 2005; Hearing: *Oil for Influence: How Saddam Used Oil to Reward Politicians and Terrorist Entities Under the United Nations Oil-for-Food Program; Report on Oil Allocations Granted to the Russian Presidential Council, Prepared by the Majority and Minority Staffs of the Permanent Staffs of the Permanent Subcommittee on Investigations*, released in conjunction with Permanent Subcommittee on Investigations May 17, 2005, Hearing: *Oil for Influence: How Saddam Used Oil to Reward Politicians and Terrorist Entities Under the United Nations Oil-For-food Program*; and *Report on Illegal Surcharges on Oil-For Food Contracts and Illegal Oil Shipments From Khor Al-Maya*, Prepared by the Minority Staff of the Permanent Subcommittee on Investigations, released in Conjunction with the Permanent Subcommittee on Investigations May 17, 2005, Hearing: *Oil for Influence: How Saddam Used Oil to Reward Politicians and Terrorist Entities Under the United Nations Oil-For-Food Program.*
167. *See Report on Oil Allocations Granted to Charles Pasqua & George Galloway*, Prepared by the Majority and Minority Staffs of the Permanent Subcommittee on Investigations, released in Conjunction with the Permanent Subcommittee on Investigations May 17, 2005, Hearing: *Oil for Influence: How Saddam Used Oil to Reward Politicians and Terrorist Entities Under the United Nations Oil-For-Food Program (France and French Officials)*; and *Report on Oil Allocations Granted to the Russian Presidential Council*, Prepared by the Majority and Minority Staffs of the Permanent Subcommittee on Investigations, released in Conjunction with the Permanent Subcommittee on Investigations May 17, 2005, Hearing: *Oil for Influence: How Saddam Used Oil to Reward Politicians and Terrorist Entities Under the United Nations Oil-for-Food Program (China)*, at 2.
168. *See* the three-volume report, *Comprehensive Report of the Special Adviser to the DCI [Director of Central Intelligence] on Iraq's WMD [Weapons of Mass Destruction]* (Sept. 30, 2004).
169. *See* the Acknowledgments section of the Duelfer Report, at 1, and Volume 1 of the Report at 1–2.
170. Volume I of the Duelfer Report at 2.
171. Volume I of the Duelfer Report, Transmittal Message, at 11.
172. Volume II of the Duelfer Report, Delivery Systems, at 7.
173. *Id.*
174. Volume I of the Duelfer Report, Regime Finance and Procurement, at 55.
175. *See, e.g.,* Volume I of the Duelfer Report, Regime Finance and Procurement, at 116 (captured documentation showing contracts between Iraq and Russian companies for the supply of weapons); *Id.* at 276 (meetings held in Iraqi Embassy in Moscow where Russian companies offered to provide technical expertise to improve and to build weapons systems, including tanks); *Id.* at 277 (Russian technical team reportedly visited Iraq to train Iraqi technicians on upgrading an air defense system); and Volume II of the Duelfer Report, Delivery Systems, at 58 (testimony that Russian President Putin agreed

to offer assistance in supplying documents that would have allowed Iraq to manufacture a certain type of accurate missile).

176. Volume III of the Duelfer Report, Chemical, at 24.

177. Volume III of the Duelfer Report, Biological, at 14.

178. Volume I of the Duelfer Report, Regime Finance and Procurement, at 56.

179. *Id.* at 111.

180. *Id.* at 217.

181. *Id.*

182. *Id.*

183. *Id.* at 65.

184. Volume II of the Duelfer Report, Delivery Systems, at 66. Parenthetically, it may be noted that certain commentators have alleged that the French government, especially Prime Minister Jacques Chirac, has itself facilitated arms sales in violation of the U.N. embargo. *See, e.g.*, RICHARD Z. CHESNOFF, THE ARROGANCE of the FRENCH 105 (2005).

185. Volume I of the Duelfer Report, Regime Strategic Intent, at 59.

186. Volume I of the Duelfer Report, Regime Finance and Procurement, at 108.

187. *Id.* at 110.

188. Samantha Power, *Missions*, NEW YORKER, Nov. 28, 2005, at 61.

189. *Dying in Darfur*, FIN. TIMES, May 9, 2005, at 12, col.1.

190. Guy Dinmore, *White House Quiet as Darfur killings Go On*, FIN. TIMES, Mar. 15, 2005, at 6, col. 3.

191. Warren Hoge, *U.N. Finds Crimes, Not Genocide in Darfur*, N.Y. TIMES, Feb. 1, 2005 at A3, col. 1.

192. *Id.*

193. S.C. Res. 1593, U.N. SCOR, U.N. Doc. S/RES/1593 (2005).

194. Warren Hoge, *International War-Crimes Prosecutor Gets List of 51 Sudan Suspects*, N.Y. TIMES, Apr. 6, 2005, at A6, col. 3.

195. *Id.*

196. For example, as noted by the *New York Times*: "After the International Criminal Court indicted Ahmad Harun, Sudan's minister of state from humanitarian affairs, for war crimes in Darfur, Sudan's president, Omas Hassan al-Bashir, refused to turn him over for prosecution. Instead, Mr. Bashir put Mr. Harum on a committee overseeing deployment of the new peacekeeping mission." *See Delay, Obstruction and Darfur*, N.Y. TIMES, Dec. 10, 2007, at A22, col. 1.

197. S.C. Res. 1590, U.N. SCOR, U.N. Doc. S/RES/1590 (2005).

198. S.C. Res. 1591, U.N. SCOR, U.N. Doc. S/RES/1591 (2005).

199. *See UMIS*, published by the Peace and Security Section of the U.N. Department of Public Information, October 25, 2007, at 8, http:www.un.org/Depts/dpko/missions/unmis

200. *Id.* at 9.

201. S.C. Res. 1706 (Aug. 31, 2006).

202. S.C. Res. 1769 (July 31, 2007).

203. *See* Harvey Morris, *Depleted UN Force Joins Peace Effort in Darfur*, FIN. TIMES, Jan. 27, 2008, at 3, col. 4.

204. *See Unkept Promises in Darfur*, N.Y. TIMES, Jan. 27, 2008, Week in Review, at 15, col. 1.

205. *See The New Rwanda*, N.Y. TIMES, Nov. 28, 2005, at A18, col. 1.

206. Statement of Nancy Soderberg, a former Clinton administration adviser and author of *The Superpower Myth*, quoted in Guy Dinmore, *White House Quiet as Darfur killings Go On*, FIN. TIMES, Mar. 15, 2005, at 6, col. 3.

207. See Report of the Secretary-General on the Deployment of the African Union-United Nations Hybrid Operation in Darfur to the United Nations Security Council, July 13, 2009, S/2009/352, para 14.
208. *Id.*, paras 14 and 15.
209. *Id.*, para 29.
210. *Id.*, para 31.
211. *Id.*, para 45.
212. *Id.*, paras 46, 47.
213. United Nations General Assembly, 2005 *World Summit Outcome*, October 24, 2005, at 30, unpan1.un. Org.inrtradoc/groups/public/documents/UN/UNPAN 021752,pdf.
214. S.C. Res. 1674 (April 28, 2006).
215. HUMAN SECURITY CENTRE, THE HUMAN SECURITY REPORT 2005: WAR and PEACE in the 21st CENTURY (2005).
216. *Id.* at 1.
217. *Id.* at 2. Even here, however, *The Economist* notes that "this picture of worldwide growth is misleading. While it is true that Asia, Latin America and Europe have all experienced more terrorist attacks than before, they are still rare. Since 2001, the Middle East has suffered more violence than the rest of the world put together." See *Briefing: The World's Silver Lining*, THE ECONOMIST, July 26, 2008, at 29.
218. See HUMAN SECURITY CENTRE, *supra* note 215, at 3. The authors note, however, that in the Middle East and North Africa the decline started much earlier, at the beginning of the 1980s. According to the authors, "[i]n part this was because the frontline Arab states recognized that fighting wars with a conventionally superior and nuclear-armed Israel was a fruitless endeavor, and in part because ruthless state repression was succeeding in crushing domestic insurgencies." *Id.* at 4.
219. *Id.* at 8.
220. *Id.*
221. According to the Report, these activities included:
    - A sixfold increase in the number of preventive diplomacy missions (those that seek to stop wars from starting) mounted by the U.N. between 1990 and 2002.
    - A fourfold increase in peacemaking activities (those that seek to stop ongoing conflicts over the same period). . . .
    - A sevenfold increase in the number of 'Friends of the Secretary-General,' 'Contact Groups,' and other government-initiated mechanisms to support peace-making and peacebuilding missions between 1990 and 2003.
    - An elevenfold increase in the number of economic sanctions in place against regimes around the world between 1989 and 2001.
    - A fourfold increase in the number of UN peacekeeping operations between 1987 and 1999 . . . The increase in numbers was not the only change. The new missions were, on average, far larger and more complex than those of the Cold War era and they have been relatively successful in sustaining the peace. With 40% of post-conflict countries relapsing into war again within five years, the importance of preventing wars from restarting again is obvious. *Id.* at 9.
222. See Michael J. Glennon, *The Fog of Law: Self-Defense, Inherence, and Incoherence in Article 51 of the United Nations Charter*, 25 HARV. J.L. & PUB. POL'Y 539–541 (2002).
223. See HUMAN SECURITY CENTRE, *supra* note 215, at 149 (citing John Mueller, *The Remnants of War* (2004)).

224. *Id.* at 150.
225. *See generally,* Michael J. Glennon, Limits of Law, Prerogative of Power: Interventionism After Kosovo (2001); Michael J. Glennon, *How International Rules Die,* 93 Geo. L.J. 939 (2005).
226. For further discussion, *see* John Murphy, *supra* note 31, at 180.
227. *See, e.g.,* William Howard Taft IV & Todd Buchwald, *Preemption, Iraq, and International Law,* 97 Am. J. Int'l L. 557 (2003).
228. A prominent (and successful) example is the economic sanctions imposed against Libya for its refusal to surrender to the United States or the United Kingdom two members of the Libyan intelligence service who had been indicted for their alleged involvement in the bombing of Pan Am Flight 103.
229. Professor Orde F. Kittrie has written widely and well on the successes and, more often, the failure, of efforts to impose effective economic sanctions against states that threaten the peace. *See, e.g.,* Orde F. Kittrie, *Averting Catastrophe: Why the Nuclear Nonproliferation Treaty is Losing Its Deterrence Capacity and How to Restore it,* 28 Mich. J. Int'l L. 337 (2007); Orde F. Kittrie, *Embolded by Impunity: The History and Consequences of Failure to Enforce Iranian Violations of International Law,* 57 Syracuse L. Rev. 519 (2007).
230. On November 23, 2005, then U.S. Permanent Representative to the United Nations, John C. Danforth, savagely excoriated the General Assembly when it decided to take no action on a resolution denouncing the human rights violations in the Sudan. *See* Warren Hoge, *Danforth Faults U.N. Assembly on Sudan Ruling,* N.Y. Times, Nov. 24, 2004, at A6, col. 8. When it became clear that the Assembly would take no action on the resolution, Danforth reportedly said:

    It's going to be inaction, it's going to be condoning atrocities, it's going to be condoning the status quo, it's going to be failure to support the African Union, it's going to be failure to support the peace process, and most importantly, it's going to be failure to support the people of Sudan, who are suffering terribly and have suffered for a very long time . . . And the message from the General Assembly, is very simple and it is, "You may be suffering, but we can't be bothered."

231. *See, e.g.,* Ivo Daalder and James Lindsay, *Our Way or the Highway,* Fin. Times, Nov. 6 and 7, 2004, at W1.
232. *Id.* Daalder and Lindsay would use criteria and rankings compiled by Freedom House and the Polity IV Project at the University of Maryland. They report that nearly five dozen countries would meet the membership standard of being "true" democracies.
233. *Id.*
234. *See* Article 53 (1) of the U.N. Charter.
235. *See* Yochi J. Dreazen, *Troop Needs Open NATO Rift,* Wall St. J., Feb. 8, 2008, at A8, col.1.
236. *Id.*
237. *See* Fidelius Schmid, Jon Boone, and Stephen Fidler, *Paris Comes to Canada's Aid With Extra Troops,* Fin. Times, Feb. 8, 2008, at 2, col. 1.
238. *See* Stephen Fidler, *US Flags up Afghanistan Terror Dangers for Europe,* Fin. Times, Feb. 11, 2008, at 4, col. 7.
239. *Id.*
240. David Scheffer, *Commentary on Collective Security, in* Law and Force in the New International Order 101, 107–08 (Lori Damrosch and David Scheffer eds., 1991).
241. *See* Leonard Meeker, *Defensive Quarantine and the Law,* 57 Am. J. Int'l L. 523, 524 (1963); Abram Chayes, The Cuban Missile Crisis (1974).

242. *See* Adlai Stevenson, *Principles of U.N.-OAS Relationship in the Dominican Republic,* 52 Dep't State Bull. 975, 976–77 (1965).

243. *Compare* John Norton Moore, *Grenada and the International Double Standard,* 78 Am. J. Int'l L. 145, 154–59 (1984) *with* Christopher Joyner, *Reflections on the Lawfulness of Invasion,* 78 Am. J. Int'l L. 131, 135–37, 142 (1984).

244. OAS Doc. OEA/Ser. F/v.1/MRE/RES. 1/91, corr.1, paras 5,6 (1991).

245. S.C. Res. 940, U.N. SCOR, U.N. Doc. S/RES/940 (1994).

246. Oscar Schachter, *Authorized Uses of Force by the United Nations and Regional Organizations, in* Law and Force in the New International Order 65, 88 (Lori Damrosch and David Scheffer eds., 1991).

247. *See* Corrine A.A. Packer & Donald Rukare, *The New African Union and Its Constitutive Act,* 96 Am. J. Int'l L. 365, 372–73 (2002).

248. For a brief discussion of problems facing other regional agencies as potential peacekeepers, *see* John Murphy, *supra* note 31, at 190–91.

249. *See, e.g., The UN Gets Tougher,* The Economist, Mar. 12, 2005, at 49 (discussing increased willingness of U.N. peacekeepers in the Congo to resort to robust use of force).

250. *See, e.g.,* Warren Hoge, *Aid Effort in Africa Undermined by New Violence, UN Reports,* N.Y. Times, Dec. 20, 2005, at A5, col. 3.

251. *See* Lydia Polgreen, *China, in New Role, Uses Ties to Press Sudan on Troubled Darfur,* N.Y. Times, Feb. 23, 2008, at A8, col. 1.

252. James Dobbins et al., The UN's Role in Nation-Building: From the Congo to Iraq (2005) (hereinafter "Rand Report").

253. *Id.,* Executive Summary, at iv.

254. The five-year war in the Congo involved the intervention of at least six foreign armies and is estimated to have claimed more than 3 million lives, primarily through disease and hunger, especially in the east where the conflict originated and U.N. forces operated. *See* Andrew England, *Uganda Told to Compensate Congo Over Illegal Incursion,* Fin. Times, Dec. 20, 2005, at 3, col. 7. On December 19, 2005, the International Court of Justice issued a decision ordering Uganda to pay reparations to the Congo for the plunder of natural resources and human rights abuses during the Congo's civil war. *See* Armed Activities in the Territory of the Congo (Congo v. Uganda) 2005 ICJ 116 (Dec. 7).

255. *See* Marc Lacey, *UN Forces Using Tougher Tactics to Secure Peace,* N.Y. Times, May 23, 2005, at A1, col. 6.

256. Rand Report, Executive Summary, *supra* note 252, at xvii–xviii.

257. Warren Hoge, *Report Calls for Punishing Peacekeepers in Sex Abuse,* N.Y. Times, Mar. 2, 2005, at A8, col. 5. In response to these reports of sex abuse, Secretary-General Kofi Annan commissioned Prince Zeid Raad al Husein, Jordan's ambassador to the United Nations, to do a study and write a report on his findings. Prince Zeid's report said that current efforts to curb abuses were "ad hoc and inadequate" and that exploitative behavior was widespread. Because the United Nations has no authority to punish violators, the report recommended, among other things, that countries contributing troops should agree to hold courts-martial of their accused soldiers in the countries where the alleged abuse occurred. *Id.*

258. For discussion, *see* John Murphy, *supra* note 31, at 190.

259. *See, e.g., Sudan, Rice Appeals to Congress on Darfur,* N.Y. Times, Dec. 17, 2005, at A10, where U.S. Secretary of State Condoleeza Rice makes a personal appeal to Congress for $50 million previously promised by the U.S. government to finance 6,000 African Union troops to keep peace in Darfur. The previous month Congress had stripped the

$50 million from a foreign financing bill. *See also,* Harvey Morris, *Depleted UN Force Joins Peace Effort in Darfur,* FIN. TIMES, Jan. 1, 2008, where reportedly Ban Ki-Moon, the U.N. Secretary-General, "lamented . . . that despite his appeals to every U.N. member state capable of providing helicopter support, none had come forward with offers."

260. HUMAN SECURITY CENTRE *supra* note 215, at 155.

261. *Id.* at 151.

262. Rand Report, Executive Summary, *supra* note 252, at xix.

263. *See* G.A. Res. 60/180, 60 U.N. GAOR, U.N.Doc. A/RES/60/180 (Dec. 30, 2005) and S.C. Res. 1645, U.N. SCOR. S/RES.1645 (Dec. 20, 2005).

264. *See* Warren Hoge, *U.N. Creates Commission to Assist Nations Recovering From Wars,* N.Y. TIMES, Dec. 21, 2005, at A25, col. 1. Secretary-General Kofi Annan told the General Assembly that "while many parts of the United Nations had traditionally been involved in helping countries in longer-term recovery after protracted conflicts, there had never been an entity to coordinate those activities, develop expertise and strategy and focus attention on reconstruction and the building of institutions." *Id.*

265. HUMAN SECURITY CENTRE, *supra* note 215, at 155.

266. *Id.*

267. *See* Warren Hoge, *supra* note 264.

268. HUMAN SECURITY CENTRE, *supra* note 215, at 153.

269. *Id.* at 9.

4

The Law of Armed Conflict

The law of armed conflict, which regulates the way armed force is employed, is also often referred to as "the law of war" or "international humanitarian law." Yoram Dinstein, an eminent authority on the subject, rejects these alternative formulations:

> Despite its popular usage today, and the stamp of approval of the International Court of Justice, "International Humanitarian Law" as an umbrella designation has a marked disadvantage. This is due to the fact that the coinage IHL is liable to create the false impression that all the rules governing hostilities are – and have to be – truly humanitarian in nature, whereas in fact not a few of them reflect the countervailing constraints of military necessity.... An alternative appellation, popular in the past – "the Laws of Warfare" (or *jus in bello*) – is equally unsatisfactory, because it is irreconcilable with the reality that the norms in question are also in effect in international armed conflicts falling short of full-fledged wars.... [1]

It is also worth noting that ambiguities raised by the terms "war" and "aggression" caused problems for the League of Nations in its efforts to maintain international peace and security,[2] and use of the term "war" sometimes had major implications in the domestic law and practice of member states.

Traditionally, a sharp distinction has been drawn between the law of armed conflict and the *jus ad bellum*, the law governing resort to the use of armed force. Under this distinction, it doesn't matter which state has been the aggressor, or has otherwise violated the *jus ad bellum*; all states that are parties to an international armed conflict are equally subject to the protections and responsibilities of the law of armed conflict. As we shall see later in this chapter, however, this distinction has recently come under sharp attack and is increasingly ignored in practice.

Moreover, one need not agree with the view of then White House Counsel Alberto Gonzales, who wrote U.S. President George W. Bush in 2002, arguing that the "new paradigm" of armed conflict rendered parts of the Geneva Conventions of 1949 "obsolete" and "quaint,"[3] to concede that in certain respects the Conventions, along with other components of the law of armed conflict, are in need of revision and reform. But as recently contended by Jean-Philippe Lavoyer, the head of the Legal Division, International Committee of the Red Cross, the current law of armed conflict is not the major problem but rather the failure to implement it in good faith.[4] Increasingly, the combatants in today's armed conflicts – terrorists, insurgents, and, most important, governments – ignore the law of armed conflict and view the law of armed conflict as irrelevant to their concerns.[5]

Much of the discussion and debate over the law of armed conflict has revolved around four international armed conflicts of the 1990s and early 2000s: the Gulf War, Kosovo, Afghanistan, and Iraq. But it is important to remember that international armed conflict is not the primary kind of armed conflict today, but rather it is internal or civil wars. In the main, these wars are being fought with no concern for the law of armed conflict or any humanitarian considerations and are largely ignored by the great powers. This is especially the case in Africa. A major reason for the failure to deal effectively with these wars is lack of political will. But it appears clear as well that the law of armed conflict applicable to internal wars – Common Article 3 of the Geneva Conventions of 1949 and the 1977 Protocol II to the Geneva Conventions – is inadequate; yet efforts to improve this law are strongly resisted.

Perhaps the most significant change in the nature of armed conflict is the rise of the so-called new terrorism, represented by al-Qaeda and its ilk. In his new book, *Terror and Consent: The Wars for the Twenty-First Century*,[6] Philip Bobbitt argues that this contemporary terrorism is so different from its predecessors that "it will take some time before the nature and composition of these wars are widely understood."[7] The new terrorism's immediate predecessor, in the twentieth century, Bobbitt refers to as "nation-state terrorism." In the twentieth century, Bobbitt explains, the nation-state obtained its legitimacy by guaranteeing the well-being of its people, under various ideologies like communism and democracy. The "terrorists of the nation-state," as he calls them, sought to destroy that order through "wars of national liberation." Terrorist groups of the time, such as the IRA and the PLO, claimed that they were engaged in such struggles and hence should be considered "freedom fighters" rather than terrorists.

By contrast, groups like al-Qaeda are not interested in national liberation. Rather their goal is to destroy the established order and replace it with another form of authority under the control of Islamic jihadists. Their strategy to this end is to be decentralized and global in their operations, prepared to "outsource" their attacks and readily trade weapons and secrets. Also, while the "terrorists of the nation-state" hesitated to kill large numbers of innocent people for fear it might undermine their efforts to gain sympathy for their cause, al-Qaeda and its imitators, "terrorists of the market state,"[8] are increasingly willing to kill large numbers of people and to make no distinction between military and civilian targets.[9] They are not seeking to gain favorable public opinion but to expand their domain of terror. To this end, they actively seek weapons of mass destruction, which thereby become much more threatening because traditional ideas of "mutual assured destruction" or MAD, have much less deterrent effect when applied against al-Qaeda rather than against the Soviet Union. This is especially the case in today's world where the global marketplace offers numerous opportunities to obtain weapons of mass destruction.

In Bobbitt's view the "new terrorism" poses an existential threat to the modern state. It attempts to replace an authority that derives its authority from the "consent of the governed" with one that has an atmosphere of "fear and horror," thereby transforming a "state of consent" into a "state of terror." Bobbitt contends it is a misconception to believe that terrorism could possibly be controlled by police action. Such an approach, he believes, overlooks the need to anticipate and prevent terrorist action rather than just punish it. Moreover, he argues, the structure of intelligence agencies is a relic of yesterday's battles and greatly needs to become more functional.

Bobbitt's negative views on the usefulness of police action illustrate another facet of the "new terrorism": the debate over the appropriate legal regime to apply to efforts to combat terrorism after the September 11, 2001, attacks. Prior to these attacks, international terrorism had been treated primarily, although not exclusively, as a criminal law matter. After September 11, however, the criminal justice approach was deemphasized and to a considerable extent supplanted by the use of military means.[10]

This shift to the military model of counterterrorism has engendered considerable controversy. Critics of this approach argue that it threatens fundamental human rights and that it is unnecessary because normal law enforcement measures can effectively combat the terrorist threat.[11] In sharp contrast, supporters of the military model contend that criminal law is "too weak a weapon" and that it was inadequate to stop al-Qaeda from planning and carrying out the attacks of September 11.[12]

A decision to employ the military model of counterterrorism in place of the law enforcement model, or vice versa, may have serious functional consequences.[13] For example, under the law enforcement model, it is impermissible to pursue and kill a suspected criminal before his capture, unless it is necessary to do so as a matter of self-defense. The goal here is to capture the suspect, subject him to trial in accordance with due process, and then, if he is convicted, impose an appropriate sanction, which, in some cases, especially under U.S. law, could include the death penalty.

Ideally, the debate over the alleged inadequacies of existing law would be resolved by international negotiations to eliminate them and substitute a more functional legal framework. But as Dr. Lavoyer and other experts have noted, the risk of this route is that it might open Pandora's box and result in a much less rather than a more satisfactory law of armed conflict. This is also a problem with the *jus ad bellum*, the law of resort to the use of force, and efforts to revise the U.N. Charter. There are now 192 member states of the United Nations, and more and more of them, especially from the so-called Third World, are demanding to be heard.[14]

This chapter begins with a brief discussion of the extent to which noninternational armed conflict in the twenty-first century presents new problems and therefore raises new challenges to the law of armed conflict. Next the chapter turns to the special challenges posed by the "new terrorism" to the current law of armed conflict as a vehicle, as well as to international human rights law. Then the chapter examines some of the reasons why states are reluctant to adapt the law to meet these challenges, and lastly considers possible ways to overcome this reluctance and allow the law to keep pace with changed circumstances.

TWENTY-FIRST-CENTURY CHALLENGES TO THE LAW OF ARMED CONFLICT

Noninternational Armed Conflict

As noted above, most of the armed conflicts in today's world are not "international" in the sense of interstate hostilities. This presents perhaps the most serious challenge facing those who seek to enforce the law of armed conflict in the contemporary international security system. The primary problem here is that "the effort to expand the application of international humanitarian law has been, and will continue to be, confronted by state reluctance to apply international norms to what has been seen as uniquely falling within their sovereign jurisdiction."[15] Because of this reluctance the only article in the Geneva Conventions of 1949 to refer expressly to "armed conflict not of an international character" is Common Article 3, which has no reference to the regulation of the conduct of hostilities.[16] For its part, Additional Protocol II Relating to the Protection of Victims of Non-International Armed Conflicts has not been ratified by a number of states, including the United States, and has such a high threshold of applicability that it will seldom be relevant to internal conflicts.[17]

Because of the perceived inadequacies of the conventional law governing noninternational armed conflicts, there is a "trend under humanitarian law to apply the established rules for governing international armed conflict to its noninternational counterpart."[18] This trend, however, has not been based on the conclusion of new conventions, or even the revision of old conventions, on the law of armed conflict. Rather, it has been based on international judicial decisions, especially the decision of the International Criminal Tribunal for the Former Yugoslavia Appeals Chamber in *Prosecutor v. Tadic*, which noted in 1995 that "it cannot be denied that customary rules have developed to govern internal strife."[19] The tribunal identified some of these rules as covering "such areas as protection of civilians from hostilities, in particular from indiscriminate attacks, protection of civilian objects, in particular cultural property, protection of all those who do not (or no longer) take active part in hostilities, as well as prohibition of means of warfare proscribed in international armed conflicts and ban of certain methods of conducting hostilities."[20] The International Committee of the Red Cross (ICRC) has also actively promoted the idea of applying the rules governing international armed conflict to noninternational armed conflict through the customary international law process, especially in its two-volume *Customary International Humanitarian Law* study.[21]

Customary international law has long played an important role in the development of the law of armed conflict, as illustrated by the Martens Clause, which was named after M. De Martens, a Russian leading international lawyer who was a Russian delegate to both Hague Peace Conferences of 1889 and 1907. The Martens Clause first appeared in the Preamble of Hague Convention (II) of 1899 and Hague Convention (IV) of 1907 Respecting the Laws and Customs of War on Land.[22] A recent example of the Martens Clause may be found in Article 1(2) of Additional Protocol I of 1977 and reads as follows:

> In cases not covered by this Protocol or by other international agreements, civilians and combatants remain under the protection and authority of the principles of international law derived from established custom, from the principles of humanity and from the dictates of public conscience.

We should remember, however, the increasingly controversial nature of the customary international law process, as discussed in Chapter 1 of this study. It should come as no surprise therefore that the methodology employed by the ICRC in its study of the customary international humanitarian law has itself come under attack. Most particularly, on November 3, 2006, John Bellinger III, Legal Adviser, U.S. Department of State, and William J. Haynes, General Counsel, U.S. Department of Defense, wrote a joint letter to Dr. Jakob Kellenberger, President, International Committee of the Red Cross, setting forth the U.S. government's "initial reactions" to the ICRC's Study.[23] The letter states that "based on our review so far, we are concerned about the methodology used to ascertain rules and about whether the authors have proffered sufficient facts and evidence to support those rules." Although noting that "[g]iven the Study's large scope, we have not yet been able to complete a detailed review of its conclusions," the authors go on to state that they thought it would be "constructive to outline some of our basic methodological concerns and, by examining a few of the rules set forth in the study, to illustrate how these flaws call into question some of the Study's conclusions."[24]

This is not the time or place to set forth a detailed discussion of the authors' concerns. For present purposes it suffices to note that the letter finds fault with both the Study's assessment of state practice and its approach to the *opinio juris* requirement. The letter also finds fault with the Study's formulation of the rules and its commentary. Significantly, the letter finds that these faults contribute to "two more general errors in the Study that are of particular concern to the United States:

> First, the assertion that a significant number of rules contained in the Additional Protocols to the Geneva Conventions have achieved the status of customary international law applicable to all States, including with respect to a significant number of States (including the United States and a number of other States that have been

involved in armed conflict since the Protocols entered into force) that have declined to become a party to those Protocols; and

Second, the assertion that certain rules contained in the Geneva Conventions and the Additional Protocols have become binding as a matter of customary international law in internal armed conflict notwithstanding the fact that there is little evidence in support of those propositions."[25]

In closing the letter the authors indicated their "appreciation for the ICRC's continued efforts in this important area, and hope that the material provided in this letter and in the attachment will initiate a constructive, in-depth dialogue with the ICRC and others on the subject."[26]

In July 2007, Jean-Marie Henckaerts responded to the Bellinger/Haynes letter.[27] His response focused largely on methodological issues and, following the structure of the U.S. comments, addressed the following questions:

1.   What density of practice is required for the formation of customary international law and what types of practice are relevant?
2.   How did the Study assess the existence of *opinio juris*?
3.   What is the weight of the commentaries on the rules?
4.   What are the broader implications of the Study with respect to Additional Protocols I and II and the law on noninternational armed conflicts in particular?

Because the U.S. comments also addressed four particular rules of the Study, Henckaerts' response dealt with the main aspects of those comments as part of the discussion on methodological issues. The rules included "Rule 31 (protection of humanitarian relief personnel), Rule 45 (prohibition on causing long-term widespread and severe damage to the environment), Rule 78 (prohibition of the use of antipersonnel exploding bullets) and Rule 157 (right to establish universal jurisdiction over war crimes)."[28]

As with respect to the Bellinger/Haynes letter, this is not the time or place to set forth a detailed discussion of Henckaerts' responses to the U.S. concerns. For present purposes it suffices to note that the ICRC rejects the U.S. contention that there is little evidence to support the assertion that certain rules in the Geneva Conventions and the Additional Protocols have become binding as a matter of customary international law in internal armed conflict. On the contrary, in the ICRC view:

. . . . the conclusion of the Study that many rules contained in the Geneva Conventions and the Additional Protocols have become binding as a matter of customary international law in noninternational armed conflict is the result of state practice to this effect. . . .

. . . . developments of international humanitarian law since the wars in the former Yugoslavia and Rwanda point towards an application of many areas of humanitarian law to noninternational armed conflicts. For example, every humanitarian law treaty adopted since 1996 has been made applicable to both international and noninternational armed conflicts....

The criminal tribunals and courts set up, first for the former Yugoslavia and Rwanda and later for Sierra Leone, deal exclusively or mostly with violations committed in noninternational armed conflicts. Similarly, the investigations and prosecutions currently under way before the International Criminal Court are related to violations committed in situations of internal armed conflict. These developments are also sustained by other practice such as military manuals, national legislation and case-law, official statements and resolutions of international organizations and conferences. In this respect, particular care was taken in Volume I to identify specific practice related to noninternational conflict and, on that basis, to provide a separate analysis of the customary nature of the rules in such conflicts. Finally, where practice was less extensive in noninternational armed conflicts, the corresponding rule is acknowledged to be only arguably applicable in noninternational armed conflicts.

When it comes to "operational practice" related to noninternational armed conflicts, there is probably a large mix of official practice supporting the rules and of their outright violation. To suggest, therefore, that there is not enough practice to sustain such a broad conclusion is to confound the value of existing "positive" practice with the many violations of the law in noninternational armed conflicts. This would mean that we let violators dictate the law or stand in the way of rules emerging. The result would be that a whole range of heinous practices committed in noninternational armed conflict would no longer be considered unlawful and that commanders ordering such practices would no longer be responsible for them. This is not what States have wanted. They have wanted the law to apply to noninternational armed conflicts and they have wanted commanders to be responsible and accountable.[29]

The Henckaerts' letter concludes by noting that the ICRC has teamed up with the British Red Cross Society and initiated a project, based at the Lauterpacht Centre for International Law at Cambridge University, to update the practice contained in Volume II of the Study. To this end the ICRC welcomes further comments on the Study in general but also information on "any further specific practice States and experts wish to share with us. This should be part of an ongoing dialogue."[30]

No doubt the dialogue shall be ongoing. Whether the dialogue will be successful in closing the considerable gap that exists between the United States and the ICRC on current norms of the law of armed conflict, especially on the issue whether the rules governing international armed conflict should be extended to internal armed conflict, or the perhaps even wider gap that exists between the developed and the developing countries, remains to be seen. Every effort should be made to this end, however, in view of the current impasse that blocks further efforts at reform through the conclusion of new conventions on the law of armed conflict.

The War(s) on Terrorism

As we have seen earlier in this chapter, there is substantial debate over the appropriate legal regime to apply to efforts to combat terrorism after the September 11, 2001, attacks. Critics of the military model of counterterrorism deny that there is such a thing as a "war on terrorism," any more than there is a "war on drugs" or a "war on poverty."[31] Such statements are mere metaphors. Moreover, states have not viewed themselves "at war" with traditional terrorist groups like the IRA or the Baader-Meinhof Gang, and only states have made war. Even civil wars are conflicts for control of a state, and are waged either by states or, if a state has collapsed, by more than one entity that claims the right of statehood. It is especially inappropriate, these critics contend, to speak of a war on terror, because terror is a strategy and not an entity. At best "a war on terror" is an inapt metaphor.

Philip Bobbitt strongly disagrees with these arguments. To him, "the phrase 'a war on terror' is not an inapt metaphor, but rather a recognition of the way war is changing."[32] Bobbitt notes that the military campaign in Afghanistan is obviously warfare and directed in part against the Taliban. He suggests, however, that the warfare is directed mainly against "a terrorist group, al-Qaeda." Moreover, he states, "I would go further, in light of the elections and the campaign to protect civilians that is ongoing as I write: it is a war against terror itself, its staging camps, its sadistic quotidian regimes, its desire to cow a (sic) entire people and to intimidate others abroad."[33]

As an illustration of the argument against recognizing the idea of a "war on terror," Bobbitt quotes a statement of Simon Jenkins, "the most articulate and compelling of the journalists writing opinions opposed to those expressed here":

> To describe what should be a relentless campaign against criminal terror as war is metaphor abuse. By hurling resources and media attention at some distant theatre, it deflects effort from the domestic front. It also insults those who fought and died in real wars, when territory was threatened and states were at risk.[34]

He then directly challenges this view as follows:

> On the contrary, when we recognize that warfare is changing; that we very much need to fight abroad no less than at home, indeed that it cannot be successfully fought by confining ourselves to either front; we will then see that the men and women who have died on our behalf in Afghanistan and Iraq and countless other places deserve the honor of soldiers for all the reasons I have given. A war against terror is not a misplaced metaphor; indeed it is not a metaphor at all.[35]

Bobbitt goes on to suggest that "an important adverse effect of refusing to recognize the struggle against terror for what it is, a war, is that it prevents us from appreciating the strategy of our enemy."[36] As an example, he cites the conclusion of many that because there have been no successful attacks on the United States since September 11, 2001, "the atrocities of that September day were a fluke, a one-off... But since 2002, al-Qaeda affiliates have killed citizens from eighteen of the twenty countries that bin Laden has identified as supporting the Coalition invasions of Afghanistan and Iraq, while at the same time avoiding spectacular attacks on the American homeland. There is every reason to believe this is a deliberate shift in strategy." Moreover, to support this argument, Bobbitt reports that, "[i]n late 2003, the Norwegian intelligence service came across an al-Qaeda strategy paper posted on an Islamist website. The paper argued that attacks on the U.S. homeland would, at this point, be counterproductive and that instead it was necessary to target American allies in Europe in order to force their governments to withdraw support for the liberation and occupation of Iraq."[37] The attacks on mass transit in Madrid and London carried out this strategy.

In concluding his argument on this point, Bobbitt quotes Lawrence Freedman to illustrate the "principal challenge this new form of warfare poses. Noting 'the difficulty the U.S. armed forces face in shifting their focus from preparing for regular wars, in which combat is separated from civil society, to irregular wars, in which combat is integrated with civil society," Freedman emphasizes that success in these wars will require that "the purpose and practice of Western forces be governed by liberal values [despite the fact that] the integration [of warfare] with civil society makes the application of liberal values so challenging."[38]

Lawrence Freedman's comment raises the issue of whether the traditional sharp separation between the *jus ad bellum* and the *jus in bello* should be maintained under current circumstances. Some have argued that in situations of asymmetric conflict, in which one party enjoys a clear superiority over the other, maintaining the distinction becomes unworkable given the lack of incentive on the part of the "disadvantaged" party.[39] The "global war on terror" is arguably the quintessential current example of asymmetric conflict, and raises in acute form issues regarding the status of the parties to the conflict and the undefined temporal limits of the "war."[40]

There is also a moral case to be made against maintaining the distinction in an asymmetric conflict like the war on terror. In the words of Jeff McMahan speaking at the Annual Meeting of the American Society of International Law:

> The fundamental reason why, as a matter of basic morality, the principles of *jus in bello* cannot be independent of those of *jus ad bellum* is that it is simply not morally permissible to fight in a war with an unjust cause. This is so for a number of reasons, one of which is that acts of war that promote an unjust cause cannot be proportionate, since any good effects they have are not of the sort that can justify being at war and hence cannot outweigh the serious forms of harm that war inflicts.
>
> Neither can acts of war that promote an unjust cause be discriminate. Let us refer to those who fight in a just war as "just combatants" and to those who fight for an unjust cause as "unjust combatants." My claim is that acts of war by unjust

combatants cannot be discriminate because just combatants are innocent in the relevant sense and are therefore not legitimate targets.

This may seem a strange claim. For in the context of war, "innocent" is usually treated as synonymous with "civilian," and just combatants are certainly not civilians. But in fact the term "innocent" has *two* uses in discourse about war that are commonly assumed to coincide. My claim involves the *other* sense, according to which the innocent are simply those who have done nothing to lose their right not to be attacked. Just combatants are innocent in this sense because people do not lose rights by justifiably defending themselves or other innocent people against unjust attack. So even when unjust combatants confine their attacks to military targets, they kill innocent people.

Most of us believe that it is normally wrong to kill innocent people even as a means of achieving a *just* goal. How, then, could it be permissible to kill innocent people as a means of achieving goals that are *unjust*?

For these and other reasons, unjust combatants act wrongly when they fight for an unjust cause. If this is right, the doctrine of the moral equality of combatants is false. And so is the idea that the moral principles of *jus in bello* can be independent of those of *jus ad bellum*. What is morally permissible to do in war (a matter of *jus in bello*) depends crucially on whether one has a just cause (a matter of *jus ad bellum*).[41]

In a somewhat different vein, Philip Bobbitt has challenged the "insipid cliché" that the ends justify the means by quoting the late Washington lawyer Paul Porter, who supposedly once remarked, "If the ends don't justify the means, I'd like to know what in the hell does."[42] Bobbitt goes on to ask, "Why do so many commentators share the assumption that ends and means must be disconnected in order for us to preserve our rights in the Wars against Terror? . . . Because we do not see twenty-first century terrorism is crucially connected to the goals and objectives of the state of terror, we are handicapped in our appreciation of the goals and objectives of the Wars against Terror of which the struggle against terrorism is a part."[43] He strongly rejects the view that terrorism is always and only a means to an end. Rather, in his view, terror can be an end in itself and not just a means to some other political goal. "In the case of al-Qaeda, the goal of the terror network is the destruction of Western values in any area where these can have an impact on Muslims. Rendering persons too frightened to act lawfully on their basic values is both a means and an end, for such a situation of terror, of terrified people in a terrified society too fearful to freely choose their actions (and thus manifest their values) is an end roughly equivalent to the total destruction of Western values."[44]

An unusual, if not unique, aspect of the al-Qaeda situation is that their use of violence is always in violation of the *jus ad bellum* and the *jus in bello*, as well as of international human rights law. Indeed, al-Qaeda and its ilk are contemptuous of Western law, national or international, and substitute as their guide Islamic law (as interpreted by them), which leads them to the use of armed force that violates the most fundamental tenets of *jus ad bellum, jus in bello,* and international human rights law. Bobbitt describes the al-Qaeda vision as "a reaction to the globalization of human rights – democracy, the rule of secular law, the protection of women's rights. It seeks to universalize the legal rules and practices by which Afghanistan was governed under the Taliban... That is to say, al-Qaeda seeks a state of terror, in one sense of the term, in order to frighten away other states, so that it may impose its own state of terror on those persons it governs. Its leaders believe that only such a state can offer Muslims the opportunity for devotion and orthodox practice that other states deny because only in such a state can the Sharia be enforced."[45]

The controversial issue remains as to the extent to which, if at all, the law of armed conflict applies to al-Qaeda. Initially, there was an internal debate within the Bush administration on the applicability of the Geneva Conventions to the conflict in Afghanistan.[46] The Department of Justice took the position that the Geneva Conventions, especially the Geneva Convention Relative to the Treatment of Prisoners of War (the Third Geneva Convention), did not apply to the conflict in Afghanistan, and therefore neither the Taliban nor al-Qaeda was entitled to prisoner of war status. In contrast, the Department of State was of the view that the Geneva Conventions, including the Third Geneva Convention, applied to the conflict because the U.S. and U.K. attack on Afghanistan necessarily gave rise to an interstate conflict between the United States and Afghanistan.

On February 7, 2002, President Bush announced the U.S. position on this issue. He determined that: (1) the Third Geneva Convention applies to the armed conflict in Afghanistan between the Taliban and the United States; (2) the Convention does not apply to the armed conflict in Afghanistan and elsewhere between al-Qaeda and the United States; (3) neither captured Taliban personnel nor captured al-Qaeda personnel are entitled to the status of prisoners of war under the Convention; and (4) nonetheless, all captured personnel are to be treated humanely and consistently with the general principles of the Convention, "to the extent appropriate and consistent with military necessity," and delegates of the International Committee of the Red Cross may privately visit each detainee.

The blanket decision to deny prisoner of war status to all captured Taliban and al-Qaeda detainees has come under sharp fire, with George Aldrich, a former Deputy Legal Adviser of the U.S. Department of State and Department of Defense lawyer, criticizing the decision and Yoram Dinstein, an eminent Israeli authority on the law of armed conflict, defending it.[47]

The president's decision to treat all captured Taliban and al-Qaeda personnel as a matter of policy rather than law humanely and consistently with the general principles of the Conventions "to the extent appropriate and consistent with military necessity" has also been sharply criticized on the ground that Common Article 3 of the Conventions protects all persons "regardless of their status, whether spy, mercenary, or terrorist, and regardless of the type of war in which they are fighting.

That same article prohibits torture, cruel treatment, and murder of all detainees, requires the wounded to be cared for, and says that any trials must be conducted by regular courts respecting due process."[48]

Assuming arguendo that Common Article 3 applies to al-Qaeda, consider the legal issues arising from the following incident.

> On November 4, 2002, an American armed surveillance drone flying in Yemeni airspace launched a missile activated by remote control. The target it struck was an automobile carrying six al-Qaeda suspects, one of them an American. All were killed. How is current international law applied to this? If the attack was part of an international armed conflict, then the law of war applies, and the persons believed to be al-Qaeda militants were lawfully subject to attack. The Government of Yemen appears to have given its consent to the missile launch. But if the attack took place outside a theater of warfare, then ordinary human rights law would apply, and Yemeni consent would be immaterial: the victims should have been tried according to ordinary criminal processes – arrest, indictment, trial, conviction, appeal – before they could have been lawfully executed. It is simply unclear at present what law applies, or indeed whether the "spatial" notion of a zone outside the theater of warfare makes any sense in a global war against terror.[49]

Bobbitt strongly suggests that the spatial notion of a zone outside the theater of warfare makes no sense in a global war against terror. "Yet rather than seeking legal reform," he notes, "the U.S. has used the inadequacy of the currently prevailing law as a basis for avoiding legal restrictions on government entirely."[50] To buttress his point, Bobbitt then quotes Rosa Brooks:

> The breakdown of these once reasonably straightforward distinctions gave the U.S. government an opening to argue, among other things, that noncitizen detainees held at Guantanamo Bay, Cuba, may be detained indefinitely without charge; that U.S. citizens (including those detained inside the U.S.) may be designated "unlawful combatants" by executive fiat and held indefinitely without charge or access to attorney; and that the U.S. may kill any suspected terrorist in any state in the world at any time.[51]

In other words, by designating members of al-Qaeda and their ilk as "unlawful combatants" in the global war on terror who enjoy no rights whatsoever under the law of armed conflict or any other system of law – national or international – the Bush administration claimed total freedom to deal with them as it saw fit, free from any legal constraints. In sharp contrast, as noted by Bobbitt, "[t]he International Committee of the Red Cross (ICRC) and Human Rights Watch... opined that if al-Qaeda terrorists – global, networked terrorists – came neither within Article 2 (which applies to armed conflict between state parties to the convention) nor Article 3 (because the conflict was very plainly international in scope), they must be civilians and thus could not be detained except as a part of the criminal process."[52]

Bobbitt rejects both the position of the Bush administration and that of the ICRC and Human Rights Watch. With respect to the later, he quotes an observation of William Lietzau that:

> [w]e must remember that the law of war [follows, not precedes, war itself]. A claim that the law's failure to recognize war's various manifestations effectively negates a particular war's existence must be acknowledged as ludicrous. Similarly, a failure of a body of law that attends war to address all its possible circumstances is hardly an argument that an entirely different body of law applies.[53]

Commenting further on this "confusion," Bobbitt notes the U.S. Supreme Court's holding in *Hamdan v. Rumsfield*[54] that "purely as a textual matter, when applied to conflicts the words 'not of an international character' plainly meant any conflict that was not between states."[55] He has mixed feelings, however, about the Court's holding: "Although I welcome the holding that Common Article 3 applies to combatants in the Wars against Terror as a provisional matter until the convention can be amended, as a matter of textual argument I confess I find this a good deal less than compelling... the Court seems not to have appreciated that Common Article 3 applies to all parties to a conflict. If a global conflict waged by a network of loose affiliates is not 'international' in nature – that is, is not fought among many different nations – then the entire nature of al-Qaeda has not been grasped."[56]

Finally, Bobbitt has harsh comments and hard questions for both the Bush administration and the human rights community about their positions and their actions:

> This is a difficult problem, and these are tense times, but it is still hard to excuse such performances. Why didn't the U.S. government simply decide what sort of rules it thought appropriate, propose these as amendments to the Geneva Conventions, and obey them in the meantime? This is how customary international law is changed by how states behave. Why didn't the human rights community acknowledge that the old rules are not really meant for the present situation (as at least some courts have recognized) and propose new rules? The result instead has been a continued derogation of the rule of law, in which both the U.S. government and its erstwhile opponents in the human rights community have had a hand.[57]

For her part, Rosa Brooks suggests that "we need to begin to imagine the basic contours of a new domestic and international legal paradigm, one that balances the need to respond to new security threats with the need to protect core rights."[58] She argues that while "[i]n the longer run, this problem can only be solved through a radical reconceptualization of national security law and the international law of armed conflict... international human rights law may offer some partial, interim solutions, and may ultimately point the way to reinventing the law of armed conflict."[59] She then discusses in detail some of the highlights of international human rights law and how they might contribute to reinventing the law of armed conflict.

Time and space constraints preclude discussing Brooks's suggestions for reinventing the law of armed conflict. Surely she is right to focus greater attention on the need to protect the rights of individuals involved in armed conflict, perhaps especially the rights of "unlawful combatants" participating in the war on terror. At the same time it is useful to bear in mind Yoram Dinstein's admonition that we should avoid creating "the false impression that all the rules governing hostilities are – and have to be – truly humanitarian in nature, whereas not a few of them reflect the countervailing constraints of military necessity."[60]

There is also considerable ambiguity regarding the precise nature of the relationship between international human rights law and the law of armed conflict. It is to this subject that we turn in the next section of this chapter.

The Relationship between International Human Rights Law and the Law of Armed Conflict

As we saw earlier in this chapter, there is considerable debate over the appropriate legal regime to apply to efforts to combat terrorism after the September 11, 2001, attacks. With the massive damage and loss of life occasioned by the September 11 attacks, the previously applied criminal justice approach was deemphasized and to a considerable extent supplanted by the use of military means. Under the criminal justice approach, international human rights law was fully applicable, subject to possible limited derogation under Article 4 (1) of the International Covenant on Civil and Political Rights, in situations of "public emergency which threatens the life of the nation and the existence of which is officially proclaimed."[61] The United States has never proclaimed such a public emergency.

Even if such a public emergency is proclaimed, certain human rights are non-derogable in wartime or in any other public emergency. Article 4 (2) of the Covenant forbids any derogation from certain specified human rights. These are the right to life; freedom from torture or cruel, inhuman, or degrading treatment or punishment; freedom from slavery or servitude; freedom from imprisonment on the ground of inability to fulfill a contractual obligation; freedom from being held guilty of any act or omission that did not constitute a criminal offense at the time of its commission, or being subject to a heavier penalty than the one applicable at that time; the right to recognition as a person before the law; and freedom of thought, conscience, and religion.

The right to life has a limited scope in times of war, of course. This is expressly recognized in Article 15 (2) of the European Convention for the Protection of Human Rights and Fundamental Freedoms, which provides an exception to the nonderogation clause "in respect of deaths resulting from lawful acts of war."[62] As for the Covenant, the International Court of Justice opined in the Advisory Opinion on Nuclear Weapons that, in armed conflict, the test of an (unlawful) arbitrary deprivation of life is governed by the *lex specialis* of the law of armed conflict.[63] During an international armed conflict, the right to life is violated by acts such as the killing of prisoners of war and the execution of hostages, but, obviously, does not prevent the killing of enemy combatants that is the inevitable result of warfare.

In its advisory opinion on *Legal Consequences of the Construction of a Wall in the Occupied Palestinian Territory*,[64] the International Court of Justice stated generally that some human rights may be covered exclusively, either by the law of armed conflict or by international human rights law, whereas others may be matters addressed by both branches of international law. Kenneth Watkin has suggested, however, that "at this stage the ultimate solution to this pressing problem is not readily ascertainable in the customary or treaty based humanitarian law. It is also not always clear whether international human rights law principles are meant to provide a governing framework of humanitarian protection during armed conflict, or if they operate merely as a form of 'fall back' protection in situations where international humanitarian law is silent."[65]

What does appear clear is that "[t]here is increasing interest by judicial bodies and human rights advocates in using human rights norms to control the use of force in contemporary security situations involving armed conflict."[66] Watkin cites as examples European Court of Human Rights decisions relating to operations conducted by Russian security forces in Chechnya.[67] He reports further that, "[i]n these cases the court applied human-rights based 'law-enforcement' principles to assess the use of aerial delivered munitions in what might ordinarily be considered, in a *de facto* sense, as operations at the armed conflict end of the hostilities spectrum. This prompted a suggestion that in respect of internal armed conflicts, 'the ECtHR(sic) will apply doctrines it has developed on the use of force in law enforcement operations even to large battles involving thousands of insurgents, artillery attacks and aerial bombardments ... These decisions will undoubtedly be the subject of critical debate, particularly since the interface between customary international humanitarian law and the convention-based European human rights regime is left unresolved."[68]

In concluding this chapter, the question that appears most poignant to me is whether the primary participants in today's armed conflicts, especially their leaders, consider the law of armed conflict to be of any relevance to them whatsoever. As Lavoyer notes, weaknesses in the law of armed conflict are not the primary problem, but rather the failure to implement it in good faith.

But, in considerable part because of the nature of armed conflicts in the current environment, many persons appear to have concluded that the law of armed conflict is now simply dysfunctional or imposes substantial constraints on the use of force they cannot accept. We have noted that states have been unwilling to accept major constraints on their freedom of action in dealing with internal or noninternational armed conflicts. Although judicial tribunals such as the International Criminal Tribunal for the Former Yugoslavia in the *Tadic* case, as well as scholars and the International Committee of the Red Cross, have contended that customary international law has developed to the point where many of the protections of the law of international armed conflict have been extended to noninternational armed conflicts, it is not clear that this proposition has been accepted by states, as illustrated by the U.S. government's argument that there is "little evidence" in support of the proposition "that certain rules contained in the Geneva Conventions and the Additional Protocols have become binding as a matter of customary international law in internal armed conflict."

The relevance of the law of armed conflict to global war or wars on terrorism has come under even sharper challenge. There is first the contention by many that there is no global war on terror and the use of violence by al-Qaeda and its ilk is a matter for criminal law and procedure.[69] Even if, as Bobbitt strenuously argues, there are wars on terror, the current law of armed conflict is hopelessly dysfunctional in dealing with them and in need of radical revision. For its part, the Bush administration made strenuous efforts to avoid any legal constraints, national or international, on its freedom of action in the war on terror. This approach bought forth a torrent of criticism from commentators and other states, although it is unclear at this writing whether this criticism and protest will bring about major changes in U.S. policy.

Thus, it appears clear that the United States and other members of the world community face some hard choices indeed with respect to the law of armed conflict. Bobbitt argues in favor of a rule of law approach:

> The U.S. can extend its influence beyond its temporary preeminence if it joins with others in crafting a system of rules to govern state responsibility for civilian well-being, preventing the proliferation of WMD, combating terrorism, and underwriting the creation of institutions that preserve civil society. To fail to do so risks more than the present mood of widespread anti-Americanism: it risks the unity of the states of consent, and all the good they can do together for the world.[70]

Notes

1. *See* Yoram Dinstein, The Conduct of Hostilities Under the Law of International Armed Conflict 13–14 (2004).
2. *See* John F. Murphy, The United Nations and the Control of International Violence 16 (1982): "The Covenant of the League of Nations prohibited members from resorting to war in some circumstances but not all; in particular, members were permitted to resort to war in cases where specified means of peaceful settlement had failed. The covenant also obligated members of the League 'to respect and preserve against external aggression the territorial integrity and existing political independence of all Members.'"
3. *See* Steven R. Ratner, *Think Again: Geneva Conventions*, Foreign Pol'y, Mar./Apr. 2008, at 26.
4. Jean-Philippe Lavoyer, *International Humanitarian Law: Should It Be Reaffirmed, Clarified or Developed?* in Issues in International Law and Military Operations 287 (Richard B. Jacques ed., Naval War College 2006). For a comment on Mr. Lavoyer's presentation, *see* John F. Murphy, *Enforcing the Law*, in *id.* at 311.
5. *See, e.g.*, Steven R. Ratner, *supra* note 3.

6. PHILIP BOBBITT, TERROR AND CONSENT: THE WARS FOR THE TWENTY-FIRST CENTURY (2008).
7. *Id.* at 3.
8. Bobbitt defines the market state as follows: "The emerging constitutional order that promises to maximize the opportunity of its people, tending to *privatize* many state activities and making representative government more responsible to consumers. It is contrasted with the current nation state, the dominant constitutional order of the twentieth century that based its legitimacy on a promise to improve the material welfare of its people." *Id.* at 4, fn.
9. For further discussion, *see* John F. Murphy, *Challenges of the "New Terrorism," in* THE ROUTLEDGE HANDBOOK of INTERNATIONAL LAW 281 (David Armstrong ed., 2009)
10. *See,* on this point, Samantha Power, *Our War on Terror,* N.Y. TIMES BOOK REV., July 19, 2007, at 1.
11. *See, e.g.,* Kenneth Roth, *The Law of War in the War on Terror,* FOREIGN AFF., Jan.–Feb. 2004, at 2.
12. *See, e.g.,* Ruth Wedgwood, *Combatants or Criminals? How Washington Should Handle Terrorists,* FOREIGN AFF., May–June 2004, at 126.
13. For an especially thoughtful treatment of these distinct consequences, *see* Noah Feldman, *Choices of Law, Choices of War,* 25 HARV. J. L. & PUB. POL'Y 457, 466 (2002).
14. An example of the kind of problems that the increasing assertiveness of developing countries can cause is the collapse of the "Doha round" trade negotiations at Cancun, Mexico, due in no small part to the resistance of the developing countries to demands by the United States and the European Union that the negotiations add foreign investment, competition, and transparency to their agenda.
15. Kenneth Watkin, *21st Century Conflict and International Humanitarian Law: Status Quo or Change ? in* INTERNATIONAL LAW and ARMED CONFLICT: EXPLORING the FAULTLINES 265, 273 (Michael Schmitt & Jelena Pejic eds., 2007).
16. Common Article 3 provides:

> In the case of armed conflict not of an international character occurring in the territory of one of the High Contracting Parties, each Party to the conflict shall be bound to apply, as a minimum, the following provisions:
>
> (1) Persons taking no active part in the hostilities, including members of armed forces who have laid down their arms and those placed *hors de combat* by sickness, wounds, detention, or any other cause, shall in all circumstances be treated humanely, without any adverse distinction founded on race, colour, religion or faith, sex, birth or wealth, or any other similar criteria. To this end, the following acts are and shall remain prohibited at any time and in any place whatsoever with respect to the above mentioned persons:
>   (a) violence to life and person, in particular, murder of all kinds, mutilation, cruel treatment and torture;
>   (b) taking of hostages;
>   (c) outrages upon personal dignity, in particular, humiliating and degrading treatment;
>   (d) the passing of sentences and the carrying out of executions without previous judgment pronounced by a regularly constituted court, affording all the judicial guarantees which are recognized as indispensable by civilized peoples.
> (2) The wounded, sick and shipwrecked shall be collected and cared for.

An impartial humanitarian body, such as the International Committee of the Red Cross, may offer its services to the Parties to the conflict. The Parties to the conflict should further endeavor to bring into force, by means of special agreements, all or part of the other provisions of the present Convention. The application of the preceding provisions shall not affect the legal status of the parties to the conflict.

17. Article 1 of Additional Protocol II provides:

     1. This Protocol, which develops and supplements Article 3 common to the Geneva Conventions of 12 August 1949 without modifying its existing conditions of application, shall apply to all armed conflicts which are not covered by Article 1 of the Protocol Additional to the Geneva Conventions of 12 August 1949, and relating to the Protection of Victims of International Armed Conflicts (Protocol I) and which take place in the territory of a High Contracting Party between its armed forces and dissident armed forces or other organized armed groups which, under responsible command, exercise such control over a part of its territory as to enable them to carry out sustained and concerted military operations and to implement this Protocol.

     2. This Protocol shall not apply to situations of internal disturbances and tensions, such as riots, isolated and sporadic acts of violence and other acts of a similar nature, as not being armed conflicts.

18. Kenneth Watkin, *supra* note 15, at 273.
19. Prosecutor v. Tadic, (Appeal Chamber) para 125 (2 October 1995), www.icty.org/x/cases/tadic/acdec/en/51002.htm.
20. *Id.*
21. *See* Jean-Marie Henckaerts & Louise Doswold-Beck, I Customary International Humanitarian Law xxix (2005).
22. *See* Yoram Dinstein, *supra* note 1, at 56.
23. *See* Letter From John Bellinger III, Legal Adviser, U.S. Dept. Of State and William J. Haynes, General Counsel, U.S. Department of Defense, to Dr. Jakob Kellenberger, President, International Committee of the Red Cross Regarding Customary International Law Study, [November 3, 2006], 46 ILM 514 (2007).
24. *Id.*
25. *Id.* at 516.
26. *Id.*
27. *See* International Committee of the Red Cross: Response of Jean-Marie Henckaerts to the Bellinger/Haynes Comments on Customary International Law Study [July 2007], 46 ILM 959 (2007).
28. *Id.*
29. *Id.* at 965.
30. *Id.* at 966.
31. For an especially strong argument supporting this thesis, *see* Michael Howard, *What's in a Name? How to Fight Terrorism*, 81 Foreign Aff. 8 (January/ February 2002).
32. Philip Bobbitt, *supra* note 6, at 133.
33. *Id.* at 133–34.
34. *Id.* at 173. The quoted statement by Jenkins can be found in Simon Jenkins, *They Opted to Bomb, It Had Better Work*, Times (London), Oct. 10, 2001, at 22.
35. Philip Bobbitt, *supra* note 6, at 173.
36. *Id.* at 175.
37. *Id.* at 176.
38. *Id.* at 177.

39. *See, e.g.*, Antoine Bouvier, *Assessing the Relationship Between Jus in Bello and Jus ad Bellum: An "Orthodox View,"* 100 ASIL PROC. 109, 111 (2006).

40. *Id.*

41. Jeff McMahan, *Morality, Law, and the Relation Between Jus Ad Bellum and Jus in Bello*, 100 ASIL PROC. 112, 113 (2006).

42. PHILIP BOBBITT, *supra* note 6, at 350–51.

43. *Id.* at 351.

44. *Id.* at 357.

45. *Id.* at 69.

46. For further discussion of this internal debate and related developments, see John F. Murphy, *Is US Adherence to the Rule of Law in International Affairs Feasible?*, in INTERNATIONAL LAW and ARMED CONFLICT: EXPLORING the FAULTLINES 197, 214–220 (Michael Schmitt & Jelena Pejic eds., 2007).

47. *See id.* at 215–17.

48. *See* Steven R. Ratner, *supra* note 3, at 27. *See also*, TOM FARER, CONFRONTING GLOBAL TERRORISM and AMERICAN NEO-CONSERVATISM: THE FRAMEWORK of a LIBERAL GRAND STRATEGY 96 (2008).

49. PHILIP BOBBITT, *supra*, note 6, at 455.

50. *Id.* at 456.

51. *See* Rosa Ehrenreich Brooks, *War Everywhere: Rights, National Security Law, and the Law of Armed Conflict in the Age of Terror*, 153 U. PA. L. REV. 675, 677–78 (2004).

52. Philip Bobbitt, *supra* note 6, at 463, citing the official position of the ICRC, *International Humanitarian Law and the Challenges of Contemporary Armed Conflicts*, report prepared by the International Conference of the Red Cross and Red Crescent, September 2003.

53. *Id.* at 463, citing William K. Lietzau, *Combating Terrorism: The Consequences of Moving From Law Enforcement to War*, in NEW WARS, NEW LAWS? 43–44 (David Wippman and Matthew Evangelista eds., 2005).

54. 548 U.S.557 (2006).

55. PHILIP BOBBITT, *supra* note 6, at 464.

56. *Id.*

57. *Id.*

58. *See* Rosa Ehrenreich Brooks, *supra* note 51, at 687.

59. *Id.* at 747.

60. *See* YORAM DINSTEIN, *supra* note 1, at 13–14.

61. *See* Article 4(1) of the 1966 International Covenant of Civil and Political Rights, 999 U.N.T.S. 171, 6 ILM 368 (1967).

62. Article 15 (2) of the European Convention for the Protection of Human Rights and Fundamental Freedoms, 1950, 213 U.N.T.S. 222, 232.

63. Advisory Opinion on Nuclear Weapons,[1996] ICJ Rep. 240.

64. Legal Consequences of the Construction of a Wall in the Occupied Palestinian Territory, Advisory Opinion, 2004 ICJ 136 (July 9). (para 106).

65. *See* Kenneth Watkin, *supra* note 15, at 288.

66. *Id.*, citing David Kretzmer, *Targeted Killing of Suspected Terrorists: Extra-Judicial Executions or Legitimate Means of Defence?* 16 EUR. J. INT'L L. 171 (2005).

67. Isayeva, Usupova and Bazayeva v. Russia, Eur. Ct. Hum. Rt., App.Nos. 57947–49/00 (24 Feb. 2005); Isayeva v. Russia, Eur. Ct. Hum. Rt., App. Nos. 57950/00 (24 Feb. 2005).

68. Kenneth Watkin, *supra* note 15, at 288–89.

69. Support for this point of view has recently come from a new book, *Leaderless Jihad*, by Marc Sageman, in which Mr. Sageman argues that al-Qaeda no longer constitutes the main terrorist threat but rather radicalized individuals and groups who meet in their neighborhoods and on the Internet to plot attacks. If Mr. Sageman is correct, then preventing terrorist attacks is "more a job for the local police and the FBI working with undercover informants and with authorities abroad . . . On the other hand, if the main task can be seen as thwarting plots or smiting Al Qaeda's leaders abroad, then attention and resources should continue to flow to the CIA, the State Department, the military and terror-financing sleuths." Elaine Sciolino & Eric Schmitt, *A Not Very Private Feud Over Terrorism*, Week in Review, N.Y. TIMES, June 8, 2008, at1, col. 1. Many experts on terrorism have challenged Mr. Sageman's views, including Bruce Hoffman, a Georgetown University historian, who wrote a highly critical review of Sageman's book for FOREIGN AFFAIRS. *See* Bruce Hoffman, *The Myth of Grass-Roots Terrorism: Why Osama bin Laden Still Matters*, FOREIGN AFF., May/June, 2008, at 133. Sageman responded to this review, and Hoffman replied in turn. *See Does Osama Still Call the Shots? Debating the Containment of al Qaeda's Leadership*, FOREIGN AFF., July/Aug. at 163–66. Hoffman contends that his view is based on "empirical evidence indicating that al Qaeda Central had reconstituted itself in Pakistan's tribal frontier areas and from that base was again actively directing and initiating international terrorist operations on a grand scale." *Id.* at 166.

70. Philip Bobbitt, *supra* note 6, at 504.

5

Arms Control, Disarmament, Nonproliferation, and Safeguards

They will beat their swords into plowshares and their spears into pruning hooks. Nation will not take up sword against nation, nor will they train for war anymore.

– Isaiah 2:4

PROBLEMS WITH CONTROLLING ILLICIT TRADE IN SMALL ARMS AND LIGHT WEAPONS

Weapons of war have become much more sophisticated than the swords and spears that were popular in the days of Isaiah. Indeed, most international efforts in the arms control and disarmament arena, with the notable exception of land mines, have focused on weapons of mass destruction – nuclear, chemical, and biological. Most wars are fought, however, and most people have been killed, not by weapons of mass destruction but by small arms and light weapons – such as pistols, assault rifles, and hand grenades. It has been estimated that some 6 million people have been killed in armed conflicts around the world in the last decade, half of them by small arms, rather than by tanks and rockets.[1] Most of these armed conflicts have been civil wars rather than cross-border conflicts.

This killing is greatly abetted by a thriving trade in arms, with between 4 to 6 billion weapons a year changing hands. The biggest-grossing producers involved in this arms trade are the United States, the United Kingdom, France, and Russia – four of the five permanent members of the Security Council. Together, these four countries export 83 percent of the world's arms.[2] The United States is the leading exporter of such weapons. In 2006 the amount of U.S. authorized small arms exports was valued at $643 million, according to the Small Arms Survey, a nongovernmental organization based in Geneva.[3]

Efforts to put constraints on this arms trade have met with limited success. On December 6, 1991, the U.N. General Assembly adopted a resolution[4] whereby it established a U.N. register of arms transfers and called on member states to provide information to the Secretary-General regarding their transfers of heavy conventional arms. The goal of the register is to limit international traffic in arms by publicizing transactions and identifying potential trouble spots by showing where arms stocks are increasing. The resolution also requests the Secretary-General to establish a group of experts to explore ways of extending the register to include lighter arms as well as production sites and national weapons stocks. This is to meet a concern expressed by many developing countries that the register would discriminate against poorer nations, which import their arms, by requiring them to disclose their purchases while protecting richer nations with indigenous arms industries against revealing their military strength. The register has not been expanded to include small arms and light weapons because of opposition by states heavily involved in the arms trade, especially the United States.

The United States has been especially opposed to efforts to conclude a broad binding international agreement on the illicit trade in small arms and light weapons. The latest effort to this end was in 2006 when the U.S. position, as well as the more restrained position of other arms exporters like China and Iran, deadlocked discussions.[5] As a result of this opposition, the most recent discussions have been limited to issues for which broader support exists, such as securing weapons and munitions stockpiles, restricting illegal brokering, and improving efforts to mark and trace weapons.[6]

THE DECLINE OF ARMS CONTROL TREATIES

Although it has not proved possible to conclude a multilateral arms control and disarmament treaty with respect to small arms and light weapons, traditionally, weapons of mass destruction have been subject to an extensive network of multilateral and bilateral treaties.[7] Many, indeed most, of these treaties were concluded with strong U.S. support. With the coming into power of the George W. Bush administration, however, there was a sea change in U.S. attitudes toward such treaties. Reflecting in large part the substantial distrust of John R. Bolton, who served first as U.S. Under-Secretary of State for Arms Control and International Security and later as U.S. Permanent Representative to the United Nations, the Bush administration "pulled out of the Anti-Ballistic Missile Treaty with Russia, scuttled an important protocol to the biological-weapons ban, ousted the head of the organization that oversees the chemical weapons ban, watered down an accord on small-arms trafficking and refused to submit the nuclear test ban treaty for Senate ratification [actually Senate advice and consent to ratification]."[8]

The view of the Bush administration apparently was that treaties on arms control, disarmament, and, to a lesser extent, nonproliferation at best do not work and at worst can endanger vital U.S. interests. It appeared especially skeptical of multilateral treaties that set up verification and enforcement regimes. In the Bush administration's view, states that cheat and violate the treaty are not prevented from doing so by the treaty, whereas intrusive verification regimes subject countries like the United States that act in accordance with the treaty's norms to infringements of their national sovereignty and to the possible loss of proprietary information from U.S. laboratories and businesses. In place of treaty regimes, the Bush administration would rely on military and other forms of U.S. power to defend against weapons of mass destruction and other possible kinds of armed attack endangering U.S. national security.[9]

At first the dramatic change of policy toward arms control and disarmament treaties by the Bush administration was sharply criticized and strongly opposed. Gradually, however, some commentators began to question the effectiveness of the arms control and disarmament treaties in coping with the growth of the weapons of mass destruction (WMD) threat in the post-Cold War period.[10]

During the Cold War period nuclear deterrence became a central feature of international relations. As pointed out by David P. Fidler:

> The bipolar international system, dominated by two ideologically opposed super-powers, created significant political/military motivations for the United States and the Soviet Union to develop, stockpile, and threaten to use nuclear weapons. Technological developments on nuclear weapons (e.g., multiple independently targeted re-entry vehicles [MIRVs]) reinforced these motivations but also provided incentives for the two countries to try, through arms control treaties, to stabilize the effect of offensive and defensive technological advancements on nuclear deterrence. One such stabilization effort – the Treaty on the Limitation of Anti-Ballistic Missile Systems of 1972 (ABM Treaty) restricted the development of anti-ballistic missile defenses in order to strengthen nuclear deterrence by increasing each superpower's vulnerability to nuclear attack.[11]

As for nuclear weapons proliferation, Fidler notes that it "did not serve the national security interests of either of the two superpowers engaged in their titanic bipolar standoff – to the contrary these national security interests were the impetus behind the creation of political and structural restraints on nuclear proliferation."[12] At the same time the U.S.-Soviet nuclear standoff led many states to support efforts to prevent the spread of nuclear weapons throughout the international system and thereby avoid exacerbating their sense of vulnerability to nuclear blackmail or attack. The Nuclear Non-Proliferation Treaty (NPT) "represented the recognition that more and more countries were acquiring the technological means (e.g., through civilian and military nuclear programs) needed to develop nuclear weapons and that the proliferation of nuclear weapons in the international system would be destabilizing."[13]

The NPT entered into force in 1970 and "[d]uring its first twenty-five years, the NPT played a central role as nuclear nonproliferation efforts met with remarkable success. In 1963, President John F. Kennedy predicted as many as 'fifteen or twenty' states could possess nuclear weapons by 1975. In fact, the number of states possessing nuclear weapons grew by only one (from six to seven) between 1970 and 1995."[14] The result was that, according to Orde F. Kittrie, "[b]y May 1995, when an NPT Review Conference voted to extend the treaty in perpetuity, a robust nuclear nonproliferation regime had arisen, with the NPT at its forefront, that seemed to have succeeded in converting the acquisition of nuclear weapons from an act of national pride into an act of international outlawry."[15] The year 1995, however, proved to be the high water mark.

The first major indications that the nuclear nonproliferation regime was at risk were the Indian and Pakistani nuclear weapons detonations in 1998. As noted by Kittrie, "[a]lthough India and Pakistan were not parties to the NPT, their flagrant proliferation, and the world's weak response, shook the NPT and did considerable damage to the nuclear nonproliferation regime."[16]

David Fidler has identified post-Cold War developments that arguably did even greater damage to the nuclear nonproliferation regime and indeed to the arms control treaty approach to weapons of mass destruction. According to Fidler, "[t]he post-Cold War period has seen a political revolution in world politics that has brought to light a WMD 'proliferation epidemic.' The political revolution has two features – as the end of the Cold War brought the bipolar, superpower international system to an end, the threat from terrorism – especially terrorism involving WMD – began to loom larger in this new world order."[17] As to arms control treaties, Fidler contends that "[d]espite its promising post-Cold War start, the arms control approach could not sustain momentum over the following decade. Instead of receding under the influence of arms control agreements, the WMD threat has grown exponentially during the post-Cold War period. This growth in the WMD threat has led to questions about the utility of the arms control approach in addressing the problem."[18]

One reason questions have been raised regarding the utility of the arms control treaty approach in addressing the problem of the growth in the WMD threat is that until very recently arms control treaties have been directed only toward state rather than nonstate behavior. The limitations of this approach were demonstrated when in the wake of the collapse of the Soviet Union the primary concern of the United States was no longer avoiding a nuclear attack by its former adversary but rather that the former adversary's nuclear weapons would fall into the hands of nonstate actors (terrorists) or of the representatives of other states hostile to the United States. An even greater concern of the United States and other Western states has been nicely identified by Fidler: "The WMD proliferation epidemic, both real and feared, posed an even greater crisis when policymakers considered the merging of the two proliferation vectors – certain states pursuing WMD capabilities have a history of supporting international terrorism, which raised the specter of a synergy between state and non-state WMD proliferation. These fears coalesced in the Bush Doctrine's declaration that the United States would confront national security threats from repressive regimes that pursued WMD as well as those that supported international terrorism."[19]

These concerns, and others, have caused the NPT to come under greater scrutiny. The first two articles of the NPT allocate responsibilities between nuclear weapons states and nonnuclear weapons states.[20] Article I requires the nuclear weapons states not to transfer nuclear weapons or devices, or control over them, and not to assist nonnuclear weapons states in acquiring nuclear weapons. Article II reciprocally obligates nonnuclear weapons states not to manufacture or acquire nuclear weapons. The key provision of the NPT is Article III, which requires bilateral so-called full scope safeguards agreements with the International Atomic Energy Agency (IAEA) on all nuclear facilities of nonnuclear weapons states that are NPT parties, and IAEA safeguards in nuclear exports by any of its parties. Articles IV and V assure nonnuclear weapons states full access to nuclear power technology for peaceful purposes. Under Article VI the nuclear weapons states agree to seek an early end to the nuclear arms race and to pursue nuclear disarmament as well as general and complete disarmament "under strict and effective international control."

In 1968 the United States, the United Kingdom, and the Soviet Union gave, in a letter to the president of the Security Council,[21] security assurances to nonnuclear weapons states that each would seek immediate Security Council action to assist any nonnuclear weapons state party to the NPT that was the target of nuclear aggression or threats. An interesting legal issue that need not be explored here is whether these unilateral statements by the three Security Council members created a legal obligation on the part of the three states. One may also ask whether the political will would be present in the Security Council to take meaningful action should the need arise to fulfill this pledge in light of the increasingly sharp divisions among the permanent members of the Council. Increasingly, many states are of the view that the political will is lacking. Also, some states are coming to the view that two of the three members of the Security Council that wrote the letter – the United States and Russia (as the successor to the Soviet Union) – are themselves the most likely threat to use nuclear weapons against nonnuclear states.

The IAEA has been subject to a number of criticisms, but a discussion of most of them is beyond the scope of this chapter.[22] For present purposes it suffices to focus on allegations that the IAEA's verification and monitoring authorities are too weak to promptly and reliably catch proliferators and that the nuclear weapons states, especially the United States and Russia, have failed to comply with their disarmament obligations.[23]

With respect to the IAEA's verification and monitoring authorities, the Article III "full scope safeguards" agreements or the "comprehensive safeguards agreement" is the principal mechanism for detecting cheating by member states on their nonproliferation obligations. Article III *requires* each nonnuclear weapons state to conclude with the IAEA a comprehensive safeguards agreement for the purpose of "verification of the fulfillment of its obligations assumed under this Treaty with a view to preventing diversions of nuclear energy from peaceful uses to nuclear weapons." Despite this clear language of obligation, Kittrie reports that "thirty NPT state parties have yet to conclude such safeguards agreements. In the absence of such agreements, the IAEA has no authority to carry out inspections in these countries."[24] Even with respect to those countries that have concluded safeguards agreements with the IAEA, critics contend they are of limited utility because they are designed only to detect a diversion of nuclear material to military uses and do not prevent a clandestine nuclear program. They have also contended that the IAEA is underfunded and understaffed, and that it has been weakened by political questions not relevant to nonproliferation.

Critics of the IAEA safeguards system especially pressed their arguments upon discovery by a U.N. and IAEA inspection team in the summer of 1991 of a secret Iraqi nuclear arms program in violation of Iraq's safeguards agreements with the IAEA. It should be noted, however, that the inspections in Iraq after the Gulf War were conducted pursuant to the extraordinary powers granted to the U.N. and IAEA inspectors by Security Council Resolution 687, which allowed for much more intrusive inspections than those under the IAEA safeguards program.

Kittrie has identified another flaw in the IAEA's comprehensive safeguards agreement:

> The IAEA's model for the comprehensive safeguards agreement is contained in an IAEA document usually referred to as INFCIRC/153. Under INFCIRC/153 safeguards agreements, parties must report to the IAEA on their nuclear facilities and the nuclear material that moves through them. The INFCIRC/153 agreements are significantly flawed, however, in that they contain no effective mechanisms for the IAEA to assess whether the reports are complete. The agreements operate on the assumption that all states declare all relevant facilities and materials.[25]

In 1997 the IAEA took a step that has the potential to mitigate the verification shortcomings of the comprehensive safeguards agreement: it issued a model protocol to be appended to the INFCIRC/ 153 agreements (the Additional Protocol). According to the IAEA: "While the chief object under INFCIRC/153 is to verify that declared nuclear material was not diverted, the chief object of the new measures . . . is to obtain assurance that the State has no undeclared activities."[26] Unlike comprehensive safeguards agreements, however, there is no obligation on NPT members to adhere to the Additional Protocol, and as of May 30, 2008, "some two-thirds of the 189 member states, including many states of proliferation concern, have yet to join."[27] Parenthetically, it may be noted that although the Senate gave its advice and consent to ratification in 2004 and passed implementing legislation for the U.S. Additional Protocol in 2006, it took until 2009 for the United States finally to ratify the Additional Protocol.[28]

Because of the weakness of the IAEA's verification and monitoring authorities, an NPT member state that is contemplating whether to develop nuclear weapons "would inevitably calculate the likelihood of getting caught as slim. Iran managed to conceal nuclear facilities, materials, and activities from the IAEA for eighteen years before an Iranian dissident group revealed them in 2002. Libya successfully hid its nuclear weapons program from the IAEA for over a decade. Iraq also kept a nuclear weapons program secret from the IAEA for more than a decade, coming within six months of a nuclear bomb before Iraq invaded Kuwait in 1990."[29] It should further be noted that North Korea developed its nuclear weapons while still a member of the NPT, "even claiming legitimacy for its weapons development based on the treaty's withdrawal provisions."[30]

In theory, it should be possible to amend the NPT to strengthen its verification and monitoring authorities. However, as Kittrie points out, "the NPT is nearly impossible to amend formally."[31] Accordingly, Kittrie favors, as the "simplest and speediest way to make legally binding changes to the nuclear nonproliferation regime," the adoption of a U.N. Security Council resolution that would impose "on all NPT parties IAEA authorities contained in the INFCIRC-153 and currently optional Additional Protocol agreements."[32]

Other commentators also have favored the use of Security Council resolutions as a tool for strengthening the nonproliferation regime.[33] The binding nature of such resolutions depends upon the Security Council being willing to determine, under Chapter VII of the U.N. Charter, that proliferation constitutes a threat to international peace and security.[34] Perhaps the closest step the Council has taken to date to creating binding changes to the nonproliferation regime is its adoption of Resolution 1540 in 2004.[35] As noted by Jack Garvey, "[i]t is the most direct, comprehensive and mandatory statement of the Security Council to date on WMD."[36]

As already noted, several commentators have identified as a weakness of the NPT, as well as of arms control treaties in general, that they are statecentric and do not address themselves to the increasingly critical problem of possible use by nonstate actors, especially terrorists, of weapons of mass destruction.[37] Until recently, the international instrument that was closest to such a treaty was the Convention on the Physical Protection of Nuclear Material, adopted in 1980 in an effort to deny terrorists access to nuclear materials.[38] In 2005 the Convention was amended to, among other things, create expanded duties to secure nuclear materials in storage and in transit and to criminalize sabotage against civilian nuclear facilities.[39]

THE INTERNATIONAL CONVENTION FOR THE SUPPRESSION OF ACTS OF NUCLEAR TERRORISM

On July 7, 2007, however, the International Convention for the Suppression of Acts of Nuclear Terrorism[40] entered into force. As noted by David Fidler, the Convention is the first antiterrorism treaty adopted after September 11, 2001.[41] According to the preamble of the Convention, it was created because "existing multilateral legal provisions do not adequately address those attacks."

Like many previous antiterrorism treaties, the Convention "requires States Parties to make certain acts criminal offenses in national law, establish jurisdiction over such offenses, prosecute or extradite persons alleged to have committed the defined criminal offenses, and engage in cooperation and mutual legal assistance with respect to objectives of the Convention."[42] A detailed discussion of the Convention is beyond the scope of this chapter.[43] For present purposes, it suffices to note the offenses covered by the Convention as well as some of its possible weaknesses.

Article 2 defines the actions that constitute offenses under the Convention. Any person who unlawfully and intentionally possesses radioactive material or makes or possesses any nuclear or radioactive explosive or dispersal device (or attempts to do so) with the intent to cause (1) death or serious bodily injury, or (2) substantial damage to property or the environment has committed an offense under the Convention. Similarly, a person commits an offense under the Convention when he unlawfully and intentionally uses any radioactive material or dispersal device or uses or damages a nuclear facility (or attempts to do so), in a manner that releases or risks release of radioactive material with the intent to (1) cause death or serious bodily injury, (2) do substantial damage to property or the environment, or (3) compel a natural or legal person, an international organization, or a state to do or refrain from doing an act. A person also commits an offense if he participates as an accomplice, organizes or directs others to commit an offense, or in any other way contributes to the commission of an offense by a group of persons acting with a common purpose.

There was considerable disagreement during negotiations on the Convention as to whether the Convention should apply to state actions involving nuclear materials or weapons. Reportedly, "some delegations had expressed concern that the convention exempts military activities and personnel from prosecution for similar offenses as those articulated in the treaty."[44]

But in order to allow the Convention to be adopted by consensus, in its final form the Convention does not address issues involving state and military possession and use of nuclear weapons and materials. Nor does the Convention address in any way the issue of the use or threat of nuclear weapons by states.

According to Fidler, the most serious weakness of the Convention is that, although state parties are obliged to prevent offenses identified in the Convention by making every effort to adopt measures to ensure the protection of radioactive material, taking into account IAEA recommendations, in light of the importance of preventing radioactive materials from being stolen or diverted by terrorists, "the Convention's very brief and general approach to prevention obligations does not advance the prevention agenda in terms of international law."[45]

Fidler points out that, with its entry into force, the Convention "becomes part of a growing array of instruments and initiatives aimed at preventing and responding to nuclear terrorism. Since the terrorist attacks of 11 September 2001, states have launched a series of efforts to address the threat of nuclear terrorism."[46] According to Fidler, these efforts have combined to create a "web of prevention" against the threat of nuclear terrorism. Nonetheless, he adds, "[t]he initiatives and instruments forming the web do not . . . eliminate concerns that the regime against nuclear terrorism still does not contain specific, detailed standards for the physical protection of radioactive materials and nuclear facilities from terrorists or mechanisms to improve physical protection efforts within States. The Convention advances neither of these tasks directly."[47]

When the Convention was still in the drafting stage, Larry D. Johnson, who was the Legal Adviser of the International Atomic Energy Agency from 1997 to 2001, urged that the weak preventive measure in the draft be revised to include more effective binding preventive measures that would go beyond the focus on the suppression of criminal acts and the extradition/prosecution of perpetrators. Commenting on both the Convention on the Physical Protection of Nuclear Material and the draft convention for the suppression of acts of nuclear terrorism, Johnson argued that "as far as terrorism treaties are concerned, they miss the mark. They focus on criminalizing the acts and punishing the terrorists, but only after the thief has let the horse out of the barn. In view of the nature of this beast – dangerous radioactive material – the point should be to make sure the thief does not get anywhere near the barn. Nuclear terrorism treaties should require specific measures of prevention to make it harder for would-be terrorists to commit acts of nuclear terrorism."[48]

As an example of a possible alternative approach, Fidler cites and quotes a proposal by George Bunn, a former General Counsel of the U.S. Arms Control & Disarmament Agency, that "[t]he Security Council, backed up by its 1540 Committee, should move ahead to establish effective standards for physical protection of nuclear facilities around the world. It should consider assigning to the IAEA the task of conducting a series of inspections to see whether these standards are being met."[49] Fidler concludes, however, that "[i]n all likelihood, addressing the perceived gap in specific, detailed, and monitored standards for the physical protection of nuclear materials and facilities will evolve through a combination of efforts within the web of prevention and will not occur through the adoption of a comprehensive, binding treaty."[50] It is worth noting that most of the instruments and initiatives cited by Fidler as constituting the "web of prevention" do not constitute binding treaties but rather nonbinding cooperative efforts between states resulting in at most written guidelines.[51] As we have seen previously in the case of other key issues of international law, with respect to nonproliferation and the prevention of the use of weapons of mass destruction by nonstate actors, the trend is away from the classic sources of international law, such as treaties, and the use of international institutions in favor of informal arrangements among interested states that eschew the creation of internationally binding legal obligations and the use of formal dispute resolution mechanisms.

THE FAILURE OF NUCLEAR WEAPONS STATES TO DISARM

As already noted, the United States and the other nuclear weapons states parties to the NPT have come under increased criticism for their alleged failure to comply with their obligations under Article VI of the NPT to seek an early end to the nuclear arms race and to pursue nuclear disarmament as well as general and complete disarmament. In particular, the nuclear weapons states have come under increased pressure to fulfill their obligations under Article VI at recent NPT Review Conferences.[52] Also, in 1996, the International Court of Justice issued its advisory opinion on the *Legality of the Threat or Use of Nuclear Weapons*,[53] in which the Court interpreted Article VI of the NPT as requiring the nuclear weapons states "to pursue in good faith and bring to a conclusion negotiations leading to nuclear disarmament in all its aspects under strict and effective international control."[54]

Despite the pressures applied by the nonnuclear weapons states at the NPT Review Conferences, and the advisory opinion of the International Court of Justice, however, there is still the question whether the United States and the other nuclear weapon states parties to the NPT truly intend to negotiate in good faith toward the ultimate elimination of nuclear weapons. At this writing the outlook for a positive answer to this question is murky at best.

To be sure, it is noteworthy that George Shultz and Henry Kissinger, two prominent former U.S. Secretaries of State; William Perry, a former U.S. Secretary of Defense; and Sam Nunn, a former chairman of the Senate Armed Services Committee, have advanced a proposal that the United States lead a global campaign to "devalue and eventually rid the world of nuclear weapons."[55] Reportedly, fourteen additional former secretaries of state and defense and national security advisers have endorsed the call, and the Norwegian government has hosted a conference to develop their ideas. President Barack Obama has embraced the proposal. Senator John McCain has not, but has called for a revival of arms control negotiations with the Russians and deep cuts in both countries' arsenals.[56]

But the tensions created between the United States and its allies in Europe and Russia by the Russian invasion of Georgia, the agreement between the United States and Poland to base part of a planned U.S. missile shield on Polish soil, the expressed willingness of the Czech Republic to accept part of the shield, veiled threats from Russia to launch a nuclear attack against Poland and the Czech Republic if they go through with this plan, as well as Prime Minister Vladimir Putin's increasingly anti-Western foreign policy, have resulted in a variety of negative developments.[57] These include, among others, the United States reconsidering whether to proceed with a landmark accord, which then President Putin and President Bush signed in 2007, that would provide a framework for greater U.S.-Russian cooperation in developing proliferation-resistant reactors and nuclear fuel banks; a possible dropping of a bid to resurrect an amended Conventional Forces in Europe treaty whose limits on troop movements Russia stopped adhering to last year; and concern that Russia may stop working with the United States and other Western countries to induce Iran to give up its plans for continuing centrifuge production and use in order to enrich uranium – for peaceful nuclear use according to Iran.

In such an atmosphere it may be difficult to agree upon a new round of cuts in strategic arsenals, much less an ambitious effort to rid the world of nuclear weapons. Still, there are current and former U.S. officials who are calling for an enhanced U.S.-Russia dialogue over key national security issues once the Georgia crisis subsides.[58]

THE GREATEST THREATS TO THE NONPROLIFERATION REGIME

At this writing, Iran and North Korea constitute the most serious challenges to nonproliferation. We turn next to a brief consideration of these crises.

Iran

Orde Kittrie has contended that "Iran's nuclear program is by far and away the number one threat to the vitality of the nuclear nonproliferation program."[59] Although some might argue in favor of North Korea's program as constituting the greatest threat, there is no doubt that both countries have engaged in actions that have created crises that remain to be resolved.

In 1970, Iran became a party to the NPT. But in September 2002, an Iranian dissident revealed that Iran was building two nuclear facilities, which it had failed to report.[60] In reaction to this revelation, the U.N. Security Council passed three resolutions[61] that "issued and reiterated an order...that 'Iran shall without further delay suspend' various 'proliferation sensitive nuclear activities' including 'all enrichment-related and reprocessing activities, including research and development' and 'work on all heavy water-related projects, including the construction of a research reactor moderated by heavy Water.'"[62] Iran, however, rejected these demands and has "openly and admittedly accelerated its enrichment activities."[63]

The Security Council has reacted by imposing economic sanctions against Iran.[64] Kittrie, however, has sharply criticized these sanctions as entirely too weak to be effective.[65] In his view, they are too weak "to coerce Iran into compliance, contain Iran's ability to advance its nuclear weapons program, or deter other states from following Iran's lead and developing their own nuclear weapons program. This is unfortunate, because Iran's heavy dependence on foreign trade – including especially on imports of refined petroleum – leaves it highly vulnerable to strong economic sanctions."[66]

Iran has steadfastly insisted that its uranium enrichment program and its other nuclear activities are solely for peaceful purposes, especially for producing fuel for nuclear reactors that generate electricity. Its claims, however, have been cast further into doubt by the recent publication of an IAEA report that disclosed activities, such as explosives, uranium processing, and a missile warhead design, that ordinarily would be associated with constructing nuclear weapons.[67]

Six nations – Britain, France, Russia, China, Germany, and the United States – have been trying to present a united front against Iran. Unlike the other five countries, however, the United States initially refused to get involved in talks with Iran, but ultimately did agree to participate.[68]

Kittrie has summarized the major reasons why the current situation is so dangerous:

> Iran's advancing nuclear program is dangerous for a number of reasons, including concern that the Iranian leadership's apocalyptic messianism and exaltation of martyrdom may make it impossible to deter Iran from using, or enabling terrorist proxies to use, nuclear weapons; the risk of rogue elements in Iran's fragmented government taking it on themselves to transfer nuclear arms to terrorist or other allies; and worry that an Iranian "nuclear umbrella" would make Iran an even more self-confident sponsor of terrorism. An equally important danger of Iran acquiring a nuclear arsenal . . . is that many of Iran's neighbors in the Middle East might feel compelled to follow suit.[69]

Perhaps the most important danger of Iran continuing its efforts to acquire a nuclear arsenal is that Israel is highly unlikely to allow these efforts to continue to the point where they are successful, in light of statements by Iranian President Ahmadinejad urging that Israel be wiped off the map. Israeli officials have informally expressed their determination to prevent Iran from obtaining nuclear weapons, if necessary by armed force. The adverse consequences of an Israeli preemptive strike on Iran's nuclear program are incalculable, but they surely would be very severe. Hence, one must hope that a combination of increased economic sanctions against Iran and creative diplomacy will be successful.

North Korea

One crucial difference between Iran and North Korea is that the latter has proclaimed its possession of nuclear weapons, and therefore whereas the effort with respect to Iran is to prevent it from acquiring nuclear weapons, in the case of North Korea the goal is to convince it to give up its nuclear weapons and to become a party again to the NPT. Moreover, whereas Iran's violation of its obligations under the NPT did not become known until 2002, knowledge of North Korea's violations came to light in 1993.

North Korea became a party to the NPT in 1985, but for a number of years thereafter it failed to conclude a safeguards agreement with the IAEA.[70] Finally, in January 1992, it reached agreement with the IAEA on the terms of a safeguards agreement, accepting six IAEA inspection visits before refusing access to two facilities near its Yongbyong nuclear reactor complex on the ground that these were conventional military facilities. Evidence began to emerge that North Korea may have used more nuclear fuel, and may have been able to separate more plutonium for possible weapons use than it had declared. As a consequence, on April 1, 1993, the

IAEA's Board of Governors ruled that North Korea had violated its safeguards agreement and referred the issue to the U.N. Security Council. For its part, North Korea gave formal notice of its intention to withdraw from the NPT. There then ensued a period of great tension that brought the United States and North Korea to the brink of war. The crisis was resolved diplomatically, however, when the United States and North Korea signed an agreement called the Agreed Framework on October 21, 1994. Under the agreement, North Korea agreed to shut down its nuclear reactors, freeze its nuclear activities, and put its nuclear materials under IAEA inspection. In return, the United States gave a pledge that a consortium of outside powers would build North Korea two modern reactors and provide it with large shipments of oil. The effectiveness of this agreement is a matter of some controversy. One commentator, however, has claimed that, "[t]hough bedeviled by problems, implementation delays, and mutual recriminations, the Agreed Framework succeeded in freezing North Korea's plutonium program for nearly ten years."[71]

Be that as it may, in October 2002, during a visit to Pyongyang, officials of the U.S. Department of State confronted North Korea with evidence of a clandestine North Korean program for the enrichment of uranium. This was a second North Korean nuclear weapons program – this one based on uranium – in addition to the plutonium program frozen by the 1994 agreement, constituting a violation of both the NPT and the Agreed Framework. Far from denying these allegations, North Korea acknowledged that it had such a program and asserted its right to pursue nuclear weapons. Thereafter, the situation rapidly deteriorated:

> In rapid succession during December 2002 and January 2003, North Korea announced its intentions to restart its long idle nuclear reactors, began to access materials and equipment that had been sealed and tagged by the IAEA to prevent their use, dismantled IAEA surveillance cameras at its nuclear facilities, and expelled IAEA inspectors from the country. On January 10, 2003, . . . North Korea declared its withdrawal from the NPT and hence its rejection of the commitment to remain non-nuclear. Later in January 2003, it was reported that Pyongyang had begun to move its 8,000 spent nuclear fuel rods, formerly safeguarded by the IAEA, out of storage facilities, raising concerns that it was about to begin "reprocessing" in order to extract the plutonium necessary for making nuclear weapons. These fuel rods contain enough plutonium for at least six nuclear weapons. Once reprocessing begins the clock will count down rapidly to the point where North Korea possesses a small nuclear arsenal: six weapons in six months is the common estimate. Meanwhile, with its reactors again running and its no longer clandestine (though still geographically hidden) uranium enrichment capacity developing at some unknown pace, Pyongyang will have future options for further augmenting its nuclear weapons capability.[72]

Although North Korea appears "extremely vulnerable to strong sanctions, so long as they include Chinese and South Korea participation,"[73] China has been concerned that severe economic pressure on North Korea could cause the North Korean regime to collapse, thereby flooding China with refugees. It therefore took the lead in preventing the Security Council from responding to North Korea's violations of its NPT and Agreed Framework obligations, withdrawal from the NPT, and announcements of a nuclear arsenal. Russia supported the Chinese position, and the two states blocked Security Council action in spring 2003. Two weeks later, as noted by Kittrie, "North Korea responded to this forbearance by declaring that it 'possesses a nuclear arsenal and might sell some of it to the highest bidder.' "[74]

Between 1995 and 2006, despite North Korea's many violations of its nonproliferation obligations, the Security Council passed no resolutions referring to these actions. As Kittrie states, "[n]ot until North Korea launched ballistic missiles on July 4, 2006, did the Security Council act. Resolution 1695 imposed missile-related sanctions, and finally condemned North Korea's 'announcement of withdrawal' from the NPT and 'stated pursuit of nuclear weapons.' "[75]

This condemnation, however, did not impress North Korea, whose response on October 9, 2006, was to test a nuclear weapon, and announce two days later: "We hope the situation will be resolved before an unfortunate incident of us firing a nuclear missile comes. That depends on how the U.S. will act."[76]

The Security Council responded to this "nuclear blackmail" by adopting Resolution 1718,[77] which President Bush categorized as a "tough" resolution.[78] Although Resolution 1718 "very significantly broadened both the range of nuclear activities prohibited to North Korea under international law and the IAEA's authority to detect such activities,"[79] and among other things, authorized all countries to inspect cargo going in and out of North Korea to detect illicit weapons, it failed to adopt the "comprehensive sanctions" that Japan had urged because of opposition by Russia and China. As a consequence, according to Kittrie, the sanctions were simply too weak to be effective, and "[r]ather than reaffirming the nuclear nonproliferation regime, the post-test sanctions on North Korea are in fact a manifestation of its decline."[80]

On February 13, 2007, North Korea concluded an agreement with the United States, China, Japan, Russia, and South Korea under which North Korea agreed to shut down its Yongbyon nuclear facility in exchange for incentives, including 50,000 tons of heavy fuel oil.[81] Kittrie, however, condemns this agreement with scant praise:

> This agreement appears to be a small step forward, in that it may help cap the size of North Korea's nuclear arsenal. But the Agreement is nonbinding (indeed, it was not even signed but simply issued as a joint statement), freezes only North Korea's plutonium facilities (which were anyway at the end of their useful lives) but not its uranium program, provides little-to-no assurance that North Korea will agree to effective verification of its compliance with the agreed freeze, does not include a North Korean commitment not to detonate or sell nuclear weapons, risks being seen by other potential proliferators as rewarding proliferation, and leaves to subsequent negotiations in the indefinite future any North Korean relinquishment of the nuclear weapons and weapons-grade fissile material it already possesses. The February 2007 agreement thus leaves nuclear nonproliferation in a far worse state

than if the Security Council had, before North Korea built its nuclear arsenal, used comprehensive economic sanctions to make it clear to North Korea that its nuclear weapons program was coming at too high a price and had to be relinquished.[82]

Similar and related criticisms have been made by other commentators on the February 13, 2007, agreement.[83] U.S. Secretary of State Condoleezza Rice has defended the agreement,[84] but her defense was written before North Korea was scheduled to make its "complete declaration" of its nuclear programs, facilities, and materials. According to John Bolton, a sharp critic of the February 13 agreement, although the agreement "states explicitly that North Korea was to provide 'a complete declaration of all nuclear programs' within sixty days, this it manifestly did not do, either in timing or in substance."[85] Moreover, at this writing, North Korea has stopped disabling its nuclear complex at Yongbyon, its only known source of plutonium, because the United States has not removed it from its list of states that support international terrorism. For its part, the United States is demanding that North Korea agree to a comprehensive method of checking whether it withheld information in its declaration before it removes North Korea from the list. The United States also is reportedly demanding full access by inspectors to all locations it suspects of being nuclear sites to ensure there are no hidden nuclear assets. North Korea has reportedly "bristled at this demand," stating that "[t]he U.S. is gravely mistaken if it thinks it can make a house search in our country as it did in Iraq."[86]

SOME CONCLUDING OBSERVATIONS

A review of the foregoing discussion in this chapter would seem to lead inexorably to the conclusion that arms control treaties, disarmament, nonproliferation instruments, especially the NPT and the IAEA, and safeguards are not functioning well and, as a consequence, the world is indeed becoming a more dangerous place. With respect to arms control treaties, it is noteworthy that the three arguably most important treaties – the Comprehensive Nuclear Test Ban Treaty, the Convention on the Prohibition of the Development, Production and Stockpiling of Bacteriological (Biological) and Toxin Weapons and on Their Destruction (Biological Weapons Convention), and the Convention on the Prohibition of the Development, Production, Stockpiling and Use of Chemical Weapons and on Their Destruction (Chemical Weapons Convention) – have serious flaws and weaknesses.

The Comprehensive Nuclear Test Ban Treaty (CTBT), for example, is currently not in force. Although a preparatory commission for the CTBT Organization was established in 1996 to set up a verification regime, including the International Monitoring System, International Data Center, and capabilities for conducting on-site inspections, and by January 2007, 138 countries had ratified the treaty, the treaty will not enter into force until all forty-four "nuclear capable" states specified in Annex 2 to the treaty have ratified it.[87] Several key countries listed in Annex 2, including China, India, Iran, Israel, Pakistan, North Korea, and the United States, have declined to ratify the treaty. Although President Clinton signed the treaty, in October 1999, the Senate declined, by a vote of forty-eight in favor, and fifty-one against (a two-thirds vote in favor being required), to give its advice and consent to ratification. The issue of advice and consent was vigorously debated in the Senate, but the arguments of the opponents of the treaty proved more persuasive to the members of the U.S. Senate.[88] The Obama administration has declared itself in favor of ratification of the treaty.

Although the CTBT is not in force, and there is little prospect at present that it will come into force, the five recognized nuclear weapons states under the Nuclear Non-Proliferation Treaty – the United States, Russia, China, France, and the United Kingdom – have maintained a voluntary moratorium on nuclear testing since 1996, when China detonated a nuclear device. India and Pakistan, nonparties to the NPT, announced their own voluntary moratoria in 1998, after each had tested nuclear devices. For their part, Bush administration officials, as part of a Nuclear Posture Review completed in December 2001, announced that the Department of Energy was accelerating its "test readiness program" to reduce the amount of time after a decision to test a nuclear device that would be required to actually carry out the test. The administration stated that the United States would continue to adhere to the testing moratorium, but critics believed that the focus on preparations for testing could undermine the moratorium.[89] At this writing this has not happened.

The primary point to be made for purposes of this study is that states have chosen to eschew a binding international treaty in favor of a voluntary moratorium on nuclear testing that is subject to being broken at any time. It is noteworthy that proponents of the treaty in the United States argued that the treaty had value as a nonproliferation measure because it would make it difficult for nonnuclear countries to develop nuclear arsenals, and some even went so far as to suggest that the treaty should be viewed as a disarmament measure as well, because it would encourage nuclear states to reduce their nuclear arsenals.[90] The treaty can serve neither of these functions, however, if it is not in force.

The Biological Weapons Convention has been in force since 1975 but has no enforcement mechanisms and is widely regarded as an ineffective mechanism for preventing the spread of biological weapons.[91] After the terrorist attacks of September 11, and subsequent anthrax attacks in the United States in September and October 2001, President Bush issued a statement that, among other things, called for strengthening the convention. The United States had been a member of an Ad Hoc Group of state parties, established in 1994, that had worked for six years on a draft protocol to the convention designed to enhance transparency and promote compliance. On the last day of the conference (December 7, 2001), however, "to the great surprise, not to say shock, of the other parties, the United States announced its opposition to continuation of work by the Ad Hoc Group. In response the parties to the convention agreed to adjourn and meet again on November 11–22, 2002."[92]

The stated reasons for the U.S. opposition to the protocol were (1) the protocol, which would have provided for inspections of facilities engaged in treaty-related activities, would not have prevented states from engaging in covert biological weapons programs, (2) inspections conducted under the convention could have resulted in the loss or compromise of commercial trade secrets by U.S. firms, and (3) the convention could have undermined the U.S. system of export controls and the multilateral framework of export controls known as the Australia Group to prevent the export both of dual-use items and others that could be used in an offensive biological weapons program.[93]

In place of the protocol the United States proposed a series of national measures or a unilateral approach to combating the risk of the use of biological weapons of mass destruction. Such measures would include "tightened export controls, an intensified nonproliferation dialogue, increased domestic preparedness and controls, enhanced biodefense and counter-bioterrorism capabilities, and innovative measures against disease outbreaks. Strict compliance by all parties with the BWC is also critical."[94] This emphasis on national controls was adopted by the Final Declaration of 2006 Review Conference, which stresses, "enactment and implementation of necessary national measures . . . [to] strengthen the effectiveness of the Convention."[95]

Once again, there has been a shift away from reliance on an arms control treaty to noninternational law measures, in this case national legal controls. Moreover, this shift may continue in effect in light of recent critical comments on the convention by an eminent authority.[96]

In sharp contrast to the Biological Weapons Convention, the Chemical Weapons Convention, which has enjoyed substantial support from the Bush administration, appears to be operating with some degree of efficiency. The convention prohibits states parties from using, producing, or stockpiling poison gas or lethal chemical weapons, and requires them to dispose of existing chemical weapons by April 2007 at the latest. Moreover, again in sharp contrast to the Biological Weapons Convention, the convention contains rigorous verification procedures administered by a new Organization for the Prohibition of Chemical Weapons (OPCW) that is located in The Hague and has been functioning since 1997. Implementation procedures include routine inspections at facilities that are declared to possess or use chemicals that may be precursors to weapons agents, and so-called challenge inspections to guard against cheating. In the first ten years of its existence the OPCW has reportedly carried out more than 2,700 inspections of chemical weapons production facilities, chemical weapons destruction facilities, and chemical industry facilities in 76 countries.[97] Both the United States and Russia, however, reported that they would not complete the destruction of their existing chemical weapons stockpiles by April 2007 and sought extensions. By September 2006, Russia had destroyed only about 3 percent of its stockpile of 40,000 metric tons of chemical agents. In the United States, environmental and other regulatory hurdles have slowed destruction activities too; as of January 2007, 40 percent of the U.S. chemical weapons stockpile of 32,000 tons had been destroyed.[98]

The Chemical Weapons Convention is a non-self-executing treaty under U.S. law and therefore required implementing legislation by Congress. Critics have contended that the convention's implementing legislation contains limitations on verification efforts by the Organization for the Prohibition of Chemical Weapons that undermine these efforts and are incompatible with U.S. obligations under the convention. These limitations give the president the right to refuse inspection of any facility on the determination that the inspection may "pose a threat to the national security interests"; narrow the number of facilities that are subject to the inspection and declaration provisions of the convention; and prohibit samples to be transferred for analysis to any laboratory outside the United States. According to the critics these limitations have had a contagion effect among other state parties to the convention.

As of January 2007, there were 181 parties to the Chemical Weapons Convention, but some countries that are suspected of having active programs of stockpiled chemical weapons, such as Egypt, Israel, North Korea, and Syria, were not among them.[99]

The foregoing discussion in this chapter of nonproliferation efforts would seem to indicate that the nonproliferation legal regime is in bad shape, and one may doubt whether the informal arrangements currently in place are an adequate substitute. Because of the great difficulties in amending the NPT identified by Kittrie, he and other experts in the field such as Jack Garvey have proposed that reforms be mandated by the U.N. Security Council under its Chapter VII powers. I have doubts, however, whether the political will necessary to adopt resolutions effecting such reforms is currently present in the Security Council. The same may be said of Kittrie's call for the Council to adopt harsher economic sanctions against the two most prominent proliferators – Iran and North Korea – especially because China and Russia have opposed such sanctions in the past.

Finally, with respect to Iran and North Korea, these crises are rapidly developing, and it is simply not possible to predict whether they can be resolved without the use of armed force. At this writing, French President Nicholas Sarkozy has publicly warned Iran that Israel may attack if Iran does not cease its efforts to develop a nuclear arsenal.[100] If anything the denouement of the North Korean crisis is even more unpredictable because of the volatile nature of its regime and its possession of a nuclear arsenal. One can only hope for a peaceful resolution of both of these critical crises.

Notes

1. *See* T.C. Fishman, *Making a Killing: The Myth of Capital's Good Intentions*, HARPER'S, AUG. 2002, at 33, 39.
2. *Id.* at 38.
3. At http://www.smallarmssurvey.org/files/sas/publications/yearb2009.html.

4. GA Res. 46.36L (Dec. 6, 1991).
5. *See* C.J. Chivers, *U.S. Position Complicates Global Effort to Curb Illicit Arms*, N.Y. TIMES, July 19, 2008, at A5, col. 1.
6. *Id.*
7. For a listing of many of these treaties, *see* L.F. DAMROSCH et al., INTERNATIONAL LAW 1077–80 (4th ed., 2001).
8. C.A. Robbins, *Disarming America's Treaties*, WALL ST. J. July 19, 2002, at A4, col. 3.
9. For a discussion of U.S. attitudes and actions toward such multilateral treaty regimes as the Comprehensive Nuclear Test Ban Treaty, the Nuclear Non-Proliferation Treaty, the Convention on the Prohibition of the Development, Production and Stockpiling of Bacteriological (biological) and Toxin Weapons and on Their Destruction (Biological Weapons Convention), and the Convention on the Prohibition of the Development, Production, Stockpiling and Use of Chemical Weapons and on Their Destruction (Chemical Weapons Convention), *see* JOHN F. MURPHY, THE UNITED STATES and the RULE of LAW in INTERNATIONAL AFFAIRS 208–18 (2004).
10. *See especially* David P. Fidler, *International Law and Weapons of Mass Destruction: End of the Arms Control Approach?*, 14 DUKE J. COMP. & INT'L L. 39 (2004).
11. *Id.* at 56.
12. *Id.* at 57.
13. *Id.*
14. *See* written testimony of Orde F. Kittrie, Before the United States House of Representatives Committee on Foreign Affairs, Subcommittee on Terrorism, Nonproliferation & Trade, at a Hearing, *Saving the NPT and the Nonproliferation Regime in an Era of Nuclear Renaissance*, July 24, 2008, at 1.
15. *Id.*
16. *Id.* at 2.
17. *See* David Fidler, *supra* note 10, at 61.
18. *Id.*
19. *Id.* at 65.
20. For further discussion of the NPT regime, *see* John F. Murphy, *Force and Arms, in* THE UNITED NATIONS and INTERNATIONAL LAW 97, 122–29 (C.C. Joyner ed., 1997).
21. *See* letter from the U.S., USSR, and U.K. to the President of the Security Council (June 12, 1968), 23 UN SCOR Supp. (Apr–June 1968) at 216, U.N. Doc. S/8630 (1968).
22. For a discussion of some of these, *see* JOHN F. MURPHY *supra* note 9, at 210–11.
23. Orde Kittrie has nicely summarized the primary reasons for the decline of the nonproliferation regime as follows: "The primary reasons for the dangerous decline of the nuclear nonproliferation regime include a lack of political will to effectively sanction proliferators, International Atomic Energy Agency (IAEA) verification and monitoring authorities that are too weak to promptly and reliably catch proliferators, the increased availability of nuclear weapons and associated technology, and a sense that the nuclear-weapon states, and particularly the United States and Russia, have not lived up to their disarmament commitments." Orde Kittrie, *supra* note 14, at 2.
24. *Id.* at 6.
25. *Id.*
26. IAEA, International Nuclear Verification Series: *The Evolution of IAEA Safeguards*, at 27, IAEA Doc. IAEA/NVS/2 (Nov. 1998) cited and quoted in Kittrie, *supra* note 14, at 7, fn. 6.
27. Orde Kittrie, *supra* note 14, at 7. According to Kittrie, "[s]tates of potential proliferation concern which did not have the Additional Protocol in force as of May 30, 2008, included

Algeria, Belarus, Brazil, India, Iran, Iraq, Malaysia, Morocco, Pakistan, Saudi Arabia, Sudan, Syria, Tunisia, Venezuela, and Yemen." *Id.*

28. *See* http://www.armscontrol.org/act/2009 01–02/usadditionalProtocol.

29. Kittrie, *supra* note 14, at 7.

30. *See* Jack I. Garvey, *A New Architecture for the Non-Proliferation of Nuclear Weapons*, 12 J. CONFLICT SEC. L. 339, 340 (2008). In fn. 3, Garvey cites to the Statement of DPRK Government on its withdrawal from NPT, http://www.Kcna.co.jp/item/2003/200301news01/11htm (last accessed 7 April 2007).

31. Orde Kittrie, *supra* note 14, at 7. One reason given by Kittrie for the difficulty in amending the NPT is the "contentiousness" of the membership, which prevented, in the 1980, 1990, and 2000 NPT Review Conferences, even the adoption of an agreed concluding statement. But "[a]n even greater obstacle is NPT Article VIII, which requires that any amendment be approved by 'the votes of all nuclear-weapons States Party to the Treaty and all other Parties which, on the date the amendment is circulated, are members of the Board of Governors of the International Atomic Energy Agency.' In other words, every member of the IAEA Board of Governors has a veto over any NPT amendment. In 2008, there are thirty-five members of the IAEA Board of Governors, including several countries with questionable commitment to nonproliferation." *Id.*

32. *Id.* at 7–8.

33. *See especially* Jack Garvey, *supra* note 30, and Vik Kanwar, *Two Crises of Confidence: Securing Non-Proliferation and the Rule of Law Through Security Council Resolutions* (April 14, 2008), available at SSRN.

34. Article 39 of the U.N. Charter provides that "[t]he Security Council shall determine the existence of any threat to the peace, breach of the peace, or act of aggression and shall make recommendations, or decide what measures shall be taken in accordance with Articles 41 and 42, to maintain or restore international peace and security." Under Article 41 the Security Council may employ measures not involving the use of armed force, and under Article 42 the Council "may take such action by air, sea, or land forces as may be necessary to maintain or restore international peace and security."

35. S.C. Res. 1540 (April 28, 2004).

36. Jack Garvey, *supra* note 30, at 354–55. To support this statement, Garvey points out that "Resolution 1540 affirms the Security Council's 'resolve to take appropriate and effective actions against any threat to international peace and security caused by' WMD proliferation. It provides a short generalized list of duties to prevent proliferation, such as physical protection measures, export and trans-shipment and financial and end-user controls." *Id.* at 355. Along the same lines, Kittrie notes that "Resolution 1540 . . . effectively filled several gaps in the NPT, including the NPT's failure to fully prohibit assisting terrorists to acquire nuclear weapons and failure to require physical protection of sensitive nuclear materials." Orde Kittrie, *supra* note 14, at 8, fn. 8.

37. *See, e.g.*, David Fidler, *supra* note 10, at 52, 57, 62, and 74.

38. Convention on the Physical Protection of Nuclear Material, 3 Mar. 1980, 1987 UNTS 125, entered into force 8 Feb. 1987.

39. *See* David P. Fidler, *International Convention for the Suppression of Acts of Nuclear Terrorism Enters into Force*, ASIL INSIGHT, August 7, 2008, at 3. On the amendment, see IAEA, Nuclear Security – Measures to Protect Against Nuclear Terrorism, Amendment to the Convention on the Physical Protection of Nuclear Material – Report of the Director General, GOV/INF/2005/10-GC (49)/INF/6, 6 Sept. 2004. As of this writing the amendment has not entered into force.

40. International Convention on the Suppression of Acts of Nuclear Terrorism, U.N. General Assembly Resolution 59/290, 13 Apr. 2005.
41. David Fidler, *supra* note 39, at 1.
42. *Id.*
43. For an excellent overview of the Convention, *see* David Fidler, *supra* note 39.
44. *Id.* at 2, quoting the South African negotiating coordinator.
45. *Id.* at 3.
46. *Id.* The efforts identified by Fidler include

- Establishment of the IAEA's Plan of Activities to Protect Against Nuclear Terrorism (2002).
- Creation by the G-8 of the Global Partnership Against the Spread of Weapons of Mass Destruction (2003).
- Launch of the U.S.-led Proliferation Security initiative to interdict WMD-related shipments and stop proliferation-related financing (2003).
- Adoption of U.N. Security Council Resolution 1540 requiring U.N. members to enact national legal measures to prevent the proliferation of WMD to non-State actors (2004).
- Amendment to the 1980 Convention on the Physical Protection of Nuclear Materials that, among other things, created expanded duties to secure nuclear materials in storage and during transit and to criminalize sabotage against civilian nuclear facilities (2005).
- Establishment of the IAEA Advisory Committee on Safeguards and Verification to explore strategies for monitoring and enforcement of the Treaty on the Non-Proliferation of Nuclear Weapons (2005).
- Creation of the U.S.-Russian Bratislava Nuclear Security Cooperation initiative to expand bilateral efforts to improve nuclear security (2005), and
- Launch of the U.S.–Russian-led Global Initiative to Combat Nuclear Terrorism (2006).

47. *Id.*
48. *See* Larry D. Johnson, *The Threat of Nuclear Terrorism and September 11th: Wake-Up Call to Get the Treaties Right*, 31 DENV. J. INT'L L. POL'Y 80,81 (2002–2003).
49. George Bunn, *Enforcing International Standards: Protecting Nuclear Materials from Terrorists Post-9/11*, Arms Control Today (Jan/Feb/ 2007), http://www.armscontrol.org/act/2007_01–02/Bunn.asp., quoted in Id. at 3–4.
50. David Fidler, *supra* note 39, at 4.
51. *See* Larry Johnson, *supra* note 48.
52. For discussion, *see* JOHN MURPHY, *supra* note 9, at 214–15.
53. Legality of the Threat or Use of Nuclear Weapons (Advisory Opinion), 1996 ICJ 226.
54. *Id.*, para.105 (2) (F).
55. *See* Carla Anne Robbins, *Thinking the Unthinkable: A World Without Nuclear Weapons*, N.Y. TIMES, June 30, 2008, at A1, col. 1.
56. *Id.*
57. *See* Jay Solomon, *Russian Nuclear Pact Stalls*, WALL ST. J., Aug. 23–24, 2008, at A1, col. 3.
58. *Id.*
59. *See* Orde Kittrie, *supra* note 14, at 3.

60. *See* Andrew J. Grotto, *Iran, the IAEA, and the UN*, ASIL INSIGHT, November 2002, www.asil.org/org/insights/2004/10insight041105.htm.
61. *See* S.C. Res. 1737 (Dec. 23, 2006), S.C. Res. 1747 (Mar. 24, 2007), and S.C. Res. 1803 (Mar. 3, 2008).
62. Orde Kittrie, *supra* note 14, at 3.
63. *Id.*
64. *See especially*, S.C. Res. 1737 (Dec. 23, 2006), S.C. Res. 1747 (Mar. 24, 2007), and S.C. Res. 1803 (Mar. 3, 2008).
65. Orde Kittrie, *supra* note 14, at 4. According to Kittrie, "[t]he sanctions imposed on Iran by the international community thus far are much weaker than the sanctions which stopped the Iraqi and Libyan nuclear weapons programs. Indeed, the Iran sanctions are thus far weaker than the sanctions imposed on South Africa in response to Apartheid, on Liberia and Cote D'Ivoire during their civil wars, Sierra Leone in response to its May 1997 military coup, the Federal Republic of Yugoslavia during the Bosnia crisis, and Haiti in response to its 1991 military coup." *See also*, Orde F. Kittrie, *Emboldened By Impunity: The History and Consequences of Failure To Enforce Iranian Violations of International Law*, 57 SYRACUSE L. REV. 519 (2007).
66. Orde Kittrie, *supra* note 14, at 4.
67. *See* Elaine Sciolino, *Atomic Monitor Signals Concern Over Iran's Work*, N.Y. TIMES, May 27, 2008, at A1, col. 6.
68. *Id.* According to Sciolino, Javier Solana, the European Union's foreign policy chief, announced that he would go to Iran soon to present a new offer of political, technological, and security and trade rewards for Iran if it halts its uranium enrichment program. These incentives were agreed upon by all six countries, but only representatives of five of the six planned to accompany Solana.
69. Orde Kittrie, *supra*, note 14, at 3.
70. This backdrop to the current North Korean crisis is derived primarily from JOHN F. MURPHY, *supra* note 9, at 211–13.
71. *See* Steven E. Miller, *The Real Crisis: North Korea's Nuclear Gambit*, HARV. INT'L L. REV., 2003, at 84.
72. *Id.* at 84–85.
73. *See* Orde Kittrie, *Averting Catastrophe: Why The Nuclear Nonproliferation Treaty Is Losing Its Deterrence Capacity And How To Restore It*, 28 MICH. J. INT'L L. 337,372 (2007).
74. *Id.* at 373.
75. *Id.* at 374.
76. Quoted in *id.*, citing in fn. 204, *Official Warns U.S. Actions Could Prompt North Korean Missile*, INT'L HERALD TRIB. Oct. 10, 2006, http://www.iht.com/articles/ap/2006/10/10/asia/AS_GEN_NKorea_Nuclear.php.
77. S.C. Res. 1718 (Oct. 14, 2006).
78. *The North Korean Nuclear Crisis: Bush Comments*, HOUS. CHRON. Oct. 15, 2006, at A19, cited in Orde Kittrie, *supra* note 73, at 374, fn. 205.
79. *Id.* at 374–75.
80. *Id.* at 378.
81. *See* Press Release, Office of the Spokesman, U.S. Dep't of State, North Korea-Denuclearization Action Plan, Press Release 2007/099 (Feb. 13, 2007) http://www.stte gov/r/pa/prs/ps/2007/february/80479.htm.
82. Orde Kittrie, *supra* note 73, at 378–79.

83. *See, e.g.,* John R. Bolton, *The Tragic End of Bush's North Korea Policy,* WALL ST. J., July 30, 2008, at A13, col. 1; John R. Bolton, *Bush's North Korea Nuclear Abdication,* WALL ST. J., June 8, 2008, at A15, col. 1.
84. Condoleezza Rice, *Diplomacy Is Working on North Korea,* WALL ST. J., June 26, 2008, at A 15, col. 2.
85. John R. Bolton, *The Tragic End of Bush's North Korea Policy,* WALL ST. J., July 30, 2008, at A13, col. 1.
86. *See* Choe Sang-Hun, *North Korea Says It Stopped Disabling Nuclear Complex,* N.Y. TIMES, Aug. 27, 2008, at A6, col. 5.
87. This information is taken from BARRY E. CARTER, PHILLIP R. TRIMBLE, and ALLEN S. WEINER, INTERNATIONAL LAW 1109 (5th ed. 2007).
88. For a discussion of these arguments, *see* JOHN F. MURPHY, *supra,* note 9, at 208–09.
89. *See* Jonathan Medalia, Congressional Research Service, Nuclear Weapons: Comprehensive Test Ban Treaty (Aug. 16, 2006), cited in BARRY E. CARTER et al., *supra* note 87, at 1109.
90. *See* JOHN F. MURPHY, *supra* note 9, at 208–09.
91. Most of this discussion of the Biological Weapons Convention, unless otherwise indicated, is taken from *id.* at 216–17.
92. *Id.* at 216.
93. *See* the statement by John Bolton, set forth in *id.*
94. *See* John R. Bolton, Remarks to the 5th Biological Weapons Convention RevCon Meeting, Nov. 19, 2001, reproduced in part in JOHN F. MURPHY, *supra* note 9, at 217.
95. *See* BARRY E. CARTER et al., *supra* note 87, at 1106.
96. *See* Jack M. Beard, *The Shortcomings of Indeterminancy in Arms Control Regimes: The Case of the Biological Weapons Convention,* 101 AM. J. INT'L L. 271 (2007).
97. *See* BARRY E. CARTER et al., *supra* note 87, at 1107.
98. *Id.*
99. *Id.*
100. John Bolton has warned that Iran is progressing in its efforts to develop a nuclear arsenal to the point where the viability of the military option for Israel to prevent this is steadily declining. *See* John R. Bolton, *While Diplomats Dither, Iran Builds Nukes,* WALL ST. J., Aug. 5, 2008, at A19, col. 1.

6

Human Rights

In previous chapters we have examined various topics that have human rights dimen-sions. Chapter 2, for example, covers the U.N. Human Rights Council, international criminal tribunals, and hybrid courts; Chapter 3 the responsibility to Protect; and Chapter 4 the nature of the relationship between international human rights law and the law of armed conflict. These subjects, however, constitute only a small part of an increasingly vast and complex field.[1]

For purposes of this chapter, therefore, it is necessary to make "hard choices" for what topics to cover. Certainly, one of the most controversial topics in the field of human rights has been the war on terrorism and international human rights, with a primary focus on alleged violations of human rights by the Bush administration, especially with respect to interrogation methods and the due process rights of detainees at Guantanamo Bay and other locations. The writings on this topic are legion,[2] and I have briefly written on this topic myself.[3] In this chapter, however, my focus is elsewhere. First, I attempt to evaluate the difference, if any, the adoption of large numbers of human rights treaties by the United Nations has made in terms of meeting the U.N.'s goal to protect and promote human rights. Next, with respect to the human rights dimensions of U.N. antiterrorism efforts, the chapter turns to the financing of terrorism, Security Council Resolutions 1373 and 1267, and the so-called al-Qaeda and Taliban Sanctions Committee. Lastly, with respect to the United Nations, the chapter examines the record of the post of the High Commissioner of Human Rights.

Turning from the United Nations, the chapter explores some recent challenges facing the institution that is generally regarded as the most successful in "promoting and encouraging respect for human rights and for fundamental freedoms for all without distinction as to race, sex, language, or religion,"[4] the European Court of Human Rights and Fundamental Freedoms. The chapter concludes with a section setting forth some hard choices that need to be made to improve future prospects for strengthening human rights on a global and regional basis.

THE EFFICACY (OR NOT) OF INTERNATIONAL HUMAN RIGHTS TREATIES

Some years ago – I have forgotten exactly when – the Annual Meeting of the American Society of International Law had a panel on the topic: "The United Nations Adopts the Covenants, So What?" Yoram Dinstein, an eminent Israeli international law scholar and practitioner, was sitting in the first row. Dinstein sat quietly until approximately two minutes before the panel was scheduled to conclude, at which point he raised his hand. Upon being recognized by the chairman of the panel, the late Frank C. Newman, also an eminent international law scholar, especially in the field of international human rights, Dinstein took note of the title of the panel and then asked, "We have had a thorough discussion of the 'what' but whatever happened to the 'so'?" Newman, not surprisingly, was taken aback by Dinstein's question and had no time to make an adequate response.

It is not surprising that an Israeli, who, like many Israelis, views the United Nations with a jaundiced eye, would make such a comment with respect to the value of the U.N.'s adoption of the International Covenant on Civil and Political Rights and the International Covenant on Economic, Social and Cultural Rights.[5] More surprising was the publication in 2002 of an article by Oona Hathaway, an international law scholar, that, on the basis of a database covering the experiences of 166 states over a nearly forty-year period in five areas of human rights law, found that ratification of human rights treaties by the countries examined had little or no effect on their human rights records.[6] Somewhat more startling, Hathaway finds that:

> Although the ratings of human rights practices of countries that have ratified international human rights treaties are generally better than those of countries that have not, noncompliance with treaty obligations appears to be common. More paradoxically, when I take into account the influence of a range of other factors that affect countries' practices, I find that treaty ratification is not infrequently associated with worse human rights ratings than otherwise expected.[7]

Not surprisingly, Hathaway's findings provoked considerable reaction, much of it hostile. In particular, Professors Ryan Goodman and Derek Jinks directly challenged both Hathaway's methodology and policy analysis.[8] They suggest that "the incorporation of human rights norms [into state practice] is a process; treaty law plays an important role in this process; and Hathaway's study does not provide a reason to reject these views."[9]

Hathaway responded to the criticisms of Goodman and Jinks.[10] I am not qualified to evaluate her arguments compared with those of Goodman and Jinks regarding the methodology of her empirical analysis, so I will leave it to the statisticians to engage in such an evaluation. It is nonetheless noteworthy, perhaps, that a later empirical analysis of the effects of ratification of human rights treaties reaches results compatible with Hathaway's findings. Eric Neumayer of the London School of Economics and Political Science and the International Peace Research Institute,

Oslo, Norway, concluded in his study that a beneficial effect of ratification of human rights treaties typically depended upon the extent of democracy and the strength of civil society groups in the ratifying country, as measured by participation in nongovernmental organizations (NGOs) with international linkages.[11] In the absence of democracy and a strong civil society, Neumayer found, "treaty ratification has no effect and is possibly even associated with more human rights violations."[12] By contrast, ratification in pure autocracies with no civil society is associated with a worsening of human rights.

In her article in the *Yale Law Journal*, Hathaway proposes, as a "first step" to combating widespread noncompliance with human rights treaties, enhancing the monitoring of human rights treaty commitments through "strengthening of the self-reporting system that currently serves as the backbone of the majority of human rights treaties."[13] She also contends that the findings of her study may "give reason to reassess the current policy of the United Nations of promoting universal ratification of the major human rights treaties" on the ground that pressure to ratify, if not followed by strong enforcement and monitoring, may be counterproductive.[14]

Interestingly, Goodman and Jinks criticize this proposal on the ground that strengthening the monitoring and enforcement of treaty obligations would undermine the effectiveness of human rights treaties because fewer states would become parties to them, and thus it would reduce the opportunities for "shallow" ratification by problem countries.[15] In response, Hathaway states that "I, like Goodman and Jinks's, believe that human rights treaties can and do change perceptions of what constitutes acceptable behavior and thereby can and do have a powerful impact on countries' human rights practices. I therefore share Goodman and Jinks's concern that any reforms aimed at enhancing the effectiveness of treaties not be made haphazardly." She goes on to add, however:

> Yet I do not agree that fostering a system of "shallow" ratification is necessary for, or always helpful to, the process of building national human rights cultures. Broad membership in the Optional Protocol to the Covenant on Civil and Political Rights, Articles 21 and 22 to the Torture Convention, and the European Convention on Human Rights belies Goodman and Jinks's assumption that stronger treaties will necessarily be shunned. Moreover, to the extent that noncompliance with many human rights treaties is widespread and accepted with little formal comment or complaint, the power of those treaties to change discourse and expectations is weakened.[16]

In my view, Professor Hathaway has the better side in this exchange. Although the International Court of Justice, in its *Advisory Opinion on Reservations to the Convention on Genocide*,[17] advised that it was important that the convention have as many parties to it as possible, and that therefore a party reserving to the convention could be regarded as being a party to the convention even if the reservation is objected to by one or more of the parties to the convention but not by others, there is no article in the convention providing for reservations. The Court also noted that a reservation contrary to the object and purpose of the convention would not be permitted. In other words, the drafters of the convention were concerned that it be effective, that is, that it induce state parties to take steps in national law and practice to fulfill the object and purpose of the convention.

It is noteworthy that the Convention on Genocide, despite the large number of state parties to it,[18] has been singularly ineffective in inducing state parties to fulfill its object and purpose, namely, the prevention of genocide or, if prevention fails, the prosecution and punishment of the perpetrators of genocide. Until the creation of the Yugoslav and Rwanda International Criminal Tribunals and of the International Criminal Court, all of which are empowered, subject to various limitations, to exercise jurisdiction to prosecute and punish the crime of genocide, no one was prosecuted, much less punished, for the crime.

The reasons for the failure of the Convention on Genocide to become an operational instrument for the protection and promotion of human rights are manifold and are beyond the scope of discussion in this chapter. Surely, however, one reason is that, unlike later human rights treaties, the Convention contains no provisions on enforcement, with the exception of Article VIII, which provides that any Contracting Party may call upon the "competent organs of the United Nations" to take action to prevent and suppress genocide,[19] and Article IX, a compromissory clause that allows disputes between Contracting Parties regarding the "interpretation, application or fulfillment" of the Convention to be submitted to the International Court of Justice at the request of any party to the dispute.[20] Article VIII, however, is unnecessary, because member states of the United Nations do not need to be parties to the Convention on Genocide to call upon the United Nations to prevent and suppress acts of genocide, and numerous Contracting Parties have filed reservations to Article IX, including the United States.[21] Moreover, until recently, situations allegedly involving genocide were referred neither to the United Nations nor to the International Court of Justice.[22]

The Convention on Genocide was an early U.N. human rights treaty, adopted in 1948. Later treaties have more or different enforcement provisions, including, at a minimum, a requirement that state parties submit reports to a committee established by the treaty on the steps they have taken to carry out their obligations and submit to a hearing in which members of the committee raise questions regarding their reports.[23] Some treaties provide that a state party to the treaty may declare that it recognizes the competence of the committee to receive and consider "communications" (i.e., complaints) to the effect that a state party claims that another state party is not fulfilling its obligations under the treaty.[24] In such a case the committee does not sit as an adjudicatory body but rather seeks to facilitate an amicable settlement between the parties and may offer its good offices to the state parties with a view to an amicable solution.[25] If an amicable solution is not found, the committee may, with the prior consent of the state parties concerned, appoint an ad hoc conciliation commission.[26] Lastly, some treaties provide that a state party may at any time "declare that it recognizes the competence of the Committee to receive and consider communications from individuals or groups of individuals within its jurisdiction claiming to be victims of a violation by that State Party of any of the rights set forth in this Convention. No communication shall be received by the Committee if it concerns a State Party which has not made such a declaration."[27] Alternatively, a state party may consent to the committee exercising such competence by becoming a party to an optional protocol, such as the Optional Protocol to the International Covenant on Civil and Political Rights.[28]

It is noteworthy that, in October 1997, Jamaica became the first, and so far the only, state party to denounce the Optional Protocol and thus withdraw the right of individual petition to the Human Rights Committee.[29] This would seem to lend a measure of support to Goodman and Jinks's thesis that overly strong procedures for the monitoring and enforcement of human rights treaty obligations may result in undermining the goal of universal or at least broad-based ratification of such treaties. On the other hand, Jamaica's withdrawal from the Optional Protocol has not been followed by the withdrawal of other state parties.

Moreover, in recent years, new approaches to the monitoring of human rights treaties have been developed that go well beyond the standard techniques contained in the International Covenant on Civil and Political Rights and in its Optional Protocol. Now, in addition to the Human Rights Committee, there are eight U.N. treaty bodies, either in existence, or soon to be.[30] Some of the new approaches to monitoring have been summarized by Steiner, Alston, and Goodman:

> Both the Convention against Torture (Art. 20) and the Optional Protocol to the CEDAW Convention (Art. 8) provide for an on-site visit, or inquiry, on an initially confidential basis, to be undertaken by one or more committee members where violations have been reliably attested and the state concerned agrees to the visit. The confidentiality may be, and consistently has been, waived once the visit has been made. Mexico, for example, has been the subject of visits under both procedures, one dealing with consistent reports of police torture, and the other concerning the killings of hundreds of young woman in Ciudad Juarez between 1993 and 2003, and both reports have been published.
>
> More recent reports have been even more creative in terms of monitoring arrangements. At one end of the spectrum is the Optional Protocol to the Torture Convention of 2002, which entered into force in 2006. Its emphasis is on prevention and it establishes a Subcommittee for Prevention which can make on-site visits at any time. It also obligates states to establish their own national preventive mechanisms (NPMs) to monitor regularly all places of detention. At the other end of the spectrum is the proposed Committee on Enforced Disappearances. In addition to the traditional functions of state reporting, individual complaints, and interstate complaints, the proposed committee, as an urgent, humanitarian procedure, is empowered to undertake on-site inquiries and may call the attention of the U.N. General Assembly to situations of widespread and systemic disappearances.[31]

Contrary to Goodman and Jinks's suggestion that more rigorous implementation procedures for human rights treaties, as proposed by Oona Hathaway, might be counterproductive, there is no indication in this excerpt that the new approaches to monitoring the human rights treaties have resulted in state parties failing to ratify them or have undermined their effectiveness. Nor is there any reference to the desirability of so-called shallow ratification.

Moreover, an observation made by Hathaway in her article bears repeating:

> In recent decades, faith in the power of international law to shape nations' actions has led to a focus on the creation of international law to shape nations' actions as a means to achieve human rights objectives. The treaties that have resulted may have played a role in changing discourse and expectations about human rights, thereby improving the practices of all nations. Yet, based on the present analysis, ratification of the treaties by individual countries appears more likely to offset pressure for change in human rights practices than to augment it. The solution to this dilemma is not the abandonment of human rights treaties, but a renewed effort to enhance the monitoring and enforcement of treaty obligations to reduce opportunities for countries to use ratification as a symbolic substitute for real improvements in their citizens' lives.[32]

An example of a country using ratification as a symbolic substitute for real improvements in its citizens' lives may be the United States' ratification of the International Covenant on Civil and Political Rights. For a number of years, the United States endured sharp criticism for its failure to ratify human rights treaties, especially the International Covenant on Civil and Political Rights. Much of this criticism came from countries with poor human rights records, such as the Soviet Union. When the United States finally did ratify, in 1992, it did so with a number of reservations, understandings and declarations, so-called RUDs. These RUDs have been subject to considerable scholarly criticism.[33] For its part, the Human Rights Committee has also weighed in heavily on the issue of the compatibility of the U.S. RUDs with the object and purpose of the Covenant.

As every state party is obligated to do under Article 40 of the Covenant, the United States submitted, on August 24, 1994, its report on measures it had taken to give effect to the rights recognized in the Covenant and on progress made in giving effect to the enjoyment of those rights to the Human Rights Committee.[34] The report contains a voluminous discussion of the political and legal structure in the United States for the protection of human rights, as well as a detailed setting forth of U.S. law and practice. In its Concluding Observations on the U.S. report, however, the Committee expresses its "regrets ... that, while containing comprehensive information on the laws and regulations giving effect to the rights provided in the Covenant at the federal level, the report contained few references to the implementation of Covenant rights at the state level."[35] More significantly, the Committee declared the U.S. reservations to Article 6 (5) and Article 7 of the Covenant, both of which relate to the death penalty,[36] "incompatible with the object and purpose of the Covenant."[37] In both reservations, the United States is proclaiming its willingness to be bound only by the constraints of the U.S. Constitution and not by the provisions of the Covenant.[38]

Moreover, in General Comment No. 24 on reservations to the Covenant,[39] the Human Rights Committee claimed that it had the competence to determine the legality of state parties' reservations. In response the United States argued that the Covenant did not "impose on States Parties an obligation to give effect to the Committee's interpretations or confer upon the Committee the power to render definitive or binding interpretations of the Covenant." The United States also rejected the determination of the Committee that "[t]he normal consequence of an unacceptable reservation is not that the Covenant will not be in effect at all for a reserving party. Rather, such a reservation will generally be severable, in the sense that the Covenant will be operative for the reserving party without benefit of the reservation."[40] In the view of the United States, this conclusion is "completely at odds with established legal practices and principles . . . The reservations contained in the United States instrument of ratification are integral parts of its consent to be bound by the Covenant and are not severable. If it were to be determined that any one or more of them were ineffective, the ratification as a whole could thereby be nullified."[41]

In its General Comment No. 24 the Committee had also implicitly criticized the U.S. declaration accompanying its ratification that the substantive articles of the Covenant were not self-executing, thereby ensuring that the Covenant could not be the basis for a lawsuit in U.S. courts, as well as the U.S. practice of reserving to any provision of the Covenant that was inconsistent with existing U.S. federal or state law. Specifically, the Committee had stated in General Comment No. 24 that, with regard to implementing the Covenant in domestic law, domestic laws "may need to be altered properly to reflect the requirements of the Covenant; and mechanisms at the domestic level will be needed to allow the Covenant rights to be enforceable at the local level."[42] In its observations, the United States (along with the United Kingdom) met the criticisms (which had also been advanced by scholars and other commentators) head on:

> First, this statement may be cited as an assertion that States Parties *must* allow suits in domestic courts based directly on the provisions of the Covenant. Some countries do in fact have such a scheme of "self-executing" treaties. In other countries, however, existing domestic law already provides the substantive rights reflected in the Covenant as well as multiple possibilities for suit to enforce those rights. Where these existing rights and mechanisms are in fact adequate to the purposes of the Covenant, it seems most unlikely that the Committee intends to insist the Covenant be directly actionable in court or that States must adopt legislation to implement the Covenant

> Second, paragraph 12 states that "[r]eservations often reveal a tendency of States not to want to change a particular law." Some may view this statement as sweepingly critical of any reservation whatsoever which is made to conform to law. Of course,

since this is the motive for a large majority of the reservations made by States in all cases, it is difficult to say that this is inappropriate in principle. Indeed, one might say that the more seriously a State Party takes into account the necessity of providing strictly for domestic enforcement of its international obligations, the more likely it is that some reservations may be taken along these lines.[43]

A comment on these U.S. and British responses is in order. Frankly, they are a bit disingenuous. The complaint of the Committee is not based on an assertion that state parties must allow suits in domestic courts based on the provisions of the Covenant. Nor is it a sweeping criticism of any reservation whatsoever that is made to conform to law. Rather, it is a criticism of the U.S. determination to ensure that no domestic law or practice, federal or state, needs to be changed because of ratification of the Covenant. In particular, the United States is determined to ensure that none of its states need change their laws because the substance of the Covenant is covered by state rather than federal law. Because a primary purpose of human rights treaties is to change the laws of state parties in such a way as to improve them, Louis Henkin argues that the U.S. reservations are incompatible with the object and purpose of the Civil and Political Rights Covenant and therefore invalid under Article 19 of the Vienna Convention on the Law of Treaties.[44]

On the other hand, Curtis A. Bradley and Jack L. Goldsmith have advanced a strong practical argument in support of U.S. declarations that the Civil and Political Rights Covenant and other human rights treaties are non-self-executing:

The ICCPR, if self-executing, would have the same domestic effect as a congressional statute and thus would supersede inconsistent state law and prior inconsistent federal legislation. Literally hundreds of U.S. federal and state laws – ranging from essential civil rights statutes like Title VII to rules of criminal procedure – would be open to reconsideration and potential modification or invitation by courts interpreting the vague terms of the ICCPR. Even if courts ultimately decided that each of the differently worded provisions in the ICCPR did not require a change in domestic law, there was concern that litigation of these issues would be costly and would generate substantial legal uncertainty. These concerns also arose, although on a narrower scale, for the other human rights treaties.[45]

When the United States ratified the Civil and Political Rights Covenant, a number of state parties objected to one or more of the reservations and understandings and in some instances found them incompatible with the object and purpose of the Covenant.[46] The objecting states, however, took the position that their objections did not prevent the Covenant from entering into force between them and the United States in accordance with Articles 20 and 21 of the Vienna Convention on the Law of Treaties.[47]

Hence, as noted previously, a large number of legal issues have arisen between the United States and the Human Rights Committee regarding the U.S. RUDs and the Committee's claim that it has the authority to determine whether the RUDs are compatible with the objective and purpose of the Covenant. There is no prospect, however, of an impartial third party issuing a binding decision in favor of one party or the other.

On November 28, 2005, the United States submitted, in a consolidated fashion, its second and third reports to the Committee.[48] In its "Concluding Observations" the Committee urges the United States to "review its interpretation of the Covenant and acknowledge its applicability with respect to individuals under its jurisdiction but outside its territory, as well as its applicability in time of war."[49] The United States replied that it "continues to consider that its view is correct that the obligations it has assumed under the Covenant do not have extraterritorial reach."[50]

Maintaining its position regarding the extraterritorial application of the Covenant, most of the Committee's concerns related to extraterritorial situations, "notably the secret detention facilities outside the U.S., the allegations of death, torture or abuse of individuals in detention facilities in Guantanamo Bay, Afghanistan, Iraq and other overseas locations, the transfer, rendition, extradition, expulsion or *refoulement* of detainees, and the applicability of the ICCPR to the situation of armed conflict in Iraq."[51] The Committee recommended that United States close its secret detention facilities and grant the International Committee of the Red Cross (ICRC) prompt access to any person detained in connection with an armed conflict. Although denying that it had any legal obligation to provide the ICRC with notice and access to these enemy combatants, the United States reported that, as of September 6, 2006, when the high-value detainees were moved from the secret detention facilities to Guantanamo, the ICRC had been granted access to them.

As had been the case with the first report of the United States, the second and third reports gave rise to numerous differences of opinion regarding legal issues between the United States and the Committee. There is no evidence that these issues were resolved between the parties, however, much less referred to a third party for a binding decision. Moreover, there was no U.S. press or television coverage of any of the public hearings on the three U.S. reports.[52] Finally, there is no evidence that the United States changed its views on these legal issues, much less its law and practice, as a result of these hearings. Accordingly, the evidence is considerable that the United States has viewed ratification as a "symbolic substitute" for real improvements in its citizens' lives.

Unlike the United States, the Soviet Union (now the Russian Federation) was an early ratifier of the Civil and Political Rights Covenant, having done so in March 23, 1976. It also ratified the Optional Protocol in January 1, 1992. The Committee considered the fifth periodic report of the Russian Federation at three meetings in 2003.[53] Its concerns with the report, in contrast to those it had with respect to the U.S. reports, did not focus on legal issues. Rather, they addressed alleged failures of Russia to carry out its obligations under the Covenant as well as to implement the Committee's views under the Optional Protocol in two cases.[54] The Committee urged Russia "to review its position in relation to views adopted by the Committee under the Optional Protocol and to implement the Views, in order to comply with Article 2 (3) of the Covenant which guarantees a right to an effective remedy when there has been a violation of the Covenant."[55]

As to alleged Russian failures to carry out its obligations under the Covenant, for example, the Committee expressed its concern regarding persistent inequality in the enjoyment of Covenant rights by women; the large number of persons in Russia who are being trafficked for sexual and labor exploitation; continuing substantiated reports of human rights violations in the Chechen Republic, including "extrajudicial killings, disappearances and torture, including rape"[56]; the provision in the Federal Law "On Combating Terrorism" that exempts law enforcement and military personnel from liability for harm caused during counterterrorist operations; the closure in recent years of independent media companies and an increase in state control of major media outlets (TV channels, radio stations, and newspapers); and journalists, researchers and environmental activists who have been tried and convicted on treason charges, "essentially for having disseminated information of legitimate public interest, . . . in some cases where the charges were not proven, the courts have referred the matter back to prosecutors instead of dismissing the charges."[57]

These and other Committee allegations of Russian violations of the Covenant paint a grim picture of the state of human rights in Russia as of 2003. The situation has not improved since then if reports by the U.S. Department of State,[58] Amnesty International,[59] and Freedom House[60] are to be believed. For example, the introductory summary of Freedom House's report states:

The 2007 State Duma elections marked a new low in the Kremlin's manipulation of the political process. The authorities sharply restricted outside election observers and ensured that the campaign environment favored Kremlin-backed parties, which won the vast majority of seats. More ominously for Russian democracy, President Vladimir Putin announced that he intended to remain on the political stage after his second term ended in 2008. [Putin was as good as his word, because he was appointed Prime Minister of Russia.] Putin's continued tenure would benefit the circle of security-agency veterans he has appointed to top positions in the government and state-owned enterprises and set Russia on a firmly authoritarian course. During the year, the authorities continued to place strict limits on opposition political parties, public demonstrations, the media, and nongovernmental organizations, and failed to launch any serious initiatives to address Russia's extensive corruption.[61]

In the same vein, the introductory summary of the Amnesty International report reads as follows:

The Russian authorities were increasingly intolerant of dissent or criticism, branding it "unpatriotic." A crackdown on civil and political rights was evident throughout the year and in particular during the run-up to the State Duma (parliament) elections in December. Given the strict state control of TV and other media, demonstrations were the flashpoint during the year for political protests, with police detaining demonstrators, journalists, and human rights activists, some of whom were beaten. Activists and political opponents of the government were also subjected to administrative detention.

The number of racist attacks that came to the attention of the media rose; at least 61 people were killed across the country. Although authorities recognized the problem and there was an increase in the number of prosecutions for racially motivated crimes, these measures failed to stem the tide of violence.

The European Court of Human Rights noted that Russia was responsible for enforced disappearances, torture and extrajudicial executions in 15 judgments relating to the second Chechen conflict which began in 1999. There were fewer reported cases of disappearances in the Chechen Republic than in previous years; however, serious human rights violations were frequent and individuals were reluctant to report abuses, fearing reprisals. Ingushetia saw an increase in serious violations, including enforced disappearances and extrajudicial executions.

NGOs were weighed down by burdensome reporting requirements imposed by changes to legislation. Torture was used by police against detainees, including to extract "confessions"; violence against inmates in prisons was also reported.[62]

The U.S. Department of State's summary of the "most notable human rights developments during the year" in Russia was especially stark:

The most notable human rights developments during the year were the contract style killings of proreform Central Bank Deputy Chairman Anrei Kozlov and journalist Anna Politkovskaya, known for uncovering human rights abuses in Chechnya. Continuing centralization of power in the executive branch, a compliant State Duma, political pressure on the judiciary, intolerance of ethnic minorities, corruption and selectivity in enforcement of the law, continuing media restrictions and self-censorship, and harassment of some nongovernmental organizations (NGOs) resulted in an erosion of the accountability of government leaders to the population. Security forces were involved in additional significant human rights problems, including alleged government involvement in politically motivated abductions, disappearances and unlawful killings in Chechnya and elsewhere in the North Caucasus; hazing in the armed forces that resulted in severe injuries and deaths; torture, violence, and other brutal or humiliating treatment by security forces; harsh and frequently life-threatening prison conditions; corruption in law enforcement; and arbitrary arrest and detention. The executive branch allegedly exerted influence over judicial decisions in certain high-profile cases. Government pressure continued to weaken freedom of expression and media independence, particularly of major national networks. Media freedom declined due to restrictions as well as harassment, intimidation, and killing of journalists. Local authorities continued to limit freedom of assembly and restrict religious groups in some regions. There were also reports of societal discrimination, harassment, and violence against members of some religious minorities and incidents of anti-Semitism. Authorities restricted freedom of movement and exhibited negative attitudes toward, and sometimes harassed, NGOs involved in human rights monitoring. Also notable was the passage and entry into force of a new law on NGOs, which has already had some adverse effect on their operations. There was widespread governmental and societal discrimination as well as racially motivated attacks against ethnic minorities and dark-skinned immigrants, including the outbreak of violence against Chechens in the northwest and the initiation of a government campaign to selectively harass and deport ethnic Georgians. Xenophobic, racial, and ethnic attacks, and hate crimes were on the rise. Violence against women and children, trafficking in persons, and instances of forced labor were also reported.[63]

It appears that the submission of five reports to the Human Rights Committee, relatively hard-hitting expressions of "concern" by the Committee regarding numerous violations of the Covenant by Russia, as well as failure to adhere to the views of the Committee about individual "communications" (i.e., complaints) submitted under the Optional Protocol have had little if any effect in improving the human rights record of Russia. In light of this failure, it may be appropriate to consider briefly some "radical" proposals for reform advanced by Hathaway in her *Yale Law Journal* article.[64]

Hathaway first suggests that the findings of her study regarding the limited effects of the ratification of human rights treaties "may also give reason to reassess the current policy of the United Nations of promoting universal ratification of the major human rights treaties."[65] She goes on to propose that "it may be worthwhile to develop, consider, and debate more radical approaches to improving human rights through the use of new types of treaty membership policies. If countries gain some expressive benefit from ratifying human rights treaties, perhaps this benefit ought to be less easily obtained."[66]

Hathaway identifies three alternative approaches to improving human rights through the use of new types of treaty membership policies. The first would require that countries demonstrate that they are complying with certain human rights standards as a condition precedent to becoming a party to human rights treaties. Second, "membership in a treaty regime could be tiered, with a probationary period during the early years of membership followed by a comprehensive assessment of country practices for promotion to full membership."[67] Lastly, "treaties could include provisions for removing countries that are habitually found in violation of the terms of the treaty from membership in the treaty regime."[68]

In principle, there is much to be said for Hathaway's proposals. Sadly, in reality there is little to no chance of their being adopted. Although it is not, strictly speaking, a "human rights treaty," the U.N. Charter contains numerous human rights provisions. More important, it contains conditions on states' admission to membership in the United Nations. Article 3 of the Charter provides: "The original Members of the United Nations shall be the States which, having participated in the United Nations

Conference on International Organization at San Francisco, or having previously signed the Declaration of United Nations of January 1, 1942, sign the present Charter and ratify it in accordance with Article 110." Article 4 (1) provides that "[m]embership in the United Nations is open to all other peace-loving states which accept the obligations contained in the present Charter and, in the judgment of the organization, are able and willing to carry out these obligations."

It is questionable at best whether the original members of the United Nations were peace-loving states or truly accepted the obligations contained in the Charter or were "able and willing to carry out these obligations." Be that as it may, it is clear that not all of the present 192 member states satisfied these criteria at the time of their admission. The reality, of course, is these criteria have been a dead letter because of the unwillingness of U.N. membership to apply them, and temporary exclusions of states from membership have been based on political factors, especially during the days of the Cold War.

Under Article 5 of the U.N. Charter, a member state against which preventive or enforcement action has been taken by the Security Council may be suspended from "the rights and privileges of membership" by the General Assembly, upon a recommendation of the Security Council,[69] and under Article 6, "[a] Member of the United Nations which has persistently violated the Principles contained in the present Charter may be expelled from the Organization by the General Assembly upon the recommendation of the Security Council." No member state, however, has had its rights and privileges of membership suspended, nor has any member state ever been expelled from the organization. In short, as the lamentable failure of member states to take forceful action against egregious violators of human rights under the so-called responsibility to protect, which we examined in Chapter 3, also demonstrates, the United Nations is reluctant to utilize coercive means against states solely because of their human rights record.

THE FINANCING OF TERRORISM, SECURITY COUNCIL RESOLUTION 1373, THE AL-QAEDA AND TALIBAN COMMITTEE, AND HUMAN RIGHTS

Terrorist fund-raising has long been noted as a major obstacle standing in the way of efforts to combat international terrorism.[70] Through a series of steps, this concern led to the General Assembly adopting a resolution on December 9, 1999, opening for signature the International Convention for the Suppression of the Financing of Terrorism.[71]

Dealing with the financing of terrorism is a delicate matter. A major problem is that terrorists often operate through "front operations" that appear on the surface to be engaged in legitimate activities or through organizations that in fact have charitable, social, or cultural goals and engage in legitimate activities to further these goals. Moreover, in some states, such as the United States, action by the government to prevent or limit the financing of organizations with charitable or similar goals could raise serious constitutional issues. In an effort to avoid such difficulties, Article 2 (1) of the convention carefully limits its scope:

1. Any person commits an offence within the meaning of this Convention if that person by any means, directly or indirectly, unlawfully and wilfully, provides or collects funds with the intention that they should be used or in the knowledge that they are to be used, in full or in part, in order to carry out: (a) an act which constitutes an offence within the scope of and as defined in one of the treaties listed in the annex; or (b) any other act intended to cause death or serious bodily injury to a civilian, or to any other person not taking an active part in the hostilities in a situation of armed conflict, when the purpose of such an act, by its nature or context, is to intimidate a population, or to compel a government or an international organization to do or abstain from doing any act.

As in the case of its predecessor "antiterrorism conventions," the principal objective of the financing convention is to require state parties to criminalize and establish jurisdiction over the offenses set forth in the convention and to extradite or submit for prosecution the persons accused of the commission of such offenses. An innovative provision in the financing convention, however, is in Article 5. It requires each state party to "take the necessary measures to enable a legal entity located in its territory organized under its laws to be held liable when a person responsible for the management or control of that legal entity" has committed an offense under the convention. Normally, the antiterrorist conventions address only the issue of criminal and not civil liability. The convention also enhances the deterrent effect of its provisions by providing for the seizure or freezing of funds and proceeds used for the commission of an offense and by prohibiting state parties from claiming privileged communication, banking secrecy, or the fiscal nature of the offense to refuse a request for mutual assistance from another state party.[72]

The financing convention, as well as the general effort to combat the financing of terrorism, received an enormous boost when on September 28, 2001, the U.N. Security Council, acting under Chapter VII of the U.N. Charter, adopted Resolution 1373.[73] By any measure, Resolution 1373 constitutes a landmark step by the Council. It has been characterized as a "minitreaty containing obligations that the majority of states had not been willing to accept in the recent past in treaty form."[74] Among the obligations that Resolution 1373 imposes on U.N. member states is to criminalize "all activities falling within the ambit of terrorist financing; it obliged states to freeze all funds or financial assets of persons and entities that are directly or indirectly used to commit terrorist acts or that are owned and controlled by persons engaged in, or associated with, terrorism; it obliged states to prevent their nationals (including private financial institutions) from making such funds available, in effect imposing strict client detection measures, STR [Suspicious Transactions Reports] procedures, and subordination to other intergovernmental institutions in order to receive the names of designated terrorist organizations or individuals; and it imposed substantive and procedural criminal law measures at the domestic level, including an obligation to cooperate in the acquisition of evidence for criminal proceedings."[75]

Arguably, the most significant step the Council took in Resolution 1373 was to establish a committee (the Counter-Terrorism Committee [CTC]) to monitor implementation of the resolution and to call upon states to report to the committee, no later than ninety days after the date of adoption of the resolution, on the steps they have taken to implement the resolution. The Council further "[e]xpresses its determination to take all necessary steps in order to ensure the full implementation of this resolution, in accordance with its responsibilities under the Charter."[76]

As early as April 1, 2003, the Counter-Terrorism Committee had received reports from all U.N. member states.[77] As might be expected, these reports varied in quality and length, "largely reflecting the different levels of capacity among states to implement Resolution 1373 and different levels of resources states have to prepare a report under Resolution 1373."[78]

At the same time, there was concern expressed early on that implementation of Resolution 1373 not be used as an excuse to infringe on human rights. Sergio Vieira de Mello, at the time the U.N. High Commissioner for Human Rights, as well as his predecessor, Mary Robinson, urged the Counter-Terrorism Committee to appoint an expert on human rights and take on the responsibility of monitoring states' compliance with human rights norms in the area of counterterrorism, with Vieira de Mello even offering to provide the Committee with such an expert.[79]

At first the Counter-Terrorism Committee was somewhat resistant to these suggestions. Its position at the time was that "the task of monitoring adherence to human rights obligations in the fight against terrorism falls outside of the CTC's mandate."[80] Human rights activists, however, continued to press for a greater focus by the CTC on human rights issues, and this pressure has had an effect.

In particular, in 2004, with the establishment of the Counter-Terrorism Committee Executive Directorate (CTED),[81] which provided the CTC with a larger, more permanent, and professional staff body to support its work, the CTC shifted to a more proactive policy on human rights. Specifically, CTED was mandated to liaise with the Office of the High Commissioner for Human Rights (OHCHR) and other human rights organizations in matters related to counterterrorism, and a human rights expert was appointed to the CTED staff.[82]

Security Council Resolution 1624,[83] which deals with incitement, stresses that states must ensure that any measures they take to implement the resolution comply with all of their obligations under international law, in particular human rights law, refugee law, and humanitarian law. "The resolution's preamble highlights the relevance of the right to freedom of expression and the right to seek asylum in the context of counterincitement measures; it also states that incitement poses a serious and growing danger to the enjoyment of human rights. The Committee is mandated to include issues related to implementing the resolution in its dialogue with Member States."[84]

As recommended by the CTED Executive Director and endorsed by Security Council Resolution 1805,[85] a working group on issues raised by Resolution 1624 and human rights aspects of counterterrorism in the context of Resolution 1373 was recently established in CTED. The working group's main objectives are to enhance expertise and develop common approaches by CTED staff on these issues, as well as to consider ways in which the Committee might more effectively encourage member states to comply with their international obligations in this area.[86]

The al-Qaeda and Taliban Committee

Before its adoption of Resolution 1373, the Security Council, concerned with the terrorist attacks initiated from Afghanistan by Osama bin Laden and al-Qaeda and the financing of such attacks by drug trafficking and money laundering, addressed the sheltering of bin Laden and his organization, as well as the cultivation, production, and trafficking of drugs in areas controlled by the Taliban, in a resolution adopted on December 8, 1998.[87] Moreover, by Resolution 1267 of October 15, 1999, the Security Council approved a series of sanctions against Afghanistan and obliged states to freeze Taliban and al-Qaeda resources, establishing for this purpose a monitoring committee called colloquially the al-Qaeda and Taliban Committee (hereinafter the "Sanctions Committee"). This committee is responsible for maintaining the list of individuals and entities against which all member states are required to impose financial, travel, and arms-related sanctions. Like the CTC this committee has attracted "significant attention from governments and nongovernmental organizations (NGOs) concerned about the human rights implications of this sanctions regime, as well as from the Council of Europe Committee on Legal Affairs."[88] Because of these concerns, reportedly, "[s]upport for the regime seems to be eroding as a result of concerns regarding the quality of information on the list and the lack of fully transparent procedures for adding and removing names from it."[89]

Despite these concerns, the Sanctions Committee has had difficulty in agreeing on procedures for adding and removing names from the list. States such as China, Russia, and the United States have reportedly argued, among other things, that the goal of Security Council sanctions is not to punish the financiers but rather to prevent the commission of terrorist acts, that the sanctions are of a temporary, administrative character, and that therefore "notions of legal due process, as enshrined in the International Covenant on Civil and Political Rights (ICCPR) and other relevant human rights instruments do not apply to those on the list."[90]

This argument stands in sharp contrast to the views of the Office of the U.N. High Commissioner for Human Rights, which has stated that "while the system of targeted sanctions represents an important improvement over the former system of comprehensive sanctions, it nonetheless continues to pose a number of serious human rights concerns related to the lack of transparency and due process in listing and delisting procedures."[91] Similarly, the Council of Europe has expressed growing concern that the imposition of these sanctions "must, under the European Convention of Human Rights and the [ICCPR]...respect certain minimum standards of procedural protection and legal certainty."[92] The Council of Europe is also concerned that "international, regional, or national courts might find the Security Council sanctions' regimes incompatible with due process norms, such as the rights to be informed of the charges against oneself, to be heard and defend oneself against these charges, and to an effective remedy."[93]

In response to these and other expressions of concern, the Sanctions Committee established new delisting procedures in December 2006 and requested the Secretary-General to establish a "focal point" to receive delisting requests and, where appropriate, to forward them to the committee. In March 2007 such a focal point was established.[94] The response to this action, however, was mixed. Although it was regarded as a step in the right direction, the decision as to whether delisting should take place was left to the committee, and in the view of one commentator, this "does not and cannot address the right of listed individuals to an effective review mechanism, which requires a certain degree of impartiality and independence in the decision making itself."[95]

As noted by a report of a leading NGO:

> Many critics believe that only the establishment of an independent panel of experts to consider delisting requests can ensure that individuals on the list are guaranteed their rights to effective review of their listing by a competent and independent mechanism and to effective remedy. The council's response, the creation of the focal point, is unlikely to be the end of the story on this issue as more and more states are faced with a situation where national or international courts are seized with complaints challenging the legality of the U.N. sanctions and their implementation by states due to the lack of a fair and effective review system. The outcome of those various challenges to the individual listings and the procedures themselves is likely to influence the council's further treatment of these issues. In the meantime, Denmark, Liechtenstein, Sweden, and Switzerland continue to push for the establishment of a meaningful review system, now advocating the establishment of a review panel within the Security Council.[96]

On September 3, 2008, the European Court of Justice, the highest court of the European Union, handed down a landmark decision[97] in which the Court set aside a judgment of the E.U.'s Court of First Instance (CFI) and annulled a regulation of the Council of the European Union implementing resolutions of the U.N. Security Council and decisions of its Sanctions Committee that called for the freezing of the assets of Yassin Abdullah Kadi, a resident of Saudi Arabia, and those of the Al Barakaat International Foundation, established in Sweden. In 2001, the Sanctions Committee had designated both Mr. Kadi and Al Barakaat as being associated with al-Qaeda.[98]

In December 2001, Kadi and Al Barakaat instituted proceedings before the Court of First Instance and originally requested annulment of European Council Regulation No 467/2001 of March 6.[99] Subsequently, they requested the annulment of European Council Regulation No 881/2002 of May 27, 2002, imposing certain specific measures against certain persons and entities associated with Osama bin Laden, the al-Qaeda network, and the Taliban, which replaced Regulation No 467/2001.

The petitioners argued that the Council of the E.U. lacked competence to adopt the regulation and that the regulation infringed several of their fundamental human rights, that is, the right to respect for property, the right to be heard before a court of law, and the right to effective judicial review.[100] On September 21, 2005, the CFI rejected all the claims of Kadi and Al Barakaat and upheld the validity of the regulation.[101]

With respect to the claim that the E.U. lacked competence to adopt the regulation, the Court of First Instance (CFI) ruled that it had no jurisdiction to review the validity of the regulation in question or, indirectly, the validity of the relevant U.N. Security Council resolution because the E.U. regulation implemented a U.N. Security Council resolution adopted under Chapter VII of the U.N. Charter. Such Security Council resolutions are binding upon E.U. member states and prevail over their obligations under the E.C. treaty because of Article 103 of the U.N. Charter.[102] According to the CFI, the one exception to this lack of jurisdiction was if the regulation at issue infringed *jus cogens* norms. The CFI concluded, however, that the restrictive measures provided in the challenged resolution did not infringe any of the Appellant's fundamental rights protected by *jus cogens* norms.

Kadi and Al Barakaat appealed the CFI's judgment in November 2005. Their appeal was based on three grounds. First, they contended that the regulation at issue lacked any legal basis in E.C. law. Second, they alleged that because the regulation directly prejudiced the rights of individuals and prescribed the imposition of individual sanctions, it had no general application, which is required by Article 294 of the E.C. Treaty. Third, and last, they argued the regulation violated their fundamental rights.

The European Court of Justice (ECJ) dismissed the first two grounds of appeal as unfounded. This part of the ECJ judgment will not be discussed further. As to the third ground of the appeal, the ECJ disagreed with the CFI's holding that it had no jurisdiction to review the internal lawfulness of the regulation and upheld, for the first time, the ECJ's full competence to review E.C. acts implementing U.N. Security Council resolutions. The Court stated:

The Community judicature must . . . ensure the review, in principle the full review, of the lawfulness of all Community acts in the light of the fundamental rights forming an integral part of the general principles of Community law, including review of measures which, like the contested regulation, are designed to give effect to resolutions adopted by the Security Council under Chapter VII of the Charter of the United Nations.[103]

The primary rationale for the ECJ's decision was the unique status of the legal order established by the E.C. Treaty. In the Court's view, "the review by the Court of the validity of any Community Measure in the light of fundamental rights must be considered to be the expression, in a community based on the rule of law, of a constitutional guarantee stemming from the E.C. Treaty as an autonomous legal system which is not to be prejudiced by an international agreement."[104] The Court emphasized, however, that "the review of lawfulness thus to be ensured by the Community judicature applies to the Community act purporting to give effect to the international agreement at issue, but not to the international agreement as such."[105] The Court added that, because the contested Security Council resolution was adopted under Chapter VII of the U.N. Charter, "it is not, therefore, for the Community judicature . . . to review the lawfulness of such a resolution . . . even if that review were to be limited to examination of the compatibility of that resolution with *jus cogens*."[106] The autonomy of the legal order established by the E.C. Treaty was further highlighted when the ECJ held that "any judgment by the Community judicature deciding that Community measure intended to give effect to . . . a [UNSC] resolution is contrary to a higher rule of law in the Community Legal Order would not entail any challenge to the primacy of that resolution in international law."[107]

Turning to the issue of whether the appellants' fundamental rights had been violated, the ECJ disagreed with the Court of First Instance and held the rights to be heard and to effective judicial review were "patently not respected."[108] The Community regulation provided no procedure for communicating the evidence justifying the inclusion on the list. Moreover, the Council of the E.U. never informed the Appellants of the evidence against them that justified including them on the list. As a result, the Appellants were not able to defend their rights before Community courts, so the regulation also infringed the right to an effective legal remedy.[109]

As to the right to property, the ECJ stated that, although the "restrictive measures imposed by the contested regulation constitute restrictions of the right to property which might, in principle be justified,"[110] . . . "the contested regulation, in so far as it concerns Mr. Kadi, was adopted without furnishing any guarantee enabling him to put his case to the competent authorities, in a situation in which the restriction of his property right must be regarded as significant, having regard to the general application and actual continuation of the freezing of funds affecting him."[111] Accordingly, in the view of the Court, the freezing of funds "constitutes an unjustified restriction of Mr. Kadi's right to property."[112]

Significantly, the ECJ authorized the European Community to maintain the regulation in force for three months to allow the Council of the European Union to remedy its deficiencies. The Court's purpose in doing so was to prevent the Appellants from avoiding the application of the freezing of their assets in the event that freezing of their assets proved to be justified.

In response to the Court's judgment, the Commission of the European Communities communicated the narrative summaries of reasons provided by the U.N.

Sanctions Committee to Kadi and Al Barakaat and gave them an opportunity to comment on these grounds in order to make their point of view known. Upon receiving comments from the Appellants, the Commission examined them and found that "given the preventive nature of the freezing of funds and economic resources," the listing of Appellants was justified because of their "association with the al-Qaeda network."[113] The Commission further held that the regulation would enter into force on December 3, 2008, be published in the Official Journal of the European Union, and apply from May 30, 2002.[114]

Not surprisingly, the ECJ's decision in *Kadi* engendered a substantial amount of commentary – some highly positive, some highly critical, and some in between.[115] Jack Goldsmith and Eric Posner, in an op-ed piece in the *Wall Street Journal*,[116] contended that "Europe's commitment [to international law] is largely rhetorical. Like the Bush administration, Europeans obey international law when it advances their interests and discard it when it does not."[117] To support their thesis, the authors refer to the *Kadi* case as an example and state that in that case the ECJ "[R]uled that the Security Council resolution was invalid." However, as noted previously, the ECJ made no such ruling. Rather, it studiously avoided commenting on the Security Council's resolution and confined its ruling to the E.C. resolution, which purported to implement the Council's resolution, holding that the E.C. Council had no authority under E.U. standards of rights protection and, as noted by de Burca, "treating the U.N. system and the E.U. system as separate and parallel regimes, without any privileged status being accorded to U.N. Charter obligations or UNSC measures within E.C. law."[118]

To be sure the ECJ's decision blocked E.U. member states from implementing the Security Council's resolution requiring them to freeze the assets of persons or entities on the Council's list and thereby to be in violation of their duties under the U.N. Charter, but this impediment lasted only the approximately three months it took the Commission of the European Communities to afford Kadi and Al Barakaat the opportunity to present their defense, as required by the ECJ's decision. After they had done so, the Commission found their defense unconvincing, and the regulation it issued resulted in their being placed on the E.C.'s list of persons and entities whose assets would be frozen pursuant to the Security Council's resolution.

Pressure continues to be brought against the Security Council to induce it to create a procedure to protect the due process rights of individuals and entities whose assets may be frozen because of a determination by the Security Council that they are supporters of al-Qaeda and the Taliban. For example, on December 29, 2008, a majority of the Human Rights Committee, in response to a communication submitted to the committee under the Optional Protocol to the International Covenant on Civil and Political Rights, expressed its view that Belgium had violated several articles of the Covenant.[119] Prior to its consideration of the merits of the claims made in the communication, the committee ruled that the communication was admissible.[120] Adopting a position reminiscent of that of the European Court of

Justice in the *Kadi* decision, a majority of the Human Rights Committee acknowledged that "the Committee could not consider alleged violations of other instruments such as the Charter of the United Nations, or allegations that challenged
United Nations rules concerning the fight against terrorism." But "the Committee
was competent to admit a communication alleging that a State party had violated
the rights set forth in the Covenant, regardless of the source of the obligations
implemented by the State party."[121]

As to the merits of the communication's claims, a majority of the committee found
that Belgium had violated Article 12 of the Covenant, which protects the right to
travel freely.[122] Belgium had frozen the assets of the authors of the communication
after their names were placed on the Consolidated List of the United Nations
Sanctions Committee. The placement of the authors' names on the sanctions list
prevented them from traveling freely. Although recognizing that Article 12 of the
Covenant permits the restriction of the right to travel on national security grounds,
the Human Rights Committee noted that Belgium had first transmitted the authors'
names to the Sanctions Committee, and this took place before the authors could be
heard. Also, the Human Rights Committee took note that a criminal investigation
initiated against the authors by the Public Prosecutor's Offices was dismissed and
that the Belgian authorities' request that the authors' names be removed from the
Sanctions Committee's list showed that the restrictions on the authors' rights to leave
the country were unnecessary to protect national security or public order.

Article 17 of the Covenant recognizes the right of everyone to protection against
arbitrary or unlawful interference with privacy, family, home, or correspondence,
and against unlawful attacks on honor and reputation. The Human Rights Committee accepted the authors' arguments that their full contact details had been made
available to everyone through their inclusion on the Sanctions Committee's list and
the availability of the list on the Internet. Even though Belgium was not competent
to remove the authors' names from the United Nations and European lists, it was
responsible for the presence of the authors' names on those lists. Accordingly, in the
Human Rights Committee's view, Belgium had violated Article 17 of the Covenant.

Lastly, under Article 2, paragraph 3(a) of the Covenant, Belgium was bound to
provide the authors with an effective remedy. Again recognizing that Belgium was
not itself competent to remove the authors' names from the Sanctions Committee's
list, the Human Rights Committee was "nevertheless of the view that the State Party
has the duty to do all it can to have their names removed from the list as soon
as possible, to provide the authors with some form of compensation and to make
public the requests for removal. The State Party is also obliged to ensure that similar
violations do not occur in the future."[123] The committee requested Belgium to
provide it, within 180 days, with information about the measures taken "to give effect
to the present Views. The State party is also invited to publish the present Views."[124]

In an individual dissenting opinion, Ruth Wedgwood expressed her view that the
Human Rights Committee should have ruled the communication of the authors
inadmissible. In her view, the "authors are complaining about the actions and

decisions of the United Nations Security Council, not the acts of Belgium. Security Council resolutions have established administrative measures to prevent the financing and facilitation of international terrorism. These sanctions extend to 'any individuals, groups, undertakings or entities associated with Al-Qaida, Usama bin Laden or the Taliban,' including those 'who have participated in financing, planning, facilitating, recruiting for, preparing, perpetrating, or otherwise supporting terrorist activities or acts.'"[125] Under Articles 48 (2) and 25 of the U.N. Charter, Belgium was obligated to carry out these Security Council decisions.

Despite the impediments to its efforts to ensure that assets of individuals or entities whose names are on the Sanctions Committee's list are frozen represented by the *Kadi* decision and the views of the Human Rights Committee, as well as the increasing criticism of the Sanctions Committee's failure to provide those whose assets are frozen an opportunity to defend themselves, at this writing, the Security Council has not yet adopted procedures that provide meaningful protection for those whose names appear on the Sanctions Committee's list beyond initially a "humanitarian exception" to allow targeted individuals to keep the funds necessary for their basic living expenses.[126] The Security Council did introduce a "delisting" procedure that allows targeted individuals and entities to submit a request for delisting to the Sanctions Committee, either through their states of residence or citizenship or through a "U.N. focal point" in the U.N. Secretariat.[127] The delisting procedure still leaves the decision whether to delist in the hands of the Sanctions Committee, and has led to greater efforts to establish a more meaningful review system, such as a review panel within the Security Council itself.[128]

Whatever form a more "meaningful" review system may take, either of the initial decision to place names on the Sanctions Committee's list, or to delist them, it is unlikely it will involve a court in the process, especially in light of the view of powerful member states of the Security Council, such as the United States, that the process is an essentially administrative procedure not requiring the kinds of due process protection afforded in criminal cases. Also, the International Court of Justice does not have jurisdiction over nonstate claims, and, as we have seen in Chapter 2, has become a highly controversial institution. It appears that a review panel within the Security Council is about as far-reaching a proposal as one could expect to have any realistic chance of adoption.[129]

Most recently, the Committee has indicated that it will vet all 513 names currently on its sanctions list for al-Qaeda and the Taliban by June 2010.[130] Reportedly, the committee also hopes to devise a process for people and entities to directly challenge inclusion on the list, which has been the subject of complaints and about thirty court cases.[131]

At this writing (December 24, 2009), the Security Council has devised such a procedure. Specifically, on December 17, 2009, the Council adopted a resolution[132] that, as reported by the *New York Times*, will "provide some recourse for individuals or organizations who believe they were unfairly blacklisted after being accused of supporting Al Qaeda or the Taliban."[133] To this end, the resolution creates an "ombudsperson" to hear complaints from those who believe they have been singled out erroneously.[134] The resolution does not, however, empower the ombudsperson to recommend whether a name should remain on the list or not. Reportedly, "[s]everal Security Council members – including France, China and Russia – felt that giving individuals the right to even raise questions about a council decision was radical enough. Allowing the ombudsman to make recommendations would be going a step too far in setting a precedent for second-guessing the Council's decisions, according to diplomats and others familiar with the negotiations."[135] It remains to be seen whether the limited powers of the ombudsperson will be sufficient to satisfy judges that persons or organizations challenging their inclusion on the list have received sufficient due process.

THE HIGH COMMISSIONER FOR HUMAN RIGHTS

The time would seem propitious to examine the record of the post of the High Commissioner for Human Rights, with the announcement on March 8, 2008, that Louise Arbour, an active and controversial High Commissioner, would retire and the appointment on July 24, 2008, of Navanethem Pillay, a South African judge, to replace her.

As noted by Henry J. Steiner et al.,[136] for more than forty years, starting in 1947, various proposals had been advanced to create the post of U.N. High Commissioner for Human Rights. The reasons such proposals got nowhere for so long were compelling: "The Soviet Union and its allies were strongly opposed, most developing countries were very wary, and the West was most enthusiastic when it was clear that the proposal was unlikely to be taken up."[137] Equally compelling were the factors that resulted in the Vienna World Conference in 1993 approving of such a proposal. They included "the demise of the Socialist bloc and associated post-Cold War optimism, the election of the Clinton Administration in the U.S. which was keen to find new ideas in the human rights area, and, curiously, the opposition of the then U.N. Secretary-General, Boutros Boutros-Ghali which reassured nervous governments that any appointee would be kept under a tight rein."[138]

Judge Pillay is the sixth High Commissioner appointed.[139] It is generally agreed that Mary Robinson and Louise Arbour have been the most dynamic.[140] Each was also controversial, and some of the reasons they were controversial are explored in the following.

Mary Robinson

Mary Robinson was appointed in 1997 as the second High Commissioner. A former president of Ireland and a human rights activist, her tenure contrasted sharply with that of the first occupant of the office, José Ayala Lasso, who was sharply criticized for failing to take forceful action.[141] No such criticisms were made of Mary Robinson. To the contrary, her appointment was widely praised by human rights NGOs, especially when she promised to "stand up to bullies" and to be a "moral voice" favoring human rights and aiming to "narrow the gap" between civil and political rights, on the one hand, and economic and social rights on the other.[142] Indeed, when asked to identify the most serious form of human rights violations in the world, she consistently replied, "extreme poverty."[143] She also pressed to see that trafficking in persons would be addressed as a human rights issue. Early in her tenure she condemned the governments of Algeria and the Democratic Republic of the Congo for human rights abuses.

Initially, the United States was enthusiastic about Robinson's appointment. U.S. President Bill Clinton called Robinson a "splendid choice" and offered her the full support of his administration.[144] The honeymoon period was brief, however, and Robinson's relationship with the United States soon took a turn for the worse. Reportedly, Robinson's conflicts with the United States were primarily in three areas: (i) her views on the Israel-Palestine conflict; (ii) her defense of and the allegedly detached way in which she presided over the Durban "World Conference against Racism"; and (iii) her criticism of U.S. conduct in its war against terror, especially her condemnation of U.S. treatment of prisoners in Camp X-Ray at Guantanamo Bay.[145]

Also, throughout her tenure Robinson was one of the most prominent critics of U.S. administration of the death penalty, and critical comments she made about the U.S. "unsigning" of the ICC Statute, as well as her refusal to consider reforms of the U.N. Human Rights Commission's election process, exacerbated tensions with the Bush administration.

The World Conference against Racism and Robinson's role in it have been the subjects that have engendered the sharpest criticism of Robinson's tenure, criticism that has not been limited to that from the Bush administration. It was held in Durban, South Africa, on August 31–September 9, 2001, concluding two days prior to the fateful al-Qaeda attack on September 11.[146] Although the U.S. government had originally planned to have Secretary of State Colin Powell participate in the conference, in the end it withdrew from the conference because allegedly it was unable to prevent the conference from turning into an "anti-American, anti-Israeli circus."[147]

According to Tom Lantos, a Democratic congressman from California and member of the House International Relations Committee, who participated as part of the U.S. delegation to the conference, the initial plans for the conference were promising, in significant part because Mary Robinson:

developed a clear vision to unify and energize the global dialogue on race in the years leading up to the convening of the conference. Her vision focused on bringing the world together to overcome fear – fear of what is different, fear of the other, and fear of the loss of personal security. In her public statements, Robinson made a compelling case that racism and xenophobia are on the rise by tying its current manifestations to growing economic and social dislocations caused by globalization. As a way to move forward, she repeatedly challenged the international community to shift its focus away from viewing diversity as a limiting factor and to discern the potential for mutual enrichment in diversity. She hoped the conference would not only serve as a catharsis for victims' groups to relieve their grievances but could also initiate a lasting dialogue between civil societies and governments focused on finding solutions to overcome hate. Robinson's public pronouncements prior to the conference also reflected an understanding that no nation is free of racism, and that all share responsibility for eradicating this pervasive and universal evil.[148]

In 1999, the General Assembly's Third Committee, which covers social, humanitarian, and cultural issues, decided that the conference would be held in Durban, South Africa, in 2001, and should be preceded by regional meetings in Strasbourg, France; Santiago, Chile; Dakar, Senegal; and Tehran, Iran. Each regional meeting was to draft a declaration and plan of action on racism that would ultimately be combined into a single set of documents to be ratified in Durban. According to Lantos, "[d]evelopments at the first three regional meetings suggested that Robinson's best hopes for the Durban conference were possible" and "[t]he documents that emerged from them attempted to tackle a range of vexing issues from the legacy of slavery to the need to confront the global resurgence of anti-Semitism."[149] These favorable developments, however, came to an abrupt end in Tehran, where, in Lantos's view, so did Robinson's effectiveness as a manager. Lantos was especially critical of Robinson's alleged failure to take forceful action in Tehran when the Iranian government barred Israeli passport holders and Jewish nongovernmental organizations, as well as Australia and New Zealand, two strong supporters of Israel, from attending. Moreover, the declaration and plan of action agreed to by the delegates to the Tehran meeting "amounted to what only could be seen as a declaration by the states present of their intention to use the conference as a propaganda weapon attacking Israel. Indeed, the documents not only singled the country out above all others – despite the well-known problems with racism, xenophobia, and discrimination that exist all over the world – but also equated its policies in the West Bank with some of the most horrible racist policies of the previous century. Israel, the text stated, engages in 'ethnic cleansing of the Arab population of historic Palestine,' and is implementing a 'new kind of apartheid, a crime against humanity.' It also purported to witness an 'increase of racist practices of Zionism' and condemned racism 'in various parts of the world, as well as the emergence of racist and violent movements based on racist and discriminatory ideas, in particular, the Zionist movement, which is based on race superiority.'"[150]

At the end of the Tehran meeting, according to Lantos, "Robinson made no visible effort to confront the breakdown that had occurred in the global dialogue that she had done so much to nurture."[151]

Despite considerable efforts, especially by the U.S. delegation, after the Tehran meeting to overcome this breakdown, these efforts were unsuccessful. As a result Secretary Powell decided to withdraw the U.S. delegation from the conference, which, according to Lantos, had become a "diplomatic farce."

After the United States departed from the conference, the European Union attempted to reach a compromise position. The "compromise, for which South Africa claimed authorship, removed some of the anti-Israeli language, but contained Mary Robinson's longed-for language that recognized the 'plight of the Palestinian people under occupation,' language that clearly would have been unsatisfactory to the United States. Not only does the final document single out one regional conflict for discussion, it does so in a biased way: the suffering of the Palestinian people is highlighted, but there is no discussion of the Palestinian terrorist attacks on Israeli citizens."[152]

It should be noted that Lantos does not assign sole or even primary blame for the breakdown in the Durban conference to Robinson. Primary blame he assigns to several member states of the Organization of the Islamic Conference (OIC), and he is critical as well of the Bush administration for its unilateral approach to world problems – although not, in this case, to the race issue – the radicalism of many foreign NGOs at the conference, the allegedly inadequate response thereto by U.S.-based NGOs, and the unwillingness of European allies to take a strong stand. Moreover, some commentators have come to Robinson's defense and responded to Lantos's criticisms, leveling a few of their own while defending the results of the conference.[153]

It is worth noting that, in addition to the issue of anti-Israel statements and anti-Semitism at the conference and in the conference's documents, another emotional issue at the conference was whether there should be reparations paid to African states because of their suffering from slavery and colonialism. According to Lantos, however, substantial progress was being made toward a compromise on these issues in the form of language to express regret short of apology or reparations, such as "deep regret and profound remorse" when OIC (Organization of the Islamic Conference) delegates drafted a "nonpaper" for consideration by the conference that "was dripping with hate." Lantos reportedly met twice with Robinson and urged her publicly to "denounce it in order to salvage the conference." But "[i]nstead of insisting that it was inappropriate to discuss a specific political conflict in the context of a World Conference on Racism, she spoke of the 'need to resolve protracted conflict and occupation, claims of inequality, violence and terrorism, and deteriorating situation on the ground.'"[154] In Lantos's view, "Robinson's intervention . . . represented the *coup d'grace* on efforts to save the conference from disaster"[155] and "negotiations on mutually acceptable language to express regret for slavery and colonialism quickly unraveled."[156]

Louise Arbour

In addition to Mary Robinson, Louise Arbour has been the High Commissioner for Human Rights commonly described as both dynamic and controversial. A former Supreme Court judge in Canada, and previously the Chief Prosecutor of the

United Nations tribunals for war crimes in Yugoslavia and Rwanda, Ms. Arbour came into the office with impressive credentials and high expectations – a situation similar to that of Mary Robinson. Upon her resignation after four years as High Commissioner, Arbour received high praise from leading human rights NGOs like Amnesty International[157] and Human Rights Watch.[158] Specifically, she was given credit because "she sharpened the profile of the high commissioner's office, not only by almost doubling its annual budget to nearly $100 million and widening its presence in the field, but also by persistently raising her own voice."[159]

To others, however, Arbour's outspokenness and persistently raising her own voice were their primary bases for sharp criticism. The Bush administration, in particular, objected to her frequent complaints about its use of torture, secret arrests, and disregard of international law as part of its campaign against terrorism. Zimbabwe's justice minister, Patrick Chinamasa, reportedly said that she had "turned her office into a 'deified oracle which spews out edicts we all must follow.'" Some supporters of Israel reportedly called her "an idiot."[160]

Ironically, Arbour herself reportedly did not regard naming and shaming as the High Commissioner's most effective tool, and admitted that she often turned to quiet diplomacy. In her words, "On my travels, I can see presidents and prime ministers and foreign ministers. A lot of nongovernmental organizations don't have this kind of access. But that calls for a different tone of interaction. There's no point in screaming if you cannot compel anything."[161]

At the same time, Arbour's assertiveness reportedly has resulted in her being admitted to places like refugee camps and prisons, or being able to see political prisoners or rape victims, "to the discomfort of her official hosts."[162] Assertiveness has its limits, however, as Arbour learned when North Korea and Myanmar refused to let her into their territories. In response to a request to visit Tibet, China told her it was not the right time. Sri Lanka, although allowing her to visit, refused her request to open a field office there, and Pakistan kept postponing her trip, finally offering a date three days before she was to leave office. She accepted and later admonished the country's president, Pervez Musharraf, and other high-ranking officials about human rights issues, including disappearances and the lack of judicial independence.

Arbour was especially concerned about what she called "a very serious erosion" of safeguards against human rights abuses in the United States. Controversy over alleged U.S. human rights abuses in the "war on terror" apparently led the presidents or prime ministers of some countries, when questioned about their own human rights records, to respond, "Why aren't you in Guantanamo? Why are you coming here?" Conversely, when she raised some human rights issues with a group of U.S. congressional aides, they complained, "Why aren't you criticizing Myanmar instead of spending your time criticizing the United States?"[163]

Arbour also had some provocative comments to make about the Human Rights Council, which we examined in Chapter 2. She reportedly stated that "pure politics" often seemed to dominate the council's proceedings. Although she welcomed the Council's new policy of universal periodic review under which every U.N. member state's human rights record would be reviewed every four years, she complained about regular attempts in the Council to gain control of her office.[164] She noted further that the Council's work had often been paralyzed and distorted by regional groups, especially the Organization of the Islamic Conference and African regional groups in the United Nations, "which not only have focused overwhelmingly on Israel's treatment of Palestinians but also have blocked discussion of such topics as sexual identity, female genital cutting and so-called honor killings," topics that these regional groups wish to avoid because their record on them is poor.[165]

It appears clear that Arbour was as least as much an activist during her tenure as Mary Robinson was during hers. One commentator, based on a report by U.N. Watch issued in December 2008, declared that "Arbour criticized governments of all types during her tenure: both in free countries and in dictatorships, as well as everything in between."[166] At the same time she was accused of having "mistaken priorities," especially in the Middle East. According to the U.N. Watch report, "in 2007–2008 the High Commissioner 'published four strong criticisms of Israel; one moderate criticism of Egypt; four moderate criticisms of Iran; three strong criticisms of Iraq (which . . . could also be criticisms or considered criticisms of the U.S.); and one weak statement regarding Lebanon.' Not one of those criticisms was directed at Saudi Arabia, a country in which this very week a women was jailed for driving a car. Additionally, she did little or nothing to stop her own organization and the Human Rights Council's craven obsession with Israel."[167]

As indicated previously, there is little doubt that human rights NGOs greatly favor an activist for the High Commissioner position. There is substantial doubt, however, as to how effective an activist approach by the High Commissioner is in promoting human rights and in protecting potential victims of human rights abuses from injury. As noted by Felice D. Gaer of the Jacob Blaustein Institute for the Advancement of Human Rights:

The advantage of independence in human rights is the ability to point to wrongs as they occur – to "tell the truth" and thus to stigmatize unforgivable action and to demand its correction. That is what NGOs continually demand of public officials who work on "human rights." But in intergovernmental (and governmental) bodies, the key to effectiveness is, in general, to be able to change behavior and reach negotiated agreements, rather than to speak out and to pass judgment according to unbending standards.

One must therefore ask: although speaking out is usually prioritized as an ideal in the field of human rights, is it always, or even usually, the most effective course of action? We would benefit from a study of violations that the high commissioner or the secretary-general, using his good offices, has identified – either publicly or privately – to see what approach has, in fact, been most effective in improving human rights. . . .

Michael Ignatieff has reminded us that human rights is itself "a politics, one that must reconcile moral ends to concrete situations and must be prepared to make painful compromises not only between means and ends, but between ends themselves. Whether and how the high commissioners made such choices, and with what results, remains a key question that must be carefully examined in order to determine the effectiveness of different approaches to leadership in human rights. The results of such an examination would provide, in turn, a guide for the protection activities of future high commissioners.[168]

Sadly, the careful examination called for by Gaer remains to be taken. Moreover, as we have seen previously in this chapter and in previous chapters, the unexamined premise that an activist approach of speaking out is the ideal, largely prevails not only in the Office of the High Commissioner but also in the Human Rights Council and the Human Rights Committee, and, indeed, in most parts of the U.N. human rights infrastructure.

It is not surprising that human rights NGOs would favor an activist, "mobilization of shame" approach because this is their standard modus operandi, and they have often enjoyed considerable success in employing it. But as suggested by Felice Gaer, this approach may well not be the most effective in an intergovernmental context, and empirical comprehensive studies of this issue appear to be sorely lacking.

Navenethem Pillay

It is too early to tell whether Judge Pillay will follow the activist approach of Mary Robinson and Louise Labour. Unfortunately for Judge Pillay, the first major challenge she faced in her new position was acting as the Secretary-General of Durban II, otherwise known as the Geneva Conference, a follow-up conference to the discredited Durban conference, in such a way that Durban II would avoid the grave problems and unhappy outcome of Durban I. Long before she became the High Commissioner, others had made strenuous efforts to avoid a repeat of Durban I, including the removal of controversial statements about Israel in the draft document for the Geneva Conference; along with statements about what constitutes defamation of religion – a position strongly supported by Muslim states – and about compensation for slavery. But a reference in the draft document that endorsed the communiqué that emerged from Durban I resulted in the United States deciding to boycott the Geneva Conference, along with Germany, Italy, Poland, the Netherlands, New Zealand, and Australia. Canada and Israel announced months before the Geneva Conference that they would not attend.[169]

At the Geneva Conference itself, which began on April 20, 2009, the proceedings were severely disrupted when Mahmoud Ahmadinejad, the president of Iran, excoriated Israel as a "cruel and repressive racist regime," at which point twenty-three diplomats from the European nations attending the conference walked out. The speech also drew a rare rebuke from U.N. Secretary-General Ban Ki-Moon, who reportedly stated that "I have not experienced this kind of destructive proceedings in an assembly, in a conference, by any one member state." For her part, Judge Pillay reportedly criticized Mr. Ahmadinejad for "grandstanding" from a United Nations dais and said his performance should not be an excuse to derail the important topic of the conference. After noting that the president's remarks were outside the scope of the conference, she added that: "This is what I would have expected the president of Iran to come and tell us: how he is addressing racial intolerance in his country."[170]

From this statement one can surmise that Judge Pillay will speak her mind, as did High Commissioners Mary Robinson and Louise Arbour, when the situation calls for it, as it surely did in Geneva. But perhaps conferences along the lines of the Geneva Conference should have hard and fast rules prohibiting criticism of individual countries in order to concentrate instead on cooperative efforts to eliminate or at least limit the problems they address. Continuation of the inflammatory statements characteristic of proceedings in the Human Rights Council or the General Assembly might be expected at a conference chaired by Libya and having Cuba and Iran as chairs but they serve only to undermine the goals of the conference. Indeed, remarks along the lines of those of the president of Iran should be sanctioned by expulsion of the country he represents from the conference. Moreover, because the tenor of President Ahmadinejad's speech was in keeping with remarks he made in the past, he should not have been selected as a headline speaker of the conference.

We shall return to human rights in the United Nations in the concluding section of this chapter. But first we turn to the institution that has been regarded as the gold standard for human rights programs: the European Court of Human Rights and Fundamental Freedoms.

THE EUROPEAN COURT OF HUMAN RIGHTS AND FUNDAMENTAL FREEDOMS

The significance of the European Convention for the Protection of Human Rights and Fundamental Human Rights, which created the European Court of Human Rights and Fundamental Freedoms, has been aptly identified by Steiner, Alston, and Goodman as follows:

> The European Convention for the Protection of Human Rights and Fundamental Freedoms (ECHR) was signed in 1950 and entered into force in 1953. The ECHR is of particular importance within the context of international human rights for several reasons: it was the first comprehensive treaty in the world in this field; it established the first international complaints procedure and the first international court for the determination of human rights matters; it remains the most judicially developed of all the human rights systems; it has generated a more extensive jurisprudence than any other part of the international system; and it now applies to some 30% of the nations in the world . . .

The impetus for the adoption came from three factors. It was first a regional response to the atrocities committed in Europe during the Second World War and an affirmation of the belief that governments respecting human rights are less likely to wage war on their neighbors. Secondly, both the Council of Europe, which was set up in 1949 (and under whose auspices the Convention was adopted), and the European Union (previously the European Community or Communities, the first of which was established in 1952) were partly based on the assumption that the best way to ensure that Germany would be a force for peace, in partnership with France, the United Kingdom, and the other European states, was through regional integration and the institutionalizion (sic) of common values. This strategy contrasted sharply with the punitive reparations-based approach embodied in the 1919 Versailles Treaty after the First World War.

Thus, the Preamble to the European Convention refers (perhaps somewhat optimistically at the time) to the "European countries which are likeminded and have a common heritage of political traditions, ideals, freedom and the rule of law" but this statement also points to the third major impetus towards a Convention – the desire to bring the non-Communist countries of the countries of Europe together within a common ideological framework and to consolidate their unity in the face of the communist threat. "Genuine democracy" (to which the Statute of the Council of Europe commits its members) or the "effective political democracy" to which the Preamble of the Convention refers, had to be clearly distinguishable from the "people's democracy" which was promoted by the Soviet Union and its allies.[171]

Although, as might be expected, some decisions of the European Court have been sharply criticized, especially by losing state parties, on the whole the record of compliance with the court's decisions has been quite extraordinary. Indeed, "[a]ccording to [Thomas] Buergenthal [a human rights expert now a judge on the International Court of Justice] the decisions of the European Court are routinely complied with by European governments. As a matter of fact, the system has been so effective in the last decade that the Court has for all practical purposes become Western Europe's constitutional court."[172]

More recently, however, this enviable record has come under serious strain. In particular, the Court has faced a dramatic increase in the number of individual applications to it. The main cause of this increase has been "the enlargement of the Council of Europe. It now has 46 member states, bringing to 800 million the total number of citizens with the right to make an application to the Court." Despite reforms introduced to cope with this problem,[173] "the current Convention system cannot cope with this level of caseload. The number of applications which can be disposed of is far exceeded by the number of new applications made, resulting in a growing backlog of cases: by the end of 2003, some 65,000 applications were pending before the Court."[174]

Among the new members of the Council of Europe contributing to the backlog of cases before the Court was the Russia Federation. The application of Russia to join the Council of Europe posed serious problems for the Council. Mark Janis has nicely framed these problems:

On 28 February 1996, Russia acceded to the Statute of the Council of Europe, becoming the Council's thirty-ninth member. . . . Russia's accession followed an extensive debate within the Council of Europe about the suitability of the applicant for membership, and occurred despite an unfavourable Eminent Lawyers Report prepared at the request of the Bureau of the Parliamentary Assembly. The report concluded "that the legal order of the Russian Federation does not, at the present moment, meet the Council of Europe standards as enshrined in the statute of the Council and developed by the organs of the European Convention on Human Rights." As a condition of joining the Council of Europe, Russia has promised to ratify the Convention for the Protection of Human Rights within one year of its accession to the Statute of the Council. . . .

The decision in February 1996 to admit Russia to the Council of Europe is commonly viewed as a result of giving greater weight to political factors than legal criteria, a realistic judgment given the importance of integrating post-Communist Russia into the more democratic liberal realm of Western Europe.

No matter how politically rational the decision to admit Russia to the Council of Europe, it must be recognized that Russia's accession will result in two important and probably negative consequences for the "legality" of the Strasbourg human rights system. First, the participation of Russia increases the possibility that European human rights law will both be disobeyed and be seen to be flouted. . . .

[T]hree aspects of Russia's accession are particularly troubling for the future of compliance with Strasbourg law. First, at the present time, as the Eminent Lawyers Report makes clear, Russia falls short of the usual standard of the rule of law and the protection of human rights. Second, given Russia's lack of experience in promoting human rights at the level of municipal law, it is likely that a great many violations of European rights law will be committed there, and that they will not be remedied domestically. Third, the same political importance of Russia that has prompted the Council of Europe to accept its admittance will make it especially difficult for Strasbourg to force the Russian government to comply with adverse findings.

The other significant consequence for the system of European human rights law posed by Russia's accession is likely to be a new challenge to what, along with Hart, we can call Strasbourg's "internal point of view." Given the difficulties of Russia effectively complying with European human rights law in its municipal legal order and of Strasbourg imposing its decisions upon the Russian government, there will be a strong temptation for the Strasbourg institutions to fashion a two-tier legal order, which would allow lower than normal expectations for Russia. This will have the likely benefit of enabling Russia's continued participation in the system, but it will threaten the perception of Hart's "officials, lawyers or private persons" that Strasbourg law "in one situation after another [is a guide] to the conduct of social life, as the basis for claims, demands, admissions, criticism or punishment. viz., in all the familiar transactions of life according to rules."

These probable challenges resulting from Russia's accession come at an awkward moment for Strasbourg. Not only is the ambit of European human rights law being widened to reach out to the former Soviet bloc, but the potency of Strasbourg law is being deepened by ever bolder Court judgments against national governments. This deepening, a welcome advance on international legal control, is proceeding just when the basic tenets of European unity are under increasing assault by nationalistic sentiments across Europe. . . . Hence, there is a danger that the failure of Russia to comply with European human rights law domestically and to obey the decisions of the Strasbourg institutions and the creation of a two-tier human rights system to accommodate Russia will give the governments of the existing member states all the more latitude in weakening their own commitment to the Strasbourg system. This all serves as a reminder that the "breakthrough" of Strasbourg law to genuine legal obligation may not be forever.[175]

Janis's comments were written in 1997. Sadly, they apply with equal, if not greater, force today. The number of cases pending against the Russian Federation constitutes the largest percentage of cases pending before the court. As of January 1, 2008, the Russian percentage was 26 percent.[176] Moreover, in numerous judgments, the European Court has ruled against the Russian Federation, and many of these judgments remain unexecuted.[177]

One of the steps taken to mitigate the overload of the European Court caused by ever increasing numbers of case filings was the adoption of a new protocol, Protocol No. 14 to the Convention for the Protection of Human Rights and Fundamental Freedoms, as part of a comprehensive reform package by the Committee of Ministers of the European Council in May 2004. A report reviewing the working methods of the European Court of Human Rights summarized Protocol No. 14's three main provisions:

It allows for a single judge, assisted by a nonjudicial rapporteur, to reject cases where they are clearly inadmissible from the outset. This replaces the current system where inadmissibility is decided by Committees of three judges, and will increase judicial capacity. Protocol 14 also provides for Committees of three judges to give judgments in repetitive cases where the case law of the Court is already well established. . . . Repetitive cases are currently heard by Chambers of seven judges, so this measure will also serve to increase efficiency and judicial capacity. Thirdly, Protocol 14 introduces a new admissibility criterion concerning cases where the applicant has not suffered a "significant disadvantage" provided that the case has already been duly considered by a domestic tribunal, and provided that there are no general human rights reasons why the application should be examined on its merits.[178]

The future of Protocol No. 14, however, is problematic. As noted by the authors of the recently published second edition of a leading U.S. casebook on human rights:

9. Protocol No. 14 will not enter into force until it has been ratified by all forty-seven High Contracting Parties. By 2006, all state parties had signed Protocol No. 14 and all but one – the Russian Federation – had ratified it. In December 2006, the Russian Parliament, the State Duma, refused to ratify the treaty. The chair of the Duma's Legislation Committee justified the rejection by pointing to the Protocol's single-judge screening procedures, which he claimed were inconsistent with collegial decisions of Russian domestic courts. The chair also stated that the protocol was "not in the interests of Russia.". . . . According to some commentators, recent judgments upholding challenges to extrajudicial killings, disappearances, and other gross human violations by the Russian military in Chechnya have soured the relationship between the Russian government and the ECHR. In addition, "given that complaints against Russia now constitute by far the largest portion of the backlog of cases pending before the Court, the question is whether the Russian authorities are genuinely committed to facilitating the efficient determination of cases by the Court."

What actions should the Council of Europe and the others (sic) High Contracting Parties take in response to Russia's refusal to ratify Protocol No. 14? Is it realistic to expect Russia to ratify the protocol given the pronounced geographic disparities in the Court's case load? More generally, how should the Council of Europe respond if Russia consistently refuses to comply with the ECHR's judgments? Would "the protection of democracy, human rights and the rule of law. . . . be better served in the long term by expelling Russia [from the Council] for such gross and flagrant violations, or by retaining it in spite of them."[179]

These questions pose in sharp relief the issues posed by Janis in 1997. Their resolution will require numerous "hard choices" to be made if the European Court of Human Rights is to continue the success it has enjoyed as the premier protector and promoter of human rights and fundamental freedoms in Europe.

SOME CONCLUDING OBSERVATIONS

The primary focus of this chapter has been on U.N. activities with respect to human rights, including human rights issues arising out of U.N. efforts to combat the financing of terrorism. To this observer, the United Nations achieves its greatest success when its goal is to assist member states that sincerely wish to improve their human rights records but need outside assistance in order to do so. In such cases, the work of the Human Rights Committee, for example, in examining the reports of the state parties to the International Covenant on Civil and Political Rights and interacting with representatives of the states presenting their reports may make a real contribution to the promotion of human rights. When it comes to dealing with states that regularly violate the rights of their citizens, as well as the citizens of other states, the United Nations has been less successful. Under such circumstances politics often interfere with effective action and generate considerably more heat than light.

The proceedings of the Human Rights Council and the breakdown of the Durban I and II conferences are salient examples.

The United Nations has been especially ineffective in dealing with the most egregious violations of human rights. In such cases, coercive action, including mandatory economic sanctions and perhaps armed force, may be required, but these are seldom employed. The continuing failures to prevent the atrocities in Darfur, Zimbabwe, or Myanmar are current prominent examples. The actions of human rights NGOs are more likely to be effective than those of U.N. human rights bodies in responding to the worst offenders.

The temptation to withdraw from United Nations human rights bodies, such as the Human Rights Council, can be substantial, but to give in to this temptation is, in my view, a mistake. The Obama administration is right to decide to run for membership in the Human Rights Council, even though the Council has many faults as we saw in Chapter 2. States of good will and a desire to protect and promote human rights should not give up the struggle to do so. This is especially true of the United States and other developed states that have the resources, in terms of financial and human capital, to make a difference.

Similarly, it would be a grave error, in my view, to expel Russia from the Council of Europe for its poor human rights record and its failure to abide by the judgments of the European Court of Human Rights. Here, too, the struggle should continue to convince Russia that the promotion of democracy, human rights, and the rule of law is in its own best interest. It is time to move away from the triumphalism that accompanied the collapse of the Soviet Union and toward exploring every possible avenue to improve cooperation between Russia and the West. A return to the days of the Cold War is in no one's interest.

Notes

1. A leading coursebook in the field, HENRY J. STEINER, PHILIP ALSTON, and RYAN GOODMAN, INTERNATIONAL HUMAN RIGHTS in CONTEXT (3rd ed. 2008), comprises 1,462 pages.
2. *See e.g.*, JORDAN J. PAUST, BEYOND the LAW: THE BUSH ADMINISTRATION'S UNLAWFUL RESPONSES in the "WAR" on TERROR (2007); DAVID COLE and JULES LOBEL, LESS SAFE, LESS FREE (2007); JACK GOLDSMITH, the TERROR PRESIDENCY (2007); MICHAEL E. TIGAR, THINKING ABOUT TERRORISM: THE THREAT to CIVIL LIBERTIES in TIMES of NATIONAL EMERGENCY (2007); JOSEPH MARGUILIES, GUANTANAMO and the ABUSE of PRESIDENTIAL POWER (2006); DAVID COLE, ENEMY ALIENS (2003); DEBORAH N. PEARLSTEIN, *Finding Effective Constraints on Executive Power: Interrogation, Detention, and Torture*, 81 IND. L.J. 1255 (2006). For a collection of essays debating both sides of the enemy combatant cases, *see* TERRORISM, the LAWS of WAR, and the CONSTITUTION (Peter Berkowitz ed., 2005).
3. *See* JOHN F. MURPHY, THE UNITED STATES and the RULE of LAW in INTERNATIONAL AFFAIRS 335–38 (2004).
4. *See* Article 1(3) of the U.N. Charter.
5. For an example of Dinstein's negative attitude toward the United Nations, *see* Yoram Dinstein, *Anti-Semitism, Anti-Zionism and the United Nations*, 17 ISRAEL Y.B. HUM. RTS. 15 (1987).

6. *See* Oona Hathaway, *Do Human Rights Treaties Make a Difference?* 111 YALE L.J. 1935 (2002).

7. *Id.* at 1940.

8. Ryan Goodman and Derek Jinks, *Measuring the Effects of Human Rights Treaties*, 14 EUR. J. INT'L L. 171 (2003).

9. *Id.* at 173.

10. Oona Hathaway, *Testing Conventional Wisdom*, 14 EUR. J. INT'L L. 185 (2003).

11. *See* Eric Neumayer, *Do International Human Rights Treaties Improve Respect for Human Rights?*, 49 J. CONFLICT RESOL. 925 (2005).

12. *Id.* at 926.

13. Oona Hathaway, *supra* note 6, at 2023.

14. *Id.* at 2024.

15. Ryan Goodman and Derek Jinks, *supra* note 8, at 182.

16. Oona Hathaway, *supra* note 10, at 199.

17. Reservations to the Convention on Genocide, International Court of Justice, Advisory Opinion, 1951, 1951 ICJ 15.

18. As of May 6, 2009, the Convention on the Prevention and Punishment of the Crime of Genocide (hereinafter "Convention on Genocide") had 140 state parties.

19. Article VIII of the Convention on Genocide provides: "Any Contracting Party may call upon the competent organs of the United Nations to take such action under the Charter of the United Nations as they consider appropriate for the prevention and suppression of acts of genocide or any of the other acts enumerated in Article III."

20. Article IX of the Convention on Genocide provides: "Disputes between the Contracting Parties relating to the interpretation, application or fulfillment of a State for genocide or for any of the other acts enumerated in article III, shall be submitted to the International Court of Justice at the request of any of the parties to the dispute."

21. The U.S. reservation reads: "That with reference to Article IX of the Convention, before any dispute to which the United States is a party may be submitted to the jurisdiction of the International Court of Justice under this article, the specific consent of the United States is required in every case."

22. On February 26, 2007, in Case Concerning the Application of the Convention on the Prevention and Punishment of the Crime of Genocide (Bosnia and Herzegovina v. Serbia and Montenegro), the Court held, by a vote of 13 to 2, that Serbia had not committed genocide in violation of its obligations under the Convention. By a vote of 12 to 3 the Court found that Serbia had nonetheless violated its obligation to prevent the Crime of Genocie pursuant to Article 1 of the Convention. For an Introductory note to the Judgment by Antoine Ollivier, *see* Antoine Ollivier, *The Judgment of the International Court of Justice in the "Genocide" Case Between Bosnia and Herzegovina v. Serbia and Montenegro*, 46 ILM 185 (2007). For the text of the Judgment, *see* 46 ILM 188 (2007). On November 18, 2008, in Application of the Convention on the Prevention and Punishment of the Crime of Genocide (Croatia v. Serbia), Preliminary Objections, the Court, by various votes, rejected the various objections of Serbia to the jurisdiction of the Court, which was based on Article IX of the Convention. A summary of the Court's judgment, prepared by the Court, can be found at www.icj-cij.org.

23. *See, e.g.*, the Human Rights Committee, established by Article 28 of the International Covenant on Civil and Political Rights, entered into force March 23, 1976, 999 U.N. T.S. 171. Under Article 40(1) state parties "undertake to submit reports on the measures they have adopted which give effect to the rights recognized herein and on the progress made in the enjoyment of those rights." Pursuant to paragraph 4 of Article 40, the Committee studies the reports submitted by the state parties and transmits these reports and "such

general comments as it may consider appropriate" to the state parties. The language of Article 40 does not spell out very clearly what powers the Committee has in dealing with state reports. But the current practice of the Committee is to adopt so-called Concluding Observations, consisting of an assessment of the state's human rights situation in light of the information provided in the state's report, the answers the Committee received to the questions posed by its members during the examination of the report, and information available from other sources, especially human rights NGOs. The Committee transmits its concluding observations to the state party concerned shortly after the hearing.

24. *See, e.g.*, Article 41 of the International Covenant on Civil and Political Rights.

25. *See, e.g.*, Article 41 (1) (e) of the International Covenant on Civil and Political Rights.

26. *See, e.g.*, Article 42 of the International Covenant of Civil and Political Rights.

27. Article 14 (1) of the International Convention on the Elimination of All Forms of Racial Discrimination.

28. Optional Protocol to the International Covenant on Civil and Political Rights, entered into force, Mar. 23, 1976, 999 U.N.T.S. 302. Article 1 of the Optional Protocol provides that: "A State Party to the Covenant that becomes a Party to the present Protocol recognizes the competence of the Committee to receive and consider communications from individuals subject to its jurisdiction who claim to be victims of a violation by that State Party of any of the rights set forth in the Covenant. No communication shall be received by the Committee if it concerns a State Party to the Covenant which is a Party to the present Protocol."

29. For discussion, *see* Natalia Schiffrin, *Jamaica Withdraws the Right of Individual Petition under the International Covenant on Civil and Political Rights*, 92 Am. J. Int'l L. 563 (1998). Parts of this article are excerpted in Mark W. Janis & John E. Noyes, International Law 384 (3rd ed. 2005), followed by notes and questions.

30. *See* Henry Steiner et al., *supra* note 1, at 918. The eight U.N. treaty bodies are as follows:

- ESCR Committee: Committee on Economic, Social and Cultural Rights (ICESCR);
- CERD Committee: Committee on the Elimination of Racial Discrimination (International Convention on the Elimination of all Forms of Racial Discrimination);
- CEDAW Committee: Committee on the Elimination of Discrimination Against Women (CEDAW Convention);
- CAT Committee: Committee Against Torture (Convention Against Torture and Other Cruel, Inhuman or Degrading Treatment or Punishment);
- CRC Committee: Committee on the Rights of the Child (Convention on the Rights of the Child);
- CMW Committee: Committee on the Protection of All Migrant Workers and Members of Their Families);
- CRPD Committee: Committee on the Rights of Persons with Disabilities (Convention on the Rights of Persons with Disabilities);
- CED Committee: Committee on Enforced Disappearances (International Convention for the Protection of All Persons from Enforced Disappearances).

31. *Id.* at 919.

32. *See* Oona Hathaway, *supra* note 6, at 2025.

33. *See especially*, Louis Henkin, *US Ratification of Human Rights Conventions: The Ghost of Senator Bricker*, 80 Am. J. Int'l L. 341 (1995).

34. *See* U.S. Department of State, Civil and Political Rights in the United States: Initial Report of the United States of America to the U.N. Human Rights Committee under the International Covenant on Civil and Political Rights.

35. Concluding Observations of the Human Rights Committee: United States of America, paragraph 267, 53rd Sess. of Committee, U.N. Doc.CCPR?C/79/Add.50 (1995).

36. Article 6(5) of the Covenant provides: "Sentences of death shall not be imposed for crimes committed by persons below eighteen years of age and shall not be carried out on pregnant women." The U.S. reservation to this provision states that "the United States reserves the right, subject to its Constitutional constraints, to impose capital punishment on any person (other than a pregnant woman) duly convicted under existing or future laws permitting the imposition of capital punishment, including such punishment for crimes committed by persons below eighteen years of age." Article 7 of the Covenant provides: "No one shall be subjected to torture or to cruel, inhuman or degrading treatment or punishment, In particular, no one shall be subjected without his free consent to medical or scientific experimentation." The U.S. reservation to Article 7 states: "the United States considers itself bound by Article 7 to the extent that 'cruel, inhuman or degrading treatment or punishment' means the cruel and unusual treatment or punishment prohibited by the Fifth, Eight and/or Fourteenth Amendments to the Constitution of the United States."

37. Concluding Observations, *supra* note 35, para 279.

38. Prior to the United States becoming a party to the Covenant in 1992, the U.S. Supreme Court held that the execution of persons younger than sixteen at the time of their offenses was an unconstitutional violation of the Eighth Amendment to the Constitution, which prohibits cruel and unusual punishment. Thompson v. Oklahoma, 487 US 815 (1988). The very next year, however, the Court upheld the death penalty for defendants aged sixteen and seventeen against claims that their execution would violate the Eighth Amendment. Stanford v. Kentucky, 492 US 361 (1989). Finally, in Roper v. Simmons, 543 US 551 (2005), the Court held that executions of persons under eighteen violated the Eighth Amendment to the Constitution.

39. General Comment No 24, General Comment on Issues Relating to Reservations Made Upon Ratification or Accessions to the Covenant or the Optional Protocols Thereto, or in Relation to Declarations under Article 41 of the Covenant, U.N. Doc, CCPR/C21/Rev.1/Add.6(1994). General Comment No. 24 may most conveniently be found in 15 Hum. Rts. L.J 422–464 (1994).

40. *See id.*, para 18, 15 Hum. Rts. L.J. at 467.

41. *See* Observations of the United States and the United Kingdom on General Comment No. 24 (52) relating to reservations, 16 Hum. Rts. L.J. at 423.

42. *See* General Comment No. 24, *supra* note 39, para 12, 15 Hum. Rts. L.J. at 466.

43. Observations of the United States and the United Kingdom, *supra* note 41, 16 Hum. Rts. L.J. at 423.

44. In pertinent part, Article 19 of the Vienna Convention on the Law of Treaties provides: "A State may, when signing, ratifying, accepting, approving or acceding to a treaty, formulate a reservation unless . . . the reservation is incompatible with the object and purpose of the treaty."

45. Curtis A. Bradley & Jack L. Goldsmith, *Treaties, Human Rights, and Conditional Consent*, 149 U. Pa. L. Rev. 399, 415 (2000).

46. *See* Henry Steiner et al., *supra* note 1, at 1143–44.

47. Article 20 (4) (b) of the Vienna Convention provides: "An objection by another contracting State to a reservation does not preclude the entry into force of the treaty as between the objecting and reserving States unless a contrary intention is definitely expressed by

the objecting State." Article 21 (3) of the Vienna Convention provides: "When a State objecting to a reservation has not opposed the entry into force of the treaty between itself and the reserving State, the provisions to which the reservations relates do not apply as between the two States to the extent of the reservation."

48. The United States had been requested to submit its second report to the Committee on September 7, 1998, and its third report on September 7, 2003. The consolidated reports were examined by the Committee in a public session on July 17, 2006. *See* Christina M Cerna, *Introductory Note to the Concluding Observations of the Human Rights Committee with Regard to the Second and Third Report Submitted by the United States and the Comments of the US Government on these Concluding Observations,* 47 ILM 586 (2008).

49. *Id.* at 587. The Concluding Observations of the Human Rights Committee may be most conveniently found at Human Rights Committee, *Consideration of Reports Submitted by States Parties Under Article 40 of the Covenant, Concluding Observations of the Human Rights Committee, United States of America,* 47 ILM 598 (2008).

50. *Id.* The response of the United States may be most conveniently found at Human Rights Committee, *Consideration of Reports Submitted by States Parties Under Article 40 of the Covenant, United States of America, Addendum, United States Responses to Selected Recommendations of the Human Rights Committee,* Oct. 10, 2007, 47 ILM 589 (2008).

51. Christina M. Cerna, *supra* note 48, at 587.

52. *Id.* at 586. According to Christina Cerna, human rights activists sought to interest C-SPAN, National Public Radio, and PBS television in covering the hearing on the first report, but failed in their mission. *Id.* at 587, endnote 1.

53. The Committee considered the fifth periodic report of the Russian Federation at its 2144th, 2145th, and 2146th meetings, held on October 24 and 25, 2003. See Human Rights Committee, Concluding Observations of the Human Rights Committee: Russian Federation. 06/11/2003. CCPR/79/RUS. (Concluding Observations/Comments).

54. *Id.* at 2. The two cases were Griden v. Russian Federation and Lantsov v. Russian Federation.

55. *Id.*

56. *Id.* at 3.

57. *Id.* at 5.

58. Country Reports on Human Rights Practices for 2006, Vol. I, Report submitted to the Committee on Foreign Relations U.S. Senate and the Committee on Foreign Affairs, U.S. House of Representatives, by the Department of State, April 2008, at 1641.

59. Amnesty International Report 2008, at 247.

60. Freedom in the World 2008, the Annual Survey of Political Rights & Civil Liberties, Freedom House, at 583.

61. *Id.*

62. Amnesty International Report, *supra* note 59, at 247–48.

63. Country Reports on Human Rights Practices for 2006, *supra* note 58, at 1641–42.

64. It worth noting that, in 2007, Hathaway published an article as a follow-up to her *Yale Law Journal article*. In this article, which examines the practices of more than 160 countries over several decades, she finds that, because domestic institutions are so central to treaty enforcement, states with robust domestic rule of law might shy away from committing to international treaties precisely because treaty commitments will be effective. Thus, the very factors that lead countries to comply with treaties can cause those same states not to commit.

65. *See* Oona Hathaway, *supra* note 6, at 2024.

66. *Id.*
67. *Id.*
68. *Id.*
69. Article 5 provides: "A Member of the United Nations against which preventive or enforcement action has been taken by the Security Council may be suspended from the exercise of the rights and privileges of membership by the General Assembly upon the recommendation of the Security Council. The exercise of these rights and privileges may be restored by the Security Council."
70. Hans Corell, then Under-Secretary-General for Legal Affairs and Legal Counsel of the United Nations, noted in 1996 that the Secretary-General of the United Nations had recognized the need for an international convention dealing with terrorist fundraising. *See* Hans Corell, *Possibilities and Limitations of International Sanctions Against Terrorism, in* COUNTERING TERRORISM THROUGH INTERNATIONAL COOPERATION 243, 253 (Alex P. Schmidt ed., 2001).
71. International Convention for the Suppression of the Financing of Terrorism, 2179 UNTS 232, entered into force on April 10, 1992.
72. For discussion of civil suits in U.S. courts against terrorists and the sponsors of terrorism, *see* John F. Murphy, *Civil Litigation Against Terrorists and the Sponsors of Terrorism: Problems and Prospects*, 28 TEX. REV. LITIG. 315 (2009).
73. S.C. Res.1373, UN SCOR, 56th Sess. UN Doc. S/1373 (2001).
74. *See* Ilias Bantekas, *Current Developments: The International Law of Terrorist Financing*, 97 AM. J. INT'L L. 315, 326 (2003).
75. *Id.* at 326.
76. S.C. Res 1373, *supra* note 73, para 8.
77. *See* Eric Rosand, *Security Council Resolution 1373, The Counter-Terrorism Committee, and the Fight Against Terrorism*, 97 AM.J. INT'L L. 333, 335 (2003).
78. *Id.* at 335.
79. *Id.* at 340.
80. *Id.*
81. *See* S.C. Res 1535 (March 26,2004).
82. *See* Counter-Terrorism Committee, *Human Rights*, Jan. 30, 2009, http://www.un.org/sc/ctc/rights.html.
83. S.C. Res. 1624 (Sept. 14, 2005).
84. Counter-Terrorism Committee, *supra* note 82.
85. S.C. Res. 1805 (March 20, 2008).
86. Counter-Terrorism Committee, *supra* note 82, at 2.
87. S.C. Res. 1214 (Dec. 8, 1998).
88. *See* Eric Rosand, Alistair Millar, and Jason IPE, *Human Rights and the Implementation of the UN Global Counter-Terrorism Strategy: Hopes and Challenges* 4–5 (Jan. 2008).
89. *Id.* at 5.
90. *Id.*
91. U.N. Human Rights Council, *Implementation of General Assembly Resolution 60/251 of 15 March 2006 Entitled "Human Rights Council: Report of the United Nations High Commissioner for Human Rights in the Protection of Human Rights on the Protection of Human Rights and Fundamental Rights While Countering Terrorism,"* A/ HRC/4/ 88, March 9, 2007, quoted in *Id.*
92. Committee on Legal Affairs and Human Rights, Council of Europe, "Provisional Draft Report on U.N. Security Council and European Union Blacklists," November 12, 2007, para 4, http://assembly.coe.int/ASP/APFeaturesManager/defaultArtSiteView.asp?ID=717, quoted in *Id.*

93. Eric Rosand et al., *supra* note 88, at 5.

94. For information regarding the role of the Focal Point for De-Listing, *see* http://www.un .org/sc/committees/dfp.shtmi; Security Council Resolution 1730, annex.

95. *See* Stefan Barriga, statement at the Open Debate of the Security Council: Briefings by the Chairpersons of the Counter-Terrorism Committee, 1267 Committee, 1540 Committee, May 27, 2007, http:// www.liechtenstein.li/pdf-fl-aussenstelle-newyork-dokumenteterrorismsecuritycouncil-delisting-2007–22.pdf.

96. Eric Rosand et al., *supra* note 88, at 6.

97. Yassin Abdullah Kadi and Al Barakaat International Foundation v. Council and Commission, Judgement of the Court of Justice in Joined Cases C-40205 P and C_402/05 P; for the full text of the judgment, *see* http://curia.europa.Eu/jurisp/cgi-brin/gettext.pl?where=&lang-en&lang=en&nu

98. *See* the Consolidated List, available at http://www.un.org/sc/committees/1267/consolist. shtml.

99. For an excellent summary of these proceedings, *see* Dr. Misa Zgonec-Rozeij, *Kadi & Al Barakaat v. Council of the EU & EC Commission: European Court of Justice Quashes a Council of the EU Regulation Implementing UN Security Council Resolutions*, ASIL INSIGHTS, Oct. 28, 2008, Vol. 12, Issue 22, http://www.asil.org/insights081028 .cfm.

100. OJ 2002 C 56, at 16; OJ 2002 C 191, at 26.

101. Judgments of the CFI of September 21, 2005, in Ahmed Ali Yusuf and Al Barakaat International Foundation v. Council of the EU and Commission of the EC (Al Barakaat CFI Judgement), Case T-306/01, and Yassin Abdullah Kadi v. Council of the EU and the Commission of the EC (Kadi CFI Judgement), Case T-315/01 (OJ 2005 C 281, at 17).

102. Article 103 of the U.N. Charter provides: "In the event of a conflict between the obligations of the Members of the United Nations under the present Charter and their obligations under any other international agreement, their obligations under the present Charter shall prevail."

103. ECJ Judgment, *supra* note 1, at para. 326.

104. *Id.*, para 316.

105. *Id.*, para 286.

106. *Id.*, para 287.

107. *Id.*, para 288.

108. *Id.*, para 334.

109. *Id.*, para 349.

110. *Id.*, para 366.

111. *Id.*, paras 368–69.

112. *Id.*, para 370.

113. *See* Commission Regulation (EC) No 1190/2008 of 28 November 2008, amending for the 101st time Council Regulation(EC) No 881/2002 imposing certain specific restrictive measures directed against certain persons and entities associated with Osama bin Laden, the al-Qaeda network and the Taliban, Official Journal of the European Union, L 322/25., paras (6) and (7).

114. *Id.* Article 2. Professor Grainne de Burca has suggested that: "It seems that the Security Council on October 21, 2008, provided the E.U. presidency, on an 'exceptional' basis, with some information on Kadi and A-Barakaat, which was relied on by the Commission to justify Regulation 1190/2008." *See* Grainne de Burca, *The EU, The European Court of Justice and the International Legal Order after Kadi*, Fordham Law Legal Studies

Research Paper No. 1321313, to be published in the *Harvard International Law Journal*, Vol. 1, No. 51, 2009.

115. For an extensive listing of commentary on the Kadi decision, as well as a probing analysis of its implications for international law and international institutions, *see Id.*

116. Jack Goldsmith and Eric Posner, *Does Europe Believe in International Law?* WALL ST. J., Nov. 25, 2008, at A.15.

117. *Id.* For similar arguments challenging the assertion that the European and American approaches to international law are so different from one another, *see* Robert J. Delahunty, *The Battle of Mars and Venus: Why do American and European Attitudes to International Law Differ?,"* St. Thomas Law School Working Paper Series No 1744 (2006), http:// law.bepress.com/cgi/viewcontent.cgi?=8181&context=expresso.

118. *See* Grainne de Burca, *supra* note 114, at 52.

119. *See* International Covenant on Civil and Political Rights, Human Rights Committee, VIEWS, Communication N. 1472/2006, 29 December 2008.

120. *Id.*, para 7.2.

121. *Id.*

122. Article 12 provides:
    1. Everyone lawfully within the territory of a State shall, within that territory, have the right to liberty of movement within that territory, have the right to liberty of movement and freedom to choose his residence.
    2. Everyone shall be free to leave any country, including his own.
    3. The above mentioned rights shall not be subject to any restrictions except those which are provided by law, are necessary to protect national security, public order (ordre public), public health or morals or the rights and freedoms of others, and are consistent with the other rights recognized in the present Covenant.
    4. No one shall be arbitrarily deprived of the right to enter his own country.

123 *See* Human Rights Committee, International Covenant on Civil and Political Rights, VIEWS, Communication No. 1472/ 2006, 29 December 2008, para 12.

124. *Id.*, para 13.

125. *See* Individual Opinion(dissenting) of Ms. Ruth Wedgwood, Id., Individual Opinions on the Committee's Decision on Admissibility, at 29.

126. *See* S.C. Res. 1452 (Dec. 20, 2002).

127. *See* S.C. Res. 1730 (Dec. 19, 2009) and S.C. Res. 1735 (Dec. 22, 2006).

128. *See* Eric Rosand et al., *supra* note 88, at 6.

129. Reportedly, Denmark, Liechtenstein, Sweden, and Switzerland are the U.N. member states pushing the hardest for a review panel within the Security Council. *Id.*

130. *See* Security Council Committee established pursuant to resolution 1267 (1999) concerning Al-Qaida and the Taliban and Associated Individuals and Entities, Open briefing on 1 July 2009, http://www.un.org/sc/commitees/1267/latest.shtml.

131. *See* Neil MacFarquhar, *Security Council Panel to Vet All Entries on Terrorism List,* N.Y. TIMES, July 15, 2009, at A9, col. 3.

132. S.C. Res. 1904 (Dec. 17, 2009).

133. *See* Neil MacFarguhar, *U.N. Measure Offers Recourse to Blacklisted,* NY TIMES, Dec. 18, 2009, at A18, col. 1.

134. S.C. Res. 1904, *supra* note 132, operative paras 20–28.

135. Neil MacFarguhar, *supra* note 133.

136. *See* HENRY J. STEINER et al., *supra* note 1, at 874.

137. *Id.*

138. *Id.*

139. The High Commissioners, in the order of their appearance and the years they served, are (1) José Ayala-Lasso (Ecuador) 1994–1997, (2) Mary Robinson (Ireland) 1997–2002, (3) Sergio Viera de Mello (Brazil) 2002–2003, (4) B.G. Ramcharan, acting-HC (Guyana) 2003–2004, (5) Louise Arbour (Canada) 2004–2008, (6) Navanethem Pillay (South Africa) 2008–present.

140. It should be noted that Sergio Viera de Mello was a highly regarded international civil servant who was expected to be an excellent High Commissioner, but tragically died in Iraq as a result of a bombing of the U.N. headquarters there.

141. *See, e.g.*, ARYEH NEUERM, WAR CRIMES, BRUTALITY, GENOCIDE, TERROR, and the STRUGGLE for JUSTICE 232–24 (1998).

142. Felice D. Gaer, *Book Review: The United Nations High Commissioner for Human Rights: The Challenges of International Protection*, by Bertrand G. Ramcharan, 98 AM. J. INT'L L. 391 (2004).

143. UNITED NATIONS DEVELOPMENT PROGRAMME, POVERTY REDUCTION and HUMAN RIGHTS: A PRACTICE NOTE iv (2003), quoted and cited in RALPH G. STEINHARDT, PAUL L. HOFFMAN, and CHRISTOPHER N. CAMPONOVO, INTERNATIONAL HUMAN RIGHTS LAWYERING : CASES and MATERIALS 1285–86 (2009).

144. Kareem Fahim, *The Education of Mary Robinson*, VILLAGE VOICE, http://www.villagevoice.com/issues/0s17/fahim.php.

145. Ian Williams, *Mary Robinson Interview*, SALON MAGAZINE, http://www.salon.com/people/interview/2002/0726maryrobinson.

146. A considerable part of this discussion of the Durban Conference is drawn from JOHN F. MURPHY, *supra* note 3, at 327–28.

147. Tom Lantos, *The Durban Debacle: An Insider's View of the UN World Conference Against Racism*, 26 FLETCHER FORUM WORLD AFF. 32 ((2002).

148. *Id.* at 33.

149. *Id.* at 34.

150. *Id.* at 36

151. *Id.*

152. *Id.* at 48.

153. *See especially*, Gay McDougall, *The World Conference Against Racism: Through a Wider Lens*, 26 FLETCHER F. WORLD AFF. 135 (2002).

154. Tom Lantos, *supra* note 147, at 42–43.

155. *Id.* at 44.

156. *Id.*

157. Amnesty International reportedly said that Arbour had been "a champion for human rights and that replacing her would not be easy." *See* Marlise Simon, *Departing Rights Official Raised Volume on Issues*, N.Y. TIMES, July 6, 2008, at A 13.

158. Kenneth Roth, executive director of Human Rights Watch, reportedly said that "Ms. Arbour had been principled and outspoken . . . and that "[our] hope is that the next commissioner not be excessively inclined to practice quiet diplomacy when outspokenness is called for." *Id.*

159. *Id.*

160. *Id.*

161. *Id.*

162. *Id.*

163. *Id.*

164. *See* Steven Edwards, *Arbour to Quit UN Job; Rights Commissioner Frustrated by Politicking*, THE GAZETTE (Montreal), Feb. 28, 2008, at A13. According to this article, Algeria,

China, and Cuba led an effort to gain as much control as possible over who's hired and the work they do. "It is part of a wider campaign that has seen them structure the council's rule so that only Israel can easily be singled out for criticism when the body – of which Canada is a member – meets. Arab and Muslim countries lobbied for Israel to be made the exception."

165. *Id.*
166. *See* Pablo Brum, *An Evaluation of the United Nations High Commissioner for Human Rights*, http://www.Cadal.org/includes /printable asp?id_nota=2457.
167. *Id.*
168. Felice Gaer, *supra* note 138, at 391, 395.
169. *See* Neil MacFarquhar, *Iranian Calls Israel Racist At Meeting in Geneva*, N.Y. TIMES, Apr. 21, 2009, at A 4.
170. *Id.*
171. HENRY STEINER et al., *supra* note 1, at 933–34.
172. *See* Dinah Shelton, *The Promise of Regional Human Rights Systems and in* THE FUTURE of INTERNATIONAL HUMAN RIGHTS 365–66, 369–70, 373, 377, 390–91, 393, 396 (Burns Weston & Stephen Marks eds., 2000), reproduced in part in RICHARD B. LILLICH, HURST HANNUM, S. JAMES ANAYA, & DINAH L. SHELTON, INTERNATIONAL HUMAN RIGHTS: PROBLEMS of LAW, POLICY, and PRACTICE 619, 624 (2006).
173. For an overview of some of these steps, *see* LOUIS HENKIN et al., HUMAN RIGHTS 657–70 (2nd ed. 2009).
174. *See* paragraph 10 of Joint Committee on Human Rights of the House of Lords and the House of Commons, Protocol No. 14 to the European Convention on Human Rights, First Report of Session 2004–05 (December 2004).As of January 1, 2008, there were nearly 80,000 pending applications. Registry of the European Court of Human Rights, Survey of activities, 2007 at 3 (2008).
175. *See* Mark Janis, *Russia and the "Legality" of Strasbourg Law*, 8 EUR. J. INT'L L. 93 (1997), reproduced in MARK JANIS, RICHARD S. KAY, and ANTHONY W. BRADLEY, EUROPEAN HUMAN RIGHTS LAW 109–11 (3rd ed. 2008).
176. Registry of the European Court of Human Rights, Survey of Activities, 2007, at 3, 54 (2008).
177. *See* Interim Resolution CM/ResDH (2009) 43, Execution of the judgements of the European Court of Human Rights in 145 cases against the Russian Federation relative to the failure or serious delay in abiding by final domestic judicial decisions delivered against the state and its entities as well as the absence of an effective remedy, adopted by the Committee of Ministers of the Council of Europe on March 19, 2009.
178. *See* the Right Honorable the Lord Wolf, Review of the Working Methods of the European Court of Human Rights 12 (Dec. 2005), http://echr.coe.int/ ECHR/Resources/Home/LORDWOOLFREEVIEWONWORKINGMETHODS. PDF.
179. *See* LOUIS HENKIN et al., *supra* note 173, at 670.

7

International Environmental Issues

In Chapter 1 of this study, there is a fairly extensive discussion of "soft law," a concept that, for reasons I discuss there, arguably creates considerable confusion and may, in some circumstances, be dysfunctional. Be that as it may, various forms of certain manifestations of soft law appear regularly in the international environmental arena. For example, it is "generally understood that 'soft' law creates and delineates goals to be achieved in the future rather than actual duties, programs rather than prescriptions, guidelines rather than strict obligations."[1] In this form, soft law is articulated in nonbinding instruments such as declarations of principles, codes of practice, guidelines, standards, nonbinding resolutions by international organizations, and international plans of action or codes of conduct. Perhaps the best known form of this kind of soft law in the international environmental law field is the Declaration on the Human Environment issued by the 1972 United Nations Conference on the Human Environment held in Stockholm, Sweden.[2] This declaration, although clearly nonbinding, contained twenty-six principles that led to the later adoption of specific binding rules.

Another example of soft law in the international environmental context is the United Nations Framework Convention on Climate Change (Framework Convention).[3] This convention, although technically a binding treaty, contains many provisions that set forth goals to be reached rather than rules to be followed. Article 4 of the convention, for example, sets forth only a general requirement that states parties adopt national programs to combat climate change, and does not provide a time frame within which such action must be taken nor specifies necessary components of such programs.

By contrast, the Kyoto Protocol to the United Nations Framework Convention (Kyoto Protocol),[4] as we shall see in some detail in the following, has as a primary goal the strengthening of the legal commitments of so-called Annex I parties (developed countries).[5] In December 2009, there will be a meeting in Copenhagen, Denmark, whose goal will be to agree on a new treaty and in general on a new climate change regime for the future.

Climate change has been described as "the defining ecological issue of the 21st century,"[6] and the first part of this chapter attempts to identify and address the most salient aspects of this issue. The second part of the chapter turns to the related problem of biodiversity, especially the United Nations Convention on Biological Diversity,[7] which was adopted at the United Nations Conference on Environment and Development in Rio de Janeiro in 1992, and entered into force on December 29, 1993. As of June 10, 2009, there were 191 parties to the convention. The United States has signed the convention but has not ratified it. It is generally agreed that there is a great need to reduce the current unprecedented biodiversity loss occurring globally.[8]

CLIMATE CHANGE

During the 1980s there was increased concern with global warming or, more precisely, climate change and the adverse effects it was alleged to have.[9] As a consequence, in 1988, the United Nations Environmental Program established the Intergovernmental Panel on Climate Change (IPCC), which was to assess available scientific data on climate change, especially change allegedly induced by human action. The IPCC is open to all members of the United Nations; it does not itself carry out research, but rather bases its assessments mainly on peer-reviewed and published scientific/technical literature. The IPCC issued a report in 1991 claiming that greenhouse gases, comprising carbon dioxide, methane, and others, could potentially cause serous climate disruptions.[10]

Not everyone agreed with the IPCC's assessment. In the words of the 1988 version of a leading U.S. law school coursebook, "[t]here is significant scientific uncertainty about whether global warming will occur, how much global warming will occur, and what the local and regional distributions of the effects of global warming will be. Moreover, there is uncertainty about the benefits and costs of actions to prevent global warming and about the efficiency of adaptive responses to global warming."[11]

Nonetheless, in 1992, at the United Nations Conference on Environment and Development in Rio de Janeiro, 167 states adopted the Framework Convention on Climate Change (Framework Convention). The United States became a party to the Framework Convention on October 15, 1992. Article 2 of the Convention commits the parties to the "stabilization of greenhouse gas concentrations in the atmosphere at a level that would prevent dangerous anthropogenic interference with the climate system." The Convention does not, however, impose any binding limits on emissions. This failure led to several conferences of the parties to the Framework Convention with a view to concluding a Protocol. But prior to the convening of the fourth conference in Kyoto, Japan, in 1997, the European Union announced its proposal for the Protocol, which called for a 15 percent reduction of the three major greenhouse gases (carbon dioxide, methane, nitrous oxide) from 1990 levels by the year 2010. The United States promptly denounced the target as "unrealistic and unachievable." This led to the passage, by a margin of ninety-five to none in July 1997, of the U.S. Senate's so-called, after its sponsors, Byrd-Hagel Resolution, which directed the president not to sign any emissions reduction agreement that (i) did not also require developing countries to reduce or limit emissions or (ii) would result in serious harm to the U.S. economy.[12]

In 1997, in Kyoto, Japan, more than 160 parties to the Framework Agreement adopted the Kyoto Protocol, which, for the first time, established legally binding limits for industrialized countries on emissions of carbon and other greenhouse gases.[13] No such legally binding limits were established for developing countries, leaving China and India – very large polluters – free from restraint. The Clinton administration nevertheless signed the Protocol on December 11, 1998, and strongly supported it. By contrast, the Bush administration announced that the Protocol was "fundamentally flawed." In its view, the Protocol was ineffective because of the exclusion of developing countries; its "precipitous" targets for the reduction of emissions were unattainable, even if the parties included all the mitigation activities that the United States wanted, such as trading in emission permits; and there were risks of "significant harm" to the U.S. and global economies. The administration cited models suggesting a drop in U.S. gross domestic product (GDP) of at least 1 to 2 percent by 2010, and up to 4 percent if certain trading provisions were not adopted.[14] There also was no change in the attitude of the U.S. Senate, so there was no chance of ratification in any event.

There is substantial support for the proposition that the Kyoto Protocol was badly flawed and in practice has not been a great success in dealing with the problem of climate change.[15] Many states that signed the treaty failed, by a substantial margin, to meet their targets in curbing carbon dioxide emissions. The United States' refusal to ratify the treaty was a major blow to progress in curbing greenhouse emissions, as was the decision to exclude developing states, especially major emitters like China and India, from any obligation to curb their emissions.

The Obama administration, however, has announced its intention to be involved in negotiations on a new treaty – to be signed in Copenhagen in December, 2009 – "in a robust way."[16] If China and some of the developing countries have their way, the Obama administration's involvement in the negotiations will have to be very "robust" indeed. Reportedly, as of this writing (May 22, 2009), China is demanding that rich countries cut their greenhouse gas emissions by 40 percent by 2020 from 1990 levels and help pay for reduction schemes in poorer countries.[17] Other developing countries have demanded emissions cuts of up to 80 percent by 2020 from certain rich nations. China has also demanded that developed countries be bound to give at least 0.5–1.0 percent of their annual economic worth to help poorer countries, including China, to cut their greenhouse gas emissions and cope with global warming. For their part other developing countries have proposed that higher percentages of the rich world's GDP be transferred to poorer countries.[18] Moreover, so far China has held firm to its position that developing countries, including China, should curb emissions only on a voluntary basis and only if the cuts "accord with their national situations and sustainable development strategies."[19]

Unlike his predecessor, President Obama has clearly indicated his willingness to agree to binding commitments to reduce greenhouse emissions. Indeed, at this writing, he has strongly supported draft legislation that would require the reduction of greenhouse gases by 17 percent from 2005 levels by 2020 and 83 percent by mid-century.[20] The draft legislation, known as the Waxman-Markey bill, would put an initial price of $10 a ton that U.S. companies would have to pay to emit greenhouse gases under a proposed carbon cap and trade system. Initially, 85 percent of these permits would be given away free to certain industries. The permits could be sold in a new "carbon market" and would have value because the overall quantity of industrial greenhouse gases emissions would be capped. Although initially most of these permits would be given away for free, later a portion of them would be auctioned off to help offset expected higher energy costs for lower to moderate income households. It is unclear at this writing whether the legislation will pass. Republicans have opposed the bill, calling it a "stealth energy tax," and some Democrats have problems with it as well.[21] Former U.S. President Bill Clinton has argued that the adoption of such legislation before the meeting in Copenhagen in December 2009 is vital if there is to be any chance of persuading China and India to agree to a new treaty.[22]

Formal negotiations on a new climate change treaty were scheduled to begin on June 1, 2009, in Berlin, Germany, with three or more meetings to be held before the final summit in Copenhagen. Reportedly, officials in the United States and Europe have privately dismissed the Chinese hardline demands as "posturing."[23] These officials note that China has taken a more helpful stance at the negotiating table by discussing the many measures the Chinese government has taken and promised to take to improve energy efficiency and expand renewable energy. Bill Clinton has claimed that China was in some respects ahead of the United States on clean energy. Mr. Clinton reportedly stated: "They're already doing a lot of things better than we are...All of their new coal plants are going to be at higher technology than our own coal stock...They have already invested more than we have in high-speed rail. The only thing they are still behind us on is vigorous energy efficiency."[24]

At this juncture the United States and other wealthy countries are reportedly willing to accept that China, India, and other emerging economies will not agree to absolute cuts in the medium term. Before they agree to help finance reduction programs in developing counties, however, they are likely to insist that, at a minimum, the developing countries commit to limit their emissions to the extent that they do not rise to the levels they would reach under a "business as usual" approach.[25]

Parenthetically, it is noteworthy that, if the current Chinese position were to be adopted, the United States and the other developed countries would be committed to a "hard law" regime, both as to their duty to cut their own greenhouse gas emissions and to finance any emissions cuts that the developing countries might decide to make, whereas the developing countries would be subject to a purely "soft law" regime. This is highly unlikely to be acceptable to the developed countries, especially the United States. A major reason that the United States failed to ratify the Kyoto Protocol was its failure to include any "hard law" commitments by the developing countries, especially China. Despite the change of administrations, and in Congress, China's change of position on this point is likely to be a *sine qua non* for the United States to ratify any new treaty that may be adopted in Copenhagen.

The Kyoto Protocol itself is not scheduled to expire until the year 2012. But as noted previously, the Protocol has not been a success. Therefore, even if there is no agreement in Copenhagen on a new treaty, the Protocol is unlikely to be much of a factor in efforts to establish an effective climate change regime.

Moreover, it is important to note that at the first meeting of the parties to the Kyoto Protocol, in December 2005, the focus was on how the climate change regime might be structured after 2012, the year the Protocol is to expire. Two separate processes were initiated: (1) an Ad Hoc open-ended Working Group to consider further commitments for developed countries beyond 2012 under the Kyoto Protocol and (2) a "Dialogue" on long-term cooperative action under the Framework Convention on Climate Change. A commentator has recently described the Dialogue as follows:

> The Dialogue, which stressed development and poverty eradication, as well as the role of technology, covered actions by *all* parties but was neither binding nor authorized to open negotiations leading to new commitments. The initiation of the Dialogue on these terms was perceived as a compromise in that whilst it would not launch negotiations on a future regime or call for an agreed outcome, it would permit discussions on future climate change to continue and it would keep non-Parties to the Kyoto Protocol, such as the United States, at the table. The title – 'Dialogue' – as well as the non-binding nature of the exchange of view also helped to bring developing countries on board.[26]

The Dialogue held four workshops and led to a report by the cofacilitators of the Dialogue to the thirteenth Conference of the Parties (COP) to the Protocol. For its part the COP decided to adopt a decision in Bali, Indonesia, on how to enhance long-term cooperative action to address climate change. This decision, known as the Bali Action Plan, was adopted in Bali on December 15, 2007.[27]

The Bali Action Plan is a decision taken by the Conference of Parties. From a formal legal perspective, COP decisions are not, absent explicit authorization, legally binding. "This does not, however, detract from the operational significance and legal influence that COP decisions have come to acquire in multilateral environmental agreements, and in particular in the climate regime."[28] In other words,

COP decisions may constitute a form of "soft law" that plays a significant role in the legal process of coping with climate change.

For example, the chapeau to the first operative paragraph of the Bali Action Plan launches the negotiation process to advance the climate regime. It reads "[the COP] [d]ecides to launch a comprehensive process to enable the full, effective and sustained implementation of the Convention through long-term cooperative action, *now, up to and beyond* 2012, in order to reach *an agreed outcome* and adopt a decision at its fifteenth session, by addressing, inter alia . . . "[29]

According to one commentator, the words "an agreed outcome" may be interpreted to suggest "a lack of agreement at this point on both the legal form that the likely outcome of this process could take, and the level of ambition it should reflect. The Berlin Mandate,[30] comparable to the Bali Action Plan, in so far as it too launched a process to advance the climate regime, explicitly specified the legal form of the outcome – 'a Protocol or another legal instrument.' The legal form that the outcome of the Bali Action Plan could take, however, is deliberately left open. It could be a legally binding 'Protocol or another legal instrument,' but it could also be a COP decision alone viz, an agreed outcome reflected in a COP decision, the precise legal status of which . . . is a matter of some debate. The legal form of the outcome assumes particular significance if the outcome, as I argue it may do, destabilizes the conceptual apparatus of the existing climate regime, and in particular of the Kyoto Protocol."[31]

More specifically, the commentator is concerned that the agreed outcome might destabilize the conceptual apparatus of the existing climate regime by "jettisoning" its two basic premises, namely, that (1) targets and timetables should be endorsed, and (2) developed countries, given their enhanced historical contributions to the carbon stock as well as their greater wealth and technological capacity, should be required to take the lead in assuming and meeting ambitious greenhouse gas mitigation targets. If an agreed outcome were to do so, the result would be "killing Kyoto softly."[32]

The commentator recognizes that "killing Kyoto softly" is not the only option. "Parties also have the option of arriving at an ambitious climate change mitigation strategy by 2009, albeit framed differently from the mitigation strategy in the Kyoto Protocol. This strategy will likely permit a range of mitigation actions, whatever their nature, stringency and extent, in a form that the United States (U.S.) and large developing countries find politically palatable."[33]

At the time of this writing, it is impossible to predict with any degree of certainty what the agreed outcome at Copenhagen will be. It appears unlikely, however, that it will take the form of a strategy of killing Kyoto softly. As part of his campaign promise, President Obama pledged to engage in post-Kyoto negotiations and "establish strong annual targets that set [the U.S.] on a course to reduce emissions to their 1990 levels by 2020 and reduce them by an additional 80 percent by 2050."[34] This position is, of course, in dramatic opposition to that of the Bush administration. If the Obama administration adheres to this position, and exerts effective leadership at

Copenhagen, the agreed outcome might indeed be the "ambitious climate change mitigation strategy" desired by the commentator quoted in the previous paragraph.

There would remain, however, the question of the form the agreed outcome should take. Should it be in the legal form of a Protocol or perhaps an entirely new treaty, or should it take the form of soft law guidelines? The likely problem facing the Obama administration if a binding treaty is adopted is the real possibility that it would be unable to get the Senate to give its advice and consent to ratification, because it would take only a one-third minority of the Senate to block such action. The likelihood of such a blocking action would be especially great, if the treaty imposed no binding obligation on China, India, and other emerging market countries to take steps to reduce their greenhouse gas emissions.

There also would remain the continuing problem of scientific uncertainty. Although there appears to be a substantial majority of scientists in favor of the proposition that climate change is real, that it is primarily caused by humans rather than nature, and that it constitutes a significant threat to humankind, there is still substantial debate over how great a threat climate change poses, the benefits and costs of actions to prevent climate change, and the efficiency of various responses to climate change.

There is also controversy about the accuracy of various scientific reports on climate change, especially those of the Intergovernmental Panel on Climate Change (IPCC). In 2007 the IPCC issued its Fourth Assessment Report, which declared that "[warming of the climate system is unequivocal. . . . " and that most of the observed change since the 1970s is likely due to greenhouse gases emitted as a result of human activities.[35] In response, however, the IPCC was accused of being a "seriously flawed" enterprise and unworthy of the slavish respect accorded to it by most governments and the media."[36] Accusing the IPCC of having been granted, "in effect, a monopoly of official wisdom," the response went on to suggest that "if governments are to get the best advice, they need information and analysis from an open and disinterested source – or else from multiple disinterested sources . . . One incompetent institution, committed to its own agenda, should never have been granted this degree of actual and moral authority over science, over public presentation of the science and over calls for 'more serious action' that go well beyond the science."[37]

Bjorn Lomborg, director of the Copenhagen Consensus, a think tank, and author of *Cool It: The Skeptical Environmentalist's Guide to Global Warning*,[38] has argued that there is a "Climate-Industrial Complex"[39] consisting of some business leaders who are "cozying up with politicians and scientists to demand swift, drastic action on global warming" in order to line their own pockets.[40] He points to Al Gore in particular, who "is a politician, a campaigner and the chair of a green private-equity firm invested in products that a climate scared world would buy." According to Lomborg, "[e]ven companies that are not heavily engaged in green business stand to gain. European energy companies made tens of billions of Euros in the first years of the European Trading System when they received free carbon emission allocations." In a concluding shot, he argues that "[t]he partnership among self-interested businesses, grandstanding politicians and alarmist campaigners truly is an unholy alliance. The climate-industrial complex does not promote discussion on how to overcome this challenge in a way that will be best for everybody. We should not be surprised that those who stand to make a profit are among the loudest calling for politicians to act. Spending a fortune on global carbon regulations will benefit a few, but dearly cost everybody else."

Elsewhere, Lomborg has suggested that rather than combat climate change through a carbon tax or a cap and trade approach along the lines of the European Trading System already in place, the focus instead should be on research and development on noncarbon-emitting energy technologies to make them cheap enough that everybody would use them. The treaty he would like to see adopted in Copenhagen would require every state party to promise to spend 0.05 percent of GDP on research and development on such technology. According to Lomborg, "[t]his would be about $7 billion for the U.S. It would be about $30 billion for the entire world. We could easily get on board because it is a fairly low amount. And it would have a much greater chance of dealing with climate change in the long run. . . . "[41]

In short, Lomborg is proposing a "technological fix" to the climate change problem. A recent Congressional Research Service Report for Congress[42] examines three starting points from which the problem of climate change may be viewed. The three starting points it calls policy "lenses." The three lenses are a technological lens, an economic lens, and an ecological lens. According to the report, "[a] technological lens views environmental problems as the result of inappropriate or misused technologies. The solution to the problems lies in improving or correcting technologies. The implied governmental role would be to provide leadership and incentives for technological development."[43] From the technological lens perspective, "policy entails the development and commercialization of new technologies; government's role can include basic research, technical support, financial subsidies, economic mechanisms, or the imposition of requirements or standards that stimulate technological developments and that create markets for such technologies."[44] The technological lens views global climate change as a problem requiring a reorientation of the energy sector from carbon-based fossil fuels to a more "environmentally friendly" energy system based on renewables and conservation. To this end, for example, the federal government has taken such steps as promoting the development of hybrid electric and fuel cell vehicles in the United States through joint government-industry research and development aimed at the introduction of high-efficiency cars and trucks, as well as tax incentives for the purchase of new advanced technology vehicles.

Viewing climate change through an economic lens, the preferred approach would be a pollution tax, or more specifically, a carbon tax. As noted by the Congressional

Research Service report, "[e]conomists observe that pollution imposes costs on society that are not incorporated in the price of the goods or services responsible for the pollution; these are called 'external' costs. An ideal pollution tax 'internalizes' these external costs by making the beneficiary of the polluting activity pay for the socially borne costs (polluter pays). As long as the polluters find it cost-effective to reduce their emissions to avoid paying the tax, they would add pollution controls until further controls would have higher incremental costs than the tax."[45]

The Economist has recently suggested that "[t]he best way to curb global warming would be a carbon tax. The money raised could be divided among citizens or used to repay the national debt. A tax on carbon dioxide (CO_2) would give everyone an incentive to emit less of it. It would be simple, direct and transparent." It then adds, however, that, "[f]or these reasons, it will never happen in America."[46] The main reason it will never happen in America, according to *The Economist*, is that "[p]oliticians hate to admit that anything they plan to do will cause pain to any voter."[47] Every voter, of course, is well aware that a tax is not pain free.

From an economic perspective, the main alternative to a carbon tax is a cap and trade system. During the 2008 presidential campaign both Barack Obama and John McCain proposed a cap and trade system, and President Obama, as we have seen, strongly favors such an approach. *The Economist* suggests that the reasons they both favor a cap and trade system is "not because it would work better than a carbon tax but because it did not have the word 'tax' in its name."[48] It also notes that neither candidate "dwelt on the fact that cap and trade will raise energy prices, that subsidies for renewable energy will have to be paid for, or that both policies will destroy jobs as well as creating them, while probably cutting growth. The Congressional Budget Office estimates that a 15 percent cut in CO_2 emissions will cost the average American household $1,600 a year."[49]

There is also debate about how a cap and trade system works in practice, as we have seen earlier with respect to the European system. There is therefore still some uncertainty, at this writing, whether Congress will support a cap and trade system through legislation or whether it will be possible to reach agreement at the international level on the details of such a system.[50]

As defined by the Congressional Research Service (CRS) report, an ecological lens approach differs significantly from either a technological or an economic lens approach. According to the CRS report, "an ecological lens views environmental problems as the result of indifference to or disregard for the planet's ecosystem on which all life depends. The solutions to the problems lie in developing an understanding of and a respect for that ecosystem, and providing people with mechanisms to express that understanding in their daily choices. The implied governmental role would be to support ecologically based education and values, as well as to promote 'green' products and processes, for example through procurement policies, efficiency standards, and regulations."[51]

The ecological lens magnifies elements that are psychological, philosophical, and theological. In contrast to the technological or economic lens view, for example, from the ecological lens perspective, "[p]ollution protection gets on the national agenda not on the basis of affordability or whether control technology exists, but because an environmental problem is recognized as a threat to human health or welfare."[52]

The CRS report nicely highlights some of the differences among the three lenses as applied to the issue of cost:

> The technological lens focuses attention on the outcome of the innovation; actions are justified if they resolve the pollution problem, and costs and benefits should be weighed in terms of the outcome, not in terms of the transitional costs. In contrast, those viewing the issue through the economic lens tend to focus on costs and benefits as the critical metric for evaluating policies; actions are justified when the benefits outweigh the costs, but not otherwise. The ecological perspective basically suggests that policy choices can be based on a recognition of "rights" rather than costs and benefits; the principles of protecting life and of preserving the ecosystem for future generations govern choices.[53]

In conclusion, the CRS report suggests:

> The effort by various interests to convince the public that their perspective is correct, and those of others reflect either the wishful thinking, misinformation, or excuses, will likely continue. Such efforts will be affected by improvements in the scientific understanding of global climate change, and of the domestic and international implications for strategies for addressing it. However, the pivotal decision-making point – whether that understanding warrants action or not – will be mediated in large part by the lens through which policymakers view the new knowledge. Ultimately, it is the balance between all three perspectives that will shape policy options and eventually determine the character and timing of any policy response to the problem.[54]

Whatever the outcome of this balancing process in Copenhagen, or in the U.S. Congress, it would appear important that any new treaty on climate change be written in such a way to allow flexibility to respond to future developments, especially those of a scientific nature that might clarify or even resolve more of the scientific uncertainty currently present. It must be kept in mind that climate change will be with us long past the conference in Copenhagen in 2009 or the 2012 expiration date for the Kyoto Protocol. With this in mind it might be desirable to have any new climate change treaty contain "soft law" provisions that are intentionally ambiguous to allow for interpretations that can meet new developing conditions without the need to constantly revise the treaty. Also, it will be necessary to have a follow-up review process, both to hold state parties to their obligations under the new treaty and to consider whether certain amendments to it are needed. There can be little doubt that resolving the problem of climate change will remain an enormous challenge involving "hard choices" for many years to come. Some of these "hard choices" have been identified by Daniel Bodansky, a leading scholar in the field of international environmental law:

> In considering the design and negotiation of future international climate efforts, a number of general issues present themselves.

FORM AND FORUM OF NEGOTIATIONS

Should international efforts continue to focus on the development of a single comprehensive global regime and, if so, does the United Nations Framework Convention on Climate Change (UNFCCC) provide the most appropriate forum? Or should negotiations proceed in a more flexible, decentralized manner, involving multiple agreements and/or smaller groups of countries or private-sector parties (for example, like-minded states or companies)? If this more variable geometry is pursued, should it be in addition, or as an alternative, to the UNFCCC process?

TIME FRAME

What is the appropriate time frame – the Kyoto Protocol's second commitment period. (Under Article 3 of the Kyoto Protocol a second commitment period is to be established to apply after the end of the first commitment period – 2008–2012), a somewhat longer medium-term time frame, or the long-term evolution and development of the regime?

MITIGATION COMMITMENTS

Approaches to defining commitments: Should the climate regime continue to operate in a top-down manner, involving the multilateral negotiation of commitments? Or should it proceed in a bottom-up fashion, seeking to encourage countries to make (and implement) pledges of domestic measures to mitigate climate change? Can the two be combined?

Type of commitments: What types of mitigation commitments should be included? Should the climate regime continue to emphasize quantitative emission targets and, if so, should they be fixed national, Kyoto-like targets, or some alternative form of target (dynamic, dual, sectoral, no lose, etc.)? Or are nontarget-based approaches preferable – for example, harmonized domestic policies and measures, development-focused approaches, financial transfers, or technological standards?

Stringency of commitments: How should the stringency of commitments be determined? Is it better to begin with relatively weak commitments to encourage broad participation, or to begin with more stringent commitments?

Differentiation and burden sharing: How should the burden of commitments be shared among countries? For example, if a target-based approach is adopted, how should targets be allocated (e.g., on the basis of population, historical responsibility, basic human needs)? What is the pathway, if any, toward global coverage? Should the differentiation in the UNFCCC and the Kyoto Protocol between developed and developing countries continue, or should additional categories of countries be defined and, if so, on what basis (e.g., per capita GDP, per capital emissions, total emissions)? Should criteria be developed for graduation of countries from one category to another?

ADAPTATION

What approach should be taken to the issue of adaptation? Can existing approaches under the UNFCCC be improved or expanded? Should a liability or insurance scheme be established to provide compensation to countries adversely affected by climate change?

IMPLEMENTATION AND COMPLIANCE

Are new institutions or approaches needed to assure that international climate commitments are implemented and enforced?[55]

NOTE: On December 19, 2009, after 12 days of "protests, posturing and seemingly endless palaver," the Copenhagen climate summit "laboured mightily and brought forth . . . a mouse. As vague as it is toothless, the accord on curbing greenhouse gas emissions that emerged from the Bella Centre this weekend imposes no real obligations, sets no binding emissions targets and requires no specific actions by anyone."[56] Andreas Carlgren, environmental minister of Sweden, holder of the rotating European Union presidency proclaimed the Copenhagen accord "a disaster" and "a great failure."[57] By contrast, Todd Stern, US special envoy for climate change, noted more than countries had backed the accord, including the EU, Australia, Japan, the African Union and the Alliance of Small Island States.[58] Whatever else may be said of the Copenhagen accord, it is clear is not a binding legal instrument. Some may regard the accord as "soft law," and there is hope that the accord will be transformed by further negotiations into a binding treaty. At this writing, however, it is by no means certain that this will be possible.

BIODIVERSITY

There has long been a concern with protecting particular species of fauna and flora.[59] More recently, however, this concern has broadened to focus on the conservation of the biological diversity of natural systems, that is, the health of ecosystems. The U.S. Council on Environmental Quality has defined "biological diversity" (often shortened to "biodiversity") as "a broad catchall term including the inter-connected and related concepts of generic diversity . . . , species or ecological diversity . . . , and habitat or natural diversity. . . . "[60] Similarly, the U.N. Convention on Biological Diversity[61] broadly defines biological diversity as "the variability among living organisms from all sources, including, *inter alia*, terrestrial marine and other aquatic ecosystems and the ecological complexes of which they are part; this includes diversity within species, between species and of ecosystems."[62]

In 1987, the United Nations Environmental Program began work on an "umbrella convention" to address biological diversity issues. The result was the Convention on Biological Diversity, which was adopted at the United Nations Conference on Environment and Development in Rio de Janeiro in 1992 and entered into force on December 29, 1993. As of June 10, 2009, there were 191 parties to the Convention. The United States has signed the Convention but has never ratified it.

The Convention provides for, among other things, the development of national strategies, plans, and programs to protect biological diversity; conservation measures; environmental impact assessments of projects for adverse effects on biological diversity; and national reports on implementing measures and the effectiveness of these measures.[63] The United States refused to sign the Convention. Among the reasons for this refusal were, first and foremost, Articles 16 (3) and 19 (2) of the Convention would require a transfer of technology, thereby risking the loss of intellectual property protection and possibly encouraging global pirating. Second, there were concerns about how the Convention would be financed. Third, the Convention created disincentives to the development of new biotechnology products.[64] These reasons reflected criticisms from biotechnology companies and their supporters, who contended that certain elements of the Convention seemed to call for the compulsory licensing of intellectual property, and that the grant of sovereign property right in genetic materials would discourage pharmaceutical research and thus would result in fewer drugs being developed. Supporters of the Convention argued that there could be no long-term pharmaceutical research without the Convention because, without conservation incentives for the developing countries, there would be very little diversity left.[65]

After Bill Clinton was sworn in as president in 1993, the Clinton administration signed the Convention on Biological Diversity and issued an interpretive statement expressing the U.S. understanding that "the Convention requires all Parties to ensure that access or transfer of technology is consistent with the adequate and effective protection of intellectual property rights."[66] This understanding was not sufficient to meet the concerns of the critics of the Convention.

At this writing, it is not clear whether the Obama administration will favor ratification of the Convention or, if so, how hard it would push the Senate to give its advice and consent to ratification. Similarly, it is unclear whether the proponents of ratification would be able to gain enough votes to have a two-thirds majority. The protection of intellectual property is a major concern of the business community.

The primary focus of the Convention on Biological Diversity is on action to be taken at the national level to conserve biodiversity. Defenders of the Bush administration's refusal to ratify the convention argued that U.S. environmental laws and regulations are "stronger in the United States than they are in any other country in the world."[67]

Although this would seem clearly to be an extravagant claim – some European laws on the environment have long been stronger than those of the United States – a less polemical commentary has suggested that "the United States has certainly participated more actively in the international environmental arena than its treaty record would suggest."[68] This participation, according to the commentary, has been through nontreaty methods where the United States can control the rules of the game. These methods include broad interpretations of U.S. environmental statutes to apply their terms extraterritorially and efforts in such international economic institutions as the International Monetary Fund, the World Bank, and the World Trade Organization, where the United States wields considerable influence, either because of weighted voting procedures or strong economic clout, to ensure that these institutions factor environmental considerations into their operations.

The "most practical aspect" of the Convention requires that state parties create a national strategy plan or program for conserving biodiversity and to integrate biodiversity conservation into economic planning.[69] National biodiversity plans have been developed by dozens of countries since passage of the Convention. They reportedly "have been effective to some extent in their goal of increasing the visibility of and political will for biodiversity conservation, as well as facilitating the coordination of international assistance and of interagency activities within a country. The plans are supposed to reflect the conservation measures identified in the Convention."[70] It has been suggested that the United States should establish a national biodiversity policy,[71] but no such action has been taken.

It appears that neither international nor national policies are currently doing the job to prevent continuing damage to biodiversity. As summarized recently by a leading U.S. casebook:

> *Fiddling while Rome burns?* The state of the world's ecosystems and biodiversity continues to decline. The Millennium Ecosystem Assessment surveyed 24 services. Four were increasing their ability to benefit humans, but three of these were agriculture, livestock and aquaculture. Fifteen services were declined. These include ocean fisheries, wood fuel, genetic resources, fresh water, air quality, soils and wetland buffers. Five were in a steady state. These were timber, cotton and hemp fibers, water regulation, disease regulation and recreation and ecotourism . . . World Watch Institute, Vital Signs 2005 86–87 (2005), reports that nearly one out of four mammals are in serious decline due to uncontrolled hunting, habitat fragmentation and loss and now global climate change. Butterfly and bird species are declining in Europe for similar reasons . . . 16,119 out of 40,177 assessed species are threatened with extinction. . . . The best one can say about rainforest loss is that the rate has

recently slowed. Of course, continued population growth continues to stress biodiversity. Experts do not expect to see the growth rates of the past century, from 1.6 to 6.1 million. Fertility rates are down, but nonetheless the developing world and the United States continue to grow rapidly. Even where population is declining, Europe, or slowing, Brazil and China, the increase in household units poses new threats to biodiversity because more resources are consumed.[72]

As the previous summary illustrates, biodiversity is a vast topic covering a great variety of flora and fauna. There are, moreover, a large number of treaties besides the Convention on Biological Diversity that have some impact, effectively or not, on the state of the world's ecosystems and biodiversity. Indeed, the Kyoto Protocol is one of these treaties. Hence, it is difficult to assess the precise impact the Convention on Biological Diversity has on the state of biodiversity. For that matter, it is difficult to assess the role that treaties and other traditional sources of international law play in protecting and conserving biodiversity. It is safe to conclude, however, that traditional international law has not played as effective a role as one might hope.[73]

To be sure, "there has been a remarkable growth, overall, in the number and range of international instruments and institutions addressing environmental problems."[74] The number of treaties has grown to the point "where some commentators have warned of treaty congestion."[75] The issue remains, however, whether the quality of these treaties matches their quantity.

Parenthetically, it should be noted that customary international law plays a relatively minor role in international environmental law. The reasons are that:

> The decentralized, and uncoordinated, nature of the customary law-making process make[sic] it ill-suited for generating the kinds of detailed rules necessary to regulate the use of hazardous materials, the trade in endangered species, or the emissions of long-range pollutants. As a result, most of the action in international environmental law relates to treaty regimes rather than custom. The customary law process is able to generate quite general principles, such as the duty to prevent transboundary harm. Apart from an occasional international or national case where norms of customary law might be invoked, these norms operate as broad principles that frame legal discourse and diplomacy – so their formal legal status is of only limited practical significance. They play a significant role in the broader process of persuasion and justification that characterizes international environmental law, rather than as rules that govern behaviour.[76]

Notes

1. INTERNATIONAL ENVIRONMENTAL LAW ANTHOLOGY 56 (Anthony D'Amato and Kristen Engel eds., 1995).
2. *See* EDITH BROWN WEISS et al., INTERNATIONAL ENVIRONMENTAL LAW and POLICY 187 (2nd ed. 2007). In the words of the authors of this casebook, "[t]he 1972 United Nations Conference on the Human Environment served both to awaken the international community to the importance of protecting the environment and was followed by a number

of institutional arrangements for that purpose (in particular, UNEP). Its formal work was embodied in a declaration (known as the Stockholm Declaration) including twenty-six principles, as well as in a more detailed Action Plan for the Human Environment."

3. United Nations Framework Convention on Climate Change, May 29, 1992, A/AC. 237/18 (Part II) Add.1, reprinted in (1992) 31 ILM 849 [hereinafter FCCC]

4. Kyoto Protocol to the United Nations Framework Convention on Climate Change, December 10, 1997, FCCC/EP 1997.L.7add.1, reprinted in (1998) 37 ILM 22 [hereinafter the Kyoto Protocol].

5. *See* Lavanya Rajamani, *From Berlin to Bali and Beyond: Killing Kyoto Softly*, 57 INT'L & COMP. L.Q. 909, 912 (2008).

6. *See* DAVID HUNTER et al., INTERNATIONAL ENVIRONMENTAL LAW and POLICY 631 (2007).

7. Convention on Biological Diversity, 31 INT'L LEGAL MATERIALS 818 (1992).

8. *See Environment: EU Expects Obama to Turn Words Into Action*, G8 Research Group, Jan. 18, 2009, http:g8live.org/2009/01/18/2285/.

9. This introductory material to the problem of climate change is taken in part from JOHN F. MURPHY, THE UNITED STATES and the RULE of LAW in INTERNATIONAL AFFAIRS 338–41 (2004).

10. IPCC, Climate Change (1991).

11. *See* EDITH BROWN WEISS et al., *supra* note 2, at 678 (1988).

12. S. Res. 98, 105th Congress – 1977.

13. For a summary of the primary provisions of the Protocol, *see* Clare Breidenich et al., *Current Development: The Kyoto Protocol to the United Nations Framework Convention on Climate Change*, 92 AM J. INT'L L. 315 (1998).

14. *See* www.state.gov/documents/organization /4584.pdf.

15. *See, e.g.,* Elisabeth Rosenthal, *Obama's Backing Raised Hopes for Climate Pact,*N.Y. TIMES, Mar. 1, 2009, http://www.nytimes.com/2009/03/01/science/earth/01treaty html?

16. *Id.*

17. *See* Jamil Anderlini and Fiona Harvey, *Tough pose held for climate talks,* FIN TIMES, May 22, 2009, at 2, col. 1.

18. *Id.*

19. *Id.*

20. *See* Ian Talley, *China Pushes for Lower Greenhouse-Gas Emissions,* WALL ST. J. May 22, 2009, at A6, col. 1.

21. *Id.*

22. *See* Edward Luce, *Bill Clinton Call for ' Strong' Climate Change Bill,* FIN. TIMES, May 14, 2009, at 5, col. 1.

23. Jamil Anderlini and Fiona Harvey, *supra* note 17.

24. *See* Edward Luce, *supra*, note 22.

25. *See* Jamil Anderini and Fiona Harvey, *supra* note 17.

26. Lavanya Rajamani, *From Berlin to Bali and Beyond: Killing Kyoto Softly?*, 57 INT'L COMP. L.Q. 909, 913 (2008).

27. Decision 1/CP. 1.3 Bali Action Plan, in Report of the Conference of the Parties on its thirteenth session, held in Bali from 3 to 15 December 2007. Addendum. Part Two: Action taken by the Conference of the Parties at its thirteenth session, FCCC/CP/2007/6/Add 1 (14 March 2008).

28. *See* Lavanya Rajamani, *supra* note 26, at 915.

29. Paragraph 1, Bali Action Plan [emphasis added] by Lavanya Rajamani, *supra* note 26.

30. Adopted by the first COP, the Berlin Mandate proposed strengthening the commitments of Annex I Parties through the adoption of a Protocol or another legal instrument. *See*

Decision on 1/CP.1, *The Berlin Mandate: Review of Adequacy of Article 4, paragraph 2, subparagraph (a) and (b), of the Convention, including proposals related to a Protocol and decisions on follow-up*, contained in Report of the Conference of Parties on its first session held at Berlin from 28 March to 7 April 1995, FCCC/CP/1995/7Add.1 (1995).

31. Lavanya Rajamani, *supra* note 26, at 918.
32. *Id.* at 910.
33. *Id.*
34. *See* Leonard Doyle and Michael McCarthy, *Obama Brings US in from the Cold*, THE INDEPENDENT, Nov. 20, 2008, at News, 1.
35. Intergovernmental Panel on Climate Change Working Group I. Climate Change 2007. The Physical Basis. 1 (Cambridge University Press 2007).
36. Clive Cook, *The Steamrollers of Climate Science*, FIN. TIMES, Aug. 3, 2007, at 5, col. 2.
37. *Id.*
38. BJORN LOMBORG, COOL IT: THE SKEPTICAL ENVIRONMENTALIST'S GUIDE to GLOBAL WARMING (2007).
39. Bjorn Lomborg, *The Climate-Industrial Complex*, WALL ST. J., May 21, 2009, at A19, col. 1.
40. *Id.*
41. *See* Gene Epstein, *Global Warming Is Manageable – If We're Smart*, BARRON'S, May 18, 2009, at 34, 35.
42. *See* Larry Parker and John Blodget, *Global Climate Change: Three Policy Perspectives*, CONGRESSIONAL RESEARCH SERVICE, November 26, 2008.
43. *Id.*, Summary.
44. *Id.* at 5.
45. *Id.* at 11.
46. Robert Guest, *Surviving the Slump*, THE ECONOMIST, May 30, 2009, at 3, 14.
47. *Id.* at 14.
48. *Id.*
49. *Id.*
50. *See* Clive Crook, *How to Do Cap-and-Trade*, NAT'L J., May 2, 2009, at 17.
51. Larry Parker and John Blodget, *supra* note 42, Summary.
52. *Id.* at 21.
53. *Id.* at 25.
54. *Id.* at 34.
55. DANIEL BODANSKY, INTERNATIONAL CLIMATE EFFORTS BEYOND 2012: A SURVEY of APPROACHES (2004), quoted in DAVID HUNTER et al., INTERNATIONAL ENVIRONMENTAL LAW and POLICY 732–33 (2007).
56. Bjorn Lomborg, *We should change tack on climate after Copenhagen*, FIN. TIMES, Dec. 23, 2009, at 9, col. 1.
57. Fiona Harvey, Amy Kazmin, Geoff Dyer, and Jonathan Wheatly, *Climate change alliance crumbles as accord is labelled 'a great failure,'* FIN. TIMES, Dec. 23, 2009, at 1, col. 4.
58. *Id.*
59. Part of this introduction is taken from JOHN F. MURPHY, *supra* note 9, at 341–42.
60. Council on Environmental Quality, Eleventh Annual Report 273 (1985) quoted in EDITH BROWN WEISS et al., *supra* note 2, at 273.
61. Convention on Biological Diversity, 31 INT'L LEGAL MATERIALS 818 (1992).
62. *Id.*, article 2.
63. *See* Daniel M. Bodanskiy, *International Law and the Protection of Biological Diversity*, 28 VAND. J. TRANSNAT'L L. 623, 627 (1995).

64. *See* United States: Declaration Made at the United Nations Environmental Program Conference for the Adoption of the Agreed Text of the Convention on Biological Diversity, 31 INT'L LEGAL MATERIALS 848 (1992).
65. *See* Daniel T. Jenks, *The Convention on Biological Diversity – An Efficient Framework for the Preservation of Life on Earth?*, 15 Nw. J. INT'L L. & BUS. 636 (1995).
66. *See* U.S. Treaty Doc. 103–20, Nov.16, 1993 VI–VIII.
67. 138 Cong.rec. Section 4896 (daily ed. April 7, 1992) (statement of Senator Dole).
68. Cyril Kormos, Brett Groskos, and Russell A. Mittermeier, *US Participation in Environmental Law and Policy*, 13 GEO. INT'L ENVTL. L. REV. 661, 691 (2001).
69. *See* DAVID HUNTER et al., *supra* note 55, at 1027.
70. *Id.* at 1027–28.
71. Walt Reid, *The United States Needs a National Biodiversity Policy*, WRI ISSUES and IDEAS (Feb. 1992), cited and partially quoted in *id.* at 1031.
72. *See* EDITH BROWN WEISS et al., *supra* note 2, at 893 (citations omitted).
73. For one area where international law has not been effective in protecting biodiversity, *see* Michael J. Glennon, *Has International Law Failed the Elephant?*, 84 AM. J. INT'L L. 1 (1990).
74. *See* Daniel Bodansky, Jutta Brunnee, and Ellen Hey, *International Environmental Law: Mapping the Field, in* THE OXFORD HANDBOOK of INTERNATIONAL ENVIRONMENTAL LAW 1, 3 (Daniel Bodansky, Jutta Brunee, and Ellen Hey eds., 2007), noting in footnote 8 that "[a] periodically updated compilation of international environmental law documents has grown to more than 20 volumes and counting. B. Ruster and B. Simma, *International Protection of the Environment: Treaties and Related Documents* (Dobbs Ferry, NY: Oceana, 1975–82, second series, 1990–present)."
75. *Id.* at 4, citing Edith Brown Weiss, *International Environmental Law: Contemporary Issues and the Emergence of a New World Order*, 81 GEO. L.J. 675 (1993).
76. *Id.* at 23.

8

Causes of the Present Malaise, Concluding Observations, and a Prognosis

In this, the concluding chapter, it is important to emphasize that there has been no attempt in this chapter or earlier chapters to identify problems and challenges facing international law and international institutions as a whole. Rather, the focus has been on subjects and challenges that arguably are the most important, as well as the most challenging, facing the world community. To be sure, the problems facing treaties and customary international law, the primary sources of traditional international law, discussed in Chapter 1, concern international law as a whole but arise in their most acute form in the substantive fields covered by this study: the maintenance of international peace and security, the law of armed conflict, arms control, disarmament, nonproliferation and safeguards, human rights, and international environmental issues. These are fields that significantly affect vital interests of states and increasingly are of great concern to nonstate actors as well. They are also the fields where states and nonstate actors are most likely to fail to comply with their international law obligations and thus belie Louis Henkin's famous declaration that: "It is probably the case that *almost all nations observe almost all principles of international law and almost all of the time.*"[1]

CAUSES OF THE PRESENT MALAISE

In the introduction to this study, it is suggested that the rapidity of change in modern life creates great instability and even chaos in some situations. The rapidity of change is particularly pronounced in the technological and scientific arenas whose considerable complexity makes it difficult for the slow-moving treaty process to adapt. A recent example of this problem is the dispute between the United States and Russia over how to counter cyberwar attacks that could wreak havoc on computer systems and the Internet. Russia favors an international treaty along the lines of those negotiated for chemical weapons and has pushed hard for that approach.[2] The United

States, however, argues that a treaty is unnecessary and instead advocates improved cooperation among international law enforcement groups. In the U.S. view, if these groups cooperate to make cyberspace more secure against criminal intrusions, this will also make cyberspace more secure against military campaigns. Trying to reach common ground over an approach to the problem is complicated, given that a significant proportion of the attacks against American government targets are coming from China and Russia. Also, Russian calls for broader international oversight of the Internet have met strong U.S. resistance to agreements that would allow governments to censor the Internet because they would provide cover for totalitarian regimes. The United States argues further that a treaty would be ineffective because it can be almost impossible to determine if an Internet attack originated from a government, a hacker loyal to that government, or a rogue acting independently. The unique challenge of cyberspace is that governments can carry out deceptive attacks to which they cannot be linked. After computer attacks in Estonia in April 2007 and in the nation of Georgia in August 2008, the Russian government denied involvement, and independent observers said the attacks could have been carried out by nationalist sympathizers or by criminal gangs. Although the United States and Russia have failed to reach agreement on the proper approach to counter cyberwar attacks, arms control experts say that major governments are reaching a point of no return in heading off a cyberwar arms race.

The Russians are pushing for a global multilateral treaty to deal with the problem of cyberwar. But even if the United States would agree to accept the Russian approach, it is not at all clear that it would be possible to get agreement on a global treaty. This is because since the early 1990s it has proven almost impossible to get agreement among the now almost 200 member states of the world community on global treaties to deal with the severest problems facing humanity, such as climate change, nuclear proliferation, terrorism, pandemics, trade protectionism, and many more. Moises Naim, the editor in chief of *Foreign Policy*, has placed part of the blame on a "flawed obsession with multilateralism as the panacea for all the world's ills."[3] In its place he has proposed a policy of "minilateralism," which would bring to the negotiating table the "smallest possible number of countries needed to have the largest possible impact on solving a particular problem. Think of this as minilateralism's magic number."[4] He suggests that the Group of 20 (G-20) would be the magic number for trade because it includes both rich and poor countries from six continents and accounts for 85 percent of the world's economy. In his view, the members of the G-20 could reach a major trade deal among themselves and make it of greater significance by allowing any member country of the United Nations to join in if it wishes to do so. The magic number for climate change would also be twenty, because the world's twenty top polluters account for 75 percent of the world's greenhouse gas emissions. He suggests other magic numbers for other problems such as twenty-one for nuclear proliferation, twelve for African poverty, and nineteen for HIV/AIDS.

One may be skeptical about Naim's minilaterist approach. The G-20 has been active in the Doha round's trade talks, but the last session failed because India failed to agree to proposals advanced by other members of the G-20. Similarly, the negotiations on climate change have so far failed because of the refusal of China and India to agree to any binding limits on emissions that would apply to them. The problem may be not the large number of countries participating in the talks but rather an unwillingness to compromise, participants preferring instead a zero-sum game.

The current debate over the process of creating a norm of customary international law and whether such norms have any relevance to how states behave, as well as the allegations that judges on international tribunals decide cases on the basis of alleged norms of customary international law that states have had no real role in creating, has served to call into question the legitimacy of customary international law, resulting in some cases in calls for its elimination. The elimination of customary international law as a source of international law, however, would raise the difficult issue of what would serve in its place to fill the increasingly large gaps in treaty law as applied to contemporary problems.

As illustrated in several of the chapters, the difficulty in reaching agreement utilizing the traditional sources of international law has resulted in an increased preference for informal nonbinding guidelines and flexible procedures in place of binding legal instruments. A recent example is the use of nonbinding declarations by the G-20 to set forth agreement on steps to be taken to resolve the current worldwide financial crisis.

In the sensitive area of international human rights, a major problem is the lack of global agreement on the definition of human rights and their importance in international relations. There is first the debate over whether emphasis should be placed on economic, social, and cultural rights or civil and political rights. As we saw in Chapter 2, during its universal periodic review session, China focused sharply on its success in reducing poverty and gave relatively short shrift to civil and political rights, an approach Russia greatly approved. There is substantial evidence, moreover, that the great majority of people in both China and Russia are primarily concerned with stability and order and their economic well-being and that only a relatively small minority demand such civil and political rights as freedom of speech, due process, an independent judiciary, or free elections. Moreover, as Fareed Zakaria has recently pointed out, China and even India are unlikely to view human rights issues as central to their foreign policy.[5] According to Zakaria, both countries "see themselves as developing countries and therefore, too poor to be concerned with issues of global order, particularly those that involve enforcing standards and rights abroad . . . they are not Protestant, proselytizing powers and thus will be less eager to spread universal values across the globe. Neither Hinduism nor Confucianism believes in universal commandments or the need to spread the faith."[6] Even in the Western countries, including the United States and Europe, human rights often take a back seat in foreign policy if they conflict with other interests such as commercial or national security considerations.

As we also saw in Chapter 2 and in other chapters, there are still a large number of U.N. member states that are dictatorships and therefore view an activist human rights program as detrimental to their interests. Bloc voting by many of these states, especially in the Arab world and Africa, can derail efforts in the United Nations and elsewhere to deal with the worst human rights offenders. Such bloc voting is also a major factor in the Council on Human Rights continuing the Commission on Human Rights' strong bias and excessive actions against Israel.

The rise of nationalism is another development that has hindered the coordination and cooperation among many countries necessary to address and resolve the numerous problems facing the world community. As Zakaria notes, "increasingly, nation-states are becoming less willing to come together to solve common problems. As the number of players – governmental and nongovernmental – increases and each one's power and confidence grows, the prospects for agreement and common action diminish. This is the central challenge of the rise of the rest – to stop the forces of global growth from turning into the forces of global disorder and disintegration."[7]

The large expansion in the membership of the United Nations and other international institutions has made many of them unwieldy and ineffective, and it contributes to bloc voting. Especially noteworthy are the problems facing the Council of Europe and the European Court of Human Rights and Fundamental Freedoms caused by the substantial increase in their membership and the participation by new members such as Russia that lack a strong tradition of respect for the rule of law. The substantial expansion in the membership of the European Union has also led to considerable difficulties.

In Chapter 1 of this study, it is suggested that the need for the rule of law in international affairs constitutes a higher order value that serves, at least in part, to provide a measure of coherence to the multifaceted nature of international law. Unfortunately, the rule of law in international affairs is not a value supported by all states. Those states that lack the rule of law at the national level are unlikely to be supportive of it at the international level.

SOME CONCLUDING OBSERVATIONS

As noted previously, it would not seem desirable to eliminate customary international law because of a lack of any other source that could fill the ever increasing gaps that exist in treaty law. Moreover, this is little prospect that states could resolve the dispute, especially between the developed and developing countries, over the kind of state practice required, how many states must participate in the creation of a norm of customary international law, how to determine whether *opinio juris* is present, etc. But perhaps the world community could take some guidance from the approach of the U.S. Supreme Court toward customary international law in the

Sosa v. Alvarez-Machain case.[8] In *Sosa* the Court was called upon to interpret the Alien Tort Statute (ATS),[9] a domestic U.S. law that provides: "The district courts [of the United States] shall have original jurisdiction of any civil action by an alien for a tort only, committed in violation of the law of nations or a treaty of the United States." Alvarez-Machain had brought an action under the statute against Sosa, a citizen of Mexico, who, along with other Mexicans, had abducted him from his home in Mexico and brought him to El Paso, Texas, where he was handed over to U.S. federal officers for trial for allegedly being involved in aiding the torture of an agent of the U.S. Drug Enforcement Agency over a two-day period, who was then murdered. In an earlier case Alvarez-Machain sought his release on the basis of a claim that his abduction violated the U.S.-Mexico Extradition Treaty, but the U.S. Supreme Court ruled against him.[10] Upon remand to the District Court for trial, however, the court dismissed the case against Alvarez-Machain on the basis of a summary judgment, and he returned to Mexico.

In his action against Sosa under the ATS, Alvarez-Machain argued that his abduction in Mexico by Sosa was a violation of the law of nations (customary international law in the modern vernacular) because it constituted an arbitrary arrest and detention. The district court and court of appeals ruled in his favor, but the Supreme Court reversed.

The Court rejected Alvarez-Machain's argument that the ATS was intended not only as a jurisdictional grant but as authority for the creation of a new cause of action for torts in violation of international law. In the Court's view the ATS could not be interpreted to give the courts power to mold substantive law. On the other hand, the Court rejected Sosa's argument that there could be no claim for relief under the ATS without a further statute expressly authorizing adoption of causes of actions. The Court found that the legislative history of the ATS indicated that the drafters had in mind the following as violations of the law of nations: violations of safe conducts, infringements of the rights of ambassadors, and piracy. Sosa had argued that only these violations were available as causes of action under the ATS, absent passage by Congress of a further statute expressly authorizing a cause of action. The Court, however, ruled that U.S. courts could consider a claim under a norm of customary international law that had developed after the 1789 adoption date of the ATS. At the same time, it stated that federal courts should not recognize violations of any international law norm with less definite content and acceptance among nations than were present with respect to the three violations of the law of nations that the drafters of the ATS had in mind.

Applying this test to Alvarez-Machain's claim that he was the victim of an arbitrary detention in violation of present-day international law, the Court found that customary international law requires a prolonged arbitrary detention, not the relatively brief detention in excess of positive authority involved in Alvarez-Machain's case. Hence, it reversed the decision of the Circuit Court of Appeals and ordered the dismissal of Alvarez-Machain's claim.

If international tribunals were to accept the approach of *Sosa* in determining the existence of an alleged norm of customary international law – a requirement of definite content and clear acceptance of the norm by states – it would go a long way to obviate the charge that judges on international tribunals are finding norms of customary international law based solely on their personal preferences rather than general acceptance by the world community.

As noted in Chapter 3, recent reports have found that there has been a substantial decline in armed conflict over the last decade. There is no guarantee, however, that this encouraging trend will continue. The global recession has "sparked fears that multiple states could slip all at once into the ranks of the failing."[11] Failed states are strong candidates for increased levels of internal and external violence, and dealing with a substantial increase in failed states would be a major challenge for the world community. Such states are also strong candidates for giving rise to genocide, war crimes, and crimes against humanity. At the time of this writing, however, the United Nations General Assembly is engaged in a bitter debate over the validity of the "responsibility to protect," or R2P as it's now called.[12] Critics of R2P argue that the whole idea is just a cover to legitimate armed interference by rich Western powers in the affairs of poor countries. Although many commentators, including this one, regard such an argument as ill founded, it resonates well with a number of U.N. member states and may diminish the already shaky willingness of states to fulfill their responsibility to prevent or at least bring to an end the commission of widespread atrocities, as demonstrated by the situation in Darfur.

Also discouraging are recent reports that postconflict peace-building efforts are facing major difficulties. Last year, for example, Guinea-Bissau slid back into political violence and assassination.[13]

In contrast, a recent encouraging development is the willingness of China to provide troops to U.N. peacekeeping.[14] Close to 2,200 Chinese are now participating in U.N. peacekeeping missions, including the United Nation's Hybrid Operation in Darfur (UNAMID). China does not provide combat troops, but it does provide medical teams, engineers, civilian police, and military observers. Some commentators see China as filling a gap that many Western powers are unwilling to fill. Others suggest that China is increasingly unwilling to be seen as a protector against genocide and other atrocities and is therefore increasingly willing to bring pressure to bear on countries like the Sudan to cease such actions.[15]

At this time there seems to be little prospect for major improvements in the law of armed conflict through the conclusion of new or the revision of old treaties. It may be that gaps in this law will be filled, as they traditionally have been, through the development of customary international law. The prospects for this development would be greatly enhanced if the International Committee of the Red Cross and major Western powers, such as the United States and Great Britain, can narrow their differences over what these customary international law norms are.

The Obama administration has put arms control, disarmament, and nonprolif-eration at the top of its agenda.[16] President Obama has embraced the proposal that the United States should join with other states to work toward a world free of nuclear weapons.[17] This proposal has engendered significant opposition, however, and its fate remains to be determined.[18] Obama has also supported the proposal to negotiate a fissile material cutoff treaty, despite increasing skepticism regarding the usefulness of arms control treaties. He has expressed the desire to strengthen the Nuclear Non-Proliferation Treaty by providing more aid for international atomic inspectors, finding new ways to punish states and their leaders that cheat, and new fueling methods for peaceful nuclear power that lower the risk of arms proliferation. As for new ways to punish cheaters, on July 16, 2009, the Security Council decided to target the heads of North Korea's nuclear industry, along with the institutions they run, with individual sanctions.[19] The sanctioned individuals will be subject to an international asset freeze and travel ban.

A PROGNOSIS

In the July/August 2007 issue of *Foreign Affairs*, on page 59, there appears an article by Azar Gat, "The Return of Authoritarian Great Powers," in which Gat argues that Germany and Japan were defeated in both world wars largely because of contingent factors rather than structural inefficiencies and that the challenge posed for Western democracies by the autocratic powers China and Russia does not face any such contingent factors. In response, the January/February 2009 issue of *Foreign Affairs*, on page 77, contains an article by Daniel Deudney and G. John Ikenberry, "The Myth of the Autocratic Revival," and the March/April 2009 issue of *Foreign Affairs*, on page 33, has an article by Ronald Inglehart and Christian Welzel, "How Development Leads to Democracy." Lastly, the July/August issue of *Foreign Affairs*, on page 150, has a debate between Gat on the one side and Deudney and Ikenberry and Inglehart and Welzel on the other, "Which Way Is History Marching? Debating the Authoritarian Revival."

One greatly hopes that Gat is wrong and that history is on the side of the lib-eral democracies as contended by Gat's opponents. There is substantial evidence, however, that in the battle of ideas, there has been an authoritarian revival led in par-ticular by China and to a lesser extent by Russia. China's great success in reducing poverty and its argument that its authoritarian form of government has been a major factor in this success resonate well in many developing countries. Moreover, as noted by Fareed Zakaria, China has developed a nuanced style of diplomacy that "empha-sizes a long-term perspective, a nonpreachy attitude, and strategic decision making that isn't bogged down by internal opposition or bureaucratic paralysis."[20] This, too, resonates well in the developed world.

From a long-term perspective, of course, the final victor in this battle of ideas remains to be determined. But the prospects for international law and functional international institutions depend upon liberal democracies being the ultimate winners. It is worth noting too that an autocratic style of government is also favored by Islamist fundamentalists, and there is evidence that they have had their successes in the battle of ideas currently under way in Islam.

As this study has sought to demonstrate, there are many "hard choices" to be made by the world community that will affect the future of international law and international institutions. Choosing to support international law and international institutions, however, is only the first step in the process. It then will be necessary to implement these choices, and I hope this study has demonstrated that implementing these choices will involve a hard struggle against opponents who favor a different set of choices, and that the outcome of this struggle is by no means certain.

Notes

1. LOUIS HENKIN, HOW NATIONS BEHAVE 47 (2nd ed. 1979).
2. *See* John Markoff and Andrew E. Kramer, *U.S. and Russia Differ on Treaty for Cyberspace*, N.Y. TIMES, June 28, 2009, at 1, col. 5.
3. *See* Moises Naim, *Minilateralism: The magic number to get real international action*, FOREIGN POL'Y, July/Aug. 2009, at 136, 135.
4. *Id.* at 135.
5. *See* FAREED ZAKARIA, THE POST-AMERICAN WORLD 84 (2008).
6. *Id.*
7. *Id.* at 31–32.
8. 542 U.S. 692 (2004).
9. 28 U.S.C. section 1350.
10. *See* United States v. Alvarez-Machain, 504 U.S. 655 (1992).
11. *See The Failed States Index*, FOREIGN POL'Y, July/Aug. 2009, at 81,82.
12. *See, e.g.*, Neil MacFarquhar, *When to Step in to Stop War Crimes Causes Fissures*, N.Y. TIMES, July 23, 2009, at A10, col. 3. *An idea Whose Time Has Come – and Gone?* THE ECONOMIST, July 25, 2009, at 58.
13. *Blue Briefcases: After the Peacekeepers Come the Peacebuilders. But They Are Struggling*, THE ECONOMIST, July 25, 2009, at 59.
14. *See* Nathan King, *China's Contribution to UN Peacekeeping Grows*, May 30, 2009, http://www.voanews.com/english/archive/2009–05/2009–05-30-voa17.cfm?renderforprint=1.
15. *See* Stephanie Klein-Ahlbrandt and Andrew Small, *China Jumps In*, INT'L HERALD Trib., Feb. 1, 2007, http://www.nytimes.com/2007/02/01/opinion/01iht-edsmall.4431580.htm?
16. *See, e.g.*, Peter Spiegel, *Obama Puts Arms Control at Core of New Strategy*, N.Y. TIMES, July 15, 2009, at A10, col. 2. William J. Broad and David E. Sanger, *The Long Arc of a Nuclear-Free Vision*, N.Y. TIMES, July 5, 2009, at 1, col. 2.
17. *See* George P. Shultz, William J. Perry, Henry A. Kissinger, and Sam Nunn, *A World Free of Nuclear Weapons*, WALL ST. J., Jan. 4, 2007, at A. 15, col. 1.
18. *See, e.g.*, Melanie Kirkpatrick, *The Weekend Interview with James R. Schlesinger, Why We Don't Want a Nuclear-Free World*, WALL ST. J., July 11–12, 2009, at A9, col. 1.
19. *See* S.C./9708, 16 July 2009, *Security Council Committee Determines Entities, Goods, Individuals Subject to Measures Imposed on Democratic People's Republic of Korea by*

Resolutions(sic) 1718 (2006). The Security Council committee acted in accordance with paragraph 24 of Resolution 1874 (June 12, 2009), which authorized the committee to decide which entities, goods, and individuals should be subject to specific measures of sanction.

20. *See* FAREED ZAKARIA, *supra* note 5.

Index

Gulf Wars, 40, 103, 138, 140, 152, 162, 186. *See also*
  specific countries

Habre, H., 94
Hague Convention, 165
Hague Peace Conference, 65
Haiti, 141, 202n65
Hamdan v. Rumsfeld, 173
Hanseatic League, 12
Hargrove, J., 71
Hariri, R., 91, 92, 93
Hathaway, O., 38, 205, 206, 209, 215
Haynes, W.J., 165
Hegel, G.F., 48n12
Helsinki Final Act (1975), 3, 21
Henckaert, J.M., 166
Henkin, L., 37, 117, 266
Hezbollah, 91, 92
Higgins, R., 1
Hinduism, 268
Howse, R., 43
Hudson, M.O., 16, 17, 28
human rights, 4, 5, 19, 44, 204–247
  armed conflict and, 173, 174–176
  Blaustein Institute, 231
  China and, 268
  Clinton administration and, 226
  crimes against humanity, 77
  definition of, 268
  Geneva Conventions and, 173. *See* Geneva
    Conventions
  Goodman-Jinks thesis, 208
  Helsinki watch commissions, 21
  High Commissioner for, 226–233
  Human Rights Council. *See* Human Rights
    Council
  Human Rights Covenants, 72
  Human Rights Watch, 64, 172, 173, 229
  intervention and, 19, 47
  Israel and, 269
  NGOs and, 238
  racist attacks and, 214
  Russia and, 238, 268
  soft law and, 20, 21
  Strasbourg system, 235
  terrorism and, 204
  U.N. and, 5, 8, 10n14, 21, 58–59, 215. *See*
    Human Rights Council
  U.S. and, 59, 61, 65, 268
  war crimes and, 8. *See also specific countries,*
    organizations
Human Rights Council, 10n14, 230
  China and, 63

  human rights and, 58, 59
  membership, 60
  U.N. and, 57–65
  UPR process, 61, 64, 65
  U.S. and, 59, 61, 65
Human Rights Covenants, 72
Human Rights Watch, 64, 172, 173, 229
Human Security Report, 136, 137, 143, 144
Hussein, S., 83, 93, 118, 119, 120, 126–127, 132, 137
hybrid courts, 7, 17, 45, 56, 75–94, 265

IAEA. *See* International Atomic Energy Agency
ICC. *See* International Criminal Court
ICCPR. *See* Civil and Political Rights Covenant;
    International Covenant on Civil and
    Political Rights
ICISS. *See* International Commission on
    Intervention and State Sovereignty
ICJ. *See* International Court of Justice
ICRC. *See* International Committee of the Red
    Cross
ICTR. *See* International Criminal Tribunal for
    Rwanda
ICTY. *See* International Criminal Tribunal for
    the Former Yugoslavia
Ignatieff, M., 231
IHT. *See* Iraqi High Tribunal
Ikenberry, G.J., 272
ILC. *See* International Law Commission
IMF. *See* International Monetary Fund
India, 3, 115, 184, 195, 250, 251, 254, 268
Inglehart, R., 272
Intergovernmental Panel on Climate Change
    (IPCC), 249, 254
International Atomic Energy Agency (IAEA), 27,
    46, 185–187, 199n23, 200n31
International Bank for Reconstruction and
    Development, 6
International Commission on Intervention and
    State Sovereignty (ICISS), 46
International Committee of the Red Cross
    (ICRC), 162, 164, 165, 167, 172, 175, 212, 271
International Convention for the Suppression of
    Acts of Nuclear Terrorism, 187–189
International Court of Justice (ICJ), 5, 17, 19, 28,
    65–75, 116, 117
  Advisory on Nuclear Weapons, 174
  armed conflict, 174
  Article 36, 66, 67
  Article 38, 10n4, 14, 15, 25, 27–30, 32
  Convention on Genocide and, 206
  discretion to decline, 69
  equity and, 28, 29

Index